THE SECRET STATE

For Irene

THE SECRET STATE

British Internal Security in the Twentieth Century

Richard Thurlow

BLACKWELL
Oxford UK & Cambridge USA

First published 1994

First published in USA 1995

Blackwell Publishers, the publishing imprint of
Basil Blackwell Ltd.
108 Cowley Road
Oxford OX4 1JF
UK

238 Main Street
Cambridge, Massachusetts 02142
USA

British Library Cataloguing in Publication Data

A CIP catalogue record for this book is available from the British Library.

Library of Congress Cataloging-in-Publication Data
Thurlow, Richard C.
The secret state: British internal security in the twentieth century / Richard Thurlow.
p. cm.
Includes bibliographical references (p.) and index.
ISBN 0-631-16066-3 (hardback : acid-free paper)
1. Great Britain—Politics and government—20th century.
2. Internal security—Great Britain—History—20th century.
3. Official secrets—Great Britain—History—20th century.
I. Title.
DA566.7.T55 1994
941.082—dc20 94-6153
CIP

Typeset in 11 on 13 pt Baskerville
by Graphicraft Typesetters Ltd, Hong Kong
Printed in Great Britain by Hartnolls Ltd, Bodmin

This book is printed on acid-free paper.

'Extremism in the defense of liberty is no vice; moderation in the pursuit of justice is no virtue.'
Senator Barry Goldwater, 1964 US Presidential Campaign.

'In your heart you know he's right.'
Republican Campaign slogan, 1964.

'In your guts you know he's nuts.'
Democratic bill sticker, 1964.

'The Chairman of the Committee of Enquiry should be a judge. The advantages are two fold:

a) on the principle of Albert the Lion 'Sum one 'ad got to be summoned so that was decided upon'. The public will feel that something is being enquired into.

b) That the public will be brought up against the dilemma of security in a free society. Almost all the accusations of the Press against the laxity of the authorities are really demands for changing the English Common Law.'

from Harold Macmillan's Cabinet paper on the disappearance of Burgess and Maclean, 1955 (CAB 129/78 CP (55) 161).

CONTENTS

LIST OF ILLUSTRATIONS

ACKNOWLEDGEMENTS

Special thanks are due to Dave Baker for reading the manuscript, and to John Hope for discussion and much correspondence particularly relating to chapters 5 and 6. I would also like to thank the following for help, advice or stimulus with regard to aspects of this book: Roger Eatwell, Pauline Elkes, Roger Griffin, Colin Holmes, Tony Kushner, Nick Lowles, Steve Ludlam, David Martin, Don MacRaild, Andy Mitchell, Andrew Moore, Pat Renshaw, Brian Simpson, John Stevenson, Jeffrey Wallder, John Warburton and Leonard Wise. I am grateful to the Record Management Services division of the Home Office, and the Cabinet Office, for assistance with this project. I would also like to thank my parents for accommodation during my research trips to London, and Irene, Hazel, Kevin and Sally for putting up with my prolonged interest in the working of the secret state. I also wish to acknowledge the financial support given by the University of Sheffield Research Fund, and the Crown Copyright of the quotations used from Public Record Office documents.

The author and publisher are grateful to the following for kind permission to reproduce photographs: the Press Association (1, 3, 4, 5, 11, 14, 16, 17, 18, 21); the Press Association–John Stillwell (18); the Press Association–Chris Bacon (20); Popperfoto (2, 6, 8, 12, 15); the Hulton Deutsch Collection Limited (7, 9, 10, 13).

LIST OF ACRONYMS

ABN	Anti-Bolshevik Bloc of Nations
ACMA	Assistant Competent Military Authority
ACPO	Association of Chief Police Officers
ALF	Animal Liberation Front
ARA	Aliens Restriction Act
BDBJ	Board of Deputies of British Jews
BF	British Fascists
BNP	British National Party
BUF	British Union of Fascists
CAB	Cabinet Office
CBI	Confederation of British Industry
CCU	Civil Contingencies Unit
CIA	Central Intelligence Agency
CID	Committee of Imperial Defence
CIGS	Chief of the Imperial General Staff
CND	Campaign for Nuclear Disarmament
CO	Colonial Office
COS	Chiefs of Staff
CPGB	Communist Party of Great Britain
DI	Directorate of Intelligence
DMP	Dublin Metropolitan Police
DNI	Director of Naval Intelligence
DORA	Defence of the Realm Act
DP	Displaced Person Camp
DR	Defence Regulation
DUP	Democratic Unionist Party
EL	Economic League
EPA	Emergency Powers Act

FBI	Federal Bureau of Investigation
GCCS	Government Code and Cypher School
GCHQ	Government Communications Headquarters
GRU	Soviet Military Intelligence
HD(S)E	Home Defence Security Executive
HO	Home Office
Humint	Human Intelligence
ILD	International Labour Defense
ILP	Independent Labour Party
IMG	International Marxist Group
INLA	Irish National Liberation Army
IRA	Irish Republican Army
IRD	Information Research Department
IS	International Socialism
IUC	Industrial Unrest Committee
JIC	Joint Intelligence Committee
JPC	Jewish People's Congress
JPC	Joint Production Committees
KGB	Soviet Intelligence and Security 1953–91
LI	League against Imperialism
LPYS	Labour Party Young Socialists
MGB	Soviet Intelligence 1945–50
MI5	Security Service
MI6	Secret Intelligence Service
MM	Minority Movement
NATO	North Atlantic Treaty Organization
NBBS	New British Broadcasting Service
NCCL	National Council for Civil Liberties
NCF	No Conscription Fellowship
NF	National Front
NICRA	Northern Ireland Civil Rights Association
NKVD	Soviet Intelligence and Security (1930s)
NUM	National Union of Mineworkers
NUPPO	National Union of Police and Prison Officers
NUW(C)M	National Unemployed Workers (Committee) Movement
OGPU	Soviet Intelligence and Security (1920s)
OMS	Organization for the Maintenance of Supplies
OUN	Ukrainian Nationalists
PIRA	Provisional Irish Republican Army

PMS2	Parliamentary Military Secretary Department, no. 2 Section
PRO	Public Record Office
PSU	Police Support Units
PWE	Political Warfare Executive
RCP	Revolutionary Communist Party
RIC	Royal Irish Constabulary
RILU	Red International of Labour Unions
RIO	Regional Information Officers
SAS	Special Air Service
SC	Strike Committee
SDLP	Social Democratic Labour Party
SDP	Social Democratic Party
SF	Sinn Fein
Sigint	Signals Intelligence
SIS	Secret Intelligence Service (see MI6)
SLL	Socialist Labour League
SOE	Special Operations Executive
SPCR	Society for the Promotion of Cultural Relations with Soviet Russia
SPG	Special Patrol Groups
STC	Supply and Transport Committee
STO	Supply and Transport Organization
SWP	Socialist Workers Party
TUC	Trades Union Congress
UDA	Ulster Defence Association
UDC	Union of Democratic Control
UDR	Ulster Defence Regiment
UFF	Ulster Freedom Fighters
UUC	Ulster Unionist Council
UVF	Ulster Volunteer Force
WRP	Workers Revolutionary Party
YCL	Young Communist League

INTRODUCTION

This book is about state management of public order and internal security in twentieth-century Britain. It is concerned particularly with the nature of policy towards what the authorities term political extremism. To a marked degree this is a subject which government would prefer that academics and others should ignore. Certainly one of the aims of the Official Secrets Act of 1989 was to discourage the leaking of information, other than that sanctioned by government, in to the public domain. The Act proposed draconian penalties for those who released classified material, those who wrote about it and those who published it. However, I believe that this is both an important topic which can help illuminate much recent political and social history and can be legitimately studied from declassified material released into the Public Record Office and other archives. Like all recent writers on such matters I make the ritualistic but nevertheless true statement that I have never knowingly communicated with or spoken to a security or intelligence officer, nor indeed asked any civil servant for improper information. Certain aspects of the subject have already been covered in the literature, but there is as yet no general study which pulls together the available material on political extremism, public order and internal security.

There are two main arguments for the development of secrecy in British government. As Ken Robertson has argued, its principal justification has been to enable the executive to direct the administration, by making ministers responsible for the actions of civil servants in their departments, in return for Whitehall being placed firmly under political control. The British have developed a more secretive approach to decision making in government than the more open systems in Sweden and the USA as a result.[1] The second argument is that police, and the intelligence and security authorities, should remain as secretive as possible so as not to hinder their activities against criminals and enemies of the state. This book is mainly about the latter form of secrecy, but also covers the relations between government, Whitehall and the police and security authorities, where the two forms of secrecy overlap. The issue is complicated by the fact that whereas the constitutional doctrine of ministerial responsibility justifies administrative secrecy, the accountability of the secret and security services is more questionable – even though both were placed on a statutory basis by recent Conservative governments.

The function of this introduction is to outline those aspects of the 'secret state' germane to this study, to define 'political extremism' and to assess the nature of the evidence for their creation and continued existence. Indeed a fair amount of useful information has become available from the opening of government records. This declassified material, available up to 1963 in some areas, can now be discussed. The topical and often controversial material that has reached the public domain and that pertains to this study can be linked to other sources to make a legitimate account. The nature of the material makes this a patchwork-quilt operation where there will inevitably be gaps, but it is nevertheless a worthwhile exercise.

a) The Secret State

The subject matter of this book involves the interplay of politicians with civil servants, the police, the military and the security and intelligence agencies of the British state. It involves a study of what is known about the security service and secret police organizations – MI5, Special Branch and the Anti-Terrorist Branch. Some consideration will also be given to the domestic aspects of the Secret Intelligence

Service (SIS), or MI6 as it is nowadays better known. This is necessary because there is a counter-intelligence section to MI6, and the authorities have linked alleged British extremist movements with control or influence by a foreign power. This has been true of three main targets of political surveillance – the Communist Party of Great Britain (CPGB); the British Union of Fascists (BUF); and Sinn Fein and its links with the Irish Republican Army (IRA).

But the secret state is more than the territory covered in the official history of domestic intelligence in the Second World War and the unofficial studies of various stages of development of the British Intelligence and Security Services by Christopher Andrew, Bernard Porter, Keith Jeffery and Nicholas Hiley.[2] It also incorporates the response of the Home Office to the administrative problems of the authorities with relation to public order concerns, particularly about advice to regional police forces and the closer relationship with the Commissioner of the Metropolitan Police. The professionalization of the Civil Service, following the introduction of competitive examination for the recruitment of staff in the 1870s, saw the emergence of a new breed of expert administrator, even if they came from the same classical Oxbridge background as their predecessors.[3]

The appointment in 1908 of Sir Edward Troup as Under-secretary at the Home Office represented both the first such high appointment in this department of state by an entrant from the competitive examination, and the beginnings of a significant increase in the influence of the civil servant in the coordination and implementation of government policy. This achievement was to be consolidated by his successor, Sir John Anderson (1922–32). The War Office (later the Ministry of Defence) was to play a reluctant role in internal security matters and a front-line function in Northern Ireland. Indeed, the colonial dimension needs some emphasis too, since both the Security and Secret Services recruited heavily from men with Empire experience.

It needs to be recognized from the outset that the growth of the secret state was a highly controversial phenomenon. Unlike much of the rest of Europe, Britain was not well-endowed with governmental machinery of political repression and social control – hence (for example) Karl Marx's freedom of action and activism. Indeed, the triumph of liberalism in the nineteenth century was seen to imply that Britain's preeminence was in some way due to the state's relatively relaxed approach to internal security and public order. Political extremism was not seen as a threat to the stability of the Victorian state and social disorder could be dealt with by the implementation of the common law. The reluctance of the authorities to develop a detective function for the emergence of police forces across the country partly represented a deeply felt revulsion by public opinion against surveillance by the state.[4]

The most serious challenge to public order was during the Chartist disturbances of the 1840s, when the military had been called out to aid the civil power, and had demonstrated that sensitive measures, rather than the repression associated with the Peterloo massacre of 1819, were best suited to manage a delicate situation.[5] In this sense Generals Napier and Arbuthnot were to bequeath a tradition of low profile yet effective public order control which General Macready and others were to develop successfully as a means of deflecting social conflict in the twentieth century. The central government's refusal to develop a centralized police force and the reliance on local control over a variety of separate authorities was also to limit the extent to which control could be exerted over potential disorder, a factor which was to worry central government as to the extent of its powers in the twentieth century. Here the contrast with Ireland was to be most marked, where a very different tradition of centralized authority over police, and the use of the military to quell public disorder was to develop, both in the nineteenth and twentieth century.[6] Yet Ireland was to play a central role in the modern re-emergence of the secret state; it was to be the Fenian bombing campaign in England in the 1880s which was to lead to the creation of Special Branch in 1887.

The development of the secret state in late Victorian and Edwardian Britain turned out to be a Janus-faced phenomenon with specifically British traits. Whilst its most obvious drawback, the lack of proper parliamentary control, produced fears for the future of democracy, both the common law and the relatively liberal influence of the Whitehall administrative machine ensured a counter to the more restrictive demands of secret policemen. Only during the period of the world wars, the special case of Ireland between 1916 and 1922 and some aspects of Northern Ireland's history since 1968, can it be said that a serious threat to the civil liberties of individuals existed. Even in these cases there were strong countervailing voices against unnecessary restrictions of freedom and what were seen as questionable police or military internal security measures. The point was that there was continuing friction between politicians, administrators, the military and the secret agencies of government throughout the twentieth century.

Bernard Porter has argued that liberals see political extremism developing in societies where moderate demands for extension of civil liberties and social reforms were ignored; conservatives, on the other hand, viewed revolution as occurring in nations where the natural paternalistic order had been undermined by 'external agencies, subversives, professional revolutionaries, conspirators'.[7] Whilst it would be too crude to label British politicians and administrators as liberals and their policemen, secret policemen and military as conservatives in this sense, nevertheless this distinction serves to explain some tensions within the government machinery. Certainly such observations were not empirically based; neither was Bernard Porter's remark that MI5 and MI6 have a distinctive right-wing view of the world, although this appears to be a plausible hypothesis too.[8]

The empirical record suggests that any working model needs to be more complex than this. The recent revelations by Peter Wright, for example, tend to suggest that one partial explanation of the Hollis affair was that some right-wing MI5 and MI6 officers became suspicious of a more liberally inclined colleague, although neither senior members of the security service nor politicians were convinced. Similarly, not all politicians were liberals. Home Office civil servants acted as a brake to the right-wing Sir William Joynson-Hicks (Jix) in the 1920s. A small minority of MI5 officers have been suspicious of the patriotism of Labour party politicians at times and have indulged in dubious political activity. Labour has sometimes been susceptible to influences outside high politics.[9] Whilst the influence of the hidden areas of government has sometimes been exaggerated it remains true that the use of information from the secret world has decisively affected events. The prize for political dirty tricks would still be awarded to Sir Reginald 'Blinker' Hall, the ex-Director of Naval Intelligence, for the use he made of secret information from a variety of sources (including the Zimmerman telegram and the Zinoviev letter) both during and after the First World War.[10]

Whilst there has been a traditional suspicion of the activities of secret policemen, and a security consciousness as to their necessity, there are also continuing tensions not only in the administration but between government departments. Traditionally this has been encapsulated in the rivalry between the Home and Foreign Offices as the senior agencies of state and their attitude to other centres of power. A good example here was the Home Office determination that the methods of government of the Colonial Office in India and Ireland (what Charles Townshend has alluded to as the 'Indian Negative') should in normal circumstances have no influence on how Britain was governed. However, because the traditional method of recruitment included a significant proportion of personnel with military or police experience in the colonies, both MI5 and MI6 advocated a tougher stance to issues of public order and civil liberties than the liberal influences of most Home Office administrations. There is also evidence that for security reasons and institutional rivalries there was little coordination or exchange of information between MI5 and MI6 before 1940.[11]

b) Political Extremism

The problem with the term 'political extremism' is that it is an emotive concept which is value loaded.[12] This book is about the British state's attitude to and management of political extremism, so an obvious approach is to define as extremist those whom different layers of the state deem to have seen in those terms. This would certainly include communists, fascists, and members of the IRA. Such a definition is one sided. Many communists and fascists would argue that they are expressing a political opinion in a strictly legal manner, and portray their activities as defence of freedom of speech. This reply may evoke scepticism, but a scepticism that was genuinely held by most alleged extremists.

Similarly, the authorities were at least equally as interested in so-called 'front organizations'; groups which allegedly had been established, infiltrated, influenced or controlled by extremist movements. Thus the state was interested in the National Unemployed Workers Movement, the Minority Movement, the Society for Cultural Relations and the League against Imperialism, and their connections with the Communist Party of Great Britain (CPGB), and the link between the January Club and the British Union of Fascists (BUF). Possible and mainly imaginary links between the Conservatives and the BUF, and Labour and the CPGB, were also of considerable interest to the Security Service, as were obvious propaganda outlets for totalitarian foreign powers like the Anglo-German Fellowship and the Link with Nazi Germany.

At moments of crisis, such as war, perfectly innocent behaviour has been viewed with alarm by the authorities. During less troubled times respectable if unconventional views of progressive groups have been subject to political surveillance; some trade union activists, the suffragettes, pacifists and nuclear disarmers spring immediately to mind. In short, the state, or at least some of its agencies, have defined as extremist or potentially extremist, organizations like the CPGB who believe in the 'dictatorship of the proletariat' in Great Britain, or the BUF who envisaged a different kind of 'leadership' under Sir Oswald Mosley, together with groups which argued for an extension of democracy. In the case of the latter it is either the use of civil disobedience or suspicions that they are being used as fronts or tools of more extremist elements which brings the attention of the authorities.

The authorities very rarely acknowledged that there might be genuine social or political grievances which explained radical criticism of British institutions. Alienation from the values of British society and political democracy, and conflict with the authorities were always seen as a law and order issue rather than a social problem. There was little sympathy with or understanding of the causes of revolt. Whilst the political and social outlook of many critics of British society was often naive, both in terms of their view of the state and of the alleged interest of classes and elites in British society, the motives of protestors were regarded as sinister, misguided, eccentric and irrelevant by the authorities – a legacy, in part, of our unwritten constitution.

However, it is not just the ends envisaged by such groups which created alarm, but the actual or alleged means employed. This ranged from underground activity, through civil disobedience to political terrorism. These methods arose from groups who felt that normal pressure group politics and working through constitutional channels would never achieve their ends. The most extreme domestic concern was with the activities of the IRA and its splinter groups, which have been involved in spasmodic guerrilla warfare with the British state since 1916. The IRA, with its use of violence, civil disobedience and conspiratorial politics, was objected to as much for its methods as for its programme of a nationalist 'free' Ireland outside the British Empire. The British state saw the IRA as political terrorists, while the IRA's self-image was one of freedom fighting.

Political violence has led the authorities to investigate other movements, such as the Animal Liberation Front, when members have engaged in illegal activity. Whatever the rights and wrongs of the differing perceptions of the British state and 'political extremists', it is quite clear that beauty or ugliness was in the eye of the beholder. Yeats's image of the 'terrible beauty' of Irish nationalism following the Easter 1916 rebellion was an evocative case in point. In terms of political ends the British establishment was centrist – the majority of the population believed in a representative government which saw a significant extension of the franchise in 1918, and became fully democratic for those over 21 in 1928. This system was based on a constitutional monarchy whose institutions were rooted in the rule of law and legal precedent involving the separation of powers between the executive, legislative and judicial functions of the state. Such ideals were suspended during periods of perceived threat to the government from internal or external forces, or the combination of the two. This had most recently arisen during the Napoleonic Wars, when habeas corpus had been suspended and the authorities had used various illiberal measures which did not conform to the constitutional expectations of the 'free born Englishman' – freedom from arbitrary arrest and imprisonment without trial and due process of law.[13]

The use of the Defence of the Realm Act (DORA) during the First World War, the Defence Regulations (DR) of 1939, and the periodic invocation of the Emergency Powers Act of 1920 during labour disputes were obvious parallels from the twentieth century, in which the military were given powers to aid the civil power. This surely represented the real 'extremism of the centre' rather more than D. S. Lewis's characterization of the British Union of Fascists.[14] The use of state powers to censor news, direct labour, detain or restrict movement of individuals without due process of law, was the establishment's response to political or social crisis. In this sense the state has used enhanced powers contrary to the general tenor of English law as a temporary measure; even if the emergency in Northern Ireland has put some strain on this concept. It is, however, necessary to point out the obvious differences between the abnormal use of limited emergency powers in the British state and the normal use of more extreme methods as the permanent basis of power in totalitarian societies.

This difference meant that the very existence of a secret police and political surveillance had to remain a state secret for as long as possible because of the fear that public knowledge would lead to public outrage. The British preference for a preventive rather than detective police, and the dislike of 'French' methods of political surveillance meant that when lack of security was perceived as weakness and as an important reason for international tension, British measures to improve internal security can be seen as an extremist form of politics.[15] In fact such behaviour was normal practice elsewhere. Governmental practice of all political persuasions produced what might be termed as a hard-nosed liberalism towards extremism – one in which political surveillance and the powers to move against threats to national security were in place but the preferred policy was to isolate, marginalize and deny publicity to such groups and to rely on public opinion to see through the utopian and illiberal dreams suggested. Such arguments even if they are heavily qualified, suggest that an interactionist approach which gives prominence to both the actions of the various levels of the secret state and the alleged activities of so-called extremists is one which at least takes into account the value problems of the emotive terminology. In short, the state has used extremist methods itself (emergency powers, internment etc.) against alleged internal enemies.

c) Sources

The material for this study is mainly to be found in the Public Record Office (PRO) at Kew, particularly in the Cabinet and Home Office papers. This to a certain extent can be supplemented from other departmental papers and from information in private collections. The PRO has released material into the public domain according to the terms of the Public Records Act of 1958 and its amendment in 1967 which has reduced the period of retention to 30 years in some cases. There are, however, a number of important qualifications which need to be borne in mind in assessing such material.

The 30-year rule is indeed not quite what it seems. Although a significant amount of new material is declassified each year there are a number of limitations on this process. All the files that are released have first to be assessed both in terms of protecting state secrets and destroying supposedly unimportant information. Given the vast amount of paper involved in the Public Records, only that part of the material can be released which the resources available have time to process. It has been estimated that 98 per cent of Public Records are routinely shredded or destroyed. This means in effect that decisions have to be taken in various government departments about the priority of relevant information with regard to release.

When such decisions have been taken, the files are weeded by officials or retired civil servants, to make them manageable for storage purposes. As there is no way of knowing the degree of historical expertise of the weeders the suspicion must remain that at least some valuable information is lost through such a process. Some files or subfiles are often retained in the department of origin or at the Public Record Office. It is thought that between 20 and 25 per cent of Home Office records and 1 per cent of Foreign Office correspondence remains classified. Privileged access may be granted to unreleased Home Office files, providing the researcher submits any publication resulting to the authorities. Once permission has been granted others can apply to see this material.[16] The HO 144 and MEPO 3 files, both of which are significant for this study, generally have a 75 or 100 year closure rule applied to them. Here again the attitude of the authorities has proved to be flexible in practice. Public pressure from an unlikely combination of Lady Mosley and left-wing Labour MPs managed to secure the early release of classified files on British Fascism in the HO 45, HO 144 and HO 283 series. The priority given to the release of government files announced by John Major on his re-election in 1992, and the subsequent Waldegrave initiative, has given hope that more papers will be released earlier than their current classification suggests.

The application of a degree of secrecy on some of the released material is covered under sections 3.4 and 5.1 of the Public Records Act.[17] The main reasons given for extended closure are national security and 'information supplied in confidence the disclosure of which would or might constitute a breach of faith'.[18] This basically means that material is held back which could compromise the identity or security of agents or the activities of the Security Service or the Secret Service. This so-called law of confidentiality has played a central role in the Peter Wright and other recent court cases, a principle which can be used to protect the identity of individuals or to prosecute whistleblowers. The government has taken on board some of the recommendations of the Wilson Committee on Public Records which reported in 1981. The third category for the retention of material causing embarrassment to living persons or their immediate descendants was subsequently dropped. However, the other major recommendation of the Wilson Committee was shelved. The government refused to set up sector panels which would have involved researchers, along with departmental interests and the PRO, in the retention and weeding process. The reasons given were a desire to avoid increasing the size of the Civil Service, a desire for economy and a belief that the present arrangements worked satisfactorily. What is perhaps equally worrying was the use of section 3.4 with regard to the release of fascist and internment files in 1986, which could be interpreted as a move toward less liberal criteria for the release of public records. This material is held back in the department of origin, and although there are procedures for review of the retention policy there is no obligation to set a time limit on the release of such information.

There is also no intention of ever releasing to public inspection the files of the Security Service or Secret Service. Although the publication of the official history of British Intelligence in the Second World War now provides much-needed information on the historical development of MI5 and MI6, it gives only a partial view of such matters. Although Hinsley and Simkins have seen all the relevant material there have been important government limitations on what they have been able to relay. The fact that the government delayed the publication of this volume on domestic intelligence shows the reluctance of the authorities to impart information about security even if it is innocuous. Information about personnel and activities is sparse, and Hinsley and Simkins is more of an administrative than an operational history. Although it does provide interesting and accurate detail on the organization of security, the restrictions on what the authors have been able to tell us of necessity limits its usefulness.[19] The researcher is not helped either by the paucity of footnotes, or by the fact that a sizeable proportion of the information released has to be taken on trust.

These reluctant disclosures of information make it necessary to handle any study of internal security with a great deal of care. Indeed, the government's attitude as recently as the Peter Wright case was made clear when they refused to confirm that MI6 continued its existence outside the period of the world wars, although thankfully the present government has a more sensible approach to such matters. This ludicrous example of being 'economical with the truth' perfectly illustrated the traditional attitude of the state to intelligence and security matters. The Stalker affair, the strange case of Colin Wallace and the grave doubts about the trials of the 'Birmingham six' and the 'Guildford four' have called into question the use of secrecy to maintain security.

Erosion of individual liberties and civil rights appears to have resulted. Whether this is too high a price to pay for the failure to deal effectively with the terrorism in Northern Ireland is questioned by some. The Ponting affair and the government's attitude to leakage of classified information shows that in spite of the new, draconian Official Secrets Act, public opinion is far from satisfied with official explanations of the continuing need for secrecy across such a broad range of political and historical issues.

From the information that has been released the often contrasting attitudes of politicians, administrators, policemen, secret policemen and security and intelligence agencies can be analysed. A fairly good idea of the attitude of different levels of state activity can be derived with regard to the suffragism, anarchism and trade union militancy before 1914; pacifists and labour unrest in the first world war; labour unrest and communism 1919–24; British fascism and the National Unemployed Workers Movement in the 1930s; and internment policy during the Second World War. After 1945 the evidence becomes patchier, although there is some useful material on labour unrest and the Cold War during the Attlee administration. There are also some valuable parliamentary papers on security issues and much public controversy and governmental policy to be assessed with regard to both public order and security issues since 1945. In addition, there are interesting examples of material which has been retained by the Home Office but released elsewhere. Some gaps are noticeable in the declassified files. The most obvious is with regard to the CPGB particularly after 1924, or renewed IRA activity since 1922. This is unfortunate because these have undoubtedly been the major areas of political surveillance since the First World War.

This book is concerned with material that has been legitimately obtained. The American National Archives in Washington have copies of security reports from Special Branch and MI5 that are not available in Britain. John Costello has drawn attention to this source in *Mask of Treachery*.[20] This material derives from the secret UK/USA intelligence exchange agreement of 1917, and represents information sent via the American embassy. The use of such material would undoubtedly infringe the Official Secrets Act, so it has not been consulted. Costello's book is valuable, however, in that it provides references to the very interesting files on communist and communist front activity at the PRO. This released material is a very small tip of a very large iceberg, but it sheds considerable light on an important area of darkness. Information from other archives also provides much needed illumination. The concern of the British government about the CPGB and their Comintern and Soviet controllers in the 1920s can only begin to be understood in a rational manner when it is realized that the Government Code and Cypher School was reading Soviet wireless traffic for much of the period before 1927.

Thus, although considerable detective work is necessary to piece together a coherent picture, the broad outlines of the relationship between the state and internal security in twentieth-century Britain are becoming clear. It is to the complex development of this process that we shall now turn.

1

THE STRANGE DEATH OF LIBERAL ENGLAND (1900–1914)

George Dangerfield's much criticized picture of social turmoil between 1911 and 1914 suggested that these years represented a transition to new public order and security concerns.[1] With hindsight it could be said that the Liberal governments of 1905–15 moved towards a more positive role for state intervention across a wide spectrum of social and political life.[2] Such activity had repercussions outside the themes of this book; yet one important consequence is central to my argument. Party, class and gender conflicts, as well as the Ulster crisis, splintered the fragile political consensus of values of British Society. This increased the pressures on the Liberals after they lost their overall majority in the parliamentary elections of 1910. It led to serious problems for the government from both within and outside conventional politics after the failure of a constitutional conference to create a bipartisan coalition government.[3] The fact that both the Liberals and Unionists were divided internally on important issues (the Liberals on defence and foreign policy, the Unionists over protection and constitutional reform) complicated the picture further.[4] The illusion of a divided ruling class no doubt encouraged unrest.

Yet overall Dangerfield's diagnosis was exaggerated. The released state papers show a flexible and sophisticated response by both politicians and administrators to the surface froth of discontent, and to complex social problems in this period. There is little evidence of a loss of confidence or control, or of low politics influencing decision making in high politics.[5] It was to be the First World War which precipitated the real crisis of liberalism. Yet the period before 1914 was to be important both for the development of new techniques of management and control of public order, and the modern origins of the secret state.

a) Public Order and the State

Although there was significant development in public order policy before 1914, the response of government was rooted in Victorian assumptions. There was a tendency to view the state as an impartial umpire between capital and labour. Social unrest was blamed chiefly on hooligans, part of the shifty residuum of the undeserving poor of Victorian imagination, rather than attributed to social causes.[6] There was an increasing move towards summary jurisdiction rather than indictment as the best means of control of the 'dangerous classes', as a conscious public order policy.[7] The magistrates' use of short terms of imprisonment, small fines and binding over to keep the peace were seen as effective deterrents which avoided the necessity of juries, who tended to remain more sceptical of police evidence and seemed unreliable from the authorities' viewpoint.

Administrative convenience was tempered by the state's concern over civil liberties and the traditional rights of 'free born Englishmen'. The Whitehall mandarins and the law officers were particularly determined that there should be as few embarrassing incidents as possible. Public opinion and MPs had to be convinced that the implementation of the law, its independence from political control and total impartiality were indisputable. Such liberal niceties were, however, under constant harrassment from those at the sharp end of the legal criminal process, in particular the police.

Here the role of the Home Office was crucial. It was ultimately responsible for the organization of the police, though control was left firmly in the hands of the Chief Constables in the shire counties and the Watch Committees in Metropolitan boroughs.[8] The Home Office provided half the cost for pay and clothing of the police in the boroughs and counties on the condition that they pass annual inspection (they always did). However, except in the case of the Metropolitan Police, the Home Office only possessed advisory powers with regard to the administration of justice, which is influenced through the issuing of circulars to police authorities.

The control of the Metropolitan Police was a direct Home Office responsibility deriving from the need to protect public order in the vicinity of parliament. The relationship between the Home Office and the Commissioner whom they appointed had led to problems, and both Sir Charles Warren and James Munro had resigned in the 1890s. Both fell victim to the Home Office's reluctance to extend the powers of the police, to restrict public meetings or to sanction unauthorized initiatives. Nominally Munro resigned over a superannuation dispute involving constables, but the real damage had been done following Sir Charles Warren's successful banning of socialist meetings in Trafalgar Square in 1886 and 1887. Munro's attempt to extend the principle to middle class groups like Temperance and Friendly Societies met with humiliating rebuff in the courts and an admonition from the Home Office.[9]

The Home Office's caution was based on recent legal precedents and the lack of a separate role for the state in English Law. Under common law the state was not recognized as a separate power and possessed the same rights as individuals and corporations. As a result the authorities possessed only loose discretionary powers. Their reactions were based on an accumulation of precedents. (It is worthwhile recalling that Max Weber, the German sociologist, pointed out that Britain was the least likely of the European powers to compromise its traditional freedoms by an expansion of bureaucratic power.[10]) The Home Office often tried to restrain over-zealous police officers who tried to extend the influence of the authorities. Rights were preserved by the absence of a written constitution, and the lack of defined powers gave the maximum administrative flexibility with response to individual problems as they arose. Thus secrecy and the lack of acknowledged rights for the state enabled law officers and the Home Office, somewhat ironically, to emerge as defenders of civil liberties against more impatient authorities who tried to whittle away individual freedoms. This defence of the nineteenth-century liberal principle of negative freedom meant that the move from localism towards centralization and a greater defining of powers in the twentieth century would be slow, particularly in the public order field.

There was a somewhat contradictory case law on public order until the 1930s, with *Beatty* v. *Gilbanks* (1882) and *Wise* v. *Dunning* (1903) decisions influencing Home Office policy.[11] The former arose out of the 'Salvation Army' riots when peaceful meetings had been broken up by publican financed gangs known as the 'skeleton army' in southern towns.[12] The court of appeal reversed a lower court judgement, and argued that the Salvation Army march was legal and not provocative, and had a perfect right to express its viewpoint. The Trafalgar Square riots of 1886 and 1887 had shown that the authorities could remove the 'rough and criminal element' to ensure the proper use of highways, but the subsequent fate of Munro showed that it was unwise for the police to restrict the freedom of the respectable middle classes.[13] The *Wise* v. *Dunning* judgement limited the freedom of demonstrations as it was successfully argued that the activities of Pastor Wise and his protestant followers had been intimidating to law-abiding Catholics in Liverpool.[14] Drink and anti-Catholicism represented concerns of nineteenth- rather than twentieth-century public order policy and became of diminishing concern to the authorities outside Liverpool and Glasgow, where Orangeism in particular continued to be an ingredient within a complex pattern of social unrest. As was typical, however, of English law both *Beatty* v. *Gilbanks* and *Wise* v. *Dunning* had been resolved on minor points of detail which left the general principle unclear.

In an era which saw a large increase in the vehemence of political debate, the intransigence of entrenched interest groups, the growth of potential conflict and the number of public meetings, it was remarkable that such a loose legal framework should prove so flexible and effective. The Public Meetings Act of 1908 showed the self-confidence of the authorities with regard to the subject. Organizers were responsible for stewarding at public meetings and police were not given the right to enter unless requested. This relaxed approach was shown to be effective almost immediately. Whilst government files, if they exist, have not been released on the constitutional crisis following the rejection of the 1909 budget, the available evidence suggests that despite the emotional rhetoric of politicians and inflamed public passions, diehards and right-wing extremist elements had few public adherents.[15] Similarly, the emotions raised by the tariff reform controversy, the national efficiency campaign and the pressure for conscription never developed in terms of methods and ideas outside the normal, acceptable conventions of influence and participation in the British political process.[16] Apart from labour disputes the main public order problems arose from a most unexpected quarter: the demand by the suffragettes of votes for women, or, at the very least, political equality with men.

The tactics of the suffragettes brought them much notoriety. Their aims, which had been encouraged by intellectuals and liberals like John Stuart Mill since the 1850s, were also those of the suffragists, who used the channels of public opinion and pressure groups to influence decision making in high politics. Although the political issues involved in extending the franchise were highly complex, the suffragettes, led by the redoubtable Mrs Emmeline Pankhurst and her two daughters Christabel and Sylvia, simplified the issue by pointing out that genteel methods of influence and cosy tea parties had not produced votes for women.[17] The suffragettes utilized stunts, civil disobedience and open flouting of the law to put pressure on government to produce reform. The tactics of struggle, publicity and the courting of martyrdom were other weapons used.

The campaign which began with the formation of the Women's Social and Political Union in 1903 soon degenerated into open revolt as the failure of minor acts of disobedience like window smashing, the destruction of letter boxes, the chaining of suffragettes to the railings of Buckingham Palace, and the open abuse of cabinet ministers, led to the advocacy of more violent means. The plausible suspicion that some Liberal politicians were guilty of prevarication and duplicity during truces in the period of direct action, led to the growth of extremist methods which included Emily Davison's death under the hooves of the King's horse at the Epsom Derby in 1913, arson at Hurst Park racecourse and several football stadiums, and the destruction of works of art.[18] The emergence of the diehard male-chauvinist Anti-suffrage Union added fuel to the fire.

The arrival of the petticoat revolutionaries was to have important consequences for public order policy. Many of the suffragettes were militant feminists, spirited respectable middle and upper class women demanding elementary rights. Some, however, adopted the tactics and fanaticism of militant anarchists. Marion Dunlop, for example, was described as an 'extremist' or 'neurotic' fanatic rather than as insane by the prison authorities at Holloway.[19] Such contradictions led to a schizophrenic official attitude towards them; police were given instructions to show firmness and tact towards suffragettes whilst upholding the law.[20] The fear that the campaign might degenerate to assault or murder of influential public figures was a factor in the expansion of Special Branch, which became increasingly involved in monitoring suffragette activities.

Growing nationalist and anarchist violence in London, including a political assassination by an Indian nationalist and the Houndsditch murders, increased fears of the emergence of a 'female Dhingra', whose extremism might lead her to an act of personal violence against Cabinet ministers or the royal family.[21] As there were no policewomen, surveillance through infiltration was difficult, although the use of plain clothes policemen, some apparently with a 'good physique', represented a half-way house in the emergence of political policing of British subjects outside Ireland. With the possible exception of the dubious framing of publishers of books on homosexuality and divorce, it appears that the suffragettes, along with anarchists, were amongst the first native targets of England's new breed of secret policemen.

The released Home Office files also make it quite clear that as suffragette intransigence became more militant, so the patience of the authorities snapped and the kid gloves came off. The refusal of suffragettes to be bound over to keep the peace led to their imprisonment. They were put in the first division initially. According to the Home Secretary in 1909, Herbert Gladstone, suffragettes took advantage of first division rules to make Holloway Jail the centre of a disorderly movement by writing to newspapers and encouraging lawlessness.[22] As this was considered highly prejudicial to prison discipline the courts subsequently committed them to the second division, with a consequent deterioration in facilities and rights.

Following the withdrawal of privileges the suffragettes retaliated by going on hunger strike. This tactic was first used by Marion Dunlop in 1909. Prison authorities had a well-developed technique of force-feeding to counter this move. Between 1904 and 1909 the authorities had used such a procedure against 82 men and 30 women, a quarter of whom had been deemed insane.[23] However, the use of such a technique against highly respectable upper class women like Lady Constance Lytton was thought to be counterproductive.[24] Although force-feeding was resolutely defended as not being a 'disgusting outrage', suffragette hunger strikers were released if there was a danger that martyrdom could be achieved by starving to death.

Such a fear lay behind the Prison Commissioners' memorandum in October 1909.[25] As a result of a truce in the militant campaign of the suffragettes, the authorities felt they were justified in adopting a conciliatory approach without appearing to give in to violence. Whilst 'political hooligans' should not be allowed first-division treatment, the fact that

LONDON CARMEN
TRADE UNION
BETHNAL GREEN
BRANCH
No 2
LIC COFFEE BAR

second division facilities were closer to the third than the first division meant that the suffragettes gained some public sympathy, before disorder turned into outrage. As a result, in April 1910, the new Home Secretary, Winston Churchill, introduced a new prison rule, 243a, which allowed suffragettes and passive resisters to be given treatment closer to that of the first division but without the ability to communicate with the outside world.[26]

Although the Home Office was very sensitive to public opinion, the political truce between the government and the suffragettes soon broke down. The suffragettes reverted to civil disobedience, the smashing of prisons and hunger strikes. Force-feeding was re-introduced and, in Churchill's words, no 'squeamishness' was to be shown to Suffragettes.[27] In all, 57 were forcibly fed in Holloway, Aylesbury and Birmingham jails by September 1912.[28]

There are also indications that prison boards of visitors thought the Home Office far too soft in their treatment of suffragettes. The visitors to Walton Jail, Liverpool, complained that Home Office advice to ignore wilful damage, such as window smashing, would be highly detrimental to prison discipline.[29] It was later alleged that Selina Hall and Leslie Martin suffered 'atrocities' at the hands of the authorities of Walton Jail, including being frog-marched, assaulted, knocked down, gagged and fed by force.[30] These complaints were dismissed as 'without foundation', although it was 'necessary to put them both under restraint'.[31]

The indiscipline of suffragettes in jail was aimed at gaining them political prisoner status. Such a change was vehemently opposed by the authorities. As Herbert Gladstone, when Home Secretary, explained in an answer to John O'Connor MP, an offender who had broken the law from good motives was likely to be more harmful to the public than an ordinary criminal because it would encourage others to follow that example.[32] Suffragettes were incensed that they were persecuted for civil disobedience whilst treasonable Ulster Unionists were not punished at all. The suffragette tactic of

---

Opposite 1 A strike meeting at Tower Hill, 1912

demanding political prisoner status was seen as imitating 'Russian' tactics (the tactics of radicals and socialists in tsarist prisons).[33] Churchill made clear that the government as a general principle would never base prison treatment on a consideration of the motives which caused illegality.[34]

As public opinion became more critical of the handling of suffragettes, the government showed resource by introducing the Temporary Discharge of Prisoners Act of 1913. This enabled the authorities to release prisoners who were in danger of inflicting permanent damage on themselves or committing suicide. They could then be rearrested to complete their sentence once they had recovered. The so-called Cat and Mouse Act ushered in a macabre sequence of events where the authorities shunted suffragettes in and out of prison. Some, like Mrs Pankhurst and Mary Richardson, responded by inciting others and committing further outrages when under temporary discharge.[35] This escalation of conflict was finally resolved by the outbreak of war: an unofficial cease-fire became permanent as many of the outstanding charges against suffragettes were dropped whilst most of the militants became more patriotic than the government in their espousal of the war, although there were significant exceptions. Sylvia Pankhurst was to become more revolutionary than Lenin in her opposition to the war, and Winifred Carney, or Kearney, became the 'typewriter of the Easter 1916 rebellion' in the Dublin Post Office. Other ex-suffragettes, such as Mary Richardson, Mary Allen, and the Pethick-Lawrences (also known as Professor and Mrs Dacre-Fox), were later to be associated with another organization deemed extremist, the British Union of Fascists.[37] Somewhat ironically, it was the executive of the highly respectable National Union of Women's Suffrage Societies, led by Millicent Garrett Fawcett, with its 60 societies and 100,000 affiliated suffragettes before the war, which split. Those pacifist members who opposed the war were to create far more problems for the state than the overdose of patriotism and white-feather fervour of Mrs Pankhurst's militants.

The suffragettes proved to be an interesting public order phenomenon. In political terms the emergence of a militant feminist approach to the suffrage question complicated and probably weakened the argument for universal suffrage in the years before 1914.[38] The government could never be seen to give in to force or civil disobedience. This meant that Die-Hards and less extreme Unionists had little difficulty in persuading the government that any alteration in the suffrage was not really on the political agenda before 1914. The division over methods and aims of suffrage reformers considerably lessened the impact of the issue.

The suffragette tactics also introduced Special Branch to sophisticated counter-intelligence techniques which more extremist groups were later to imitate. Sinn Fein, for example, were to copy the 'shadow' system whereby every official in the suffragettes organization had a replacement who could immediately assume responsibility if the authorities acted against individuals.[39]

What released government files suggested was that the militant campaign produced little if any movement by the state to accommodate suffragette claims. The authorities proved adept at modifying their tactics so as not to allow the suffragettes to appear martyrs in the eyes of the public. The limits of such flexibility had been approached by the time war broke out; however, the most belligerent suffragettes had become so extreme they were increasingly counter-productive. Criminal behaviour could not be condoned in however noble a cause. An interesting example of official attitudes towards the suffragettes was shown with the discovery that one of the prison inspectors, Dr Mary Gordon, was a suffragette sympathizer. In spite of official pressures she managed to keep her post, probably because all the suffragette prisoners were released in 1914.[40] It was significant that the performance of women in the war effort should be given as the official reason for the extension of the franchise to some women in 1918. But even here the inequality of women was emphasized: only those over 30 who satisfied a property qualification were to be included. Just the same, this included many suffragettes. The suffragette political demands were not met until 1928, on the 'leaping Niagara' principle: gradualism and as few concessions as possible to violent behaviour were the time-honoured responses of the state to commotion.

b) Labour Unrest

The issue which caused most public order problems for the authorities before 1914 was labour unrest. The succession of serious disputes between 1910 and 1914 led to important changes in the role of the state in containing potential conflict between capital and labour. Throughout the period the government maintained the liberal position that it was a neutral force between employers and employed. As late as 1914 the Board of Trade emphasized that both entrepreneurs and trade unions were against compulsory arbitration to resolve industrial disputes and the state authorities were still reluctant to intervene, and to be specific in limiting the rights of pickets.[41]

There was also a considerable hesitation on the part of government to employ troops to control labour disturbances, no doubt as a result of the Featherstone 'massacre' in 1893, when two miners had been shot.[42] This problem was decisively faced in the South Wales disturbances of 1910–11, the outcome of which was that all future requests for troops had to be notified to both the War Office and Home Office.[43] Local authorities and chief constables still had the statutory right and duty to summon troops if satisfactory agreements over the loan of police from other areas could not be negotiated under the terms of the 1890 Police Act. According to the Home Office in 1908, 27 counties and 30 boroughs had entered into such agreements. The report of the select committee on employment of the military in case of disturbance suggested they should be extended so that ten per cent of any county police force could be sent in an emergency.[44] Similarly the Permanent Undersecretary at the Home Office, Sir Edward Troup, was highly critical of the assumptions of many South Wales businessmen and magistrates (the two categories overlapped) in 1910 that the purpose of imported troops and police was to act in their interest and at their direction.[45]

Whilst the state authorities tried to distance themselves from the direct interest of employers, their attitude towards Labour represented a mixture of ancient prejudices, political calculation and a resolve never to be seen to give in to industrial force. Thus labour unrest was usually seen as having economic causes, particularly with the relative decline of real wages amongst important groups in this period. We now know this pattern was more complex and that low rates of unemployment were also a key factor which encouraged labour militancy.[46] There was no recognition by the government of the social causes of the most important and intransigent dispute in South Wales; nor that it was rooted in abnormal working practices and deep class division.[47] The frustration and social alienation which led to attacks on Chinese and Jewish immigrants in South Wales was seen mainly in public order terms as the work of hooligans, although the authorities expressed concern that respectable shopkeepers were conniving at the looting of successful ethnic competitors.[48]

This anxiety reflected the ambivalence over political concerns about trade union power. The Liberal Party at the national level were worried about the growing working class vote, and wanted local associations to choose one worker in two-member constituencies, where appropriate. The secret agreement between Herbert Gladstone and Ramsay MacDonald in 1903 developed a more concrete form with the passing of the Trade Disputes Act of 1906, which made clear that unions could not be sued for restraint of trade during industrial disputes, and made the restrictions on picketing more problematic.[49] Although the Osborne judgement in 1909 showed that the legal status of unions was still in question, and further threatened the survival of Labour representation in parliament, for most Conservatives the Liberals had weakened the state against union militancy.

If the balance of power was swinging in the Labour movement's favour, and economic and political factors were polarizing attitudes, the growth of union militancy caused increasing concern. Yet the evidence suggests that labour troubles were not perceived as an organized threat which extremists manipulated against the political system. Although uniformed police were increasingly used to monitor socialist and trade union demonstrations,[50] there was little evidence that the labour movement became a concern of Special Branch, or of military intelligence, before 1914.[51]

If the state was to maintain a plausible neutrality between capital and labour it needed a more positive framework within which to exercise an influence. In the more bitter confrontations, like that in the North Wales lead mines (1903), and the Hemsworth Colliery dispute (1907), the Home Office adopted a more traditional role of proferring advice when requested and was careful not to intervene outside the framework of the law or accepted practice. With the disputes of 1910–11, however, the initiatives of Winston Churchill as Home Secretary were to leave an indelible mark on state attitudes towards labour and public disorder, and to redefine the control and management of the public order authorities by the state. It was to mark the beginning of a change in relationship between central government and local authorities over public order, and the emergence of a slow but definite trend towards more centralized management of an essentially locally controlled police force.

The issue which triggered the reappraisal of the state's role in industrial disputes was a seemingly innocuous strike in Newport docks in 1910. This arose when an employer, Houlder Brothers, broke an agreement which would have ended a strike, by importing so-called scab labour after sacking their own workers. The authorities felt unable to control passions after failing to get outside police reinforcements to bolster the hard-pressed local constabulary. The advice from Whitehall was that police should not be used to protect the imported labour because local resentment was so strong, and there was a continuing danger of civil conflict if they were used to protect Houlder Brothers' interests.[52] This was at variance with the spirit of all previous advice, since never giving into force had always been given a higher priority than state neutrality.

After the settlement of this dispute, Winston Churchill, the Home Secretary, who had been absent for much of the period of the Newport Strike, was determined that the state should never again abdicate its responsiblity for the maintenance of public order. He intervened decisively at the outset of the next major dispute in South Wales. The Cambrian Combine dispute began as an industrial confrontation over working practices in the South Wales coalfield, and rapidly spread to other employers as an issue of payment for working in abnormal places.[53] The Home Office records do not even mention the origins or nature of the problem in four boxes of material which relate to this file.[54] Trade union leaders and syndicalists developed the issue into a demand for a national minimum wage for miners. This was to spread from South Wales to other mining areas like north-east England and Scotland.

The deeply ingrained and volatile class prejudices in South Wales had a long history. The public regarded the local police, more so than in other working class districts, as agents and upholders of the local landholding and entrepreneurial interests.[55] In Glamorgan, the centre of the problem, the Chief Constable between 1896 and 1935 was Lionel Lindsay, who had succeeded his father in the post. In Monmouthshire Victor Bosanquet, and in Carmarthenshire W. Picton Phillips, were similarly long-serving, entrenched and autocratic policemen who ruled in a rigid and high-handed fashion to maintain law and order.[56] The Home Office came to view Lindsay's overzealous policing policies as a factor in worsening the alienation of the community in South Wales.

Churchill's role in the dispute began when as a result of an interdepartmental conference between the Home and War Office, he dramatically stopped the troops requested by Lindsay, and arranged for Metropolitan Police officers to be sent instead. Troops were then sent under the Director of Personal Services, Sir Nevil Macready, to act as a force of last resort if the police could not contain the situation. Churchill's intervention and his direction of the Metropolitan Police, who had not been allowed by the Home Office to enter into agreements with other constabularies under the Police Act of 1890, emphasized that the police should be primarily responsible for maintaining public order. The other novel result of the intervention was that Winston Churchill made Macready responsible for the maintenance of public order, and he was given control over both the police and army forces in South Wales as a combined responsibility.

What is quite clear from Macready's autobiography, the Home Office files and the Blue Book on the dispute, is that

2 Sir Basil Thomson, 1938

although Macready had a military suspicion of politicians, he followed the spirit of Churchill's instructions to the letter.[57] Macready was even happy to work with a Home Office 'spy', John Moylan, who reported regularly to Whitehall about the public order situation in South Wales.[58] Macready's influence on policy was to be seminal, and reinforced the nineteenth-century trends toward a lower profile for the military in managing civil disorder.[59]

Macready viewed his appointment in neutral terms. He was determined not to be seen as supporting either side in the dispute. After arriving in South Wales he refused to send troops or to act on the demands of the employers unless, in his judgement, based on independent assessment, the situation warranted it.[60] He was very critical of the mine owners and forbade his staff from accepting any hospitality from them.[61] Whilst recognizing the delicate situation of

Lindsay he thought Lindsay was too much influenced by the employers.

The sceptical approach adopted by Macready owed much to the information he was receiving from his own intelligence network. He recognized from the outset that information from interested parties in the dispute would be tainted, and that unless troops and police could be shown to be neutral their presence could only inflame, rather than defuse, the situation. Whilst Moylan's role was to provide an objective viewpoint for the Home Office, Macready adopted the same approach to the parties in the dispute. He insisted on independent factual information not coloured by the prejudices of participants. What was perhaps of equal significance was that two of Macready's team played important roles in public order and internal security policy in the 1920s, which extended Macready's influence. His role in strike control (1910–11), as Adjutant-General in the First World War, Commissioner of the Metropolitan Police (1918–19), and Commander in Chief in Ireland (1919–22) left an indelible mark on the management of internal security. Brigadier-General Horwood was Metropolitan Police Commissioner between 1919 and 1928, and Captain (later Major-General) Childs, the Chief Intelligence Officer in South Wales, became head of Special Branch between 1921 and 1928. Childs was such a devoted admirer of Macready and his methods that his autobiography was dedicated to him. Such was his obsequious attitude that his nickname in the Home Office was 'Fido'.[62]

It has to be emphasized that Macready's intelligence network was not political surveillance, nor did it involve Special Branch. However, the security implications of domestic intelligence were foreshadowed in his final report. As well as outlining his role as a public order umpire, Macready implied that political strikes were unacceptable. He emphasized that in his view 'extreme socialists' were responsible for increased tensions and for prolonging the dispute.[63] They should be firmly dealt with. Macready's role in crushing the police strikes in London in 1918 and 1919 demonstrated that he was even more determined that the representatives of law and order should not side with the unions or employers in industrial disputes.[64] Neutrality in the liberal state meant disregarding politely the more irresponsible of the demands of the employers, whilst using uniformed officers to provide intelligence of the moods and plans of the strikers. Any attempt by the representatives of law and order to show partiality to unions or to force the authorities to give in to workers' demands were to be severely punished.

It was ironic that Winston Churchill, the main architect of new initiatives to control public order, was the main victim of the successful intervention. The violence in Tonypandy was to be forever associated with his name – despite his imaginative policy, and implementation by Macready which led to a minimal use of troops and the emergence of efficient Metropolitan Police techniques of crowd control. Although the bitter strike lasted for nearly a year, troops were withdrawn after a few months. While the Home Office policy was successful in public order terms, the response of the local community was more double-edged. The local authority refused to pay the bill for the cost of the Metropolitan Police officers drafted into South Wales on the grounds they had asked for troops and not policemen.[65] This complaint was upheld, although Glamorgan were still forced to pay the cost of police imported from other authorities. The Home Office lost face over the issue, but the success of the operation gave the government grounds to ask parliament for powers to send police on their own initiative, even when not requested to do so.

The lessons learned in South Wales were almost immediately used in controlling wider outbreaks of industrial unrest. The troubles of 1911–12 saw serious strikes of the railwaymen, coal miners and dockers. The coordinating role of the Home Office, the continued use of the military as a force of last resort and the increased controversy over the alleged violence and brutality of imported policemen led to the organization of a loose countervailing alliance of transport workers, dockers and miners in the Triple Alliance (formed 1914). Although there were syndicalist undercurrents to this development, it owed more to deep-seated industrial unrest than socialist rhetoric or the ideas of Daniel de Leon.[66] Even in South Wales, where the publication of the *The Miners' Next Step* gave impetus to such ideas, the transition to demands for a national minimum wage did not really develop a widespread syndicalist movement. Before the First World War there was little coordination of strike action. The unrest was treated as separate disturbances by both Churchill and his less innovative successor as Home Secretary, Reginald McKenna (1911–15).

Separate strikes by dockers, carters, seamen, railwaymen and miners threatened public order in 1911. The Home Office responded by sending Metropolitan Police when the local forces of law and order requested them, and where reinforcements negotiated through exchange schemes under the Police Act proved insufficient. Macready was also sent to direct where the military had been called in to aid the civil power. Metropolitan Police were sent to Hull and Cardiff, troops to Salford and the London docks, and HMS Antrim to Liverpool.[67] After a disastrous confrontation between troops and strikers at Llanelli the authorities saw a disciplined police force trained for riot control and maintenance of public order, as the answer to problems provoked by industrial violence. Eight people died at Llanelli during the rail dispute, and the incident highlighted the lessons of the Featherstone massacre: that the Riot Act was a clumsy bludgeon in twentieth-century conditions.[68] Again Macready's successful application of minimal force and the psychological use of troop dispositions at Salford during the carters' dispute proved to be more useful in controlling the situation and defusing tension. Macready's response in the 1910–11 crisis revived the tradition of firm yet low-profile military response to crowd control that had been pioneered by Generals Napier and Arbuthnot during the Chartist disturbances of the 1840s.[69]

In all these disputes the state tried to maintain its role as an impartial arbiter between capital and labour. What is noticeable, however, is that government intervention sometimes followed employers' complaints about intimidation of their workforce by strikers (Liverpool 1911, London 1912); incidents of arson (Cardiff 1911); threats by employers to provide vigilante protection for their own property; or concerned questions from the new King, George V, about the strikes.[70] Although the Home Office always denied that it had acted in response to such pressures, it appeared to have been influenced more by such complaints than by allegations of police brutality from socialists or the London Trades Council.[71] An interesting variation on this theme occurred in Liverpool, where an irate Liberal member wrote to the Home Office to complain of police brutality by imported Birmingham policemen. The police, he alleged, had deliberately broken up a peaceful demonstration of strikers with a baton charge.[72] He blamed brewing interests (the supposed power behind local Conservatives) for such behaviour.

There were signs that the authorities were more nervous about the degree of conflict in 1911. The Home Office was concerned by reports of alleged seditious language used by Fred Knee of the London Trades Council and by the dockers leader Ben Tillett at a strike meeting. However, it was decided not to prosecute Knee under the Incitement to Mutiny Act of 1797 because – although his language was extreme – the meeting was a 'fiasco' and the government did not want any publicity given to such sentiments.[73] Tom Mann, the charismatic syndicalist militant, was prosecuted following a separate incident, and imprisoned. A close interest was also taken in the legal proceedings taken against the anarchist magazine *Dawn* in Ilkeston, Derbyshire, in 1913. Here the seditious writing of anarchist shopkeepers was kept in check by the magistrates.[74] The use of summary jurisdiction, small fines and binding over to keep the peace was sensibly seen as the best means of exerting social control over a relatively trivial incident.

Yet if the government realized that direct action, neo-syndicalist threats and political revolution were little more than hot air in 1911–12, they were more concerned about the threat to the food supply and feared that the 'respectable classes' might be sympathetic towards the strikers. This was particularly the case in South Wales, where the authorities felt that public opinion did not always aid the military or civil power in maintaining order.

Such fears no doubt were behind the Home Office advice to the magistrates in 1911. Although in theory there was no connection between the will of the executive branch of government and the operation of the judicial process, Sir Edward Troup sent a letter by circuitous route to magistrates to inform them that the Home Office expected stiff sentences to be handed down in cases resulting from the industrial unrest. The clerks of the court were instructed to show the letter confidentially to magistrates.[75] Where such methods failed to deter strikers, such as during the Agadir crisis of 1911, Lloyd George used the patriotic gambit, urging workers to return in the national interest.

Whilst there was a relatively sophisticated response to industrial problems, caution and nervous concern about upsetting public opinion were always paramount in the administration of public order policy. The minimal force principle, inherent in the King's Regulations, was spelt out clearly in a 1908 enquiry following a violent clash between rioters and the cavalry in Belfast.[76] The principle was enshrined in its classic form by the law officers Rufus Isaacs and John Simon in 1911.[77] They advised that the military use the minimal force necessary to maintain public order during the dock strike, and that any greater response would make them answerable to the authorities and subject them to the rigours of the common law.

This principle was almost immediately applied to the police. In response to a request for a judicial enquiry, the authorities (somewhat surprisingly, given the Home Office reluctance to question police behaviour) granted one with respect to charges of brutality at Rotherhithe during the dock strike of 1912.[78] Mr Chester Jones QC allowed the use of public funds to enable critics of the police to air their grievances. Charges of brutality were found unproven. Workers who had been dismissed for allegedly giving evidence in support of the strikers were ignored by the enquiry after it was submitted by management that they had been sacked for lax supervision of a warehouse. The police were exonerated because they had used their capes to disperse a threatening crowd, and this, it was argued, had caused less damage than drawing truncheons would have done.[79] Hence the police were justified in using the minimum force necessary in the circumstances. Although the hearing had set a precedent, given the novel use of public funds, the conclusion was similar to that of several later investigations. The word of the police was accepted rather than that of their critics. This was the conclusion of most future enquiries up until the Wapping affair of 1987.

Although released government files give the impression that the main problems were posed in the strikes of 1911–12, the great labour unrest produced more strikes in 1913 and the first seven months of 1914 than at any other time.[80] These included the violent Black Country engineering strike, the bitter Dublin labour disturbances of 1913–14, and the London building lock-out in 1914.[81] Whilst the state reacted in an *ad hoc* fashion to all these individual disputes, the aim of remaining in control of the situation was achieved. The state merely wished to hold the ring, to maintain public order, whilst allowing the disputing parties of capital and labour to come to a compromise. However, the innovations of Churchill, despite the fact that they were little developed by his successor, did provide a framework which was gradually used to increase Home Office powers after the First World War.[82] There was little desire before 1914 for the state to adopt a corporatist role between capital and labour. It did not want to follow some of the Dominions in establishing arbitration services. Indeed, labour unrest appeared to make both Lloyd George and Churchill less liberal in their view of trade unions.

The experimental and largely successful techniques of public order control in the period show that the liberal state was far from being undermined by social crisis. It proved more flexible than the proverbial leopard, and reacted by changing its spots. Positive liberalism with a degree of centralized coordination which would not significantly undermine local control enabled the Home Office to manage labour conflicts within British society without recourse to measures which would destroy traditional liberties. In that sense public order initiatives bolstered the social control aspects of the welfare reforms of the Liberal government.[83] Whether, without the impact of the First World War, such measures would have been sufficient to defuse the multitude of problems facing the government is more debatable. The Great War brought about the real political crisis of the Liberal party.

c) The Birth of the Secret State

It was somewhat ironic that the surface froth of a crisis of public order in Edwardian Britain should play little part in the formation, in the years before 1914, of what proved to be the new security arm of the secret state. The security arm had arisen, rather, in response to changes in foreign policy and military strategy. The organization was originally set up as a counter-espionage agency ('Mot') to deal with the threat of what proved to be imaginary or incompetent German spies,[84] but rapidly developed techniques which could monitor public order and internal security. The silent revolution of 1909–11, draped as it was in secrecy and duplicity, was hidden from view by the terms of the Official Secrets Act of 1911, which made it an offence for individuals to leak

3 Suffragette incident at Buckingham Palace, 1914

information into the public domain which the authorities had not sanctioned.

To understand the transformation of security issues within the Edwardian state it is necessary to examine the interaction between public opinion, the decline of Britain as a great power and increased national rivalries. The benefits of Victorian liberalism had been called into question by the less than glorious victory in the Boer War (1899–1902), where a nation of peasant farmers had kept 350,000 British soldiers stretched for three years before finally succumbing to the logic of superior force. This signalled the end of 'splendid isolation' and a call for 'national efficiency'. As a result better relations were developed with France, the traditional enemy, through the Entente Cordiale in 1904, and with Russia, through an agreement in 1907.

The decision by Germany to challenge Britain's naval supremacy increased international tensions. This had important domestic implications because it forced the Liberal government to finance the building of double the number of new dreadnought battleships it intended, in order to maintain Britain's supremacy.[85] By refusing to abandon its social welfare programme in order to pay for this expansion it precipitated the tax changes of the 1909 budget, which led in turn to a constitutional crisis with the House of Lords. Demands for more controls on the dissemination of information were already being made. Germany's success was seen to be based partly on its secretive, bureaucratic and authoritarian mode of government. The victory of the inscrutable Japanese, with their obsessively closed society, over the Russians in 1904–5 also seemed a good advertisement for the military of the virtues of secrecy.[86] This led to increasing military pressure on the government to make Britain's defences more secure.

The tension coincided with continued pressure from foreign governments to end Britain's policy of political asylum for foreign refugees. The increase in anarchist violence in continental Europe, the murder of Sir Curzon Wyllie in London by Indian nationalists, a perceived threat from Egyptian nationalists and the activities of suffragettes provided the necessary ammunition by which Patrick Quinn argued successfully for the expansion of Special Branch.[87] In addition, the security and protection duties with which Special Branch was becoming associated ensured its survival and expansion, despite the fact that the need to combat Irish terrorism, for which Britain's secret police had been formed in the first place, was not a major problem in the Edwardian age. The fact that Superintendent Quinn made successful annual requests for the continued employment of extra officers shows that the authorities saw both the necessity for it, and were still reluctant to sanction the permanence of the still small Special Branch (a staff of 114 in 1914).[88]

Public opinion played a crucial role in inducing official security consciousness. Popular journalism and the genre of alarmist spy novels pressured the authorities to adopt a less liberal security policy. This had its root in Francophobic spy mania and the furore over the imaginery 'Battle of Dorking' when fictional concern about the traditional threat of French invasion was transferred to the Prussians. The Entente Cordiale reinforced this sentiment, and the dastardly Hun became the villain in the immensely popular invasion scare literature of the early twentieth century. Erskine Childers, *The Riddle of the Sands* (1903), E. Phillips Oppenheim, *A Maker of History* (1905) and William Le Queux's *Spies of the Kaiser* (1909) were representative of a truly dreadful genre. Le Queux, a con man with a vivid imagination, made a living out of his invasion scare stories. The serialization in 1906 of his account of an imaginary German invasion in 1910, in the columns of Northcliffe's *Daily Mail*, was both targeted at increasing the circulation of the newspaper in those unfortunate towns and cities supposedly captured that day by the Germans, and at increasing military preparedness and security consciousness.[89] Le Queux and 'Oppy' were connected with the popularization of Lord Roberts' campaign for the formation of the Territorial Army. P. G. Wodehouse wrote an amusing spoof of this type of literature called *The Swoop, or How Clarence Saved England*, detailing how an alert boy scout saved the country from nine invading armies. The point, however, was that whereas *The Invasion of 1910* sold over a million copies, and was translated into over 20 languages, Wodehouse's far superior work was a total flop. Popular opinion, if not respectable liberal views, took such fears and fantasies about invasion by foreign armies seriously.[90]

The evidence suggests that such phobias permeated upwards into the establishment itself. This began in 1906, when a conference of officials set up by the Admiralty and War Office to consider the powers of the executive during emergencies recommended an immediate strengthening of laws against espionage. The War Office's Directorate of Operations ('MO2') then investigated reports of German espionage. Its conclusion was that a counter-espionage bureau was needed to prevent spying. In 1909 a subcomittee of the Committee of Imperial Defence examined the evidence.[91] The Director of Military Intelligence, Colonel James Edmonds, persuaded the Committee that there was a serious threat to Britain's security posed by German espionage which his pitiful resources were powerless to check. However, the evidence provided by Edmonds was derisory: it conjured up foreign sounding men with false beards, wigs and guttural accents and alleged their involvement in suspicious activity. Much of it appeared to have been derived from Le Queux either directly or indirectly. Such was the mood of the time that the normally sceptical Lord Haldane finally agreed that a small department should be established in the War Office to examine the nature of German espionage activities in Britain, whether or not there actually was any threat to national security from aliens.

What was significant was that such innovation was introduced furtively with a degree of reluctance. Only a small unit was to be provided in conditions of great secrecy. The 'Secret Service Bureau' was established and within two months the division between intelligence and counter-intelligence was recognized. Edmonds' protégé Captain Vernon Kell became head of MO(t) (domestic counter-espionage) and Commander Smith-Cumming of foreign intelligence.[92] The report of the Committee failed to mention these all-important indications of the humble origins of the twentieth-century British secret state, of what were to become MI5 and MI6. This was to prove no hindrance. Kell, or 'K' as he was known in the secret world, was an assiduous empire builder, a man with a 'golden tongue', who spoke six languages, and fanatical about security measures which would surely have met with the approval of Le Queux.[93] Kell proved less charismatic than his colleague and rival Smith-Cumming. Whereas the head of the secret service was always to be known as 'C', ' K' disappeared forever when Kell was sacked in 1940.

Kell's appointment, together with the growth of Special Branch, marked the beginning of an organized security presence. This could be used by the state but was independent from parliamentary scrutiny. What differentiated the new security developments from the loose personal espionage and domestic surveillance arrangements that had operated between the reign of Elizabeth 1 and 1850, was the fact that the new security service was not to be officially acknowledged until the 1960s, and its activities could always be denied.

Two of Churchill's secret directives during his tenure as Home Secretary played crucial parts in the survival and growth of 'MO(t)'. Kell was convinced that the main function of a counter-intelligence agency was to monitor the activities of aliens in Britain. The military saw the main threat to Britain's interests as emanating from foreign enemies rather than native radicals. As it was implausible before 1914 to link authoritarian foreign governments with domestic social unrest, it was the supposed devious activities of actual or potential German agents in Britain which were said to need monitoring. Two other influences reinforced this attitude. Although there was considerable interest on the radical right in the supposed bureaucratic efficiency of the German state, belief in Prussian virtues was only skin deep and merely considered that Britain might need to copy German models in order to compete with her. Secondly, Liberals still frowned on the activities of 'detectives' and 'French methods' of policing. It was thought that political surveillance, if it was considered necessary, should only be directed at the activities of foreigners or those who advertised the flouting of the law.

New methods of policing were tolerated which had the potential to be adapted to the greater control of domestic problems. Robert Anderson, a Home Office bureaucrat, as early as 1898 had admitted in a Home Office minute that

Special Branch sometimes used questionable methods which were not sanctioned by the law.[94] The suspicions over the use of *agents provocateurs* and planted evidence – particularly in the Daly and Walsall bomb cases of 1884 and 1893 – added to this belief.[95] MO5(g) (as Kell's empire came to be known) also developed what liberals considered dubious practices. Here the crucial innovations were the introduction of an unofficial aliens register and of general powers to intercept mail.[96]

Churchill's first directive was to create the most potent and controversial weapon in the British counter-intelligence armoury. As knowledge of it would have provoked hostility it was constructed in secrecy, with Kell contacting chief constables and asking for a list of addresses of known aliens in their jurisdiction. The police in urban areas were often not contacted, because Watch Committees in the Boroughs were considered less discreet than Chief Constables, being more accountable to the electors. This was the origin of the infamous Registry of MI5: the file index of unchecked information, gossip, rumour and innuendo which was collected by British counter-intelligence and which originally related to aliens but extended to so-called subversives in the latter stages of the First World War. The list was to prove invaluable to the authorities during the roundup and internment of aliens in 1915. It was to ensure a meal ticket for Kell until he was sacked as director-general of MI5 in 1940, and gave employment to an ever expanding number of upper class female clerks, or 'queens', as they became jocularly known, in what was to become the hub of British counter-intelligence.

The second secret directive of Churchill made it easier for counter-intelligence to use general warrants to intercept the post. This had suspect foreign persons in mind. Reading other gentlemen's mail, like espionage in peacetime, was not considered cricket in respectable circles, but the growing war clouds in Europe and the developing feeling of unease at home necessitated drastic measures to monitor the situation. Whilst the police were able to intercept suffragette mail, it was not always clear whether this was a result of raids after obtaining search warrants or through the use or abuse of these new powers. Some aliens' mail was tampered with, and the steam iron became an early if crude implement in the new security technology.

Such ethically dubious practice was hidden from view by a series of preemptive strikes by the government which stopped prying eyes from suspecting that the cherished liberties of Englishmen were being undermined. Secrecy, duplicity and chicanery were the means used and both formal and informal channels were employed. The first of these arose as a result of the apoplexy of the Director of Military Intelligence in 1898 when he read the order of battle of the British fleet in *The Times.* This was considered as threatening national security. Hence the military impressed on successive governments the demand for legislation which would drastically restrict the right of the media to comment on matters pertaining to the operations of the armed forces. This, however, was met with resistance from liberal-minded administrators and politicians who objected to any muzzling of the press. Such legislation would be difficult to justify or push through parliament. The solution discovered by the military was to appeal to the patriotism of newspaper owners. If arm twisting proved counter-productive or inappropriate then flattery was to be the key. The D-Notice committee was set up in 1909, whereby the newspapers provided their own self-censorship.[97] Here the authorities could apply pressure to the press to prevent sensitive material from being published.

The conjunction of national and international crises in 1911 provided the background to the passing of the Official Secrets Act, the legislative teeth behind recent government secrecy in Britain. This provided the steel behind the self-censorship of the D-Notice committee. The defunct Official Secrets Act of 1889, which applied only to actual spies, was revamped. Under the terms of the notorious section 2, government permission had to be sought for the release of information. This meant that the menus in staff canteens or parliamentary dining rooms were theoretically state secrets. Such draconian legislation was hurriedly pushed through one sultry summer afternoon in 1911 during the Agadir crisis, when German gunboats were sent to Morocco, and after most MPs had already departed for the weekend. That

4 Police and troops escorting a convoy by a strike meeting, 1911

it was the government pulling a fast one was shown by its insistence that all stages of the bill be pushed through immediately. One MP called it the end of Magna Carta in response to government claims that it did not restrict liberties. Most of the few MPs who stayed for the debate ignored this threat and voted for the bill.[98]

If the military were demanding tighter control over security matters, then there were also pressures which suggested both political and military intrigue behind the scenes. The Liberal government, having lost its overall majority in the elections of 1910, became dependent on Irish Nationalist and Labour party support for its survival. The Parliament Act of 1911 and the Home Rule Bill of 1912 deeply alienated the Unionist and military hierarchies. Many who prided themselves on their patriotism began to plot against the elected government and to threaten mutiny. This was signalled by organized gun-running. The threatened mass resignation of military officers, including Sir Henry Wilson during the Curragh Incident in 1914, was enough to force the Secretary of State for War to give a written limitation of the government's power to coerce Ulster, although the document was repudiated by the Cabinet and Seely, the Secretary of State for War, resigned.[99] The problem was only finally defused by the outbreak of war and agreement to put the problem on ice for the duration of hostilities.

Such tactics, aimed at the authority of the Liberals, suggested that 'patriots' had a higher level of allegiance than that of the legally elected government of the day. It also implied that Conservatives and Ulster Unionists would turn to extremist methods if they felt that there was no alternative or redress by constitutional means. The tactics also weakened both the case against trade unionists, who tried to use industrial muscle against the government, and the suffragettes. In spite of the failure of interparty conferences on both the constitutional and Irish issues, the country was still able to unite behind the war effort in 1914. This suggests that compromise, rather than conflict, was still the preferred means of settling disputes. Having seen the abyss, the disputing parties retreated from it.

The security revolution of 1909–11 was a byproduct of the threat of war rather than social unrest. A more prominent role for the new security watchdogs and secret policemen was signalled with the appointment of Sir Basil Thomson, sometime Prime Minister of Tonga and prison governor of Dartmoor penitentiary, as Assistant Commissioner of the Metropolitan Police in charge of Special Branch in 1913.[100] This appointment, together with the outbreak of the First World War, marked the end of the birthpangs of the age of secrecy. From 1914 the confluence of increased threats from foreign powers and renewed fears of domestic unrest increased security consciousness with a vengeance. However, the golden age of liberalism left behind it important residues which ensured that the old prejudices about intelligence and the work of secret policemen biased national perceptions of both these activities. The pretence that Britain did not indulge in using underhand methods, although more or less true between 1850 and 1900, was becoming difficult to maintain. The cover-up was based on two assumptions: that the state would be embarrassed at admitting a betrayal of the continuing hostility of public opinion to such methods; and (the intelligence and security communities, belief) that a secret service should remain secret. Thus the state adopted an evasive and hypocritical approach to the existence of the secret world, believing that it would be in the national interest if everybody was left in the dark about the new institutions designed to protect them from foreign danger.

The modern origins of the secret state were to influence its development in other ways. Most notable was the continuing belief that the chief threats to the state came from foreign sources and that domestic subversion should primarily be seen as an agency of foreign powers, controlled by money or ideological sympathy. Thus German aliens in Britain, revolutionary socialists and fascists were seen as being manipulated from Berlin, Moscow or Rome. Even problems with a more obviously domestic genesis, such as IRA activity or labour unrest, also were interpreted in that light. Domestic concerns about the nature of power in British society, and arguments that economic and social problems caused unrest, were not recognized as significant by the authorities. The obsession with foreign influence and public order concerns developed from political conflict before 1914: in Charles Townshend's phrase, it was an era of 'flawed equipoise'.[100] But although the origins of the modern institutions of state security are to be found in this period, they remained a weak and pallid growth until the trauma of the First World War inaugurated a period of massive expansion in security activities.

2

THE FIRST WORLD WAR (1914–1918)

The First World War transformed the relationship between civil liberties, public order, security and the state on both a permanent and temporary basis. Firstly and permanently, the outbreak of hostilities saw an inversion of the mid-Victorian liberal ideological disregard for security and political surveillance and a return to older traditions.[1] It ensured the survival and massive wartime growth of the still secret security arms of the state, the Metropolitan Police Special Branch and MI5, as well as a mushrooming of political surveillance. Indeed, the domestic success of the primary protection, security and counter-espionage functions of these agencies against either an imaginary or incompetent foe combined with growing warweariness developing from the failure to break the stalemate on the western front with a knockout blow, and this combined with the progressive breakdown of law and order in Ireland after the Easter 1916 rebellion and its aftermath, to lead to a seismic shift from the priority of anti-German measures to monitoring industrial and domestic political discontent.[2] Many of the prejudices against policing methods and the use of secret police disappeared in official circles, even if the change of heart could not be admitted in public.

Secondly, and more temporarily, the passing of the Defence of the Realm Act (DORA), and its attendant regulations for the period 1914–20, meant that a watered-down form of martial law was superimposed on the workings of the common-law and civilian jurisdiction.[3] This legislation gave the naval and military authorities virtually unlimited powers. DORA gave the government the ability to impose regulations without the consent of parliament, and greatly extended the influence of the executive at the expense of the legislature and judiciary. The regulations did not need parliamentary approval, and became law through Orders in Council, authorized by an omnibus act of parliament. Three separate acts in the summer and autumn of 1914 codified these powers. DORA turned the British constitution upside-down during the First World War. Parliament declined into a relatively uninfluential mouthpiece of public opinion, and the executive increased its influence at the expense of the legislative functions of government.

DORA became the model for the Defence Regulations of the Second World War and the similar elastic powers conferred on the executive by the Emergency Powers Act of 1920. These were to be used during proclaimed national emergency: in practice a euphemism for war, strikes and strategic industrial disputes. At such times the draconian powers of the state envisaged in this legislation replaced the workings of the common law, which defended the rights of individuals against encroachment by the state and other corporations. However, there can be little doubt that the increase in state powers in the First World War through the use of DORA, the greater direction of industry through the Ministry of Munitions, the coming of conscription in 1916, and the activities of the Department of National Service, had long-term effects, even if the more explicit examples of state political extremism, such as internment, ended before the demise of wartime regulations.[4]

The introduction of Regulation 14B in June 1915 by Sir John Simon, the Home Secretary, marked the most radical break with the liberal tradition. This Order in Council, framed as a response to the sinking of the *Lusitania*, complemented the decision to intern all enemy aliens; naturalized aliens through the regulation could also be subject to executive detention as well. Probably about 160 persons were detained under 14B during the First World War, with a peak of 125 in the summer of 1917. It was the fear of a fifth column in our midst, combined with the knowledge that there was insufficient evidence to convict, which led to the radical break from the fundamental precepts of British law. Whilst the impact of this was for the duration of the emergency, other administrative changes which limited the civil liberty of the subject were considered suitable for more permanent change. The experience of 'war socialism', in however diluted a form, convinced the Home Office of the need to coordinate better the various police forces for public order and other functions, and as a result the Police Department was set up as part of the Police Act (1919).[5]

The relative neglect by historians of the undermining of civil liberties and its impact during the First World War is partly due to secrecy which is still maintained by the authorities. Although some material on the treatment of aliens has been released, the fact that some of the surviving DORA papers have been unhelpfully catalogued in the Ministry of Air files at the PRO has done little to improve the historical study of this important subject.[6]

a) The Security Framework

The First World War saw the rapid growth of security consciousness and political surveillance. Indeed, the outbreak of hostilities proved a landmark for those who wished to keep undesirable immigrants out and to stop objectionable views being broadcast abroad, as it marked the introduction of passports. This was the most obvious sign of the developing political paranoia directed by the state at those with German connections. The First World War also saw an expansion of MI5 (MO5(g) until 1916) from four officers, three detectives and seven clerks to almost 850 employees, whilst Special Branch grew from 112 to 700 secret policemen.[7] Yet the security and surveillance arms of the state were not restricted to the expansion of these organizations. The Ministry of Munitions developed its own labour intelligence branch after 1916 with the help of Sir Basil Thomson, the Assistant Commissioner of the Metropolitan Police, who was responsible for the Special Branch. Thomson was then recruited by the Cabinet to provide fortnightly, and later weekly, summaries of intelligence on the growth of pacifist and revolutionary organizations after 1917.[8] The Ministry of Labour also supplied the Cabinet with weekly intelligence reports on labour unrest from May 1917, which were often more prosaic and analytical and less colourful than Thomson's descriptions of the same events. The Admiralty and GHQ (General Headquarters, Great Britain) also provided material on public opinion and political surveillance.[9]

This plethora of information represented both a planned expansion of the sources of domestic intelligence and a haphazard growth of new agencies. These resulted from Lloyd George's changes in the structure of Cabinet government and the growth of executive authority. Who the consumers of such diverse material were, how it was analysed and what conclusions were drawn is problematical, although the War Cabinet and Ministers tended to interpret the often contradictory reports in terms of reinforcing their own preconceptions and prejudices. Certainly there was much overlap and waste in the collection of domestic intelligence in the First World War, which was the main point behind the appointment of 'the invaluable sleuth hound' (the phrase is Lord Curzon's), Sir Basil Thomson, as the Director of Intelligence in 1919. This new post had been suggested by the Chief Constable of Sheffield, Major Hall-Dalwood, in 1917. He argued that the success of the Army and Navy secret services and the civil authorities during the war in obtaining domestic intelligence should be continued in peacetime. His one caveat was that collection of such information should be continued openly because secret policemen threatened the liberty of the individual. Thomson, no doubt already sensing he would be the ideal candidate for the appointment, showed a degree of enthusiasm for a limited collection of 'unrest intelligence'.[10]

The civilian disquiet occasioned by war weariness, delays in demobilization, strikes and the impact of the Russian Revolution, led to Walter Long, the first Lord of the Admiralty, sending a memorandum to the War Cabinet arguing for an 'efficient secret service on the civil side'. The Secret Service committee was set up and reported to the War Cabinet in January 1919 that a directorate of civil intelligence should be established immediately and reviewed when civilian unrest declined. It should be directed by Sir Basil Thomson, who would be responsible to the Home Secretary. This was accepted by the War Cabinet in March 1919.[11]

The significance of the new post was that it represented the transition of political snooping from military to police control after the war. The important point, however, was that the state accepted the need to monitor civilian unrest in peace as well as in war. Thomson and the Directorate of Intelligence survived only for two years, but its monitoring of political extremism was then taken over by Special Branch. Thomson fell foul of Brigadier-General Horwood – the Commissioner of the Metropolitan Police, who resented his independence – and the Treasury Committee under Warren Fisher, in 1921. Under pressure of financial stringency Fisher attacked the inaccuracy of many of Thomson's reports on overseas revolutionary movements, and suggested the incorporation of the Directorate of Intelligence in a general reorganization of the Metropolitan Police. Horwood then wrote to the Home Secretary arguing that the Directorate was a menace to the discipline of the force and that its intelligence was often inaccurate. He also argued that the public resented domestic espionage. Thomson was forced to resign, and Harwood successfully resisted the alternative proposal that Vernon Kell should combine the military security function of MI5 with civilian surveillance.[12] Institutional rivalry, frictional hostility, ambition and pride delayed the emergence of a coordinated Security Service until 1931. Even then, overlapping areas of counter-espionage and counter-intelligence with MI6 caused continuing organizational problems.

More temporary than the surviving if reduced influence

of MI5 was the experience of military control during the First World War. DORA, which gave the government powers to rule through proclamation, led to a martial law which was partially lifted in 1915 when the right to trial by jury was restored. However, all security measures still needed the consent of the military to be implemented. The nation was divided into administrative areas under the control of the 'Competent Military Authority'. These were responsible to General Headquarters and enforced the regulations made under the emergency regulations.[13] The military were given authority to control and enter public buildings, investigate unrest, regulate drinking hours and arrest without warrant, and given the powers of preventive detention. The summaries of the contravention of the DORA regulations suggest that they were unnecessary for the British population and cast suspicion on a large number of imaginary German spies and a few incompetent real ones.[14] The authorities claimed that so many cases of accidentally flickering lights were reported that it was impossible to identify those who were trying to help the enemy. Most of the reported infringements of the regulations represented minor misdemeanours and were treated summarily by court martial, or, if handed over to the civil power, dealt with by magistrates.

The difficulties and increased pressures faced in 1918 led to a bureaucratic reorganization. A Home Office circular reduced the number of Competent Military Authorities whilst at the same time providing an Assistant Competent Military Authority (ACMA). He would be responsible for the administration of DORA; the scheme for control of dangerous persons in an emergency; liaison with the civil authorities in case of social disturbance; and military intelligence with relation to the civil population.[15] Much of the surviving documentation from military intelligence was produced by the local ACMAs, and amply illustrates that security meant counter-intelligence against the Germans, and monitoring and controlling civilian unrest in the domestic population.

Although the failure to break the military deadlock led to the fall of the Liberal government in May 1915, and its replacement, firstly, by a coalition with the Conservatives and

Labour representatives under Asquith, and, after December 1916, a new coalition under Lloyd George which was dominated by the Unionists, civilian direction of the war was jealously preserved by 'the frocks'. The Home Office was determined not to let military authority usurp civilian control even in wartime. A strong objection was lodged in March 1915 to the military assumption that if called in to aid the civil power in any potential disturbances in London it would assume the responsibility for law and order.[16] This view was a mistaken interpretation of the position agreed at a Home Office conference in January 1913. Sir Edward Troup had sent a circular at the outbreak of war to chief constables stating that if alien disturbances, unemployed demonstrations or price riots necessitated the military being called in to aid the civil power, then the Home Office must be informed and strict adherence to pre-war arrangements must be met.[17]

Thus the First World War saw a Jekyll and Hyde attitude to internal security. Harsh regulations introduced the structure of a police state under military control. Although the regulations were considered useful to control labour unrest, and necessary to attempt to pacify the Irish, the government proved reluctant to relinquish the direction of power to the military. The military themselves were less than enthusiastic about aiding the civil power, a point later forcefully made by Lord Ironside, who asserted that there was no more distasteful duty for the Army.[18] This was to be shown most emphatically after the war, when rapid demobilization combined with serious national strikes led both Sir Douglas Haig, the Commander in Chief of Home Forces, and Sir Henry Wilson, the Chief of the Imperial General Staff, to argue that the army did not have the resources in 1919 to aid the civil power. Haig argued it was no part of military duties to engage in domestic espionage;[19] and Wilson that the police, buttressed by civilian guards or special constables, should undertake all protection duties.[20] To an alarmist like Wilson – whose response, if his diary is any guide, was to advocate the shooting of Sinn Feiners, communists and trade union leaders – such a firm stance could regrettably no longer be the duty of the Army.[21]

b) Aliens

The security consciousness of the First World War developed out of the imagined need to protect the state against espionage and sabotage by German agents, aliens and naturalized Germans in Britain. The work of Captain Vernon Kell in counter-espionage before the war had included not only building up a detailed knowledge of the German spy network in the United Kingdom, which enabled him to round up 21 alleged agents on the outbreak of war, but also developing a central registry of 30,000 aliens in Britain, collected with the help of Chief Constables, and behind the cloak of the Official Secrets Act.[22] Growing pre-war fears of rivalry with Germany had also induced a sub-committee of the Committee of Imperial Defence to prepare in 1910 an Aliens Restriction Act (ARA), which gave the authorities powers to transfer aliens away from sensitive areas and to control refugees and immigrants who wished to enter the country.[23] The ARA was passed on the first afternoon of war, enacted immediately by an Order in Council, and, together with powers added during the war under DORA, became the blueprint for Britain's aliens policy. The British Nationality and Status of Aliens Act of 1914 enabled the executive to order the internment of aliens under the Royal Prerogative.

The fear of aliens (particularly Germans) reached ridiculous proportions in the First World War. It has recently been argued that no national group in Britain has ever been so systematically vilified, abused and attacked as the Germans were in the First World War. At one stage the authorities, consumed by fears of German sabotage against 'vulnerable points', used 70,000 police, special constables and reservists to protect the railways.[24] But, although there were accidental explosions at munitions factories, there was never any evidence that there was any German inspired sabotage on mainland Britain during the First World War. This fact did not stop the authorities and public opinion becoming obsessed with the supposed threat posed by German agents, and German hairdressers, clerks and waiters. In the eyes of the authorities all foreigners were immediately suspect. At Felixstowe in 1914 a 6 foot 5 inch, 21 stone director of a London company was considered suspect as he was thought to be a clever German (because his parting words to a boatman on a fishing expedition, said 'with a curious grin', were 'Goodbye, I shall be back again'). The same file also reports a mysterious tunnel under the Chiltern Hills which was allegedly dug out on the orders of two suspicious Germans eight years previously.[25] From Colchester in September 1915 illicit signalling was suspected from the Post Office engineering department, and it was noted that one of the employees had a German sounding name.[26] In 1915 an Edouardo Ziegler was reported as constantly hanging around the Chilworth gunpowder factory, and it was thought that his car stopped and appeared to throw its light upwards as if signalling.[27] These represent the tip of a huge iceberg of innuendo, hearsay evidence and ludicrous rumour that passed as intelligence in the initial stages of war.

Such examples highlighted the prevailing Germanophobia. Even pigeons were not exempt. When Mr Hammerschmidt of Mitcham, a naturalized Austrian citizen of 20 years, tried to register his homing pigeons under DORA, the police came and killed them. He later received £2 7s. 6d. compensation.[28] Two Special Branch officers were sent on a fruitless week's visit to Harwich to search for suspicious pigeons.[29] German aliens were even arrested for being near pigeons.[30]

This, then, was the background to the decision to intern or repatriate as many Germans as possible during the First World War. Thirty-two thousand enemy alien men were interned and up to 20,000 men and women and children were repatriated out of a total of 75,000 in the United Kingdom. By 1919 the numbers expelled had reached 25,000.[31] Alien and naturalized Germans became the scapegoats for the failure to deliver the knockout blow, and became the victims of anti-enemy propaganda. The Home Office, although the bastion of British civil liberties, was under pressure from public opinion, and orchestrated the demand for internment of enemy aliens from the outset of the war. They were particularly interested in interning German and

5 Sir Nevil Macready

Austrian reservists who remained in this country after the declaration of war, and those who were made unemployed on the outbreak of hostilities and who might become desperate through destitution. Reginald McKenna, the Home Secretary in 1914, wanted to intern enemy aliens both because they were security risks and to protect them from the chauvinistic wrath of British citizens.[32]

So keen was the Home Office to lock up Germans they even tried to pressure the ultra-security-conscious War Office to speed up the rate of internment. Lord Kitchener pointed out that there were difficulties of accommodation and the reception centres could not cope with the large numbers envisaged. Indeed Sir Edward Henry, the Metropolitan Police Commissioner, wanted to arrest aliens at the rate of 4,000 per day even though the Olympia reception centre could only cope with 1,500. Even when in 1915 Prime

Minister Asquith gave the order for a return to more general internment, Kitchener, as Minister for War, insisted on the release of as many non-security-risks as possible. Henry objected to a general release policy both on the grounds of protecting vulnerable points from 'alien enemies', and the need to save released detainees from the wrath of public opinion, which had led to serious anti-German riots during the First World War.[33] These occurred in August 1914, October 1914, May 1915, June 1916 and July 1917. They resulted in the most widespread disturbances in twentieth-century Britain, with towns and cities as diverse as Glasgow, Winchester, Liverpool and London experiencing violence. Thousands were arrested during the disturbances in 1915 and total damage was estimated at many hundreds of thousands of pounds. The War Office was forced to compromise and to argue that it could only release detainees with the consent of the Metropolitan Police Commissioner.

What was alarming about the infringement of basic liberties was the compliance of the judiciary with the convenience of the executive. In the important test case of *Rex* v. *Halliday exparte Zadig* (March 1917) it was ruled that the courts had no powers to question the decision of the executive to intern those whom the authorities deemed security risks unless it could be shown that the action was without due cause. This was a turning point in British law: since 1917 the courts have very rarely questioned the actions of the executive in eroding British liberties in the name of good government. What restraint there has been was usually the result of the Home Office or the law officers acting as a brake on overzealous policemen, politicians or administrators. The internment of aliens represented the reaction of the Liberal government and Whitehall to perceived political pressure, public opinion and the security arguments of the Metropolitan Police Commissioner and MI5.

There was also rampant class prejudice in the initial Home Office decision to intern in 1914. Men of 'good position' could be left at liberty if they were given satisfactory character references by two British citizens of good repute. Aliens of 'no standing', like waiters, hairdressers and mechanics, were to be handed over to the military forthwith.[34] There were other voices which utilized more bellicose arguments, however. Military Intelligence argued that there was no reason to suggest that some classes of German were more potentially dangerous than others – they were all 'alien Germans' and should be watched. Hence the notorious press campaign against Prince Louis of Battenberg and Sir Edward Speyer, and the attacks on the Germanophile cabinet minister Lord Haldane in 1914–15. Some of the arguments were blatantly racist; naturalized Germans were considered to be the most obnoxious in some quarters, and potentially the most dangerous.[35]

The failure to win the war quickly, the hardening of popular opinion and the replacement of the Liberal government by a national coalition under Asquith, in May 1915, led to a more tightly organized aliens policy. There was cross party agreement on the necessary measures. Asquith and Bonar Law both accepted the need to increase anti-alien measures, and the Home Office took over from the War Office the administration of internment. The new Home Secretary, the Liberal Sir John Simon, a man of known moderate and humanitarian views, became responsible for internment policy.[36] He established the bureaucracy which was to provide the procedure for internment of aliens and others in both world wars.

An advisory commission was set up comprising two judges four MPs and two additional members. They were to hear the appeals of those interned, and had the duty to advise the Home Secretary on granting or refusing applications for exemptions from internment.[37] Although much more documentation has been released on internment in the Second World War, the evidence suggests the advisory committee system worked relatively smoothly. Although many decisions on internment, repatriation and exemption in the early days of the Advisory Committee's operations were based on inadequate information, they became increasingly sceptical of the quality of the evidence presented by anti-alien propagandists and the security authorities.[38] Sankey, the Advisory Committee Chairman, and his colleagues won the respect of most parliamentarians and the emigré groups for their impartiality and their critical response to the diehard voices of William Joynson-Hicks ('Jix'), Henry Page Croft and Richard Cooper in Parliament; and the British Empire Union, the National Party and MI5 in general.

Conditions of internment during the First World War appear to have been reasonable for most of the time. The American embassy was allowed to produce reports on conditions in reception centres and internment camps. An early report on aliens and prisoners of war at the Frimley outdoor stockade camp and at Queensferry, commented on the good rations, and observed that inmates were well treated. They had few grumbles except their loss of freedom.[38] A more comprehensive report in 1915, based on inspection of nine ships and thirteen other internment centres, reported that up to one-third of all Germans in the United Kingdom had been interned but ten per cent had been released. Treatment seemed to be as good as possible in the circumstances, but there was a shortage of fresh vegetables in the diet, although in general the health of camps was good.[39] A police report on an Islington camp arrived at much the same conclusions.[40]

However, not all internment administrations were as smooth as the reports suggested. In fact, the attention to conditions which the authorities showed owed much to the bad publicity from initial reactions from internees in the Isle of Man camps. In November 1914 a riot took place in the Douglas camp which led to the death of six internees with fourteen injured. The causes were deemed to be general frustration, inadequate tented accommodation, cold and wet weather, and bland diet.[41] The historical treatment of aliens by the authorities and the Home Office has proved to be the Achilles heel to their argument that they have always protected civil liberties. The draconian immigration legislation of the post-war period owed much to the very serious anti-German riots of the First World War, and anti-Jewish and anti-Chinese violence between 1911 and 1920.[42] At best it can be said that the Home Office has an ethnocentric liberal ideology which becomes strained in conditions of crisis and industrial unrest. The First World War not only saw the collapse of the Liberal Party but marked a weakening of Britain's liberal traditions.

c) Pacifism and Pacificism

If aliens were seen as potential German spies or saboteurs then pacifists were deemed equally likely to be controlled by the same 'hidden hand'.[43] A vast German conspiracy, the reason for the emergence of the British secret state, was seen to be behind the British peace movement. In fact during the First World War the authorities distinguished little between those who objected to fighting any war (pacifist), and those who opposed the reasons for this war, or who wished for a compromise peace (pacificist).[44] The latter were considered more dangerous, as they included some MPs and men with influence, but both groups were considered pacifists by the authorities and potential traitors.

This becomes obvious in the surviving general and personal files relating to pacifists in the First World War. It is quite clear that the anti-war movement was viewed quite differently by Liberal and Unionist politicians, a factor of some consequence in the internal strains of the Asquith (1915–16) and Lloyd George (1916–22) coalitions. Thus, for example, Sir John Simon, the Liberal Home Secretary, was unaware of the decision taken by the Unionist Attorney-General, Sir Edward Carson, to seize copies of E. D. Morel's *Ten Years of Secret Diplomacy* in July 1916. The Permanent Secretary, Sir Edward Troup, argued it was the Home Office's responsibility to deal with legal proceedings with a political object, and the Director of Public Prosecutions was forced to hand the book back.[45]

Special Branch and MI5 provided material which was designed to show radicals in a poor light or to appeal to the prejudices of right-wing politicians. Thus E. D. Morel, the main force behind the Union of Democratic Control (UDC), the most important peace movement, was smeared by Sir Basil Thomson in a personal report as 'George Edmund Morel-de-Ville, alias E. D. Morel'. Thomson argued that the stated aims of the UDC, of open diplomacy and a negotiated compromise peace settlement, were merely a front. The real policy was that of 'all the peace cranks' and 'pro-Germans', to persuade public opinion that British participation in the war was a 'criminal and absurd act'.[46] Morel was later imprisoned on what appeared to be a technicality, if not a trumped up charge. Similarly Norman Angell's ('alias Ralph Lane's') personal file also implied that he held unconventional if not treasonable views.[47]

Indeed Angell's file is very interesting because it contains fascinating material showing differences of attitude between the security authorities, ministers and government aides towards the politics of the peace movement. Norman Angell was a progressive liberal whose rationalistic and optimistic book *The Great Illusion* (1910), on the futility of war, had obtained cult status and spawned an Edwardian pacifist movement.[48] He was one of the founder members of the UDC, but had distanced himself from the organization. Sir Basil Thomson objected to Angell being allowed to visit the USA in February 1917, on the grounds that he was a founder of the UDC which opposed the war, 'that he habitually writes and speaks as if he had no nationality', and that he overestimated his influence on the Americans.[49] His objection was seconded by MI5.

Angell's request for a passport was backed by Philip Kerr, who wrote as an aide to Lloyd George from 10 Downing Street, and who later was to be an ambassador in both Moscow and Washington. Kerr argued that Angell was not pacifist like Bertrand Russell or the *Labour Leader*, and his whole argument was based on international cooperation to prevent war. Since war broke out he had stated that neutrality was an impossible position for the Americans to maintain, that the USA should support the allies and come to a naval understanding with the British Empire as a foundation for the permanent pacification of the world. The Home Secretary, Sir George Cave, decided not to let him go to the USA in February 1917, despite the fact he had been on a lecture tour the previous year.[50]

This decision was challenged in May 1917 by the Minister for Blockade at the Foreign Office, Lord Robert Cecil, who granted Angell a passport.[51] He argued that Angell's visit would do much to strengthen the resolution of those who wished to bring the war to a satisfactory conclusion. Also it would prevent him from drifting back into an alliance in

England with those pacifist groups from which he was now clearly separated. What this minor episode demonstrated was the degree to which security consciousness could influence policy in periods of crisis.

The surviving personal files also present other prominent individuals in a critical light. Although they have been weeded, both the files on Charles Trevelyan MP and Philip Snowden MP, Chancellor of the Exchequer in the Labour governments of 1924 and 1929–31, are of interest. Trevelyan, a leading member of the UDC and a supporter of a negotiated peace, had two wireless messages to the USA intercepted, because the Home Office thought they were trying to avoid censorship, and they had notes on a 'very objectionable speech'.[52] Philip Snowden, a leading peace campaigner for the Independent Labour Party (ILP), was also monitored by the authorities. Extensive verbatim reports were made of speeches he made in Glamorgan in December 1916. Although the speeches were considered objectionable, the Home Office, after consulting the Law Officers, thought a prosecution would be undesirable; while Vernon Kell, for MI5, thought that such a course would do more harm than good.[53] The personal file of Ramsay MacDonald, the future Labour Prime Minister, to whose ILP and UDC meetings there are numerous references in the general files, has not survived, and indeed he appears to have been refused access to it in 1924.[54]

Interesting light is shed on why files should be started on respectable or influential people with controversial or opposition opinions in a report from military intelligence. Scottish Command reported in March 1918 that new life had been breathed into labour agitation on the Clyde by the letter of Lord Lansdowne to *The Times* advocating a compromise peace. This (according to Military Intelligence) gave the extremists their opportunity and they joined forces with the 'moderate people' to increase their influence.[55] The surviving security documentation also implies that Special Branch and MI5 in particular smeared as cranks or worse those with moderate demands, like a negotiated peace.

The general files are also of interest with regard to the surveillance of pacificist groups like the ILP and UDC, of pacifists like the No Conscription Fellowship (NCF), and of the range of techniques pursued to control their propaganda. This included snooping on those 'most dangerous women', highly respectable feminist suffragist opponents of the war like Catherine Marshall, who once calculated that her work for conscientious objectors meant she was liable to 2,000 years imprisonment. There is evidence that MI5 intercepted the mail of the 'Stop the War Committee' in July 1915, although they found no evidence of anti-British sentiments.[56] A Special Branch report described a raid on the NCF in June 1916 and MI5's seizure of records, addresses, correspondence and leaflets of the group. There was also evidence to suggest that the authorities were so keen to visit the NCF headquarters that they had not told the City of London police in whose jurisdiction it was, and who should have been the arresting authority.[57] Lieutenant Golding, an ex-military officer who denounced the war in a series of public lectures in 1918, was arrested and sentenced to six months' imprisonment. The Home Office disliked his anti-war stance and argued that he had been forced to resign in 1917 for being inefficient and unreliable.[58]

A very different approach was adopted to the protestations of Lionel Lindsay, the Chief Constable of Glamorgan, who complained to the Home Office that 42 cases submitted to the Competent Military Authority in 1917, and relating to anti-war meetings in South Wales, had not been proceeded with. Lindsay argued that the loyal majority of the population would become disheartened if nothing was done about the disloyal minority. The failure to do anything would make the disloyal become more truculent and aggressive and the middle ground of public opinion apathetic or supportive of extremism. The Home Office thought Lindsay alarmist and argued that inflammatory language in South Wales would have little effect on the rest of the country.[59] It was not only what was said that determined whether action was taken but whether more harm than good would result from publicizing such views. The Inspector of Constabulary, Lionel Dunning, investigated Lindsay's complaints and drew attention to his argument that the people of Glamorgan were like those of Ireland. If firm steps were not taken against disloyalty, then lawlessness would become as great a problem in South Wales as across the Irish Sea.[60]

If some of the authorities showed intermittent concern about the potential public order effects of the peace movement, the failure to break the stalemate on the western front in 1917 led Unionist politicians to accuse pacifists of collusion with the Germans. Sir Edward Carson submitted a memorandum to the War Cabinet requesting an investigation of the sources of funding of anti-war movements. Sir Basil Thomson found no evidence of German funding, but phrased his report in such an inconclusive manner that the War Cabinet decided to receive fortnightly, and later weekly, reports on pacifist and revolutionary movements.

There were those, however, who refused to fight any war, and conscientious objectors became an important problem for the authorities. The First World War represented the first conflict in which an organized minority refused to recognize the state's right to conscript men for the armed forces and to direct labour for work in war industries. This was seen as a form of political extremism by the authorities, organized by cranks, cowards and those with possible links with the enemy. Whilst it was recognized that religious opposition, such as that demonstrated by the Quakers to warfare, was a justified reason for conscientious objection, the sincerity of this belief had to be proved. Political or humanitarian grounds were not considered as acceptable, and life had to be made as difficult as possible for those who objected in principle to aiding the war effort. The No Conscription Fellowship (NCF) became the main political organization for those pacifists who objected to fighting in all wars.[61] The prejudice against conscientious objection was so profound that even in April 1919 one of the two main reasons for a War Cabinet decision to delay the release of the last of the conscientious objectors was that a 'large proportion' of those remaining had 'thoroughly bad characters'.[62]

Conscientious objection became a serious problem for the authorities when the Lord Kitchener-inspired 'Your Country Needs You' voluntary recruiting campaign began to flag in 1915. The 'Derby Scheme' in autumn 1915 failed to boost numbers to the required level, so the introduction of compulsory recruiting with the first Military Service Act or 'Bachelors Bill' in 1916 (for all unmarried men not working in essential wartime industry) was seen as the thin end of the wedge. The failure to win the war, and the crisis of spring 1918, led to the 'comb-out' of all available manpower up to the age of 51 in the third Military Service Act, 1918.[63] Conscription was also a key issue which led to the split in the Liberal Party, and it is not surprising that conscientious objectors should be seen by public opinion, the military tribunals and the authorities as a scapegoat for the frustrations of a long war.

The Military Service Acts provided tribunals where individuals could object to being conscripted into the army. There were 5,944 conscientious objectors who either failed to accept the tribunal's decision or refused to apply to the tribunal on the grounds of conscientious objection.[64] Once handed over to the military, conscientious objectors were dealt with by the office of the Adjutant-General, General Macready, and the Director of Personal Services, Lieutenant-General Wyndham Childs. It was they who were to set the framework for the treatment of conscripted soldiers who conscientiously objected.[65]

As in South Wales in 1910, they were to show considerable skill in their management of a problem which defied a solution, with a mixture of firmness and individual consideration.[66] Childs, who was directly responsible, could not understand why the Cabinet allowed the NCF to continue when victory might depend on conscription, but his conscience and personal sympathy led to rigorous intervention, when cases of personal mistreatment of conscientious objectors were proved. The Macready–Childs regime was also alive to the propaganda war – as far as possible conscientious objectors were not allowed to become martyrs, and no defaulters were shot.

Indeed, many of the conscientious objectors of the NCF deliberately courted martyrdom. Hunger strikes in prison and the immediate rearrest of conscientious objectors after their sentence led to a situation similar to the state's attitude to suffragettes before 1914.[67] For those who did not object to working for the authorities, a Home Office scheme

6 Sir Wyndham Childs with Lady Childs, at their home at Kimpton, Hertfordshire, 1929

of labour was introduced, which provided employment for 4,522 men during the war. This proved unsatisfactory, as a man died at Dyce, the first camp in Aberdeenshire, and many found the physical labour demeaning and useless. Living conditions were also poor and work and morale suffered.[68]

Many conscientious objectors suffered greatly at the hands of the state in the First World War, although some of the suffering was self-induced. The fact that absolutists, like many suffragettes, were placed in the Third Division Prison category, together with the banalities of the Home Office scheme, meant many lost weight, and like Clifford Allen of the NCF, had their health undermined. Most had few contacts prepared to push their case, although some, like

Stephen Hobhouse, had friends in high places. His mother, through the family's connections, persuaded Lord Milner to become involved. He presented a long memorandum to the War Cabinet in May 1917 condemning the present policy as too lenient for unscrupulous people trying to shirk conscription, and too harsh for those whose convictions were genuine.[69]

Although Childs was able to persuade the War Cabinet not to alter military regulations, further persistence enabled Hobhouse to be released.[70] The story of conscientious objectors between 1914 and 1918 showed that although the state stood firm against the principles of those who refused to fight, it lost the propaganda war. The authorities learned from the treatment of those pacifists who refused to fight in the First World War, and the treatment of conscientious objectors after 1939 was far less traumatic as a result.[71]

d) Labour Unrest

As the failure to win a decisive victory became manifest and the home front came to pose more problems, internal security shifted decisively towards surveillance and management of British citizens. Foremost amongst the developments which gave the authorities cause for concern were labour problems and the growth of socialist movements opposed to the war. This situation was unforeseen by the authorities. Indeed, prior to the war there was little evidence that Britain's secret policemen, except in the special case of the suffragettes, had much to do with monitoring or controlling unrest. Military intelligence summaries for the first two years of the war do not mention labour problems, not because there was a lack of disputes, but because of the ingrained liberal phobia that political surveillance was a nasty and unnecessary habit of Continental policemen. Civilian unrest during the war altered that perspective, and the security-conscious military, and Unionist politicians, oversaw a massive expansion of the secret state, with an increasing function of surveillance and political policing of Britain's more troublesome citizens, as defined by the authorities.

Labour unrest during the war derived from several sources. Its basic cause was economic and not political. After a period of relatively full employment and declining real wages – itself a recipe for industrial trouble as the period 1911–14 had demonstrated – wartime inflation had eroded and threatened living standards still further. Morever, labour was becoming increasingly organized and had developed a countervailing power that industry and government needed to take into account. Small unions had been amalgamated into larger units such as the National Transport Workers Federation in 1910 (the Transport and General Workers Union in 1922), while the National Union of Railwaymen had been formed in 1913. Syndicalist ideas had taken root amongst the rank and file in certain groups, such as the South Wales miners and shop stewards in the engineering unions.

There were also growing links between unions. In June 1914, miners, railwaymen and transport workers formed a 'Triple Industrial Alliance'. This developed into a more formal though loose arrangement, whose members pledged in December 1915 to coordinate industrial action with regard to national disputes or matters of principle.[72] Given full employment in the war, organized labour determined to flex its muscles and defend its pre-war gains and traditional rights, and with the increasing realization by wartime governments of the need to gain the cooperation of the workforce, it is not surprising that membership of unions more than doubled between 1914 and 1920 from four to eight million.[73]

What was seen increasingly during the war was the need to incorporate the working classes into the national consensus. The state was concerned to gain the support and enthusiasm of labour in the organization of government and industry to obtain victory. As the failure to gain a rapid knockout blow turned hostilities into a life and death struggle, the authorities were forced to revolutionize the relationship between the state and civil society. Greater government direction and management of industry was seen as imperative so that production of munitions for the overriding aim of winning the war could be achieved. Conscription of labour for both military and industrial needs was seen as vital after 1917. As a result, an *ad hoc* corporate state developed piecemeal in the latter stages of the war under the dynamic leadership of Lloyd George. Prior to 1914 the state, employers and labour were all equally hostile to a greater role for government in industrial relations. The changes brought about by war necessitated the cajoling of organized labour into accepting the necessary sacrifices for winning the war. Industrial restructuring was to be achieved by agreement, not revolution.

Politically this was attempted through the inclusion of Arthur Henderson, as a representative of the Labour Party in Asquith's coalition government of May 1915, and as a member of Lloyd George's War Cabinet in December 1916. Yet the Labour Party was divided, with a minority led by the ex-leader, Ramsay MacDonald, opposing the war, and the majority suspicious of the need to end restrictive practices and Union agreements in industry. The issues of conscription and dilution were to sour relations between organized labour and the governments during the war and gradually the Labour Party, although it never formally opposed the war, became steadily more influenced by the ideas of the UDC.[74] Indeed, it was Henderson's fear, after a visit to Russia, that the Kerensky government would collapse unless a negotiated peace was immediately achieved, and that this would have disastrous consequences for the western front, which led him to push for Labour Party representation at the Stockholm meeting of the Second International in 1917. His intention was to help promote the idea of a compromise peace, which led to his forced resignation and the weakening of the involvement of the labour movement in Lloyd George's coalition.

It would, however, be wrong to suggest that the labour movement was in any way unpatriotic or not wholly committed to the war. Lloyd George, in particular, realized the complexities of the situation. He saw the necessity of gaining the consent of organized labour in 1915 for the radical changes in the organization of industry that were deemed necessary to win the war. As a result, legislation was put in place which both increased trade union power in negotiating settlements, whilst imposing draconian punishments on those who opposed the war. As Minister of Munitions in 1915 Lloyd George negotiated the Treasury Agreement with the Unions which substituted arbitration for stoppages of work and relaxed trade union restrictions.[75] These no-strike agreements were formalized in the Munitions of War Act (1915), which also forced workers to obtain leaving certificates before accepting new work.[76]

This was a compromise solution to the issue of industrial conscription, and was only agreed after attempts had been made to limit employers' profits. Organized labour used its influence in the Manpower crisis of 1917–18. The need to placate labour was a key factor in shaping government policy pertaining to the introduction of conscription and the dilution in industry. 'War socialism' meant both expanding the labour supply and ensuring disruption to production be kept to a minimum, while at the same time increasing recruitment for the armed forces and increasing output of munitions.

The solution was firm direction, and a willingness to compromise and to attempt to gain the confidence of union leaders and organized labour. From the Trade Card scheme to the final 'comb-out' of manpower in 1918, agreement with the Unions was paramount in the eyes of the Government. Dilution of industry, with skilled work being performed by unskilled workers, and increasing numbers of women being employed, proved an effective solution, although there was considerable resistance, particularly in Clydeside and in the engineering industry. The solution proved temporary and was reversed at the end of the war. From the Bachelors Bill (1916), to the third Military Service Act of 1918, when military conscription combed out the last nonessential workers under 51 for the armed forces, the leaders of the Labour movement reluctantly cooperated with the Government.[77]

Agreement was only won at a price. Lloyd George's strategy of coaxing cooperation and agreement out of union leaders ignored shop-floor suspicion, the conservatism of restrictive practices and deeply entrenched union rights. Whilst Lloyd George charmed and cajoled labour leaders, there was increasing hostility both towards the Government and the trade union establishment from militant minorities who felt that their living standards were threatened and their rights infringed, and who were in some cases opposed to the war. Outbreaks of militancy began in 1915 in key areas such as South Wales, where a solid strike of 200,000 miners forced Lloyd George to agree to give in to wage demands rather than invoke DORA or the Munitions of War Act.[78] An unofficial Clyde workers committee organized by shop stewards led a series of disputes in 1915 and 1916 in Glasgow, and similar disputes occurred in the engineering industry in Sheffield, Coventry, Barrow and Lancashire in 1917.[79] Resistance to the comb-out in 1918 also produced a series of clashes between an increasingly aggrieved Labour movement and the Government.

It is this background which explains why the secret state became more concerned about domestic unrest than the activities of the enemy on mainland Britain after 1916. Political surveillance became almost an obsession of the authorities, with the growth of intelligence agencies attached to many of the departments of state. On the whole, the results of increased snooping were encouraging for the authorities. The Ministry of Munitions reports for 1917 on trade unions, Labour, Socialist and Shop Stewards movements were broadly reassuring, and the Ministry of Labour reports in the Cabinet papers gave detailed accounts of the decline of militant influence.[80] The two Russian revolutions of 1917 appear to have had different effects; the March 1917 revolution encouraged dissidence and revolt, whilst the Bolshevik coup in October 1917, paradoxically, soon led to a decline in revolutionary feeling.

Lord Milner and the Unionists in the War Cabinet became increasingly alarmist or conspiratorial in their interpretation of labour unrest. Milner circulated a memorandum to the War Cabinet entitled *Labour in Revolt*, by Professor Arnold of Bangor University, arguing that the unofficial strike movement needed to be crushed, as the 'angelic anarchy' of its opposition to conscription and support for the Russian Revolution, and the spread of its influence, meant that there would be a 'serious conflict'.[81] The War Cabinet asked the Workers Educational Association for its opinion. Its secretary argued that sensible reforms like nationalization of the mines and railways, and extension of unemployment insurance, would defuse industrial unrest.[82]

The Commission of Enquiry into Industrial Unrest established by the War Cabinet in June 1917 proved to be the most extensive wartime examination of labour problems in the First World War.[83] Under its chairman, George Barnes, a Labour MP, it established eight regional commissions which held between ten and thirty meetings in each case. Each commission saw between 100 and 200 witnesses. Barnes concluded in July 1917 that there was a strong feeling of patriotism amongst both employers and employed, and all were determined to help the state in the war. Barnes emphasized that the large majority of the workforce were loyal and did not want a revolution.

There was, nevertheless, a growing criticism of the war and some demand for a negotiated peace. Although there were regional differences in emphasis, the main causes of industrial unrest included the high cost of living, restrictions on personal freedom, large wage differentials between skilled and unskilled men, dilution of skills, poor housing conditions, alcohol restrictions, industrial fatigue, decline in community spirit, low women's wages, delay in war pensions, the need to raise the limit of income tax exemptions and inadequate workmen's compensation. The Commission recommended an immediate reduction in prices and the implementation of the Whitley report, which recommended the continuation of industrial partnership. It further suggested that labour should be granted due respect, and not be seen merely as a servant of the community. The state immediately reacted by authorizing an increase in wages in government controlled munitions factories.

The significance of the Barnes Commission was that it provided the most authoritative and exhaustive examination of state attitudes towards increasing working class unrest in the First World War. It represented the saner and less alarmist response, which on the whole was accepted by the Lloyd George government. But it was not the only view. Unionist politicians, aided and abetted by the security authorities, suggested a more conspiratorial interpretation of events. This emphasized that behind the unrest was the 'Hidden Hand' of the enemy. The 'Hun' was manipulating all sources of discontent to his advantage and was partially responsible for its organization. Such a view developed into a more plausible theory after the two Russian revolutions of 1917, when industrial unrest could plausibly be transferred to new management, the Bolsheviks. The peace treaty of Brest-Litovsk, which took Russia out of the war, together with the call for international working class revolution, were the impetuses for the great red scare which was to dominate security and public order policy until 1990. It is to this issue that our attention must now turn, but to understand its significance it is first necessary to fit the Irish dimension into the jigsaw of the development of the twentieth-century secret state.

3

JOHN BULL'S OTHER ISLAND (1910–1923)

The missing dimension in the account of the years before 1923 is – with regard to internal security, public order and political extremism – the severe problems posed by the Irish troubles. This is important because, as Bernard Porter has shown in *The Origins of the Vigilant State*, it had been the export of Irish Fenian terrorism to Britain in the 1880s which had led to the formation of Special Branch, Britain's first secret policemen. For our purposes it is the contrast between the state's attitude to security in England, Scotland and Wales, and its attitude to problems in Ireland which is of particular significance, as well as the impact of actual rebellion in Ireland during the troubles of 1916–22.

The comparison could hardly be more stark. This difference tells us much about the nature of the liberal state. The fact that a solution of a kind was found for the 'Irish problem', that a temporary patching up of irreconcilable positions was achieved, illustrates well the relationship between force and the necessity of compromise in a liberal system. The Irish troubles, and their political, military and administrative dimensions, became an important negative influence on government in the rest of the United Kingdom.

Political violence, institutional challenges to state authority, the establishment of private armies and guerrilla warfare were features which the British authorities and their security services became concerned with defusing in their management of what it termed political extremism.

The British state in the twentieth century, as in less recent history, aimed to ensure that knowledge of the nature and the methods of Irish disturbances was kept off mainland Britain. This objective was achieved (with exceptions particularly in 1923 and 1939) until 1968, as much by virtue of the fact that the cultural and religious factors at the root of the Irish troubles were far less potent issues in the rest of the United Kingdom, than by political or security measures.

The collapse of British power, which the loss of Ireland signified, was to be masked by the illusion of the return to normality which became the style and substance of the British government in the interwar period. At root this meant that the British Empire would develop according to negotiation and compromise and, for white settler dominated and geographically distant dominions, self-governing status, rather than be maintained by indiscriminate force. The atrocities associated with the Black and Tans and Auxiliaries in Ireland, and the Amritsar massacre in India, were deemed to be beyond the pale, and Britain lacked both the will and resources to use such methods elsewhere.[1] The rule of law was to be firmly upheld at all costs, both within the Empire and (particularly) at home. Civil liberties, the administration of justice and freedom of opinion were to be observed to the maximum extent permissible with internal security needs.

The fact that the 'Irish troubles' are still a contemporary security issue in the British state has effaced the role of the issue in continuing government secrecy. About one-third of the files are still retained on the troubles, although significant releases have been forthcoming from the Cabinet Office, Colonial Office and Home Office. In spite of this, the underlying problems remain much the same today as in the First World War, particularly the centrality of the Ulster problem.

In the nine counties of Ulster in 1911 there were 891,000

Protestants and 691,000 Catholics. In the three southern provinces there were 250,000 Anglo-Irish Protestants amongst a Catholic population of 2.5 million.[2] Irish nationalism and independence from the United Kingdom became associated mainly with Catholicism, and 'Orangeism' with the 'more British than the British' Ulster Protestants. It was somewhat ironic that the military leader of the Irish Volunteers in 1916, Eoin McNeill, was an Ulsterman, and Sir Edward Carson, the parliamentary leader of the Ulster Unionist MPs, was an Anglo-Irish barrister from Dublin.

Such facts illustrated the complexity of the problem. The supposedly ultra-loyal Protestants of Ulster threatened rebellion against the British state in 1913–14, and many were implicated in gun-running and the receiving of illegal arms shipments. This was financed by the Carson Defence League and Lord Milner.[3] These preparations for civil war and armed insurrection against Home Rule were supported by the Conservative Party, and indeed, much of the army command in Northern Ireland, who threatened to resign over the issue during the Curragh Incident in 1914 (an attempt to blackmail the Liberal government to drop the Home Rule bill in 1914). Ireland was to reinvigorate Diehardism as a British adjunct to the cause of Ulster Unionism. Whilst local politicians were worried by the potential unreliability of Conservative support, there was little chance of that whilst Bonar Law, who saw the issue purely through Ulster spectacles, remained leader of the Conservative Party.

The First World War radically altered the nature of the Irish Question. The parliamentary opposition of the Irish Nationalists gave way to Sinn Fein (SF), who refused to recognize either Westminster or Dublin Castle as the legitimate government of Ireland. Just as significantly, much of the Irish Volunteer Force, formed in imitation of the Ulster Volunteer Force (UVF), became the military wing of SF, and after the first meeting of the Dail in 1919, changed its name to the Irish Republican Army (IRA). Constitutional Opposition was replaced by secret society plotting, guerrilla warfare, armed insurrection and civil disobedience. The harsh response of the British authorities to the Easter Rising in 1916, and the attempt to extend conscription to Ireland in 1918, alienated Catholic opinion and provided the background to the undeclared war with the British state between 1918 and 1921.[4] It took all Lloyd George's negotiating skills, as well as the logic of the situation, to produce a highly controversial solution which continued to be opposed by substantial minorities on both sides. 'Solving' the Irish problem did not end the civil war in Ireland, nor did it provide a long-term resolution to the difficulties. Ireland was to prove the most intractable security problem for the British state in the twentieth century; it also provided lessons which reinforced long-held liberal views about not transporting the methods needed to rule Ireland to the rest of the United Kingdom.

a) 'Ulster will fight and Ulster will be right'

The Ulster problem before the First World War mobilized right-wing political extremism throughout Britain, and threatened to turn the constitutional issue of the powers of the House of Lords to one of outright rebellion. This situation arose as a direct consequence of the parliamentary disputes over the 1909 budget and the Parliament Act of 1911, which reduced the powers of the House of Lords to delaying tactics only. The Conservatives had lost power in 1905 and were frustrated over their inability to regain it. They were also concerned about alleged Liberal 'weakness' in their social and labour policy, and in foreign affairs. They saw themselves as guardians of Ulster. Twice, in 1886 and 1893, Liberal attempts to introduce Home Rule had been defeated: frustrated, firstly, by Joseph Chamberlain's split and defection to ally himself with the Conservatives, and, secondly, by the Tory peers. The Parliament Act had now removed the House of Lords as a permanent block against Home Rule.

What had placed the Ulster problem back on the political agenda were the two indecisive general elections of 1910. The outcome was a continuation of the Liberal government, with the support of the Irish Nationalists and the Labour Party, despite the fact that both Conservatives and Liberals had the same number of seats. One of the conditions for this support was an understanding that Home Rule would be given to Ireland. The situation was made more intractable when the new leader of the Conservatives, Andrew Bonar Law, publically committed himself to the maintenance of Ulster within the United Kingdom in 1911. However, he was powerless to prevent the Liberals from using their new parliamentary powers to override the veto of the House of Lords, and thus to be on course for the introduction of Home Rule in 1914.

As a result the Conservatives and Ulster Unionists instigated a last ditch campaign to stop the implementation of Home Rule at any price. It combined the low politics of Orangeism, the annual flaunting of the Protestant ascendancy during the summer marching season, with high politics intrigue at Westminster. This affected the entire spectrum of political behaviour in Britain. The severity of the political crisis was illustrated by the pressure placed on the new King, George V, by Bonar Law, the Conservative leader, to dismiss Asquith as Prime Minister if the Home Rule Bill of 1912 passed into law. It involved a stratagem according to which Conservative peers would defeat the Army Annual Bill and leave the government unable to control or pay the Army.[5] The crisis saw military intrigue which forced the government to agree not to use the army to coerce Ulster into Home Rule in 1914.[6] The conspiracy involved Lord Milner and Sir Henry Wilson, the Adjutant-General, working with Bonar Law to support Generals Paget and Gough against the orders of the War Minister, J. E. Seely. The 'Curragh Incident', or mutiny, led to the forced resignation of Seely. Asquith, the Prime Minister, then took over the responsibility for the War Ministry for a time, before the gathering war clouds enabled him to appoint Lord Kitchener to the post, an icon who could be accepted by all.

The degree of political blackmail was also reflected in the internal security and public order problems which emerged around the matter. Mass plebiscitary politics reached its apogee over the issue in the lead up to the war. The Unionists adapted the popular resistance of the convention in 1892 to a more democratic framework in September 1912, and issued a covenant which most Ulster Protestants signed, saying they would defend Ulster against the imposition of Home Rule. Many Englishmen also pledged themselves to defend Ulster under the Covenant, and the Orange lodges on both sides of the water underwent a revival, in both Ireland and England. Ulster intransigence was led by the Ulster Unionist Council (UUC), founded in 1905.

When Walter Long resigned the leadership of the Ulster Unionists, defence of Ulster was given a practical priority by the new leaders, Sir Edward Carson MP (elected unanimously in February 1910), and Captain James Craig MP. They immediately established practical resistance to the threat of Home Rule, involving preparations for an alternative government, the establishment of an armed force to prevent any weakening of the Union, and a series of gigantic meetings to alert Ulster Protestants to the threat of being forced to become a minority in a Catholic Ireland. At Craigavon in September 1911 Carson stated that the day Home Rule became law, the Ulster Unionists must be prepared to be responsible for the government of Ulster.[7] To that end the UUC, eight months before the passing of the third Home Rule Bill, established a committee to draft a constitution for a provisional government of Ulster. The draft was approved by them in September 1913.[8]

Equally worrying for the authorities, the Ulster Unionists took practical steps to ensure they could defend themselves. In 1911 the UUC revived the Unionist Club Movement, which rapidly became the nucleus of a more militant approach to the defence of Ulster. With the aid of the Orange lodges, by the end of 1912 there were 297 clubs with 55,596 members, many of whom were trained to shoot rifles.[9] These became the nucleus of the Ulster Volunteer Force (UVF) when it was formed in January 1913 under the direction of Lieutenant-General Sir George Richardson. The Peace Preservation or Arms Acts of 1881 and 1886, which had been renewable annually, had been allowed to lapse after the Liberals won the election of 1906. These had placed restrictions on the traffic and possession of arms in Ireland. As a Colonial Office minute graphically put it, this discontinuance proved 'disastrous to the maintenance of good order throughout Ireland',[10] nowhere more so than in Ulster after 1910. During

1912 and 1913 a significant quantity of arms was smuggled into Northern Ireland. By December 1913, 20,000 rifles were in the possession of the Ulster Volunteers, and the number rose to 24,879 by April 1914. The figure was again dramatically raised to an estimate of 51,600 rifles after the gun-running to Larne, Bangor and Donaghedee, on 24 April 1914, by the *Fanny* (Doreen), and *Clydevalley* (Mountjoy).[11]

The direct challenge to law and order placed the authorities in a quandary. The fact was that Ulster Unionists, supported by English Conservatives and elements in the Army, were deliberately pressing their luck, becoming openly involved in potential sedition and disregarding the law, challenging constitutional rule and the authority of the government. It was one thing to isolate and apply the law to defuse suffragette and labour challenges to the state; it was quite another to move against His Majesty's parliamentary opposition, who professed loyalty to the crown. That the Unionists and Conservatives were seditious was made quite clear both by the rhetoric spouted by Carson and leading Conservatives in Ulster between 1912 and 1914, and the evidence of the gun-running. F. E. 'Galloper' Smith, later Lord Birkenhead, told a large crowd at Ballyclare on 21 September 1913, that if the 'corrupt and guilty' Liberals chose to coerce Ulster, the Conservatives would stand shoulder to shoulder with 100,000 organized, drilled and armed men to protect its liberties, and refuse 'to recognize any law, and prepar[e] with you to risk the collapse of the whole body politic to prevent this monstrous crime (Cheers)'.[12]

The authorities were fully aware of the gun-running, although they tended to underplay its significance until the Larne incident. The Royal Irish Constabulary (RIC), as early as July 1912, were informing the Colonial Office that it would be dangerous to assume that rumours of imports of arms were mere bluff.[13] The British police kept active surveillance of gun-running, but they were often powerless to intervene. A large consignment of ammunition was taken from Gravesend to Birmingham and hidden in a consignment of cement from the Stockton works.[14] Special Branch discovered that elements within the Conservative party were also implicated in the gun-running. Four members were named, including

Captain Budden, who had the key of the Windsor Castle Hotel, Hammersmith, where the guns were stored and loaded before being sent to Lord Cavan's estate in Ireland.[15]

The Colonial Office in fact obtained intelligence about all levels of the Unionist campaign. This included a mole in the Ulster Unionist Council, where it was reported the Unionist Clubs were for arming, Lord Londonderry was against, and Sir Edward Carson would put himself in the 'hands of his Unionist friends'.[16] The authorities also learned about the activities of the Enniskillen Horse, their request for lances and weapons, and their military drill.[17] In 1913–14 the RIC produced weekly reports on the Unionist Movement and Home Rule. One which has survived was a review of the year 1912–13. Inspector Chamberlain concluded that the Orangemen, and even some of the more respectable classes in Belfast, were prepared to go to extremes in their resistance to Home Rule. However, he felt that a large proportion of the Ulster farmers only signed the Covenant on the understanding that they would never have to face the forces of the crown. Many regarded the formation of the UVF as a political move to force the authorities to abandon the idea of Home Rule.[18]

The evidence suggests that the government took seriously Ulster Unionist intransigence and the political pressure imposed by their Conservative allies. As early as 1911 the law officers had ventured the opinion that if arms had been imported to intimidate parliament from enacting new laws under the constitution, or for resisting by force, or promoting civil war or any unlawful purpose, then the perpetrators could be indicted for sedition.[19] Whilst such a broad-ranging opinion was difficult if not impossible to implement, the authorities became so worried that in December 1913 a Royal Proclamation prohibited the importation into Ireland of arms, ammunition and warlike stores.[20] Whilst the Proclamation was revoked at the beginning of the First World War, it is quite clear that the gun-running at Larne was illegal. The government was anxious to be seen not to be giving in to political blackmail or the threat of force, but was prepared to offer concessions to take the heat out of the situation.

Hence General Macready was held in readiness to take over the Belfast Command in 1914. Macready believed that when the military was called in to aid the civil power, it was the soldier's duty to maintain law and order and not to take sides in political disputes. He was also the most senior military figure to hold less than enthusiastic views about Ulster Unionists in general, and military personnel who refused to carry out orders in particular.[21] Asquith also put pressure on Redmond, the Nationalist leader, to agree to allow Ulster counties to opt out of Home Rule for up to six years if they wished. This was to allow time for up to two general elections to see if there was still a mandate for Home Rule in the country as a whole. However, Liberals, Conservatives, Nationalists and Unionists had very different ideas about which sections of Ulster should be excluded. For Unionists, Home Rule was not an issue which could be achieved by democratic means, as the majority Protestant community in Ulster were totally opposed to the concept of Home Rule and equated it with Catholic control from Dublin.

The fact that the Ulster Crisis of 1913–14 did not lead to serious civil strife was mainly due to luck. The attempts by the King, George V, to keep the lid on the situation through informal contacts with politicians in 1913, and by convening a Buckingham Palace Conference in July 1914, ended in failure.[22] These were unsuccessful and constitutionally debatable, but impressed on all parties in the dispute the need for moderation to avoid precipitating a conflict against the express wishes of the king. The Sarajevo crisis of summer 1914 overtook events and replaced the threat of civil war with actual war. All the parliamentary parties declared a truce on the issue, and Home Rule was put on ice for the duration – at least as far as the main participants in the Ulster crisis of 1912–14 were concerned.

The revolt of the Orangemen had important consequences for our theme. It blurred the distinction between treason and loyalty, and set a precedent which nationalist extremists were quick to seize upon in Ireland during the First World War. The challenge to the Westminster parliament, the British constitution and the rule of law, by the supposedly loyalist Conservative and Unionist parties, compromised the moral high ground and provided a precedent for revolt by more subterranean forces in 1916. Even before 1914 the Nationalists had seized on the example of the UVF, to form the Irish Volunteers. This in turn divided into two factions at the outbreak of war.

After an argument in the committee of the Irish Volunteers, some dissociated themselves from Asquith's and Redmond's call in Dublin on 25 September 1914 to recruit for the British Army. About 10,000 enrolled members adhered to a new committee under Eoin McNeill, and became the Irish or Sinn Fein Volunteers.[23] Small consignments of arms and ammunition were imported for them in November and December 1914.[24] The First World War replaced a constitutional crisis with a potential revolutionary one and an underground threat which blew up in the face of the authorities at Easter 1916. Their over-reaction to that event and the introduction of conscription in 1918 destroyed the authority of the British government, undermined law and order, and turned Ireland into a case study, in a nationalist context, of Lenin's concept of 'revolutionary defeatism'. It was ironic that the Ulster Unionists in 1914, who desired the complete antithesis of an independent Ireland, should have provided so many precedents for methods and organization of revolt which could be copied effectively by their enemies.

A second interesting consequence of the Ulster crisis was the influence several of the leading participants had on the organization of national security in the First World War and beyond. Whereas leading intransigents like Sir Edward Carson, Walter Long and Viscount Milner were expert forgetters of their own attempts at political blackmail, or sedition against a lawfully elected government, they became the leading advocates of security measures against the Sinn Fein volunteers and the challenge of organized labour in 1917. It was Carson and Milner who carefully orchestrated the response to the alleged German plot, the 'Hidden Hand', behind Sinn Fein, pacifism, and labour unrest in the First World War. Walter Long threatened resignation in 1916, if Home Rule was to be granted as part of the price for maintaining lines of credit to the USA after the Easter Rising.[25]

He also demanded measures to suppress sedition in Ireland in 1918, so that if the Germans landed they would not be supported by a Sinn Fein rising.[26] It was Long's memorandum which led to the formation of the Directorate of Intelligence in 1919. Sir Henry Wilson, the brain behind much of the intrigue surrounding the Curragh Incident, was also to prove himself an advocate of the shortest possible shrift being granted to all security troublemakers. Thus it was that yesterday's sedition mongers came to be super patriots and exert a mainly doleful influence on the twentieth-century secret state.

b) Easter 1916

The poet W. B. Yeats intuitively saw the significance of the insurrection centred on the Dublin Post Office in April 1916. In his poem 'Easter 1916', written in September of that year, his understanding of Irish romantic nationalism led to the realization that the execution of the rebel leaders by the British authorities would turn them from terrorists in to martyrs. Yeats' poetic licence saw clearly and almost immediately the real meaning of the Easter 1916 rising in Dublin. This was more than could be said for the actions of Dublin Castle, the military authorities or the British government. Whilst the revolt proved a damp squib in the short run (the six-day rebellion failed to ignite sympathetic action outside the city), the heavy-handed response of the British signalled the beginning of the loss of credibility of the forces of moderation in the struggle for Irish nationalism. The ruthless repression of the uprising, justified by the exigencies of war, alienated Irish public opinion. This was compounded by the internment of Sinn Fein members and other leading opponents of British rule. Further, many individuals who had nothing to do with the uprising were sent to detention camps in England, and this helped sour British relations with nationalists and encouraged the growth of extremism.

The misinterpretation of a supposed German plot led to the locking up of moderates whilst the leading exponents of physical force remained free in 1918. The failure of British policy was an intelligence débâcle; because the authorities did not have the traditionally good sources of information as to what Irish nationalists were planning, conspiracy and fantasy provided an excuse for repression. The entire situation played into the hands of those in the Irish Volunteers who advocated physical rather than moral force.

Extremism was then legitimized by the effects of the extension of conscription to Ireland in April 1918. This was borne out by the collapse of the Irish Nationalists in the Coupon election of November 1918. Sinn Fein won 73 of the 105 Irish seats, with the Ulster Unionists winning most of the remainder. The response of the British became a study in how not to influence or manage Irish public opinion. It also showed the dangers in subordinating political factors so completely to security considerations. The traditional repressive military measures adopted by the British since Tudor times merely drove resistance underground and the secret societies and subterranean organizations used new counter-espionage and guerrilla warfare techniques in a far more devastating manner than any previous insurgency.

The lack of subtlety and flexibility in the British response was as much a political as an intelligence failure. Colonial rule in Ireland was centred on Dublin Castle, which supervised the administration of a turbulent country. Overpopulation, the land problem, the ethnic conflict between Protestants and Catholics, Nationalists and Unionists, had made Ireland difficult to govern in the nineteenth century. The furore over Home Rule illustrated the nature of the Irish problem. The measure, which involved little more than giving Ireland the self-governing powers of a county council, and left most of the important decisions firmly under Westminster control, created passions which bordered on civil war in Ulster, and constitutional strife at Westminster.

The two Irish police forces, the Royal Irish Constabulary (RIC), and the Dublin Metropolitan Police (DMP), were centrally controlled, established intelligence networks to monitor political subversion. The RIC was armed.[27] They had more in common with the repressive policemen of most continental European states than their counterparts in the rest of the United Kingdom. The military, too, were called in much more often than in England to aid the civil power. In terms of administering security, the Westminster parliament, like a latter day Pontius Pilate, had washed its hands of the issue, so as not to contaminate itself with the more dubious aspects of the Irish problem. This was the devolved responsibility of the Irish Secretary and his administration in Dublin Castle. Sadly, in 1916 the Irish Secretary was Augustine Birrell, a reforming Liberal whose 'softness' was to be held responsible for the rising by Unionists and the military authorities. General Sir Joseph Byrne, the Catholic head of the RIC, came under suspicion in 1919, partly because of his belief that the Irish problem could not be resolved simply by repressive policing.[28] They were to be made the scapegoats, and political control was to be subordinated to the unsophisticated methods of the military – until it was too late.

The Easter rising in fact could not be blamed on either an intelligence failure or the supposed political deficiencies of Dublin Castle. Basil Thomson, in an intelligence report for Sir John French in September 1916, concluded that there were too many sources of political surveillance in Ireland, seven in all, and too much overlapping of intelligence.[29] This was wishful thinking but reflected one of the crucial problems: the poor quality of much existing intelligence. The sources included the Admiralty, War Office (MI5), Irish Command, the DMP and RIC. Throughout the troubles the quality of information was very variable. Unlike nineteenth-century Irish nationalism, Sinn Fein and other secretive organizations conducted an efficient counter-espionage operation which severely restricted reliable information about their activities percolating through to the authorities. Rumour and innuendo further compounded the problem. It was therefore difficult to distinguish between hard intelligence and the background noise. The two RIC sources, 'Chalk' and 'Granite', both correctly informed the authorities in March and April 1916 that the Irish Volunteers were storing arms, and that younger members, together with elements from James Connolly's Citizen Army, and the Irish Republican Brotherhood, were demanding 'business', and that events were moving to a crisis.[30] 'Chalk' even informed the authorities that emergency rations were being issued to some members of the Irish Volunteers on Easter Sunday, and that Macdonagh, one of the leaders of the Easter Rising, was telling members that some would not return. Thus Dublin Castle appears to have been kept better informed than Eoin McNeill, the organizer of the Irish Volunteers, as he had already cancelled secretive plans for a rising on Easter Sunday. However, inability to distinguish between relevant intelligence, rumour and innuendo, meant that a persistent weakness of British administration was its inability to get reliable information about the activities of Sinn Fein and the various secret societies and paramilitary organizations.

The military authorities had also been told that Easter 1916 was to see significant developments from another source. On 17 April General Stafford in Cork informed Dublin that he had heard 'casually' from Admiral Bayly that the Germans were to land arms for the Irish Volunteers.[31] This event had enormous impact on British security policy – the landing of Sir Roger Casement from a German submarine and an attempt to supply rebels with munitions from the German ship, the *Aud*. It proved the significance of the cracking of the German codes by Rear Admiral Sir Reginald 'Blinker' Hall's cryptographers in Room 40 of the Admiralty.

The informal notification of the authorities was unorthodox but preserved Hall's chief concern, the security of his source. The decision was amply vindicated when Hall later intercepted the Zimmerman telegram which was crucial in bringing the USA into the war. However, other aspects of Hall's behaviour and the use he made of this intelligence source were more controversial. After removal to London and interrogation by Hall and Thomson, Casement's request that a message cancelling the proposed rising should be made known in Ireland was refused. Casement's plan appeared to be to discourage plans for a rising, but nevertheless Hall circulated part of Casement's diaries with details of his alleged homosexual encounters, to ensure he went to the scaffold.[32] Recent examination by a handwriting expert under restricted access in the Home Office suggests the diary was not forged, but Hall's intention was clear. The aim, which was successful, was to encourage the ruthless suppression of any proposed rising, as well as to punish an alleged traitor. The most significant consequence was that it provided the petrol to fan the flames of that great Unionist bogey man, the German-Sinn Fein plot.

It was not that the Germans failed to use Irish nationalism against the British – the sending of Casement and arms to Ireland proved that. The point was that the security authorities wildly exaggerated its significance. From 1916 to the end of the war, all Irish and social unrest in Britain was blamed on German machinations, was stigmatized as disloyal and explained by right-wing politicians and internal security forces as a conspiracy. In fact, the low priority given by Germany to aiding the IVF was shown by an RIC report in June 1918 which said that there was no evidence of any illegal landing of arms in Ireland during the war.[33] Yet Hall frequently passed on information to Dublin Castle alleging such activity, after wireless interception of German–American communications ceased in 1917, when the USA came into the war and Hall had lost his reliable source on German intentions.

Such ill-founded rumour was seized upon by Walter Long and others to justify renewed internment in 1918, with disastrous consequences.[34] Ireland was to set a pattern. Future native political extremism was to be seen as the work of deluded agents of foreign powers, rather than an expression of disillusion and alienation from parliamentary government and the British Constitution. The tendency to see all social unrest in Ireland after 1916 as a Sinn Fein conspiracy was another symptom of this mentality. The failure to distinguish between physical and moral force advocates, moderates and extremists, secret society plotting and legal opposition, was to make a mockery of constitutional rule. By outlawing opponents of violence, as well as attempting to crack down on terrorism, the British government played in to the hands of the extremists. The tendency to simplify Irish politics and the failure to distinguish between membership of Sinn Fein and terrorism had disastrous consequences.

The crushing of the Easter 1916 rebellion can be seen in

retrospect as a failure of political imagination and an over-reaction. By proclaiming martial law in Dublin on 25 April 1916, extending it to the whole of Ireland four days later, and renewing it for much of the rest of 1916, the British government temporarily withdrew its political responsibility for events in Ireland.[35] The result was confusion rather than military dictatorship. Indeed, the security measures taken by the army were taken under the Defence of the Realm regulations rather than martial law.[36] General Maxwell, appointed Commander in Chief of the Forces in Ireland, put down the rebellion with ferocity, and maintained law and order through harsh punishments against those who had rebelled against the state, and through mass internment of Sinn Fein members. This led to the intervention of the government authorities. Maxwell found it necessary to send his internees to England, and the government began to realize that absolving itself of responsibility for the knee-jerk reaction to the rebellion, whilst being popular in Ulster, became increasingly counter-productive, and was viewed with less than rapture in the rest of Ireland.

In the immediate aftermath of the rebellion 160 persons were convicted by courts martial, of whom 90 were sentenced to death. Fifteen of these were executed including the seven signatories of the Proclamation of the republic. Many of the others were sentenced to life imprisonment or fixed terms of ten years or more.[37] 1,850 individuals, either involved in or alleged supporters of the rebellion, were sent to England after arrest in May 1916, as Maxwell judged them to be 'prejudicial to the safety of the realm'.[38]

Sending Irishmen to England presented the Home Secretary, Sir Herbert Samuel, with a difficult legal problem in May 1916. He justified the action as an urgent military necessity in order to promote law and order in Ireland following the crushed insurrection. However, it was felt that a writ of habeas corpus from any of the internees could cause problems for the authorities. The prisoners could not be brought before the courts in England because their offences were committed in Ireland. They could not be tried in England by court martial because martial law could not be specially applied for that purpose, and if proceedings were taken under the Defence of the Realm Act (DORA), any British subject had the right to elect to be tried by a civil court. Whilst this right had been suspended in Ireland by Proclamation in 1915, it had not, and could not be, suspended in Great Britain. The prisoners could not be sent back to Ireland because, even if the civilian legal system was restored, juries could not be relied upon for justice, and trial by court martial would meet strong objections. The answer was to intern the prisoners in England by amending Defence Regulation 14B, which applied to aliens. The internment orders were reviewed by the Advisory Committee on Internment, which were justified by the argument that the known link between Sir Roger Casement and Germany, and the attempt to land arms justified linking Sinn Fein with 'hostile associations' through the proved connection with the enemy.[39]

As a result of the difficulties which the law officers assessed, the Cabinet decided to use existing legislation, DR 14B, without amendment. The Advisory Committee was split into two, with Mr Justice Sankey, Mr Justice Ross and Mr Mooney MP dealing with the Sinn Feiners.[40] This procedure appears to have worked fairly smoothly, as the Advisory Committee discharged 1,272 of the prisoners, and most of the rest were released by Christmas 1916.[41] This suggests, in the absence of the relevant papers, that the Advisory Committee was not impressed by the lack of evidence of wrongdoing by many detainees. Most of the internees had been sent to an internment camp at Frongoch in North Wales, although 30 leaders were sent to a similar establishment at Douglas, Isle of Man. MI5 starred some names on the list as 'especially dangerous'.[42] The conditions of internment were similar to those of prisoners of war, but the two groups were kept entirely separate. Women internees were held in Lewes and Aylesbury jails. The significance of the first mass internment of Irish detainees was that it provided a working model for the internment of British citizens, particularly fascists, during the Second World War. The last detainees were released in 1917, in an unsuccessful attempt to help the Irish Convention produce a better atmosphere for the emergence of a workable solution to the Irish problem.[43]

The second internment of Sinn Fein prisoners in May 1918 caused more problems for the authorities. One hundred and fifty Irish men and women were interned as a result of the discovery of the non-existent Sinn Fein–German plot, in the wake of Irish discontent over the extension of conscription to Ireland.[44] The men were held in Birmingham, Durham, Gloucester, Lincoln, Reading and Usk jails, and the women at Holloway.

The difficulties experienced by the authorities arose mainly from two sources. The death of Thomas Ashe, in Dublin, after forcible feeding during a hunger strike in jail in September 1917, and the death of Terence MacSwiney, the Mayor of Cork, after a hunger strike, created a new propaganda weapon for Sinn Fein to add to the martyrs of Easter 1916.[45] Although, by March 1918, the authorities decided that the release of hunger strikers made it impossible to maintain security, the authorities remained very concerned about Sinn Fein propaganda over prison conditions.[46] This threat remained a real one after the decision, taken in October 1916, that Irish internees and convicts were not to be given the privileges of Rule 243a, which the suffragettes had been granted. Secondly, political offences were not recognized in English law, and treason and sedition were considered much more serious offences than the misdemeanours of the suffragettes.[47] De Valera had already instituted a work strike amongst Irish prisoners at Lewes jail in May 1917 in an attempt to put pressure on the authorities. The Irish prisoners were then almost immediately released. Both de Valera, whose death sentence was commuted in 1916, because he was born in the USA, and Sinn Fein wrongly interpreted this as a response to their militancy, rather than the political circumstances of the Irish Convention. When the Sinn Fein leaders were interned again there was greater resistance to the prison regime.

Indeed, a growing intransigence was noticeable on both sides. The personal files of the detainees released illustrate a hardening of attitudes on both sides as to how internment could affect public opinion in Ireland and the inflexible mind-set of the British government. There was a wide variety of reaction. Arthur Griffith, the founder and deputy

President of Sinn Fein, refused to apply for release and, when brought before the Advisory Committee, disputed the right of the tribunal to examine his case.[49] Sankey felt there was no alternative but to confirm his order for internment even though he abhorred violence and opposed physical force. Winifred Carney, or Kearney, the ex-suffragette who had been James Connolly's chief assistant in the Textile Workers Union since 1911, and had acted as 'the typewriter of the 1916 rebellion', refused to give an undertaking not to engage in acts of a seditious nature, and was refused permission to become Countess Markiewicz's companion in prison when her death sentence was commuted.[50]

Two cases which illustrated differences of opinion within the British government provide an interesting contrast. Ernest Blythe, a principal organizer of the Irish Volunteers, had been arrested before the Easter Rising under DORA regulations for hostile associations with the enemy. Kell, the head of MI5, who signed the warrant as the Competent Military Authority, argued that the rebel Sinn Fein and Irish Volunteers organization had been deliberately aided and financed by Germany.[51] Pat Maloney, however, was released on the argument of the Advisory Committee, because he was a 'respectable' follower of Parnell and Redmond, who thought the Nationalists had sold out in 1914, but who took no part in the armed insurrection. None the less, he was not given back his diary of internment at Frongoch, and a Home Office minute queried the Advisory Committee's recommendation of the release of 'this bitter pro-German'.[52]

There was also disagreement over the case of John Richmond. When released from internment at Frongoch he was granted permission to visit the USA. The Irish authorities wished to stop him returning to the United Kingdom, but the Home Office decided that this was not possible if he wished to come back. He could only be issued with an order under DORA regulation 14E which prevented him returning to Ireland. This was granted.[53]

A somewhat similar view was taken in the case of George Noble, 'Count' Plunkett. Although there was no surviving internment order, he was sent to reside in England, and was not allowed to return to Ireland until January 1917. He was the father of Joseph Plunkett, executed after the Easter Rising, and was the victor of the Roscommon by-election in 1917, which first heralded the significance of Sinn Fein as a political force. Interned in 1918, he was released in December because the authorities were afraid that his frail health would attract influenza, and did not want to create more martyrs for the Irish cause.[54] There was nothing in his file which suggested that the authorities were aware of the significance of his decision to boycott Westminster after his election in 1917. This caused much dissension in Sinn Fein and was a classic example of the lack of unity in the organization. By portraying Sinn Fein as a monolithic conspiracy the authorities failed to develop a sophisticated perspective on it.

Many of these reactions were repeated in the case of Maud Gonne Macbride. Her ordeal demonstrated the range of attitudes and influences on the authorities. Her file showed traces of character assassination, suspicion bordering on paranoia, the influence of respectable opinion and the martyr fear of the authorities. Maud Gonne Macbride was the estranged widow of Major John Macbride, who had been executed for his part in the Easter Rising. He was a member of the Irish Republican Brotherhood, was second in command at the Jacob's Biscuit factory during the Rising, and had led the Boer's Irish Brigade in 1900. His double treason was perhaps the reason for his execution. Maud Gonne was a tall, gaunt débutante daughter of a British Army Officer who saw herself as an Irish Joan of Arc. She was the unrequited passion of the poet W. B. Yeats. A Home Office minute queried whether she was married to Macbride, from whom she was separated.

The suspicions of the authorities about Maud Gonne combined concerns about the possible treacherous behaviour of an upper class renegade, with the propaganda concern about the impact of a seemingly respectable Irish romantic nationalist in the United States. Indeed the authorities had some cause to be concerned, as Gonne appeared to have been implicated in a plot to shoot Edward VII in Gibraltar during her honeymoon. The authorities were extremely worried about the visit she and James Connolly's daughter made to the USA in 1916, and MI5 and General Maxwell stopped her from returning to Ireland.[55] The move was of doubtful validity, as they were prevented from entering Ireland before the order prohibiting them from returning under Defence Regulation 14E had been granted. The Home Secretary was so concerned about her that even after the last of the internees had been released and allowed to return to Ireland in June 1917, the 14E order on Maud Gonne Macbride was not lifted. Neither was that on her adopted daughter and cook when she wished them to return to Ireland to look after her affairs. The three finally returned to Dublin in January 1918 in contravention of the order against her.[56] She was not arrested because the authorities did not want to give additional propaganda to Sinn Fein.

Maud Gonne was later interned following the conscription controversy and the alleged Sinn Fein plot. Whilst interned at Holloway Jail her solicitor asked whether she could have a meeting with her son to discuss his education. This was allowed under strict conditions, as Edward Shortt, the Home Secretary, was concerned that a code could be used in conversation which would not attract the attention of a prison official present at the meeting.[57] The visit was satisfactory, except when the prisoner complained about the injustice of her imprisonment and the poor conditions in Holloway. This lament was no doubt related to a worsening lung condition which resulted in the diagnosis of tuberculosis. It led to pressure being applied to the new Home Secretary, Sir George Cave, by the literary elite. A letter organized by Lady Cunard, and signed by W. B. Yeats, James Joyce, T. S. Eliot and Wyndham Lewis asked whether death in prison or permanent injury to her health would be in anyone's interest given the current situation in Ireland.[58] The following day Maud Gonne Macbride was released from prison and entered a nursing home, where she gradually recovered her health.

The government also was scrupulously correct in assessing the culpability of civil servants implicated in the Easter Rising. A special enquiry was held in Dublin in August 1916 to assess the degree of involvement of 42 civil servants. In order to avoid the charge of a witch hunt the enquiry was not held at Dublin Castle. Judgement of the individuals' suitability to remain in government employment was not only based on possible continued commitment to Sinn Fein, but also depended on their activities, their attitude to the rebellion and a promise to subordinate their political beliefs to their professional duties as government officials. Following the enquiry 23 were dismissed, one was pensioned off and 18 were reinstated.[59]

What the released documentation on the Easter 1916 rising and its aftermath illustrated was that purely military and security responses to the crisis merely worsened the situation by driving resistance underground. The efforts of military counter-insurgency, although able to prevent the widening of the insurrection, played a crucial role in losing the propaganda war. The harsh and confused response of the martial law administration, the inability of politicians at Westminster to get to grips with the worsening problem led to a slow disintegration of British rule in Ireland. For the British government, the Irish troubles were an unwelcome irritant, beside the problems of stalemate on the Western Front. The executions, the hunger strike of Thomas Ashe, the absurdity of the alleged German plot, and the conscription controversy all played into the hands of Sinn Fein. The development of public disobedience and obstruction, and the sabotage of British rule, hastened the slide into guerrilla warfare and the undermining of British influence in Ireland.

The response of the authorities and the pressures of the First World War destroyed the credibility of the Irish Nationalists. The failure of the Irish Convention of 1916, when Nationalists and Unionists were unable to resolve their differences over Home Rule, resulted from the intransigence of the Ulster Unionists. This had highlighted the political bankruptcy of the Irish Nationalists, a fact established by the emergence of Sinn Fein as a credible political as well as an insurrectionary force in the by-elections of 1917. Lloyd George's failed political wizardry at the Irish Convention was to be followed by the harsh measures of his administration in 1917. The dual policy of olive branch and security clampdown, although inevitable during the war, made Irish politicians as well as others distrustful of Lloyd George's sincerity.

The 1916 rebellion led to experimentation with regard to government in Ireland. Although Birrell was succeeded by H. E. Duke as Chief Secretary, his failure to pacify Ireland and to check the rise of Sinn Fein led to a change of policy. The appointment of Lord French as Viceroy in 1917, and the establishment of proconsular government which subordinated the role of the Chief Secretary to the executive authority of the committees under the new structure, gradually alienated moderate opinion in Ireland. 'Johnny' French, despite his reputation as a believer in Home Rule, proved in practice to be an authoritarian modernizer who believed in firm military discipline. A system of internal passports was introduced to try to control nationalist and republican elements. This endeared him to the Ulster Unionists, and his regime saw the reaffirmation of Protestant control in the Dublin Castle administration, after the attempt to placate the Catholics in the wake of the rebellion. The lack of democratic control and the administrative chaos produced by Sir John Taylor's failure to delegate work, reinforced by the rigid financial control insisted upon by the Treasury Remembrancer, Maurice Headlam, produced a crisis in government which added to the problems of the deteriorating security situation. The failure of proconsular government led to more reforms in government in 1919–20.[60]

The compound mistakes of Irish policy were to lead to the collapse of British power in Ireland. The British governments during the First World War, and Dublin Castle, misunderstood the significance of Sinn Fein. The obscure rebellion of a splinter group in the Irish Volunteers, allied to a ragbag collection of ill-disciplined elements in the so-called Irish Citizen Army and to a conspiratorial secret subversive society, the Irish Republican Brotherhood, was turned from political farce into an Irish tragedy by the response of the authorities. Political and security errors during the First World War played into the hands of the extremists in Irish society. The scene was set for the weakening of the British Empire and the attainment of Irish independence in the aftermath of the First World War.

c) The Collapse of British Power (1919–23)

The attainment of Irish independence in 1922 represented the end product of one of the darker episodes in recent British history: the 'troubles' of the 1919–21 period in Ireland. This illustrated the political bankruptcy of the Irish administration centred on Dublin Castle, the intelligence and security failure of the authorities, and the collapse of law and order. It saw the more moderate Irish Nationalists replaced by the radical Sinn Fein as the motor behind the drive for independence. This signalled the demise of politics and its replacement by the use of force as the means by which such ends could be achieved. New types of resistance were improvised to undermine the military. The ideology of guerrilla warfare, pioneered by the Boers in South Africa, was adapted to the Irish situation by Bulmer Hobson and J. J. O'Connell.[61] It was developed, somewhat against Hobson's wishes, by the Irish Volunteers and the Irish Republican Army (IRA), as they became known, after the first Dail in 1919. Michael Collins, of the Irish Republican Brotherhood, proved himself an organizer of genius, and demonstrated to the British, even more than the Bolsheviks, what a ruthless intelligence and security apparatus could achieve.[62]

Ireland proved a political and military graveyard. The troubles were directly or indirectly responsible for the deaths of Collins, Griffith and that implacable foe of Irish nationalism, Sir Henry Wilson. They also played a significant role in the removal of Lloyd George as Prime Minister, and the political eclipse of Austen Chamberlain and Lord Birkenhead in the Conservative Party. In the military sphere the troubles saw the failure of the British attempt to pacify Ireland. Although not defeated, the British held power only through the use of draconian force and the reimposition of martial law in the south and west in 1920. The reprisals and atrocities of the Black and Tans, and the Auxiliaries, lost the British the propaganda war. Unauthorized reprisals and the failure to punish the loss of control by elements in the police cost the British dear. In the end a military stalemate forced both the Irish and the British to the conference table. Violence and counter-violence between 1919 and 1921 led to 600 deaths and 1,200 wounded for the IRA.[63]

What the activities of Sinn Fein and the IRA demonstrated was how insurrection and civil war could effectively challenge a weakened British state through intelligence and security measures. Successful resistance to British rule was achieved by a dual strategy. The establishment of a 'state within a state', the emergence of an alternative administrative structure based on the Dáil Eireann, represented a positive attempt to set up a new government. Whilst initially the decision of the elected Sinn Fein representatives to boycott Westminster and to establish their own government was viewed with derision rather than concern, the British were quickly forced to take the challenge seriously. The intimidation and political terrorism practised by the IRA reinforced the growing adherence of Sinn Fein to the activities of the IRA in rural areas. This arose from the second part of the strategy: the assault on law and order, and the undermining of Dublin Castle.

All forms of British power were attacked in Ireland. Traditional forms of unrest, such as cattle drives and other agrarian 'outrages', were stepped up in the southern and western counties. These reached their peak in 1920 and 1921, with few being arrested.[64] The monthly number of outrages against the police rose from 57 in June 1920 to 589 by July 1921. In that latter month there were 11 deaths, 54 resignations, 24 dismissals, with a total wastage of 92 officers. These were replaced by 8 recruits from Ireland and 202 from England.[65] The war on the police was particularly effective, as these statistics demonstrate. Michael Collins' counter-subversion strategy kept the IRA leadership informed of British plans by the placing of agents in Dublin Castle, and through the murder of the DMP's political detectives in such incidents as 'Bloody Sunday' in 1920.[66] Such activity brought home to the British the importance of an effective 'secret state'. Whereas in the past the authorities had found it relatively easy to infiltrate Irish secret societies, Collins' counter-intelligence precautions were to undermine the basis of British power. IRA attacks on the police in 1920–1 led to the destruction of nearly 470 barracks.[67] In essence the IRA took advantage of the pressure on resources available to the British state; hence the success of the boycott of British munitions on rail and road transport, which further tied up scarce manpower in the police and British army.

The purpose of the assault on the police was to destroy British control over law and order, but it also had the side effect of inviting reprisals. The morale of the DMP in particular, and to a certain extent that of the RIC, was undermined, except in Ulster. The problem in terms of personnel was partly relieved by the recruitment of demobilized British soldiers and volunteers, who formed the basis of the infamous 'Black and Tans' and 'Auxiliaries'. Their actions alienated public opinion completely.

The difficulty was that ever since the Easter Rising neither the politicians, the military nor the police had provided an effective military or political response to the problems posed by Sinn Fein. Public opinion in Ireland had become progressively alienated by the pressures of war, which led to the draconian response to the 1916 rebellion and the problems caused by the extension of conscription to that country in 1918. The victory of Sinn Fein in the general election of December 1918 undermined the moral legitimacy of British rule everywhere outside Ulster. The situation was not helped by the failure of the military response. Martial law in 1916 had been unnecessary outside Dublin, and the inflexible and unimaginative security measures of General Maxwell and Field Marshal Viscount French (who was created Lord Lieutenant in 1918, with the brief of restoring law and order, and exposing German intrigues), created neither efficient political nor security responses to the deteriorating situation. The appointment of Macready as General Officer in Command in Ireland, with a parallel reform of Dublin Castle, with Hamar Greenwood acting as Chief Secretary, was too little too late. The most significant development was the appointment of Sir John Anderson as Joint Undersecretary at Dublin Castle. His Irish experiences influenced his very important role in developing internal security measures in the United Kingdom in the 1920s, as Permanent Undersecretary at the Home Office from 1922–32.

The significant changes and reforms instituted after the

failure of proconsular government illustrates also the limits of administrative influence on British politics. The enquiry by Sir Warren Fisher into the structure of Irish Government produced one of the most damning reports ever on any aspect of British administration. Whilst the government was persuaded of the need to radically restructure the way in which Ireland was administered, the Cabinet took not the slightest account of Fisher and his fellow civil servants' plea for a political initiative which would acknowledge the political fact that the majority of Irishmen now supported Sinn Fein. The Government of Ireland Act of 1920, Unionist in origin, provided the framework for two Home Rule governments based in Dublin and Belfast. Ironically, Fisher's reforms were a success; the administrative structure and the personnel set in place by Sir John Anderson proved invaluable in the new governments, in both Dublin and Belfast.[68]

All these changes signified was the necessity of a change in direction of Irish policy. This was emphasized by the law advisor, W. E. Wylie QC, to Dublin Castle in 1920. He argued that Ireland was becoming ungovernable because British law had been framed for a law-abiding people, on constitutional principles. At present there was no public opinion behind the administration which could only be achieved by political measures such as the establishment of Home Rule. In particular Ireland should be governed constitutionally, and in his opinion all anti-democratic and 'semi-martial' measures should be dropped. However, where lawbreakers were apprehended prompt punishment should be meted out to all those tried and convicted. The return of law and order could only be attained by the granting of colonial Home Rule.[69] Politically, Lloyd George, Anderson and Macready were amenable to such a suggestion; but the fact that Lloyd George was dependent on the Conservatives, who backed Ulster Unionist opposition to Home Rule, and that Sinn Fein was anti-British, divided amongst itself, and increasingly republican, meant that both political and military solutions to the Irish problem were extremely difficult to achieve. It was not until the security situation had deteriorated so badly, and the military stalemate made it in the majorities' interest on both sides to come to an agreement, that a compromise became possible.

7 Michael Collins as Sinn Fein candidate for Cork, 1919

That public opinion outside Ulster could remain apathetic to the administration at Dublin Castle, no matter how intimidating, murderous and illegal the activities of the IRA became, owed much to the increasingly unofficial reprisals of elements in the security forces. The lack of an overall command structure in military and police in Ireland proved to be an insuperable handicap. Macready, despite the success of his leadership in such a policy in South Wales in 1910, categorically refused to be given responsibility for a command structure which included the police.[70] This was unfortunate, because he failed to get on with Major-General Tudor, the head of the RIC.

No doubt this was because Macready considered the RIC to be an ill-disciplined rabble, a view that was reinforced by the unauthorized reprisal by the Black and Tans and Auxiliaries against the IRA. After the outrage in Cork in December 1920, where the centre of the city was burned down in retaliation for an IRA atrocity, Macready issued instructions that where the RIC or Auxiliaries were accommodated in army barracks they must come under military discipline. After a further reprisal in March 1921, Macready was adamant that young soldiers must not see police riots such as the bombing, shooting and burning at Westport. Other notorious reprisals took place in Balbriggan and County Clare, following an ambush at Rineen. Macready acknowledged the deterrent function of reprisals. His point was that if such a policy was decided upon it should have the full force of the state behind it, as unauthorized actions created anarchy.[71] Tudor, in his report of the fire at Cork, argued that it was a regrettable but understandable reaction to an earlier attack on the Auxiliaries.[72] Although intelligence improved as a result of Colonel Ormonde Winter being given responsibility, 'O's show' failed to reverse the decline, as his secretive behaviour failed to endear him to Macready.

The problem of joint command of the security forces was further complicated by the imposition of martial law in December 1920. Macready was against martial law because it would require too much manpower to administer adequately and would not be effective unless it was ruthlessly applied. It was also restricted to cover only most of Munster, whilst Macready thought that if it was implemented it was vital for it to be applied to the ports, particularly Dublin.[73] Yet even in the martial law area it was found impossible in practice to subordinate the RIC to the military because the provisions for administration of the order were so vague. Lloyd George was particularly worried that civilian control should not be relinquished, and that the same mistakes should not be made as in 1916.

In fact the military stalemate encouraged both sides to sit down at the negotiating table. The British government was forced to talk with those whom it deemed terrorists, a movement it had proscribed in 1919, and to forsake its principle that it should never compromise with the threat of force. The fig-leaf of a cease-fire provided the pretext for such a development. Lloyd George cleverly used the full range of his political skills to cajole both his Conservative allies and Sinn Fein to the negotiating table. Austen Chamberlain and Lord Birkenhead were persuaded to back Lloyd George's efforts to encourage the moderate elements in Sinn Fein. Lloyd George also listened to his special negotiator, Andy Cope, and the Cabinet Secretariat, under Sir Maurice Hankey and Tom Jones, who encouraged him to make unofficial contacts with Sinn Fein, as they were convinced that the more responsible leaders would settle for a form of Home Rule.[74] The Dominions, particularly through General Smuts, also applied pressure to produce a settlement with Ireland to become a self-governing state within the Empire.

As Lloyd George had to outmanoeuvre the opposition of Diehards like the CIGS, Sir Henry Wilson and the Ulster Unionists, so Sinn Fein leaders had to be cajoled into agreeing to a settlement. On the British side, Bonar Law, the leader of the Conservatives, told Tom Jones that coercion was the only policy, as the Irish were an inferior race who only understood force.[75] Other Conservatives found it difficult to sit down with those they considered to be seditious rebels. As for Sinn Fein, whilst pragmatists like Arthur Griffiths and Michael Collins were prepared to compromise for the sake of the establishment of a self-governing Ireland, intransigents like de Valera, sentenced to death by the British in 1916, and Austin Stack, Erskine Childers and Cathal Brugha, were not to be satisfied with any solution except complete independence for the whole of Ireland. The bitterness of the divisions led to civil war in Ireland, after the narrow agreement of the Dáil to the terms of the 1922 treaty, which led to the death through overwork of Griffiths, the murder of Collins and the shooting of Childers.

After the repression of 1919–21, it was the British who offered the olive branch. In return for a truce, talks took place to try to provide a solution to the Irish problem. It was the timely intervention of George V which provided the impetus for compromise. His speech at the opening of the Belfast parliament in 1921, and the displeasure he expressed to the Cabinet and Imperial Conference about the activities of the Black and Tans, and organized reprisals, were the catalyst which gave Lloyd George the necessary leverage to persuade the Cabinet to agree to sup with the devil, albeit with a long spoon.[76] The negotiations with the delegates of Sinn Fein were fraught with difficulty and only with complex manoeuvrings and political pressure, particularly with relation to the idea of a Boundary Commission to decide the border of Ulster, was an agreement reached with the more pragmatic members of the Irish delegation, in December 1921.[77]

In many ways the subtle and devious negotiating skills of Lloyd George, aided by the administrative support of liberal civil servants like Andy Cope, Sir John Anderson, Maurice Hankey and Tom Jones, and the realism of Churchill, Birkenhead and Austen Chamberlain, produced a settlement which preserved the ability of two-thirds of historic Ulster to remain within the United Kingdom, whilst the rest of Ireland became a Dominion within the Empire. The refusal to countenance the loss of Empire was the sticking-point for Unionists, Diehards and Conservatives; the establishment of the Boundary Commission to determine the border between the Irish Free State and Northern Ireland was the necessary compromise which enabled a solution to be found. Even then more blood was spilt, the Free State became a Republic outside the Commonwealth, and the problems of Ulster were to rumble on throughout the twentieth century without a final resolution to the problem.[78]

This outcome satisfied neither Diehards like Sir Henry Wilson, nor some Ulster intransigents. It split Sinn Fein irrevocably. Yet it was a result which allowed the British state to restore the rule of law throughout the new boundaries of the United Kingdom during the interwar period. Somewhat ironically, it was the failure to export IRA terrorism to the rest of the United Kingdom until 1939, despite the murder of Sir Henry Wilson in London in 1923, which kept the

Irish troubles over the water. The birth of the Irish Free State was marked by civil war and continuing guerrilla warfare. The occupation of the four courts in Dublin by those in the IRA who refused to accept the 1922 treaty saw the renewal of hostilities until the final defeat of the rebels in 1924. Those who continued to ignore Irish and British realities were driven underground and continued bloody rebellion against both countries. The unfinished business of the Irish problem later returned to haunt both British and Irish governments after 1968.

The consequences of the 'loss of Ireland' were to be very important for British politics, public order and internal security. Few of those most involved in the political solution displayed 'teflon' characteristics. Lloyd George's political skills were increasingly seen by the Conservative rank and file as being morally reprehensible and lacking in principle. Many never forgave him for negotiating with rebels, despite the fact there was little option. The treaty of 1922 proved disastrous for all involved in the settlement. Birkenhead, Austen Chamberlain and Churchill were all politically damaged by their close association with Lloyd George, and their involvement in 'solving' the Irish problem. The future, in the interwar Conservative party, was to belong to those who had kept their political distance from Lloyd George. The disastrous split in Sinn Fein was to lead to even worse consequences: the tragic deaths of Arthur Griffiths and Michael Collins, and the Civil War.

In terms of public order and internal security, Ireland proved a case study in how not to influence and manipulate public opinion. As in the nineteenth century, methods of dealing with the rebellious Irish played little part in managing affairs in the rest of the United Kingdom. The lessons of Ireland were not lost on Home Office administrators like Sir John Anderson, who had himself been an Undersecretary in Dublin Castle in the crucial years 1920–1, or the police. The Irish problem reinforced important lessons of counter-subversion strategy. Opposition or extremist groups should never be allowed to build up a state within a state, or to organize an administrative structure which provided an alternative law and order jurisdiction to that prescribed by the authorities. It was interesting to note that it was where organized labour tried to control movement of supplies in Northumberland and Durham during the General Strike that the authorities cracked down hardest. Similarly, Special Branch and MI5 were particularly interested in monitoring attempts by both communists and fascists to establish their own controlled economic and political organizations.

The authorities carefully monitored political violence, and were particularly keen not to drive either communist or fascist organizations underground. The Home Office in fact blocked the attempts by Metropolitan Police commissioners to outlaw political extremism, on the grounds that it would be more difficult to monitor a secret society than a legal political party, a tactic learned from the Irish experience. The denial of publicity, and the concern that public opinion should remain insulated from all forms of political extremism, were counter-subversion tactics taught by the Irish situation. Above all, law and order had to be upheld and all attempts to undermine it stoutly resisted. Liberty and freedom of speech were to be defended provided criticism of the state was within the law and did not encourage unconstitutional action. Even when it did, the authorities would let sleeping dogs lie if it was concluded that more harm than good, or more publicity, would be generated for extremism if their activities were prosecuted. Mistakes made with the IRA were to be avoided: political martyrdom was to be avoided at all costs and unconstitutional behaviour was to be isolated. Finally the Irish troubles had shown the necessity for coordinated control of the forces of law and order and the desirability of military discipline in the security forces. In so far as the authorities learned from their political and security mistakes in Ireland, political violence was never to be such a problem in John Bull's island as it had proved to be in her politically divided colonial appendage.

4

REDS IN THE BED (1917–1939)

The survival of the new security apparatus after the First World War resulted from a change in the perception of the threat to the British state. Subversion was deemed to be under new management as a result of the Russian Revolution. Discontent following conscription and the failure to deliver a knockout blow to it led to increased industrial unrest during the war itself, and for the first time political surveillance by un-uniformed security agencies was extended to left-wing radicals, reformist socialists and trade unionists, as well as revolutionaries and potential terrorists. Attila the Hun was replaced by the red web in the demonology of the security buffs. Moscow, rather than Berlin, was seen as the new centre for subversion of the British state. This threat was to justify the survival of snooping and the political police until the demise of the perceived international communist menace in 1990, by which time there were plenty of other problems to ensure its permanent if somewhat less secure survival.

The rise of the Comintern octopus was preceded by increased concern about the threat of revolutionary activity under domestic management. It appears that following the Clydeside unrest of 1915–16 the Ministry of Munitions investigation of the dispute used Special Branch officers to monitor opponents of dilution, following the replacement of skilled by semi-skilled or unskilled workers.[1] Macassey's investigation for the Ministry of Munitions recommended swift action against the Clyde Workers Committee, and subsequently ten of the strike leaders were deported. This had the effect of defusing the situation on the Clyde but of exporting unrest to other engineering centres. The Commission's fears about an 'anti-British conspiracy', and of possible German influence, led to the establishment of a national intelligence network in the Ministry of Munitions. This was to be developed out of the MI5 anti-aliens and anti-sabotage organization. It was known by its cover name as PMS2 (Parliamentary Military Secretary Department No. 2 Section).[2]

This short-lived organization was important because its history demonstrated the lack of a credible threat from political extremists in Britain and the suspicions with which public opinion tended to view secret service work. Its use of agents like the notorious 'Alec Gordon' (William Rickard) to try and trap shop stewards and socialists into sabotage plots, led to the arrest and conviction of four naive idealists framed in a 'murder plot' against Lloyd George and Arthur Henderson. This was viewed with grave suspicion by the entire labour movement. An ex-journalist working for Military Intelligence in 1918 argued that the use of *agents provocateurs* by the government was one of the main causes of working class unrest, particularly in the north.[3] Joe Toole, at the Leeds Conference on the Russian Revolution, argued against the setting up of soviets in Britain because they would be infiltrated by the likes of Alec Gordon, who would manufacture a pretext for the authorities to move against them.[4] A report on public and working class opinion in the London district by Lord Willoughby de Broke, for Military Intelligence, argued that the working classes were very resentful of the implication that every striker was in German pay, and that they lacked patriotism.[5] Similarly, the uncovering of the London radical W. F. Watson as a source for Special Branch after the war rapidly terminated his credentials with the left, despite his claims that he was feeding the authorities disinformation. Such state suspicions of the patriotism of the left, which allegedly justified the use of such underhand methods, were to make a reappearance as late as the 1984 miners strike when Mrs Thatcher was to attack 'the enemy within'.

There were more alarmist voices. Sir Edward Carson's call for an investigation into a possible German plot behind pacifist and revolutionary activities in 1917 brought Sir Basil Thomson's views on the behavioural psychology of the working classes to the attention of the War Cabinet. Although he could find no evidence of the 'Hidden Hand', he blamed working class unrest on the curtailment of traditional amusements like horse racing and football, and on the reduced hours of public houses. Hence the frustrated working classes became an easy prey for agitators – a situation which could be defused if other outlets of excitement could be introduced (Thomson suggested premium bonds).[6] Thomson's patronizing views were developed over three more years of reporting on revolutionaries.

Other jaundiced interpretations were also paraded before the War Cabinet. Lord Robert Cecil circulated a long report on the 'Leeds Soviet' by an anonymous agent.[7] This emphasized hostile public opinion in Leeds and the attempt to stop delegates lodging in local hotels. The content of speeches by MPs, such as W. C. Anderson, Ramsay MacDonald and Philip Snowden, which made reckless comments, and the general anti-British tone of the proceedings, was denounced. Particular significance was attached to demands for immediate revolution, the setting up of Soviets and Noah Ablett's call for the establishment of Soldiers' and Workers' Councils. Speakers were also alleged to imply that legislation was passed not to win the war but to enslave the workers after hostilities had finished. Although several in the War Cabinet were alarmists, the Prime Minister viewed the proceedings with caution. Lloyd George argued that the 1,151 delegates represented only themselves and were not a significant voice of public opinion, and that more would be gained by ignoring the conference than by attempting to move against the organizers of the meeting. If it achieved no publicity the general public would soon forget the event, whereas attempts to suppress it would give revolutionary activity unwanted attention.

Thus unrest on the Home Front in the First World War provided the motivation for the retention and expansion of the security arrangements, put in place originally for the monitoring of aliens. It was to be the problems of transition to peace, and the emergence of a much more sophisticated and dangerous enemy than the intelligence services of Imperial Germany that ensured the survival, in a reduced form in the interwar period, of internal security and counter-intelligence agencies in the British state.

a) The Transition to Peace (1918–21)

The aftermath of the First World War was the heyday of alarmists and security buffs fearful of imminent revolution in Britain. Events in continental Europe and in Ireland, as well as the seemingly intractable labour problems in Britain, meant that the coalition government became very concerned about civilian unrest.[8] The problems of demobilization, police strikes in 1918 and 1919, the revival of the Triple Alliance in 1919, and rail, transport, dock and coal strikes between 1919 and 1921, led to considerable unease amongst politicians, the military, the police and the Home Office. These fears were articulated particularly by leading Unionist politicians such as Sir Edward Carson, Lord Curzon, Walter Long, Sir Auckland Geddes and Lord Birkenhead, and at times their leader Bonar Law and the then coalition Liberal, Winston Churchill. Their tough stance, at least in rhetorical terms, was orchestrated by the CIGS, Sir Henry Wilson, Air Marshal Trenchard, and the two Metropolitan Police Commissioners, General Macready and Brigadier-General Horwood. Interestingly, Sir Basil Thomson was sometimes more sanguine than many in government at this time. Fortunately Lloyd George was more astute, devious and less alarmist than many of his cabinet colleagues, and a subtle mixture of coercion, confrontation, duplicity and compromise was to characterize the government's response to labour problems.

These views are best illustrated by the account of the Assistant Secretary to the Cabinet, Thomas Jones, of a Cabinet Conference on industrial disturbances on 2 February

1920.[9] This appeared to encompass the full range of prejudices and phobias. Auckland Geddes implied that the universities were stuffed full of trained men who would cooperate with clerks and stockbrokers to resist the revolution. Bonar Law appeared to see battalions of stockbrokers willing to come to the help of the government. Edward Shortt, the Home Secretary, talked of raising a temporary force of 10,000 men for a national emergency. Trenchard pledged the 20,000 mechanics and 2,000 airmen of the RAF to help maintain order. On another occasion his Cabinet colleagues appeared to take seriously his call for the death sentence for aliens who brought revolutionary propaganda into Britain, and a proposal to bomb strikers. Macready said there were a large number of trained men who could use rifles in the Metropolitan Police. Wilson, the 'Lost Dictator', suggested shooting strikers and trade union leaders.[10] With such extreme views amongst his colleagues, according to Tom Jones, Lloyd George ironically indulged in 'a lot of unsuspected leg pulling' as he did not believe in the imminence of revolution and thought that the Home Office had been got at by the War Office, in order to provide an excuse to boost recruitment.[11]

That party politicians and the military were influenced by such fantasies no doubt owed much to the over-reaction to the Russian Revolution. Certainly there appeared to be a contradiction between the political views of the intelligence and security communities and right-wing politicians, and the much more reassuring reports on public opinion which emanated from government departments, Military Intelligence and the Directorate of Intelligence (DI). 'Terrific anti-Bolsheviks' like Kell (MI5), Smith-Cumming (MI6), Thomson (DI), Hall and Sinclair (both Directors of Naval Intelligence (DNI)), grossly exaggerated the threat posed by soviet propaganda after the war.[12] 'Bolshevism' soon became a political swear-word used by right-wing politicians and brass hats against the political and social changes which had been set in motion by the First World War. It was used to explain the lack of social deference, high taxation or the 'nationalization of women'.[13] Sir Basil Thomson summed up many of these phobias. For him, Bolshevism was an 'infectious disease' which 'spread like a cancer', and destroyed the tissue of society.[14] This is the language of contemporary racism and perfectly illustrates the close proximity of race and class as two sides of the 'alien menace' coin.

Whilst there was industrial unrest after the war, too much should not be read into the fears of Unionist politicians, right-wing generals and law and order policemen. Throughout the interwar period more sophisticated views, like those of Lloyd George and Baldwin amongst the politicians, Sir John Anderson and other Home Office officials, and most of the law officers, prevailed and successfully restrained the more outrageous restrictions on civil liberties demanded by some diehard anti-communists. Political surveillance, the Supply and Transport Organization, piecemeal legislation to restrict extremist propaganda and influence, and selective arrests rather than outright repression of revolutionary movements were the main methods used to control subversive influence. The bald statistics of the development of the Communist Party of Great Britain (CPGB), suggest that a relatively subtle approach to the problem was a wise decision. At no stage during the interwar years did the CPGB ever have more than two members of parliament elected to the House of Commons. The Membership of the CPGB fluctuated from 4,000 at its foundation in 1920, to 2,000 in 1921, 3,000 in 1924, 10,730 in October 1926 to 3,200 in 1929.[15] The party expanded steadily in the 1930's, mainly as a result of its United Front anti-fascist campaign, from 7,500 in 1936 to 18,000 by August 1939.[16] These statistics suggest the degree of concern was exaggerated, particularly as the communist mania was more widespread in the 1920s.

Certainly successive governments were not taken in by the security hysteria. Neither the police forces, Whitehall nor the intelligence communities were immune from the anti-waste campaign and the financial retrenchment of the interwar years. Although the Desborough Committee had rectified the low pay of policemen in 1918, the Geddes axe in 1922 reduced the size of police forces by 5 per cent (raised to 7 per cent in 1923), and police expenditure by 12 per cent.[17] Although the policy was altered in 1925, practically all police forces remained significantly below establishment levels throughout the interwar period. Whilst emergencies such as the General Strike brought in many volunteers, the Special Constables Act of 1923 failed to provide sufficient recruits in those industrial areas where they where were most needed. By 1925 MI5's staff had fallen from 800 in 1918 to 30. Even though there was some expansion in the 1930s, by September 1938 MI5 had only 30 officers, 120 secretarial and registry staff and a surveillance section of 6 men.[18] It survived a takeover bid by MI6 in 1925 and important further rationalization took place in 1931.[19]

In this year the Secret Service Committee, at the suggestion of Sir John Anderson, transferred Scotland Yard's civilian intelligence staff to MI5 to create a new security service which would centralize information on revolutionary and subversive activities. This important change was designed to reduce expenditure as much as increase efficiency, and secret service work was seriously underfunded and ran on a shoestring.[20]

Such evidence helps to place state anti-communist activity in a less irrational context. Whilst the military too were less than keen to aid the civil power between 1918 and 1939, heightened fears about civil disorder were countered by less rather than more expenditure.[21] Political extremism was not considered to be a significant threat for much of the interwar period, except by those in the intelligence community whose professional interests meant that it was necessary for it to be seen as a continued menace. The state, however, saw its intelligence product as a useful tool in the planning of counter-extremist policies.

This combination of paranoia and parsimony on the right led to MI5 cooperating with private organizations in political surveillance and anti-revolutionary operations after the First World War. John Hope has shown how respectable middle class organizations like the British Empire Union (BEU), the National Citizens Union (NCU), the Anti Socialist Union, the National Security Union, the Liberty League and the Economic League (EL), cooperated with the security authorities through the coordinating function of National Propaganda, and played an important role in the groups set up to aid the Supply and Transport Committee in the strikes of 1919, 1921 and 1926, and through the research facilities set in place by the anti-Semitic conspiracy theorist, Nesta Webster. Apparently National Propaganda provided much of the often inaccurate material for the Directorate of Intelligence and Special Branch reports on left-wing extremism. Its role in political surveillance represented one of the many contributions to anti-subversion activity by one of its earliest directors, 'Blinker' Hall. The EL took over much of this work in 1924. Key personnel in MI5 anti-communist operations, like Maxwell Knight and James Mcguirk Hughes, were recruited from the private intelligence network based on patriotic middle class societies like the BEU and the EL, and these appear to have formed the backbone of the Organization for the Maintenance of Supplies during the General Strike. Knight and Hughes were also to be the respective Directors of Intelligence in the British Fascists and the British Union of Fascists; this suggests that until Munich MI5 had ambivalent feelings about British fascists: they were to be put under political surveillance because of their connections with foreign powers, and the public order problems which their existence posed; but also because some, at least in the security community, saw them as allies in anti-communist operations.[22]

The major problem with determining the extent to which the authorities were concerned with communism derives from the secrecy which still surrounds the subject. There is no doubt that communism and soviet propaganda were the main security preoccupation of the state in mainland Britain. But this is not at all obvious from the released records after 1924. The discrepancy is apparent because we know that until at least 1928 there was a regular survey of revolutionary movements in the United Kingdom issued by the Cabinet or Home Office.[23] By November 1933 this had been downgraded to a three-monthly Civil Security Intelligence summary. The released documentation is particularly thin for the 1930s. The memoirs of Sir Basil Thomson and his successor as head of Special Branch, Sir Wyndham Childs, reflect the official concern about communism in the 1920s.[24] Most informed reports suggest that what has been released represents the tip of an iceberg of political surveillance material emanating from Special Branch in the interwar period. It is also quite clear that the tunnel vision of Special Branch and the Security Service after 1931 interpreted its intelligence product in too cavalier a fashion and used it to reinforce its preconceived image of the grave danger of the Soviet plot to undermine the British Empire. The loss of the Soviet intercepts in 1927, after an orgy of indiscretion following the reading of wireless interceptions in the House of Commons, compounded the difficulty.[25]

What the somewhat ambiguous attitude of the state signified was that even the most liberal politicians and administrators were influenced by security concerns. In particular, left-wing extremism was only perceived in law and order terms. There was little appreciation of the social context of labour unrest or British communism, and little comprehension that they represented a protest against the inequalities and injustice in British society. British communism was a movement of struggle, of class conflict and discontent against capitalism and the state. The authorities tended to view the CPGB as a monolith under 'Bolshevik discipline' and controlled by a foreign power. There appeared to be insufficient appreciation of the ongoing conflict between institutional and party loyalty; 'Hornerism', for example, became from Moscow's perspective a right-wing deviation for communists who put reformist and trade union functions above party discipline. Arthur Horner, the South Wales miners' leader, whilst submitting to party discipline for putting his trade union loyalties above those of the CPGB, in fact did not alter his behaviour. Similarly, there was little appreciation of the significant differences in outlook between those who joined the CPGB in the 1930s to defend the interests of the Soviet Union, and those who saw it as the most militant source of anti-fascism. The internal problems of the 'class against class' period, and the Nazi–Soviet pact between 1939 and 1941, appear to have been little exploited by the authorities. This has to be compared with the subtle and devious psychological recruitment by the Soviet intelligence and security organizations, the OGPU (until 1934) and NKVD, of upper class renegades within the British establishment.

Whilst the Comintern undoubtedly dictated policy and

tactics, the authorities failed to recognize that the CPGB reflected alienated British working class aspirations as well as Soviet intrigue. The first academic history of the CPGB, Henry Pelling's *The British Communist Party*, provides a similar interpretation to the less alarmist views of the state perspective of British communism. However, there is some truth in the criticism of this work by Rajani Palme Dutt, the leading British communist theoretician, that it is like a film of a wrestling match with the exertions of one of the combatants blacked out. This has to be contrasted with James Kluggman's official history, which, although it admirably outlines the domestic context of the origins of British communism, nevertheless reads like the Rosencrantz and Guildenstern version of Hamlet. Its failure to properly analyse the role of Moscow and the Comintern in the origins of British communism meant that it suffered from the opposite defect to that of Pelling's book.

The opening of the CPGB archive to non-party researchers, and the acquisition of executive minutes sent to Moscow, has led to a considerable revision of our knowledge of the CPGB. Recent research by Kevin Morgan and Nina Fishman leads this author to suggest that despite the massive surveillance operation organized by Special Branch, the failure to properly analyse the product of such intelligence only reinforced the stereotyped views already examined. The reality was that there were shifting alliances within the CPGB leadership, that the degree of manipulation and control by Comintern and Moscow Centre did not always lead to bovine obedience from British communists, and that the CPGB exhibited within limits some initiative in political developments. Reading between the lines of released intelligence reports suggests that the authorities did not see the significance of this. Thus the period of the 'bolshevization' of the party, from 1922–30, under the direction of Harry Pollitt and Rajani Palme Dutt, was not differentiated from the struggle between two very different groups of Stalinists in the 1930s, between the rightist 'revolutionary pragmatist' united front trade unionist strategy of Pollitt, Campbell, Hannington and Horner, and the unreconstructed leftist 'class against class' warriors, Rajani Palme Dutt, William Rust and Dave

Springhall. The dearth of reference to Salme Palme Dutt, the wife of Rajani, in declassified material, as well as most accounts of the CPGB, suggested this was another secret the party kept well hidden and which is now revealed in CPGB archives.[26]

Whilst the publication in 1990 of the CPGB minutes of the crucial debates on the Nazi–Soviet pact is to be applauded, mention of the fact that the man who brought the news of the change of line from Moscow, 'Dave' Springhall, was later convicted of espionage for the Soviet Union in 1943, was relegated to the glossary, illustrated the point that even Glasnost has its limits. The establishment perspective of British communism ignored an important aspect of the party's function in British life; as a result, some in the state apparatus took a demonological view of its operations. The hostility of the state also affected the behaviour of the CPGB; as a small minority party it was concerned about staying within the law, avoiding proscription or being closed down by the authorities, and this limited its range of legal options when it set about advocating a revolutionary programme.

In the aftermath of the First World War, however, the advocates of a less alarmist view had the upper hand in policy formulation. The Department of Labour under Sir Robert Horne (1919–20) continued to produce sober, well balanced and judicious reports of labour unrest which stressed the economic and not political causes of discontent, even though Horne himself at times was influenced by the alarmist tide of right-wing politicians. For example, Military Intelligence, which reported relatively objectively on domestic unrest between 1918 and 1920, stated in June 1919 that Northern Command found that there was a growing desire in all classes to return to normal working conditions and that 'the more intelligent' of the working classes were becoming alarmed at the activities of extremist syndicalists. According to this source, the 'great majority' of the working classes wanted government action against the British Socialist Party and other revolutionary bodies, so long as it was made clear to all that the legitimate aspirations of labour were to be encouraged.[27] The Assistant Competent Military Authority (ACMA) at Stafford in April 1919 commented on the public's 'growing weariness' of industrial unrest and suspicion that it was manufactured.[28] More workers were said to be seeing through the hot air spouted by extremists: although John McClean, the leading Scottish revolutionary agitator, generated large crowds at meetings in 1918 and 1919, he was 'reported to be going mad'.[29] Thomson argued he was seen as 'mentally unstable'[30] and that 'sober working men' saw him as 'insane'.[31] Whatever the objective merits of this judgement, and most labour historians would certainly dispute this assessment, it certainly displayed the inbuilt bias of the intelligence agencies in the aftermath of war. Apparently McClean believed the authorities were trying to poison him when he was imprisoned in 1918, and this response was interpreted as a clinical symptom.

Even though the tone of military intelligence from the regional commands was jittery at times, particularly with regard to the attitude of troops towards labour unrest, the overwhelming impression was one of the complete reliability of the forces, particularly in areas of tension like Scottish Command, and public opinion's hostility to industrial conflict.[32] In most areas the response of the reports on subjects under the headings 'Revolutionary Activity' and 'Acts of Disloyalty' was 'nil'.[33]

In the same vein, Thomson's more colourful and idiosyncratic weekly reports to the Cabinet, as well as titillating some of the more alarmist sensibilities of the consumers of such material, also commented on the 'steadying' influences which kept most of the working classes immune from the effects of revolutionary rhetoric. These included, in addition to the 1917 list, the popularity of the royal family, bad weather and the 'ill feeling' between the 'saner Labour elements from the forces' and the 'shirkers'.[34] Thomson's flamboyant contributions contained enough worrying material to ensure his immediate survival; after the Coupon Election when the massive coalition majority of 410 forced socialist opposition to go underground and advocate a policy of direct action. The obvious conclusion to be derived from his obsession with a miniscule revolutionary movement was that the Directorate of Intelligence was a waste of time and money, a view which Lloyd George came to in 1921.[35] In general, political surveillance generated more heat than light; it increased working class suspicion of the government, and public opinion became increasingly hostile to the domestic spying activities of a Special Branch directed by the energetic Thomson. However, Thomson's demise in 1921 did not see the end of Continental practices; political surveillance returned to a secret underworld, increasingly outside parliamentary, if not entirely Home Office, control.

If unrest intelligence provoked critical comment, then the increased powers of the state and the means by which public order and internal security were managed also provided much controversy. This represented a mixture of formal and informal measures. Formally, such legislation as the Official Secrets Act, the Emergency Powers Act and the Firearms Act (all 1920) gave the authorities the ability to replace the lapsed DORA regulations with similar powers during states of emergency proclaimed by the government.[36] In effect the principles of habeas corpus and the workings of the common law could be suspended during periods of crisis at the behest of the authorities. The Emergency Powers Act and its attendant regulations enabled government to declare a state of emergency for one month and to make any regulation necessary to secure essential services.[37] Its powers were soon to be invoked in the coal strike of 1921. Whilst the state could now resurrect wartime powers in peace by declaring a state of emergency, it also revamped the machinery of state and gave new powers to the authorities through the Police Act (1919) and, more informally, through the tightening of Home Office control of public order.

The Police Act (1919) had resulted from the two police strikes, the first over wages and conditions of service in the Metropolitan Police in 1918, the second over the refusal of the government to allow the unionization of the police. This strike affected several police authorities, most seriously at Liverpool, where 50 per cent of the force came out. There had been unrest and a challenge to military discipline at Dover, Folkestone, Calais and several other army camps in January 1919 over demobilization, and this combined with continuing labour unrest, particularly in the mines.[38] In Glasgow and Belfast the authorities took drastic steps with military intervention, to ensure state control over the machinery of law and order.

Of seminal importance was to be the replacement of Sir Edward Henry by General Macready as Metropolitan Police Commissioner in 1918. Although he only retained that position until 1920 before being sent to Ireland, Macready was the chief influence on the future organization of police forces in Britain, as a consequence not only of his actions in crushing the police strike in 1918, but because of the fact that he militarized police tactics and increased the deployment of mounted officers, and also because the Desborough Committee, set up to investigate the causes of the strike, and the important Police Act (1919), which implemented its findings, largely followed his recommendations. As a result, a Police Council was established which was to be consulted in national negotiations about pay and conditions of service. A significant pay rise to help offset wartime inflation was immediately given to Metropolitan Police officers. The Exchequer grant was now increased to cover half the cost of the police rather than just pay and clothing. The Police Federation was set up to represent lower ranks, but policemen were forbidden to join a trade union and it was made a criminal offence to attempt to induce a policeman to strike.[39]

The concern of the authorities was highlighted by the dismissal of all police officers who refused to leave the National Union of Police and Prison Officers (NUPPO), which had recently changed its regulations to allow for strikes if passed with a two-thirds majority. The changes were enacted in response to Macready's objections to the union takeover of the consultative board of the Metropolitan Police, which, he argued, was undermining the discipline of the force. The War Cabinet backed Macready, and dismissed all those officers who came out on strike – 2,365 officers in all, from London (1,156), Liverpool (954), Birmingham (119), Birkenhead (114) and Bootle (63).[40] They were never reinstated.

The strike was crushed, but not without serious problems in Liverpool, where half the force was out and a battleship and two destroyers were sent to the Mersey. Although a general strike there failed to materialize public order broke down; the disorder led to both the final reading of the Riot Act in Britain and the death of the last man to be killed by the military in aid of the civil power on the mainland.[41] As a result of these developments future organization of the police was to be administered more on military example, in line with Macready's argument to the Desborough Committee.[42]

The second report of the Desborough Committee in 1920 recommended the establishment of the Police Department in the Home Office and suggested that the Home Secretary should have the power to approve the appointment and dismissal of Chief Constables, and to standardize the procedures for the provision of police from one authority to another. Tighter Home Office supervision of the localized control of the police developed, although municipal authorities objected successfully to plans to give borough police chiefs the same power as their county counterparts.[43] Just the same, greater Home Office influence was achieved by the back door. More emphasis was placed on legal advice which stressed the independent powers of Chief Constables.[44] This helped further to erode police accountability to elected borough councils, some of whom had acquired a Labour majority on their Police Committee for the first time. Such a development was aided by the institution of separate district meetings of county and borough Chief Constables which had first been established in 1918 at a central conference in the Home Office.[45] This was established on a permanent basis at the fourth meeting in December 1920.[46] The point was that Whitehall strengthened ties with chief constables in order to support them in possible confrontations with local authorities who opposed government policy. The Home Office Inspectorate of Constabulary was also increased from two to three to oversee the new responsibilities.

The crisis in public order in 1919 was made more pressing by the rapid demobilization of the troops and, somewhat paradoxically, by both the bellicosity and reluctance of the brass hats to provide aid to the civil power. The Adjutant-General, Sir George Macdonagh, although objecting to the pressures placed on the military, argued forcefully that the main reason for the reluctance of the military to aid the civil power was that it strained the British Constitution.[47] Yet such was the panic over the national railway strike in September 1919, and the threat to mobilize the Triple Alliance (a mythical general staff of organized labour), that 23,000 troops were called out to protect food convoys, and a further 16,000 were kept back in barracks.[48] However, little disorder resulted.

Following the railway strike of 1919 the Home Office attempted to move quickly in response to the War Office's extreme reluctance to continue aiding the civil power except as a last resort. Edward Shortt, the Home Secretary, told a conference of civic leaders that although the extremists had suffered a severe rebuff in the railway strike, experience had shown that the preservation of law and order was not easily attained by the civil authority rather than by a display of military force. He argued that a new Citizen Guard should be formed which would absorb the Special Constables to help protect the food, fuel and public health of the community during periods of crisis.[49] However, when the proposal was circulated to other authorities the Home Office changed its mind. Industrial districts complained that the Citizen Guard would be seen as a semi-military force, would be resented by the local community and might affect recruiting to the Special Constabulary.[50] The Home Office decided to expand the recruitment of Special Constables instead, a power derived from the Special Constables Act (1831) and used to recruit temporary officers in the First World War.

Most of these changes in the nature of controlling public order were demonstrated in the 1921 coal strike. As in the 1919 railway strike, there was a marked contrast between the degree of organization adopted by the authorities to control the strike and the lack of political violence by the strikers themselves. This was most graphically illustrated in South Wales, where both Lindsay and Bosanquet, the Chief Constables of Glamorgan and Monmouthshire, applied for troops and borrowed police. Under the state of emergency that was proclaimed, the police could prohibit marches and meetings, arrest without a warrant or take action against anything which would hinder the emergency measures.

Lindsay in particular used his new powers liberally. His borrowed police, using the 'Macready formation' tactics of 1910, broke up without provocation or orders 'the political extremists of 1921'.[51] He served over 500 summonses relating to acts likely to cause sedition under Emergency Regulations. Whilst the Home Office emphasized that large crowds themselves could be construed as evidence of intimidation, and there were problems in Yorkshire and Derbyshire,[52] it was quite clear that Lindsay went right over the top, particularly with his complaints about the dismissal of charges against, or the leniency of sentences on, strikers who had not adopted violent means. Such strikers, in Lindsay's view were 'disloyalists' who tried to make ex-soldiers discontented with their return to civilian life.[53] Lindsay's actions showed that the new powers could be abused by the authorities and that there were dangers in the new Home Office view that law and order was the responsibility of the Chief Constable and not the Watch or the Police Committee. Nevertheless, it remained true that in most areas the new emergency regulations did not cause public order confrontation. Autocratic policemen rather than political extremism (whether generated by socialist agitators, syndicalists or state powers) were the main cause of friction in 1921.

At a deeper level the state developed a permanent organization to deal with industrial unrest, as a response to the problems of the post-war period. This was in essence a secret organisation for the maintenance of supplies. It had been formed in the wake of what the Secretary of State for Scotland, the Coalition Liberal, R. Munro, called a 'Bolshevist rising', referring to the near general strike in Glasgow which began on 27 January 1919. The decision to form an Industrial Unrest Committee (IUC) on 4 February 1919 was a more prosaic response to a London bus and underground strike, and a threatened electrical engineers' stoppage which never materialized. Formed under the chairmanship of Edward Shortt, the Home Secretary, the IUC worked out a national plan to coordinate the distribution of supplies, organize local facilities and set up a series of subcommittees to deal with public utilities, transport, security, communications and electrical power. Interdepartmental arrangements were made with the Ministry of Food and the Coal Control department to ensure maintenance of essential services. In essence the IUC became the government's response to the reactivation of the Triple Alliance in February 1919. It organized plans to counteract a miners' stoppage in 1919, but the publication of the Sankey report in June 1919 and the continuing subsidies defused the situation, and relative peace was bought at a price.

The railway strike, beginning on 26 September 1919, and the threat of sympathy action by other members of the Triple Alliance, persuaded the government to prepare for a general strike. The IUC was disbanded and replaced by the Strike Committee (SC), chaired by the dynamic troubleshooter, 'the man of push and go' (according to Lloyd George), the Transport Secretary, Sir Eric Geddes. Under Geddes, and with a leading contribution from Churchill, now Minister for War and Air, an impressive and efficient coordination of services was planned. Civil Commisioners were designated for each region, who were responsible for maintaining supplies and law and order. The ending of the strike meant the lack of necessity for implementing many of the schemes, but the experience had demonstrated the advantages of forward planning when dealing with national emergencies. A Supply and Transport Organization (STO), which was controlled by the new Supply and Transport Committee (STC), was formed on a more permanent basis, even if it remained dormant after 1921.[54] The IUC, SC, and STC were all basically euphemisms for the real purpose: the creation of a strike-busting organization which would resist industrial blackmail by organized labour.[55]

The STO was to prove the effectiveness of government by committee. Its key personnel tended to be not the politicians nor the military, but the civil servants who serviced the committees and subcommittees and provided continuity. These included Christopher Roundell, seconded from the Ministry of Health in 1920, and Sir John Anderson, the Permanent Undersecretary in the Home Office (1922–32). Neither the politicians nor the military seemed too keen on administering the new organization despite its proved usefulness. Sir Eric Geddes divested himself of the Chairmanship at the earliest possible opportunity, and Sir Henry Wilson, despite his 'Blimpish' views, twice used its meetings to reduce military involvement in any civil emergency arrangements.[56] In spite of any political embarrassment it may have caused, the secret organization worked well. Its detailed planning proved invaluable, even if its machinery was not needed, in both the railway strike of 1919 and the coal strike of 1921. Even when the STC was wound down after 1922 its blueprint remained, and was resurrected after a report by Anderson in 1923. It was to prove important in planning the government resistance to the General Strike in 1926. The important point was that its organization remained a secret. Even the first Labour government in 1924 did not inform the Labour movement or the TUC of its existence. Formed as a response to the Triple Alliance, it was to prove a highly efficient organizational and planning committee to counter the effects of strikes. Syndicalist ideas had only influenced a small minority of labour activists; indeed, when Lloyd George asked the Triple Alliance leaders in 1919 what they intended to do if they defeated the state, they had no answer.[57] It was the secret organization of the STC which provided an effective answer, not to political extremism, but to industrial disruption.

b) Why Was There No Revolution in Britain?

The changes that war brought about in the management and control of internal security, public order and political extremism inevitably raise the question of what role the state played in maintaining social stability. Most of the important changes in the structure of government brought about by the war did not survive the fall of Lloyd George and the coalition government in 1922, so they can hardly be described as revolutionary. 'War Socialism', DORA, the 'garden suburb', the 'men of push and go', Lord Milner and other innovations which were difficult to square with the British Constitution all disappeared before or after Lloyd George's demise. Other more radical schemes, like a Ministry of Reconstruction, 'homes fit for heroes to live in' and education reform, bit the dust with financial retrenchment and the Geddes Axe in 1921.[58] If social reform was a victim of retrenchment then so were defence, internal security and the police. The Cabinet Secretariat and the Emergency Powers Act (1920) were the main elements of continuity from the war, but in most cases the illusion of the 'return to normalcy' was the key to the structure of British politics and society for much of the interwar period. The post-war deflation leading to the return of the Gold Standard at pre-war parity in 1925 was the great totem of this mood.

The war reinforced the conservatism rather than the political extremism of the right. The same holds true for the left. Although the authorities became alarmed at the potential for disruption of the Triple Alliance and, after 1920, the activities of the CPGB, these challenges were mainly in the industrial rather than the political arena. The fact that Britain was on the winning side in the war, and that the sacrifices could be justified as worthwhile, strengthened belief in traditional institutions. Britain had eventually emerged as a victor in the war, she had not been stabbed in the back, and the euphoric nationalist mood was 'Hang the Kaiser' and 'squeeze Germany until the pips squeak', rather than a resentful nostalgic belief in past glories. This was reinforced by the effects of the Representation of the People Act in 1918 and its extension in 1928, to enfranchise practically everyone over the age of 21, apart from royalty, the peerage, prisoners and lunatics. The war did not result in a Leninist revolutionary defeatism but in political democracy. Industrial discontent did not develop political overtones. The survival of the coalition government in the transition to peace, Lloyd George's unsuccessful attempt to lead a new centrist party, did not undermine the British Constitution or the belief in parliamentary institutions, despite the widespread disillusionment felt when the brave new world failed to materialize. Whilst frustrated rising expectations created discontent, this proved to be no more than the froth on the surface of political life. Only small minorities were attracted to a political fringe which did not succeed in breaking the mould of British politics. An alienated few equated the Conservative Party with fascism, or the Labour Party with communism, but neither view had any plausibility for the interwar period, despite the conspiracy theories of Stalinists with regard to the former, and of the intelligence and security communities with regard the latter.

Whilst the sociology of revolution is far from an exact science, the potential for undermining the state involves a number of factors. These include a divided ruling class, worsening living standards and/or frustrated rising expectations, class consciousness, political leadership of a revolutionary cadre and the undermining of the security and political structure of government institutions. Some of these criteria were present in the aftermath of the First World War, but the British government showed remarkable resource in adapting to crisis and change. The liberal structure of the British state proved far from flabby or decayed, while the divisions within the ruling class proved to be more apparent than real. Whilst the First World War shattered the Liberal Party, the wartime coalitions, under Asquith from May 1915, and Lloyd George from 1916 to 1922, governed effectively. Although the manpower crisis, conscription, and the relationship between 'frocks' (politicians) and 'gowns' (military) proved a source of friction between Liberals and Conservatives, and the Labour Party became steadily disillusioned with both the war and the government, political tensions were for the most part contained. The problems in Ireland remained a sideshow for most politicians. Lloyd George in particular provided effective leadership and maintained the credibility of his 'mongrel coalition'. Lenin recognized that Lloyd George was a subtle, devious and skilful opponent, hence the dedication to him in *Left Wing Communism, An Infantile Disorder*, a tract partially aimed at British comrades.

Although the Conservatives dumped Lloyd George in 1922 the basic structure of British politics, while changed, was to survive. Whilst the post-war political scene saw the decline of the Liberals and the disappearance of the Irish Nationalists, the Labour Party became the second party of state. In the coupon election of 1918, the coalition won 537 seats, of which the Liberals won 127.[59] Labour only attained 60 seats, but following the Spen Valley by-election in 1920 it rapidly rose to become the most important opposition party. In 1922 the Conservatives returned to power and set the Baldwinian agenda for interwar politics: 'Safety First', to keep Lloyd George out of power at all costs and to mould the Labour Party into constitutional respectability as the second party of state.[60] This agenda was also implicitly followed by Ramsay MacDonald, the Labour leader, when in power.

Between 1918 and 1921 Lloyd George papered over the cracks in the coalition and was forced by the collapse of the post-war boom in 1920 to tone down his radicalism. Lloyd George's chief crime in the eyes of the political establishment was that his methods and behaviour had become politically and personally disreputable. He had also 'lost' Ireland through 'solving' the problem, his foreign policy objectives in Greece were not those of Conservatives and the sale of honours demeaned political life. The split in the ruling class was resolved by getting rid of Lloyd George.

For those who survived the war the evidence suggested that living standards were improving rather than worsening. Indeed, for the civilian population in the war life expectancy increased, the infant mortality rate declined, working conditions improved, alcohol consumption was curbed and, in 1915, rents were officially controlled.[61] Although the statistical improvements were not unalloyed, they cumulatively helped to maintain morale. Since government propaganda directed public attention to the imaginary atrocities of the 'Hun', and security and news management prevented the civilian population from learning about the true nature of the war on the western front, conditions were not conducive until 1918 to the emergence of a significant anti-war movement or the increased criticism of organized labour. Living standards had been maintained chiefly by trade unions using their bargaining position to increase wages to help offset wartime inflation. The poorest gained from the war; inflation eroded the incomes of skilled rather more than unskilled workers.[62] Lloyd George had brought industrial peace through compulsory arbitration procedures in munitions factories. The labour shortage ended unemployment and encouraged women to re-enter the workforce.[63]

Whilst the post-war slump (1920–1) and the long-term

structural unemployment of the interwar years brought poverty to many, there was to be no return to the destitution and misery of the Edwardian era. War pensions, unemployment insurance and the extension of the dole to all without work and their dependants, provided a cushion, however meagre, to the problems of the interwar period.[64] Also, despite the mythology, unemployment produced more apathy than revolutionary activity amongst the working classes; a fact both communists and fascists were to learn.

The economic difficulties of the interwar period certainly created frustrated rising expectations. Between 1918 and 1921 the problems of demobilization, disillusionment, the collapse of the boom, and the militancy of organized labour made reconstruction promises sound hollow. Trade unions reasserted their traditional rights, restrictive practices reappeared and many women returned to domestic life.[65] Yet the transition to peace had a positive side for many. New industries and employment opportunities developed with the growth of consumer industries in the south and east of England, even if unemployment remained a curse in the traditional heartland of British industry. The suffrage had been extended to all working class men in 1918, and women by 1928. The Labour Party was becoming the second party of state and was reflecting the aspirations of much of organized labour and the working classes. Whilst there were many frustrations, the avenues of change and influence were not closed to aspiring and talented members of the lower orders.

There was also negligible evidence which suggested that many in the working classes had developed more than a trade union consciousness. Whilst the Labour Party had adopted a socialist constitution in 1918, there was little to suggest that the working classes were becoming more politically militant. In fact the Labour Party, although it stood in more seats, did little better in the 1918 coupon election than it had in 1910. Most workers voted for the couponed Conservatives and Lloyd George Liberals. Also, the Labour Party proved indelibly reformist, not revolutionary, and accepted parliamentary institutions and the constitutional monarchy. Most workers were patriotic, loyal and 'social chauvinist', with an ingrained belief in the hegemonic values and ideology of a liberal society. Political surveillance and intelligence reports suggested most were deferential, conservative in outlook, yet resentful of insults and condescension and willing to fight for their rights and defend hard-earned privileges. Ethnic as much as class tensions featured as a main ingredient in working class unrest in 1919. There were race riots in nine British cities in that year, the most serious of which – in Glasgow, Liverpool and Cardiff – were in centres where working class unrest had been prevalent since 1910.[66]

There were also obvious status and group divisions within the far from homogeneous working class. Skilled and unskilled workers had very different outlooks, as the dilution controversies were to illustrate in the war. Blue and white collar workers had separate aspirations, and there were significant regional variations in militancy. The Celtic fringe, particularly the South Wales miners and engineers on Clydeside, was a hotbed of industrial discontent and socialist opinion. A shop stewards' movement developed in the munitions industry, but there was little sign of a coordinated attempt to link up spontaneous disruption into a political strike during the war.

Groups of workers, like the police and the railwaymen, who had lost out in the inflationary scramble during the war, had their wage disputes settled even if their demand for a policemen's union was ruthlessly crushed. Others with more muscle, like the miners, were bought off with the Sankey Commission in 1919, which extended wartime subsidies for a time, before being confronted with the secret organization of the STC in 1921. The miners blinked first on Black Friday and the threatened strike failed to materialize. None of these strikes had a political purpose. The 'Jolly George' incident in 1919 was, however, a successful attempt to stop Britain's aid to Poland, to withdraw troops from Soviet Russia, and to end assistance to the White armies.[67] London dockers, fired by the young Harry Pollitt, the future Communist leader, threatened to close the port. Portrayed as a great victory for the 'Councils of Action', they were in fact no more successful than the 'Soviets' of 1917. Lloyd George had already come to the conclusion that intervention in Soviet Russia was counter-productive and backed off accordingly.

If class consciousness was problematic, then the lack of credible leadership cadre of British revolutionaries was both a symptom and a result of this fact. The tortuous negotiations in 1919–20, which eventually led to the formation of the CPGB, reflected this. Proceedings were dominated by personality clashes, political differences, tactical manoeuvring and quarrels over the relationship with Soviet Russia and the newly formed Comintern. The various factions in the British Socialist Party, the Socialist Labour Party, the Shop Stewards Movement and the Workers Socialist Federation endlessly debated the issue of how to form a united revolutionary party; all had miniscule political influence.[68] Sylvia Pankhurst, the ex-suffragette, considered that participation in British politics would corrupt the revolution, and for this she was roundly condemned by Lenin.

The attempt in 1919 to form a united communist party was a failure. When British revolutionary politics finally got its act together it did so with considerable prompting from Moscow, after shipping representatives from most of the factions to the second congress of the Comintern in 1920. The mixture of persuasion and a head banging exercise enabled a relatively united CPGB to come into existence the following year. The authorities were delighted to be able to discredit the enterprise from the outset. By showing that the CPGB was funded almost entirely by Soviet money, initially by the illicit and illegal sale of Tsarist diamonds smuggled into the country, the government was able to prove that left-wing political extremism had relatively weak roots in British society.[69] The working classes were suspicious of security agents and *provocateurs*; they were even more hostile to organizations which could be shown to be funded, and arguably directed and controlled by, a foreign power, particularly given that the Communist International was little more than a front for the interests of the Soviet Union. The 'bolshevization' of the British party in 1922 under the influence of Rajani Palme Dutt and Harry Pollitt, further reinforced the image of the CPGB as an agent of international revolution, a stereotype that was to dominate the state image of British communism.

Given all these difficulties for the emergence of a revolutionary organization in Great Britain, it would seem unnecessary for the British state to have diverged from the virtual Victorian disregard of internal security. Yet the machinery was already in place: MI5, Special Branch and Military Intelligence had evolved as counters to both the Irish and German threats to the British state. The Metropolitan Police, in particular, had shown itself to be a well trained, disciplined force which could maintain public order. Whilst some politicians and civil servants in the Home Office were suspicious of the growth and influence of secret policemen, other more alarmist politicians were not. By exaggerating the red menace, the security community would ensure its survival in peacetime.

New public order tactics, greater legal powers and the decision, forced both by financial cutbacks and military reluctance to aid the civil power, to make the police responsible for the monitoring of civilian unrest, were the flexible methods by which the Home Office could increase its influence over the maintenance of public order. DORA, the Official Secrets Act, the Emergency Powers Act, the STO and the decline of local accountability and increase in central direction of internal security and public order control, meant the state was well endowed to deal with political extremism, internal security and public order. Although there were considerable problems, particularly with labour unrest between 1917 and 1921, the authorities managed and controlled civilian disturbances during this difficult period. The security authorities' tendency to label pacifists, aliens and strikers as actual or potential political extremists meant an exaggerated view of disturbances was taken.

In fact, geographical factors made it relatively easy for MI5 and Special Branch to control entry to the country at British ports, by firstly German and then Soviet agents. MI5's aliens register was also instrumental in securing its survival. Not only was the register expanded to include domestic as well as foreign personages whom MI5 considered necessary to monitor, but the authorities could never be sure that the lack of sabotage and the failure of espionage activity in the First World War was due to the competence of counter-intelligence or the incompetence of the enemy. The soviet challenge provided a much more searching test for an under-resourced, bureaucratically efficient but somewhat unimaginative counter-intelligence and security organization.

c) The Red Card

The different levels of the British state viewed the social disruption of the post-war years with varying degrees of alarm and suggested a range of remedies across a spectrum from the politically sophisticated to the ruthless. Three particular problems were isolated. Firstly, the political challenge of the Labour Party, which since the by-elections in 1919 and 1920 was increasingly seen by politicians as having replaced the divided Liberals as the second party of state. Secondly, the industrial challenge posed by organised labour, particularly the renewal of the Triple Alliance in 1919, trade union militancy between 1919 and 1921, and the crisis generated by the General Strike in 1926. Thirdly, the virtual non-existent political threat posed by revolutionaries fired up by the Russian Revolution in 1917, whose aim was to overthrow the state.[70] Some confused all three problems and assumed all were directed from, or at the very least used by, Moscow. Most correctly differentiated between the three problems and adopted alternative strategies for containing the issues posed by each.

Politicians viewed the 'challenge of labour' in different ways. The Coalition government in 1918 was partly maintained to try and contain this very problem. Lloyd George knew his strongest suit with the many Conservatives who distrusted him was his legendary ability to control and manipulate organized labour. He could play the 'Red Card' to push through controversial legislation which many Conservatives would never accept under any other circumstances. His schemes for social reconstruction, and 'Homes fit for heroes to live in', were partly seen as a Bismarckian 'cheap insurance against Bolshevism', as well as a personal expression of his residual radicalism.[71] It was an attempt to provide a coherent programme for an anti-Labour coalition, after the relative failure of the British Workers League and the National Labour Group to undermine the Labour Party in the coupon election of 1918.

Hard line anti-communists in the coalition, the military and the security services were even more alarmed by Lloyd George's insistence on pushing through the Anglo-Soviet trade agreement in 1920. This was because Lord Curzon, Winston Churchill and Walter Long had become enraged after the successful decoding of Soviet radio intercepts by the Government Code and Cypher School in 1920.[72] This early source of sigint (signals intelligence) had shown that the Soviets were using the trade delegation as a front to spread revolutionary propaganda in the British Empire, were financing subversive organizations and the *Daily Herald*, and had close links with the Council of Action designed to stop military intervention in Russia. The Chief of the Imperial General Staff (CIGS), Sir Henry Wilson, was particularly apoplectic, and confided to his diary that Lloyd George could be considered a secret Bolshevik given the calm manner with which he dealt with the issue. Churchill, the Minister for War, allegedly claimed Lloyd George was dragging the Cabinet towards Bolshevism, and both Thomson and Trenchard agreed with Wilson, that he was a 'traitor'.[73] As with the Ulster crisis in 1914, Wilson hinted that if such perfidy was ignored, the loyalty of the armed forces to the government could not be assumed.

Lloyd George adroitly compromised. He would not allow Kamenev, the head of the trade delegation, to return to Britain after his visit to Moscow. A selection of messages were then published, which compromised the 'Marta' cipher, particularly as *The Times* admitted the source of such information had been wireless intercepts. Fortunately the Soviets failed to realize the extent to which their codes had been broken until the orgy of political indiscretion following the Arcos raid in 1927, when intercepts were read out in parliament by Stanley Baldwin, the Prime Minister, and by Sir William Joynson-Hicks ('Jix'), the Home Secretary.

Thus the intelligence community lost the goose that laid the golden egg through the indiscretions of politicians, although for its failure to protect the security of its source and for egging on politicians in 1920, it could not be entirely exonerated from the responsibility for its loss.

In fact protecting the security of the source had been Lloyd George's motivation in 1920. He considered it an advantage to know what one's enemy was up to. He hoped that by opening up the Soviet Union to international trade, it would improve their behaviour as well as help solve Britain's unemployment problem, a root cause of social discontent.[74] Lloyd George's views represented a peculiar mixture of subtlety and naïvety which his more obdurate colleagues could not comprehend. They viewed soviet actions as both duplicitous and aimed at undermining the British Empire, the chief barrier to international Bolshevism. Several ministers' prejudices and preconceptions were bolstered by the security and intelligence community. The best defence against Bolshevism seemed to be to take advantage of geography and not let them in in the first place; as the Aliens legislation, and the use of MI5 and Special Branch officers at ports and passport control offices in the war had proved its efficiency against German agents.

Organized labour also came to distrust Lloyd George and his policy. Suspicion of his cajoling, the dilution of their traditional privileges in the war, and the financial retrenchment of the Geddes axe in 1922 disillusioned those who saw him as a radical and a friend of the working man. The Welsh Wizard became a pariah figure detested both by the left and right in British politics, the goat forever consigned to the political wilderness once he was ousted as Prime Minister in 1922. No longer needed as the man who could save Britain from Bolshevism, his Irish and anti-Turk policy, together with his dubious slush fund derived from the sale of honours via seedy intermediaries like Maundy Gregory, signalled his political demise. The Conservative rank and file dumped him at the Carlton Club.

After Lloyd George's anti-Labour coalition had collapsed it was replaced by Bonar Law's, and then Baldwin's Conservative governments in 1922 and 1923. This signalled the recognition of a new respectability for the Labour Party. Baldwin saw the need to tame Labour and to make them the main constitutional opposition in the traditional two party system of government. This strategy appeared to be the approach implicitly followed by Ramsay MacDonald in the 1920s. It meant in effect that the Labour Party should be encouraged to distance itself from the political aims of industrial militants and revolutionary extremists. It meant re-educating much of the Conservative Party, the establishment and the security machine to accept that the Labour Party was reformist, constitutional and the alternative government in Britain's new democracy. In effect Baldwin's strategy was to lock the Labour Party into accepting the established rules of British constitutional government, and not becoming allied with protest movements whose main interest was in class struggle and mass demonstrations. Unlike France and Spain in the 1930s, there was to be no Popular Front, no 'United Front from above', with Labour cooperating with the communists. This was demonstrated by the first Labour government in 1924, even if suspicions remain about the involvement of intelligence or security personnel in the background to the Campbell case and the Zinoviev letter.[75] The former arose from MacDonald's dithering about prosecuting a communist for inciting servicemen to rebel. Whether the latter was a forgery or not, and the evidence is not conclusive (as its contents, urging the working class to smash British capitalism and to rise up against the state, were typical of both Soviet propaganda and White Russian fabrications), it was used to devastating effect by 'Blinker' Hall and Conservative Central Office, and was a key factor in the election victory of the Conservatives in 1924. It was interpreted as a crude attempt by the Soviet Union to subvert the British state, and a sign that Labour could not be trusted. Diehardism temporarily gained the upper hand, while Baldwin's moderate agenda for making Labour the respectable second party of state was put on the back burner for the duration of the election campaign.

The extent to which the Labour Party was deemed to have gained respectability was dramatically shown with the inclusion of MacDonald as Prime Minister (between 1931 and 1935) and Snowden, his Chancellor of the Exchequer in 1931, in the National Government. Ironically, both of them had been placed under political surveillance during the First World War. It was also very clear that the Labour Party was vehemently opposed to the Communists.[76] Individual membership of both organizations had been forbidden by the Labour Party in the 1920s, the CPGB had been officially proscribed by 1926, and was never recognized as an affiliated organization. Whilst the declining Independent Labour Party and Stafford Cripps' Socialist League called for a United Front with the Communists in the 1930s, both groups were proscribed by the Labour Party. Any movement which advocated a popular front with the CPGB was viewed with grave suspicion by the parliamentary party, including the Left Book Club.[77] The International Department of the Labour Party became especially concerned about the network of interlocking fronts organized from Paris by the Comintern propaganda genius, Willi Munzenberg, and tended towards a paranoic interpretation of any international anti-fascist organization as a result.

Labour constantly refused to let the CPGB affiliate either as an organization or through individual membership. Communists who tried to join the Labour Party were rapidly expelled when uncovered, and the leadership by its opposition to the CPGB showed that it accepted incorporation into the hegemonic values of the establishment with respect to official hostility to left-wing political extremism.

Whilst the respectability of the Labour Party was not accepted by all in the state apparatus, and the left-wing in particular was seen as a potential communist Trojan horse, the authorities encouraged the maintenance of the perceived social distance between Labour and political extremism, and worked to isolate the CPGB. This meant that one of the aims of political surveillance was to monitor what contacts there were between the Labour left and the CPGB, and the areas of joint participation in front organizations. This was of particular concern after the failure of the CPGB's 'class against class' policy, in which the Labour Party were portrayed as 'social fascists'. The policy had been foisted on the CPGB by the Comintern and its Soviet masters in 1929.

Even before the 'United Front' campaign in 1935, British Stalinists had tried to manipulate and influence all progressive forces in a concerted campaign against fascism. An implicit policy of 'revolutionary pragmatism' developed under the management of Harry Pollitt and Johnny Campbell, reassessed the failure of calling all reformists 'social fascists' in the trade union movement, three years before the Comintern changed its line to the Popular Front in 1935.[78] The state become increasingly concerned about the attempts by the CPGB to manipulate and lead the progressive left in the 1930s.

Conservative politicians increasingly saw Labour as a reformist barrier against political extremism. The trend was encouraged by civil servants. During the interwar period an administrative revolution completed the professionalization of Whitehall.[79] The Home Office under the legendary Permanent Secretary, Sir John Anderson (1922–32), organized the means by which political extremism, public order and internal security were managed.[80]

Anderson was responsible for the revamped STC, which secretly organized the state's response to continuing industrial militancy in 1926. It was Anderson, too, who seems to have argued successfully against the demands of the Metropolitan Police Commissioner and Special Branch to outlaw the CPGB in the 1920s.[81] He also appears to have persuaded the most right-wing Home Secretary of the interwar years, Sir William Joynson-Hicks (1924–9), to moderate his anti-communist policies, if not his rhetoric. The absence from, or less than enthusiastic reference to, Anderson in both Childs' autobiography, and the authorized biography of Jix is strange, given that the uncharismatic Anderson was one of the century's greatest civil servants. Anderson argued that freedom of speech, provided that the law was not being broken, was a fundamental right, and that more damage was done by persecuting extremist groups than by denying them the oxygen of publicity and letting them spout hot air to the small number of true believers.[82] This line was also taken by his successors, Sir Russell Scott (1932–8), Sir Alexander Maxwell (1938–48), and Sir Frank Newsam (1948–58) in the Home Office, and by other important administrators like Norman Brook and Sir Arthur Dixon, who were heavily influenced by Anderson. Although there were marked differences in approach to the problems faced by his successors – Maxwell had a reputation for a genuine concern for civil liberties, whilst Newsam's main preoccupation was to keep his minister out of trouble – all broadly followed the restrained liberal conservatism of Anderson.

The Home Office, usually backed up by the cautious advice of the law officers, acted as a brake against the impatient demands of the Metropolitan Police Commissioners, the massed ranks of the security authorities and right-wing politicians like Jix, who were itching to deal a final blow against the CPGB. The Home Office told Horwood it was easier to manage and control a legal organization through political surveillance than to outlaw it, driving it underground and turning it into a revolutionary organization committed to direct action. Piecemeal harassment (like the arrest of 12 leading members of the CPGB in 1925), intelligence gathering and secret emergency organizations were the preferred method of isolating the CPGB and left-wing political extremism.

While politicians were divided and administrators cautious in their response to the CPGB, the police and the security service view was more forthright. In general terms the function of operations was to keep the authorities informed through surveillance of the activities and intentions of communists and their allies, and to discourage the emergence of a 'United Front from below', of cooperation between the membership of the CPGB and other groups. All the Metropolitan Police Commissioners were unsympathetic towards political extremism in any form. The reluctance of the military to aid the civil power after 1918 was countered by the appointment of brass hats with a strong commitment to law and order as Commissioners of the Metropolitan Police. General Sir Nevil Macready (1918–19), Brigadier-General Horwood (1919–28), General Byng (1928–31), Lord Trenchard (1931–5), and Sir Philip Game (1935–47), were all critical of the tolerance shown to disruption and disorder caused by mainly left-wing protest processions and demonstrations, and all were vehemently opposed to the attempts to unionize the police and the military. Whilst the nature of policing remained firmly under civilian direction, the tactical administration of the police became subject to a more military discipline, mainly as a response to increased concern about civil disorder.

Similarly, Special Branch under Sir Basil Thomson (1913–21), and Major-General Sir Wyndham Childs (1921–8) provided political surveillance of left-wing extremist groups which reinforced these attitudes. The reports on revolutionary organizations which were circulated to Cabinet members until 1924 outlined the conspiracy, orchestrated from Moscow, to undermine the British Empire.[83]

What is particularly interesting was the key role played by Sir Nevil Macready in the 1920s and Lord Trenchard in the 1930s. Both Horwood and Childs were acolytes of Macready, and although General Sir Joseph Byrne had been the first choice to replace Thomson in 1921, the net effect was to stamp Macready's authority and discipline on public order and internal security in the 1920s.[84] He also admired Anderson and worked with him in Ireland in 1920 and 1921. Macready's relatively even handed approach to industrial matters in South Wales in 1910 had developed into a tough anti-union policy to break the police strike in 1919. His hard nosed liberalism meant a ruthless approach to protecting the authority of the police, the introduction of military discipline into the organization of the constabulary, keeping extremist movements under surveillance and control. This policy was diligently followed by his disciples, Horwood and Childs, in the Metropolitan Police during the 1920s.

Although his reports on revolutionary organizations were models of clarity and less opinionated than those of Thomson, Childs' intrinsic anti-communism was manifest in his autobiography.[85] For him communists were 'social pariahs' against whom all political parties should wage a 'ceaseless war'.[86] Childs, before he became obsessed with communism, could be subtle as well as militaristic. His careful emphasis on the threat of communist infiltration into the Labour Party in his reports of 1924 was instrumental in converting Ramsay MacDonald to the value of Special Branch.[87] Childs' long career in monitoring extremists came to a premature end in 1928. It appears that although he was highly regarded, he finally cracked under the strain of a developing obsession with communism. He was persuaded to resign by Jix at the early age of 53. According to a Treasury minute he was granted a reduced pension in 'exceptional circumstances'.[88] Anderson explained that Childs exhibited the effects of an intense mental strain on a highly strung temperament.

Thus Macready, Horwood and Childs established a firm attitude towards communism in the 1920s. Later Lord Trenchard and his hand picked successor, Sir Philip Game, applied further pressure on the state to crush political extremism in the 1930s. They were appointed partly to restore police morale and to strenghen the authorities' control of public order. Trenchard in particular thought Anderson's successors in the Home Office to be administrative lightweights, and he appealed over their heads to the Home Secretary, Sir John Gilmour, to create a more professional police service, to give the police greater powers to impose law and order, to ban communists and fascists, and to control demonstrations and meetings.[89] Although Game held an equally dim view of extremists and demonstrators he was less authoritarian than Trenchard, and proved more responsive to Home Office advice.

The released documentation on the activitities of the security service is patchy for the interwar period. We know more about its organization than about its operations. In general, however, it may be said that MI5 under Kell fought a successful rearguard action against both its security rivals and the CPGB. Having survived the 1921 investigation by the Secret Service Committee, it was reduced from its wartime role to one of counter-intelligence in the armed services with a brief to prevent communist influence. In this it was highly successful. Only the Invergordon incident in 1931 (when ratings protested against wage cuts) could be seen as mutinous, and here the CPGB were as surprised by the naval demonstration as the authorities.[90] MI5 appears to have spearheaded the campaign to update the Mutiny Act of 1797 and to re-enact Regulation 42 of DORA, which had been pigeonholed in 1921. Pressure finally resulted in the Incitement to Disaffection Act of 1934.[91] In his surviving 'lecture notes on socialism' Kell argued that although there was little scope for communist activity in the British Army, given the conditions of service and good relations with the officers, there was a need for constant vigilance, because discontent in the forces of Hungary, Finland and Russia had played a key role in revolutionary activity in those countries. Disaffection was prone to increase in the armed forces during industrial crises. For Kell, revolutionaries driven underground were difficult to find and the authorities needed to locate the secret cells from which their operations emanated.[92]

Kell's anti-communist watchdog role on the armed forces meant he played a key part in censoring political propaganda in the 1920s and in counter-subversion activities. Most interesting is a file on the part played by MI5 and other security organizations in putting pressure on the British Board of Film Censors to refuse to grant certification to Soviet films like 'Panzer Kreuzer Potemkin' and 'The End of St. Petersburg', as they dealt with mutiny against properly ordered authority and depicted scenes showing the armed forces firing on the civilian population.[93] Although the Home Office and Special Branch were willing to allow the film 'Storm over Asia' to be given a certificate, MI5 successfully appealed to the censor not to allow it as it reflected unfairly on the British Army.[94] In the 1930s the CPGB and the Labour movement found loopholes in the law to enable working class organizations to show Soviet cinema and to enable socialist filming of mass demonstrations, recruitment for the International Brigade and anti-Mosley marches. There proved to be a limit to the secret power of MI5 to manipulate the news and prevent the dissemination of communist propaganda.

Kell's success in diligently ensuring that the armed forces were kept clear of communist contamination allowed him to recreate his First World War security empire in the 1930s. Having fought off attempts by SIS (MI6) to takeover his counter-intelligence roles in 1923 and 1925, Kell became the beneficiary of a security review in 1931 which merged some of the counter-intelligence activities of Special Branch and MI5. Although Kell had lost control of Passport Control operations to SIS in 1919, his expansion of the aliens register to include revolutionaries and other suspicious persons made the Registry Card Index, despite its inaccuracies, the indispensable reference tool of British counter-intelligence. As penny pinching as his rivals, Kell provided an efficient counter-intelligence and counter-subversion operation on a shoestring.

Kell became the head of the Security Service in 1931, with undisputed control of all civilian and military counter-espionage in the British Empire, except with relation to Ireland and anarchism.[95] Special Branch was reduced to the effective police arm of the Security Service, with MI5 now directing operations and interpreting the results of surveillance of both communist and fascist movements. These activities were still handled by secret means, whose operation could be denied, if dubious methods were brought to the attention of prying eyes.

c) The Secret War

The tension between moderates and extremists in the state with respect to the CPGB was reflected in the methods used to contain the supposed revolutionary threat in the 1920s. The issue was seen purely in terms of the influence of Soviet power, and as a law and order rather than a social problem, both by those who wished to strike a final blow against the tiny CPGB, and those who favoured more subtle and sophisticated means. Political surveillance conducted apparently on a significant scale supplied the necessary intelligence from which the authorities decided policy. Special Branch provided much of the domestic surveillance and SIS most of the intelligence from Moscow.

An important additional source was provided by the Government Code and Cypher School (GCCS) before 1927, until the soviets realized the extent of British telegraphic eavesdropping. Whilst there was an increasingly professional approach adopted to the raw material of intelligence, not all of it proved to be reliable. The authorities successfully adopted the mirror image of the infiltration tactics of the CPGB, but they were sometimes taken in by anti-soviet

8 Harry Pollitt, Secretary of the British Communist Party, reading the *Daily Worker* at Party H.Q. in London

forgeries.[96] Tunnel vision analysis also often failed to appreciate the changing nature of soviet aims in the interwar period. Whilst the Comintern was responsible for exporting soviet revolutionary ideas in the early 1920s, the decline in its authority after the General Strike and its more limited

9 The 'Communist twelve' at the Old Bailey in 1925: the men who were on trial, with their wives. Harry Pollitt is third from the left in the front row

agenda were not entirely appreciated. Although Soviet secret police and military intelligence (the Cheka, OGPU, NKVD, MGB and GRU) were not underestimated, the degree of their subtlety and deception was never fully realized by British counter-intelligence.[97]

The failures of British counter-intelligence against the communist threat resulted from an inability to draw the correct conclusions from its political surveillance operations. British counter-intelligence surmised that the soviets were adopting a strategy which operated on at least three levels. The first was open support for all revolutionary and trade union groups under the leadership, control or influence of the CPGB, or engaged in spontaneous activity against the British state or Empire. The second was the use of legitimate trade as a front for industrial espionage, the distribution of funds and the spread of propaganda. The third objective was the conversion and infiltration of as many institutions as possible within the British state, with particular emphasis on government, civil service and universities. Evidence from the public records suggests that all these areas were closely monitored by British counter-intelligence, at least in the 1920s.

Such a view was supported by documents from Moscow intercepted by Special Branch and SIS. One such document, entitled *Strike Strategy in Britain* (1925), discussed how the CPGB and its industrial front organization, the National Minority Movement (MM), should argue within the TUC for a planned strike, which would use surprise to develop a general strike to initiate class warfare. The aim would be to bring about 'revolutionary combats' and civil war. Although Britain had a 'very clever capitalist class', it must be goaded to introduce repressive measures which would lead to sympathetic strikes.

A Foreign Office minute noted that the author had underestimated the 'good humoured decency and common sense' of British workers. Whilst the government and the somewhat patronizing Foreign Office official learned not to make that mistake, there was every indication that the state took such conspiratorial fantasies seriously; there appeared to be no appreciation of the tension between the left and the CPGB nor of the contradiction between the trade union and political functions of party members.[98] As industrial crisis developed so did the mind set of the governing class: communists and revolutionaries were seen to be the beneficiaries if not the cause of class conflict and a hard attitude to concessions developed as a result.

Such rigidity was reinforced by the interpretation of the evidence of political surveillance. Special Branch stressed how the soviet government used the Third International to operate openly against the British Empire, which it saw as the main obstacle to world revolution. Working through couriers and banks the Comintern had financed the development of the CPGB. Subsidiary organizations like the Young Communist League (YCL), the 'Hands off Russia' Committee and the National Minority Movement (NMM), which were also directed from Moscow by the International, or the Red International of Labour Unions (Profintern), spread the revolutionary message, and funds, to a wider audience.

The extent of Moscow domination was illustrated by documentary evidence that the CPGB had received £60,000 from Moscow for propaganda purposes, compared with £1,699 1s. 10d. from subscriptions between August 1920 and April 1922.[99] The exact amount specified suggested the degree of surveillance and infiltration by the authorities. SIS claimed also to have received from a trustworthy paid agent in Moscow the minutes of the Financial Commission of the Fourth Congress of the Third International, which voted £80,000 and £120,000 to the CPGB and Indian Communist Party in 1923. A Scotland Yard agent in the CPGB reported that by January 1923 they had received £75,000.[100]

The near obsession with discovering Soviet funding behind extremist activity led to an extraordinary memorandum entitled 'Russian Money' during the General Strike. Jix alleged that the strike was a plot organized and financed by the executive of the International and RILU during 1925. He argued that the Comintern, through its agents the CPGB and the MM, had been able to capture the TUC. Revolutionary activity had been stepped up amongst the unemployed, allegedly the nucleus of a Red Army in Britain, in February 1926. At the beginning of May the Bank for Russian Trade had engineered currency transactions worth £300,000 at the Cooperative Wholesale Society to enable trade unions to fund strike pay.[101]

Jix's conspiratorial view of the General Strike failed to square with the facts when it became clear that the TUC had refused Soviet financial assistance and that £302,000 had been made available from trade union funds.[102] What it did show was that the authorities believed that the General Strike was a plot engineered by Profintern and the MM. Somewhat ironically, the Soviets, too, were very much concerned about the ability of British communists to squander vast amounts of secret funding in the 1920s without any appreciable effect. Agents like Jan Valtin were sent over to investigate the alleged 'fat cats' of British Communism.[103]

As well as the obsession with Soviet financing of

revolutionary activity, the authorities were also concerned about legitimate trade. The significance of trade resulted from the absence of full diplomatic recognition before 1924. Since 1921 the Anglo-Soviet Trade Agreement had represented the basis of Soviet activity in Britain. The Soviets had used this to disseminate propaganda and to organize communist activity. The British government had embarked on a series of diplomatic manoeuvres to try to undermine the Soviet government.[104] The Third International urged members of the CPGB to work for the ratification of Anglo-Soviet treaties so that trade facilities could be used for transmitting Soviet propaganda, which, according to Zinoviev, was a necessary preliminary for armed action.

The Special Branch report on the Arcos raid in 1927 showed how the Soviet organization had become a sophisticated espionage agency. In spite of the lack of compromising material in the documents judged suitable for publication, the police found a wealth of evidence which confirmed their suspicions. Separate rings were alleged to organize a variety of intelligence activities. The Kirchenstein organization was purported to control the MM, which had been the principal group, according to Special Branch, behind the industrial unrest in Britain, prior to, during and after the General Strike. Piaznitsky, the head of the Finance department, also ran a secret organization.[105] The financial activities of the Narodny State Bank were so complex that it was difficult to trace the means by which Soviet transactions were completed. According to leaked security sources the documents discovered in the Arcos raid were so revealing that Special Branch was able to uncover the genetic code of Soviet operations planning.

The interest in trade and banking operations which is merely hinted at in the declassified files was a significant element in the activities of Special Branch. One example will suffice of what the authorities were prepared to release, although it was quite clear that this area was central to Special Branch's concern about Soviet activity in Britain. In 1924 Russian Oil Products was established with a nominal capital of £100,000. According to a report in 1932 it was established as a legitimate business distributing Soviet oil and petroleum products in Britain, but it was so inefficiently managed that it never made a profit and had to have several injections of capital to keep it in business. It was the 'extensive overhead charges' which made it of special interest to the authorities, particularly after the sacking of its commercial staff in 1930 and their replacement by hand picked communists. Special Branch was particularly scornful of its 'inefficiency and incompetence'. Guy Liddell in MI5 was worried about this organization at the outbreak of war in 1939 because it collected information about oil supplies in Britain, and had 'potential [as an] agent for sabotage'. He noted, however, that the official Soviet trading delegation with its official contacts and semi-diplomatic status was a valuable cover behind which agents could collect information.

The importance of Soviet commercial activity in Britain is now seen as particularly significant. Not only was it a crucial activity in both the legitimate transfer of technology and equipment to the Soviet Union, but it was often used by the OGPU, NKVD and the GRU to steal industrial secrets. It also now appears that soviet business was also used as a front to smuggle the 'illegals' in to manage espionage rings after the Arcos raid necessitated the closing down of spying organized from official soviet premises. It is not thought that there are files on 'The American Refrigerator Company' in the MI5 archive. This, according to John Costello and Oleg Tsarev, whose information is based on NKVD files, was the front run by 'William Goldin', better known to Western intelligence as the soviet defector, or 'non returner', Alexander Orlov. He disappeared in 1938 when recalled to Moscow from Spain, where he was in charge of NKVD operations mainly directed at liquidating anarchists and Trotskyists, and reappeared in Cleveland, Ohio on the death of Stalin. In the 1950s he told the Americans about the general rationale behind soviet espionage in the 1930s and the recruitment of upper class renegades in capitalist countries. According to the NKVD files he was operating in Britain in 1934–5 and was directly responsible for managing the 'three musketeers', Kim Philby, Donald Maclean and Guy Burgess, as well as supervising their operations when he returned to Moscow between 1936 and 1938.[106]

Special Branch were also able to trace the manner in which Soviet and communist influence allegedly captured reformist organizations, permeated progressive societies and established front organizations. The communist cell organization was allegedly used to undermine trade unions and other institutions. The fixation on communism displayed by some of the security authorities was made clear during the General Strike. Childs circularized a secret report to Chief Constables entitled *Communism and the General Strike.* This purported to show it was a communist plot, although the evidence produced to support this conspiracy theory was very weak. Only 183 of the 1,388 arrests during the strike were communist, and despite regional disparities, both the low total of arrests and the relatively small numbers of communists involved undermined the whole argument of the document.[107] Although both MI5 and Special Branch were supported by Jix and other hardliners like Churchill, wiser voices like Baldwin's ensured that public opinion was not alienated by repressive policies which totally undermined civil liberties. Tom Jones, the Deputy Secretary to the Cabinet, and others persuaded him not to rush through anti-trade union legislation during the General Strike, although the right eventually obtained its pound of flesh with the Trade Union Act of 1927 which outlawed general and sympathy strikes.[108]

The authorities were particularly concerned that secretive underground working class activities should be ruthlessly suppressed. Whilst moderates successfully argued that any attempt to ban the CPGB and its fronts would lead to a mushrooming of that threat, Special Branch monitored the attempts by the CPGB and NMM to establish their own defence force between 1925 and 1928. In order to protect itself against alleged assaults by fascist and capitalist forces, such as the kidnapping of Harry Pollitt and the abduction of a *Daily Herald* van by the National Fascisti in 1925, attempts were made in some quarters to establish a Workers Defence Corps.[109] The surviving evidence was rather thin and it was not surprising that the authorities acted very cautiously. A few units appear to have been established in South Wales, London and Durham, and the Labour League of ex-Servicemen was seen as an extension of such an idea.[110] The Home Office view was that so long as such groups confined their activities to the marshalling of processions and demonstrations, and did not infringe the Unlawful Drillings Act of 1819, proceedings could be counterproductive. No action should be taken unless a successful prosecution was assured.[111]

Although the Comintern was very keen on British workers building their own self-defence organization, the CPGB was more worried about protecting its legal status, so it did not overtly challenge the state by developing such a group. However, Childs remined suspicious. In December 1927 he wrote to the Home Secretary stating that reliable sources had informed him that the CPGB sent its cadres to be trained in 'the theory of street fighting' and revolutionary tactics, to a 'school on the continent outside Russia'.[112] This was later discovered to be a 'hut in the Jura'.[113] No doubt such vague allegations helped persuade the Home Office that Childs should retire prematurely.

Soviet propaganda to influence liberal and radical middle class opinion was also monitored by Special Branch. Although White Russian sources manufactured many forgeries, Comintern documents and wireless intercepts show this was a key area of Soviet, Third International and CPGB activity in Britain,[114] the failure to stop Soviet infiltration of the establishment after 1935 was not entirely the fault of the intelligence authorities. Although this now represents the most secret part of anti-communist operations, one can reliably surmise that the authorities were aware of the problem. As early as 1921 Sir Basil Thomson had reported on 'parlour Bolshevism' and the establishment of communist influence at the University of Cambridge.[115] A thick file on Soviet film propaganda in the years 1926–9 has been released, and some of that is about the activities of the Cambridge Film Society. It includes copies of intercepted mail between the communist academic, Maurice Dobb, and Ivor Montagu in February 1929 about the screening of the Soviet film, 'Mother'.[116] This shows that Special Branch were investigating Soviet influence at Cambridge in the 1920s, and that Dobb's possible role as a 'talent spotter' was already bringing him to the attention of the authorities. It is noteworthy that Palme Dutt, the leading CPGB functionary, was highly critical of Dobb's attempt to recruit intellectuals during the 'class against class' period.

Special Branch also monitored Soviet scientific propaganda and its attempts to influence British academics. The released file on Bukharin, who attended the conference on the History of Science and Technology in London in 1931, showed that Special Branch had a 'specially secret source' at the proceedings.[117] It was reported that many of the younger British scientists were impressed with dialectical materialism and the prestige of science in the Soviet Union.

A file on the alleged agent and correspondent in the Press Department of the Soviet Mission in London in 1926, Anna Goldfarb, outlined how the Comintern controlled propaganda front organizations like the Society for the Promotion of Cultural Relations with Soviet Russia (SPCR). The Special Branch report alleged that the Society (formed in 1924) had 353 members, including CPGB members, representatives from the Russian Trade delegation and 'advanced people and the miscellaneous cranks' who attached themselves to such organisations. The meetings of the executive committee were allegedly dominated by extremist elements, such as one in February 1925, when five employees of the Soviet government under the Anglo-Russian Trade Agreement – one of whom was Andrew Rothstein, 'the most dangerous agent of the Soviet government in this country' – met to formulate policy.[118] Evidence from raids following the arrest of leading communists in 1925 shows that the CPGB was working in close contact with the SPCR.

Special Branch also closely assessed Soviet influence on peace movements in the 1920s. The International of War Victims and War Veterans was described as a pseudo-independent body which was subject to communist direction and control, and Guy Liddell, then at Special Branch, requested that Hans Richter should not be allowed into the country to attend an international conference.[119]

These isolated examples from files that are now declassified must act as samples from the mass of unreleased documentation illustrating the level of political surveillance in the 1920s, and the communist phobia of many in the administration and the security services. What is revealing is the discrepancy between the facts revealed and interpretations based on them. The relatively objective reporting of Special Branch, which shows quite conclusively that communist influence and control was not very significant in British politics and society, even if there was a problem in the trade unions, nevertheless portrays communism as a serious threat which was undermining British institutions. Whilst there obviously were communist front organizations, Special Branch tended to suggest that practically all groups which had communist members were under Soviet influence or control. The communist threat, such as it was, was exaggerated by the security authorities, and wiser politicians ignored much of the advice from that quarter.

Unfortunately we know very little about the nature of surveillance of left-wing groups and of communist and united front organizations in the 1930s because so few files have been released. Apart from some innocuous material on demonsrations supporting the Spanish Republic, on the anti-fascist campaign particularly in the East End of London and on the hunger marches, there is little declassified material relating to disturbances, the recruitment of the International Brigade in the Spanish Civil War, the emergence of a 'United Front from below', or a 'People's Front', and the monitoring of left-wing political extremism. It must have been extensive and relatively successful in controlling and managing most forms of unrest. What is clear is that the continuous expansion of the CPGB and the success of the United or People's Front after 1938 meant the authorities' concern about the switch in tactics to the 'Popular Front from Below' was considerably increased in the later 1930s, although this is not at all obvious from the released material. It is also not entirely clear to what extent the authorities altered their conception of the communist menace as a result of the change to Popular Front tactics. The evidence from the Second World War, when the activities of the CPGB were still interpreted in the light of the original revolutionary agenda of the Comintern, suggests that MI5 never really understood that Stalin had different priorities to his predecessors, and that both 'Socialism in One Country' and the takeover of the Comintern by Soviet Intelligence in the 1930s meant that greater sophistication and subtlety, as well as collective security, became the hallmarks of Soviet policy.

If knowledge of the extent of secret political surveillance would have horrified many with liberal sensibilities, then the formation of a secret organization designed to combat strikes would have worried those who were concerned with civil liberties, as well as increasing tension with organized labour. The Supply and Transport Organisation (STO), although officially wound down in 1921, was kept on ice and resurrected on the advice of Sir John Anderson, who conducted an enquiry into its use in 1923.

He concluded that as a preventive measure it would be advisable to have a skeleton organization which could prepare plans to coordinate the responses of government departments if the Emergency Powers Act of 1920 should be put into operation. Anderson argued that a Chief Civil Commissioner of Cabinet rank should be appointed in London, and that subordinate Regional Commissioners should be appointed to coordinate local services. There should be five separate subcommittees to deal with food, fuel and transport, protection, communications, finance and publicity, as well as the main committee (STC). Anderson thought that such an organization should remain as secret as possible, although financial retrenchment meant there were no longer large numbers of local officials of central government through which the scheme could be worked. Such an organization in future would depend on the voluntary cooperation of local businessmen. Nevertheless, the aim was to keep the organization as secret as possible, and to rely on the good sense and discretion of those who were enrolled in it.[120] Anderson's report was accepted by Baldwin's Cabinet, and J. C. C. Davidson, the Prime Minister's trusted troubleshooter, became the first Chief Civil Commissioner.[121]

The revival of the STO was important because it enabled the state to manage and control industrial unrest. The first Labour government found it a useful tool to help organize state responses to the effects of dock and transport strikes in 1924. Neither the Labour Party nor moderate trade unionists appointed to the STO in that year informed their more militant successors in the TUC of its existence.[122] Although neither the new Chief Commissioner, Josiah Wedgwood, nor Anderson appear to have been keen to advertise its presence in 1924, there was little doubt that its survival ensured its permament role on Baldwin's return to power, and Davidson's assumption of his former position.

The STO also played an important role in the state's management of the General Strike. The government establishment of the Samuel Commission in July 1925 following 'Red Friday' was partly due to the need to rally public support and to ensure that the administrative machine of the STO was workable. The Samuel Commission was in part a delaying tactic, to allow time for public opinion to be brought behind the government's seemingly conciliatory approach to industrial confrontation.[123] The aim was to blame any breakdown in conciliation on the unions, so that the counter-organization of the state to a national strike could be easily justified. Ironically, the state used the privately sponsored Organization for the Maintenance of Supplies (OMS) as a kind of mirror image of the alleged communist front organization. Whilst insisting that in any national emergency the OMS must hand over all its information to the state and become immediately subordinate to government control, it found it a convenient device to siphon attention away from the secret preparations being finalized in the STO behind the scenes.[124]

As well as engaging in secret preparations, the Cabinet also examined the present law with regard to sedition and strikes in 1925. Although it decided not to revamp the law of seditious libel, seditious conspiracy and incitement to mutiny, the Attorney-General and the Director of Public Prosecutions thought there was sufficient evidence to successfully charge the leaders of the CPGB, following the discovery of anti-military leaflets in barrack towns.[125] The trial was notable for the defence's use of the Curragh Incident to suggest that alleged sedition was not a monopoly of the left, and the ludicrous attempt by the judge to reduce sentences if the defendants would renounce their communism.[126] The effect was to detain the national leadership of the CPGB at His Majesty's pleasure during the period of the General Strike.

There was also a pronounced anti-communist phobia developed by more right-wing members of the government and security services whose hawkish views acted as pace-setters behind the scenes. Although Baldwin's more moderate viewpoint was receptive to advice which differentiated between trade unionism and communism, the General Strike nevertheless proved to be the finest hour of Colonel Blimp. The strike report of the Civil Commissioner argued that the government should take action to control the media, because although the BBC were acting responsibly it was necessary for the state to publicize its case. Hence the use of the *Morning Post*'s presses to print the British Gazette because the Trade Unions were adopting the 'Soviet system' in all newspaper offices so that their agents could act as self regulating censors.[127]

The insistence that the government should control the media, organize the distribution of supplies and establish a comprehensive intelligence network to monitor strike activities was paramount in government policy. This accounted for the harsh government and police response to the strike in the one area of the country where the trade unions attempted a coordinated organization of their activities. The Northumberland and Durham Joint Strike Committee was ruthlessly harried by the authorities. Harry Bolton, the chairman of Blaydon UDC, and Will Lawther, a Labour county councillor from Durham, were both imprisoned after allegedly trying to interfere with food distribution.[128] Both were wrongly smeared in court as being 'connected with the communist movement'.[129]

Although the authorities were prepared to let sleeping dogs lie in the various 'little Moscows' on the Celtic fringe, attempts to take over the role of the state elsewhere were immediately challenged.[130] The north-east, which saw little public disorder in 1911 and 1921, saw much more social conflict than South Wales during the General Strike.[131] Whereas the autocratic police chiefs of South Wales fretted about the possibility that the solidity of the stike would create communal consensus, the authorities deliberately broke up the Durham coalfield's attempt to control the movement of supplies.

The authorities monitored all developments and reacted immediately to control dangerous situations. As in the 1921 coal strike, the Home Office received daily intelligence reports from the Regional Civil Commissioners.[132] Military intelligence was also reactivated through the seconding of 12 MI5 officers to obtain information on the civilian population in London. The War Office report on the General Strike said this was a great success and that in future civil disturbances intelligence reports should include a section on communists, as one of four headings.[133]

Political extremism came close to being defined as being all social activity not immediately under the control of the state during the General Strike. The authorities strengthened the mechanism whereby the police and the reluctant military authorities combined to maintain order during the 1920s. Far from undermining the state, the first Labour government in 1924 was to play a key role in accelerating the coordination of the authorities. The Home Secretary, Arthur Henderson, refused to reinstate the 1919 police strikers, who were sacked for failing to give up union membership. Henderson also pressed local authorities to enter a General Mutual Aid agreement, as recommended by the Desborough Committee in 1919.[134] This was implemented by all police forces and began operation in October 1925.

This had two important consequences. Firstly, it ended the use of the military to aid the civil power except as a force of last resort. Apart from the use of troops in the London docks in 1926, the armed forces played a psychological rather than an active role during the General Strike. Secondly, it greatly increased the importance of the newly created Section F, the Home Office department under Arthur Dixon. This was to coordinate the movement of police during strikes, to help the recruitment of Special Constables, to organize the protection of vulnerable points in emergencies and to establish the new Civil Constabulary Reserve, which helped augment the police and troops during May 1926. The large temporary expansion of the forces of law and order created problems over the supply of truncheons for the police. Scotland Yard improvised by purchasing a lorry load of chair legs which were fitted with lengths of rope to imitate truncheons.[135]

Although the General Strike marked the definitive transition to the use of police as the frontline public order force, with the numbers of Special Constables rising from 98,000 to 226,000, it nevertheless remained true that 26 battalions of troops, about a quarter of the army's strength, was out on emergency duty during the General Strike.[136] The Navy, too, played a vital role in security and protection duties. At the beginning of the strike, battleships were sent to the Clyde, the Mersey and Rosyth, and destroyers to other harbours.[137]

The relative lack of violence, except for isolated intances at Hull and Southampton, illustrated the greater control over public order by the Home Office through the Police Department. This increasingly bypassed the local Watch Committees in the boroughs and accelerated the process whereby the Chief Constable was increasingly encouraged to exert control independent of the police authority.[138] Sir John Anderson's administrative policy was partly aimed at troublesome Labour controlled authorities in areas such as South Wales.

Whilst enhancing the role of Chief Constable the Home Office was reluctantly forced into filling the power vacuum by coordinating the patchwork quilt of police forces through the regular Conference of Chief Constables, and the work of the Police Department. Such changes certainly did not mean an increase in democratically accountable police behaviour. The Home Office unconsciously developed a creeping centralization policing policy, though a national police force was still anathema, and the independence of local constabularies was strongly upheld at Whitehall.

e) The National Unemployed Workers Movement

The relative scarcity of government papers with regard to state attitudes to left-wing political extremism in inter-war Britain increases the necessity to review the declassified surviving material on a specific case on which there is sufficient evidence to come to a considered judgement. The National Unemployed Workers Movement (NUWM) (Committee until 1929) provides an example for which there is not only copious state documentation, but interesting surviving memoirs and a large sympathetic secondary literature that provide the necessary antidote to the hostile and suspicious view painted in Special Branch reports, and Ministry of Health and Cabinet papers, and which illustrates well the state bias against militant protest.

The NUWM is important because it was the largest communist sponsored and influenced organization, and had a claimed throughput of between 500,000 and one million members during the interwar period. Although these figures mask the near collapse of the movement on several occasions, and belie the fact that the great majority of members joined for only short periods of time, it remains true that the NUWM was the most creditable of all the movements that were subject to CPGB influence.

The NUWM was formed in April 1921 as a response by socialist, communist and militant shop stewards to the slump following the post-war boom. It became a national movement under the dynamic leadership of an unemployed engineer and member of the CPGB, Wal Hannington. Between 1920 and 1936 it was the main left-wing workers' organization to protest against unemployment, and it organized six hunger marches.[139] The labour movement regarded the NUWM as an embarrassing conscience, while the Labour Party viewed it suspiciously as a communist front organization and later as a proscribed movement. The TUC established an Unemployment Joint Advisory Committee with the NUWM between 1924 and 1926, but then distanced itself from the movement. Both the TUC and the Labour Party were loath to appear on the same platform as NUWM speakers, even during the United Front period and the joint campaign against the means test and the National Assistance Boards. If the NUWM's purpose was seen purely as a means by which communists could become Trojan horses within reformist organizations, then it was to prove unsuccessful.

Whilst organized labour's view of the NUWM oscillated

between suspicion and outright hostility, the state treated the organization with a mixture of Bismarckian *realpolitik* and Victorian attitudes towards the unemployed. The extension of Edwardian unemployment insurance to cover practically the whole of the working population in 1920 was of enormous importance in providing a safety net for the destitute in the interwar period.[140] Even if the government's attitude towards unemployment insurance dictated that the programme should be self-supporting, and although after 1921 the insurance fund ran heavily into debt, the important battles of thc interwar period were about the levels of relief and not the principle.[141] The provision of the dole, and the abolition of local control by the Boards of Guardians in 1929, meant that despite the means test after 1931 and the attempt to lower many of the rates of relief by the National Assistance Board in 1934, the unemployed became apathetic towards their plight rather than militant or revolutionary. There is little evidence that either private or state sponsored unemployed organizations played any major role in providing constructive alternatives for those without work or successfully challenging the political role of the NUWM. Although the British Union of Fascists had ostensibly been formed to solve the unemployment problem, the Fascist Union of British Workers conspicuously failed to get off the ground and was unable to challenge the services provided by the NUWM even in areas of high unemployment. The more officially sponsored National Council of Social Service, and the Unemployed Clubs, also were unable to occupy the jobless with organized social activity like physical education or other attempts to maintain morale. The political space provided by high unemployment was to be most adequately filled not by the activities of the state, but by an unemployed movement viewed as extremist and under the domination of the CPGB.

Fear of this appears to have been behind the concern exhibited by the authorities. Both Sir Basil Thomson and Sir Wyndham Childs placed unemployment at the top of their causes of revolutionary activity in Britain, and they often headed their reports with lengthy opinionated accounts of unemployment and NUWM activities.[142] For Thomson,

10 Sir Vernon George Waldegrave Kell, founder of MI5

the National Administrative Union of the Unemployed, a forerunner of the NUWM, took its orders from Moscow and was to prepare for world revolution. Yet his meticulous national survey of the unemployed in September 1921 convinced him that the jobless showed no disposition to revolutionary activity although he claimed the cold weather could make them the tools of unscrupulous agitators.[143] As Thomson usually argued that hot weather was a cause of revolutionary activity, the degree of consistency in his comments was somewhat suspect. For Childs, his intelligence sources in Moscow and the CPGB had convinced him that the Soviets regarded the organized unemployed as the nucleus of the future Red Army in Britain. Such stereotyped views ignored the reality that although the CPGB played the most important role in the history of the NUWM there were always tensions between communists, reformists and syndicalists in the organization, and on more than one occasion its leaders were disciplined by the party. Most serious of all, the NUWM resisted the attempts by the Comintern to merge it with the MM during the 'class against class' period between 1928 and 1933.[144]

The Home Office view of the unemployed appeared to have developed little from the image of the undeserving poor of Victorian imagination. In 1923 the Chief Constable of Sheffield was asked to explain the remarkable increase in larceny in Sheffield compared with Rotherham, where similar economic conditions existed. He argued that the large number of unemployed and the leniency of the courts were the chief factors. The Home Office officials commented that unemployment, together with a large amount of communist oratory, had led to a great increase in dishonesty. Sheffield had been one of the most active areas in the hunger march of 1922, and the return of many of the bad characters associated with the NUWM meant it became a magnet for people with criminal tendencies.[145] This rather dubious exercise in social psychology was typical of official attitudes in the 1920s.

For the state authorities the NUWM represented two mutually reinforcing negative stereotypes. Not only was it a Soviet controlled communist front organization, but it was also a threat to public order, and an alleged cause of the increase in ordinary crime. It was for these reasons the NUWM was subject to the same surveillance and infiltration that the CPGB experienced. The MEPO 2 files show quite conclusively that police spies, informers, informants and *agents provocateurs* were operating at all levels of the NUWM in the interwar period, and that most of the information they passed to the authorities exaggerated the potential for violence and criminality of the organization. As well as political gossip from leading figures passed on by narks, Special Branch appears to have regularly received information from private meetings of the NUWM National Administrative Council, the NUWM Party fraction, the movement's London District Council, and the London Reception Committee.[146] It appears that a national leader may have been a police spy.[147]

The police use of narks and special agents, the 'pernicious toad-like species', as Wal Hannington called them, certainly weakened the NUWM and caused dissension and suspicion in its ranks.[148] Several leading personalities were wrongly accused of informing to the authorities. Hannington alleged that a member of the Central Council of the 1922 hunger march was an *agent provocateur*, and that Special Branch spied on his walks across Hampstead Heath with his daughter. He also alleged that Special Branch were morally responsible for the suicide of Harry Johnstone, as they refused to help him after his actions were unmasked. Harry Pollitt also wryly suggested that Special Branch surveillance of CPGB and related organizations was so intrusive that they even followed him on his honeymoon.[149] There are also suspicions that the events and accusations which led to the resignation of Sid Elias from the movement resulted from a classic Special Branch dirty tricks operation.

The authorities' approach to the NUWM was blanket political surveillance, the use of police to maintain law and order during periods of disturbance (like the hunger marches, the cut in the dole in 1931, the agitation against the Unemployment Act of 1934), and a curious mixture of what may be termed secret dubious manoeuvres to discourage the organization. In general terms, the NUWM gained support as a result of administrative attempts to cut the level of relief or to alter benefits or make them more difficult to obtain. The use of direct action in 1931, with the staging of processions and demonstrations outside labour exchanges to protest the cuts in the dole, led to the 'Trenchard ban' on meetings in the vicinity of public buildings.

This had arisen as a result of NUWM protests, where demonstrators allegedly armed with sticks and staves were interfering with the work of labour exchanges, and truncheons had to be drawn at several sites.[150] The Ministry of Labour requested the Metropolitan Police Commissioner, Lord Trenchard, to ban meetings, which he readily agreed to. The Home Office argued that he had the authority to do this under the Highways Act (1835) and the Metropolitan Police Act (1839), where the police had been given powers to prevent obstruction of the thoroughfares in the vicinity of palaces and other public offices.[151] This important limitation of the right of public meetings was later extended in *Duncan* v. *Jones* (1936), where police power to close down demonstrations and disturbances of a type which had resulted in violence in the past was declared legal.[152] The Trenchard ban was challenged in 1934 by the newly formed National Council for Civil Liberties (NCCL). Lord Trenchard, like the Home Office, viewed it as a communist front organization, and refused to discuss with them the principle behind the ban.

The hunger marches of 1922–3, 1929, 1930, 1932, 1934 and 1936 became the main areas of confrontation between the NUWM and the state. The disorder surrounding NUWM demonstrations in Glasgow, Keighley and Rochdale in January 1932, and violence with two deaths in Belfast, several days' rioting in Birkenhead, as well as serious disturbances in Glasgow, Bristol and Merseyside in the summer of that year, alerted the authorities to the problems posed by the hunger march.[153]

The hunger march aimed at delivering a monster petition to parliament, protesting about the means test and opposing unemployment. Such was the concern of the authorities that more police were called out to the demonstrations in London than at any time since 1848. On 1 November 1932, when the petition was taken to the House of Commons, 3,174 constables guarded central London and 792 Specials were called in to relieve police officers from normal duties. There were also 1,724 officers called out for the 30 October demonstration in Trafalgar Square.[154]

Many of the police precautions were based on highly

coloured Special Branch sources. Allegations that the unemployed would sabotage restaurants by ordering and not paying for meals, that communists were planning window smashing and looting in the West End of London, and that the unemployed had been told to attack the Special Constabulary were erroneous.[155] The peaceful intentions of the marchers was demonstrated after the arrest of Hannington. Amongst the documents seized was the response of all the contingents to the idea of carrying sticks or cudgels after the violence of 27 October. Only three were in favour of it.[156]

Indeed, the Home Office was so concerned about demonstrations of the unemployed that a circular was sent to all police authorities on 9 October 1931 asking them to send in reports of disorder however minor in character. This order was not lifted for the Metropolitan Police District until October 1939. The hunger marches and the response of the authorities to the unemployed led to the Cabinet and Home Office giving serious consideration to limitations on public meetings and processions.[157] Although after much discussion new laws were not introduced, Commissioner Trenchard strengthened the tactical deployment of mounted police officers to control demonstrations and acted rigorously to preserve public order. So strongly did he feel about the necessity for such tactics that when they were mildly criticized by Sir John Gilmour, the Home Secretary, Trenchard was only persuaded from resigning by the King. The response to the hunger marches was stern and authoritarian, and the misery of those who were driven to such a despairing act was forgotten by the authorities. There was little compassion shown to the hunger marchers, either by the state or the official Labour movement, and certainly not in the surviving Metropolitan Police Commissioner's papers.

One of the major ironies of the NUWM was that its one significant victory over the government surprised both the communists and the authorities. This was the success of the agitation against the Unemployment Act of 1934.[158] More was lost than gained by the reorganization of the rates of unemployment pay doled out by the National Assistance Board, and public demonstrations around the country forced the government to issue a standstill order. This immediately raised worries about the resuscitation of the NUWM, and the authorities again over-reacted to the 1934 and 1936 hunger marches.

Devious stratagems were used against the hunger marches. It was made as difficult as possible to take part and so-called vagrants were not allowed to draw the dole when on the march. Hunger marchers were also supposed to accept the often demeaning workhouse regulations if they used Poor Law or casual ward facilities on their travels.[159] Lord Trenchard and Sir Philip Game arm twisted the film companies in to not showing news coverage of demonstrations in cinemas or publicizing the 1932, 1934 and 1936 marches.[160] The authorities, on the other hand, recognized the smaller, non-political Jarrow march in 1936, which was smaller than any of the hunger marches. There was even a letter of thanks for the sympathetic treatment given to the Jarrow contingent at Hendon, a feature absent from reports of the hunger marchers.[161] As the Jarrow crusade was officially condoned by the parliamentary parties it received far better treatment than the NUWM sponsored marches. Even then, Baldwin ensured that the leaders of the Jarrow march were sent on a sightseeing tour of London when the issue was discussed in parliament.[162]

The police also broke up numerous processions and demonstrations of the NUWM, baton charged crowds, arrested organizers and used summary jurisdiction to bind over alleged troublemakers to keep the peace, particularly in 1931 and 1932. Leaders such as Sidney Elias and Wal Hannington were jailed on several occasions, the former for two years and the latter at the peak of the hunger march in 1932.[163] The important *Elias* v. *Pasmore* (1934) judgement ruled that although the police had acted illegally in confiscating documents from the NUWM, because some of them gave details of a 'crime', propaganda designed to cause disaffection in the police and society, it was justified even if the search warrant related to another matter.[164] Many on the left believed that the NUWM was being persecuted, and this led to the formation of what became the NCCL in 1934, to defend popular rights and freedoms.[165] It exists today under the name of Liberty.

The Labour Party and the TUC had only a marginally more sympathetic view of the NUWM than the government.[166] Comintern directives and intercepted instructions from Moscow in the 1920s could certainly be interpreted in this light, but such a view exhibits a blinkered perspective on the organization. In retrospect Sidney Elias claimed that the most valuable work achieved by the NUWM was at the local level, where the representation provided at Unemployment Appeals ensured that many of the unemployed received all the payments they were legally entitled to.[167] Revisionist views like that of Harry Harmer have emphasized this aspect of NUWM activity. [168] Cases backed by the NUWM had a much better rate of success than those that were not.[169]

It was this aspect of NUWM activity which explains why the unemployed joined the organization in such numbers and

11 A food convoy with military escort, passing through the Docks on its way to Hyde Park, 1926

why they left once their entitled benefits had often been attained by the excellent representation before the Umpire and Referees. The NUWM was a relative success as a reformist organization despite the cold shoulder it received from the Labour Party and the TUC. Indeed, both Wal Hannington and Sid Elias were punished for their achievement. Hannington was twice removed from the executive of the CPGB for right-wing deviations. The somewhat schizophrenic Comintern was impressed by the success of the NUWM in recruiting a mass membership, but less happy at times with the failure to make a more direct challenge to the state. In the eyes of true believers in Moscow both Hannington and Elias were more interested in helping the unemployed than in promoting revolutionary activity. The British state acted on an opposite delusion. By massively exaggerating the revolutionary potential of the NUWM, and by overestimating its responsibility and propensity for disorder, the British state came close to persecuting an organization which performed valuable work to ensure that claimants gained their maximum entitlement under the law. It increased morale and provided support for those who refused, if not to starve in silence, then at least to maintain low living standards.[170]

The story of the NUWM provides a graphic illustration of the pitfalls of writing history from state papers. There are other questions which continuing secrecy on all sides imposes on the study of communism in Great Britain. No doubt reasons of national security and confidentiality still dictate the reluctance of the authorities to disclose more on political surveillance, infiltration and the nature of the anti-communist phobia in the interwar period. On the other hand, there are important gaps in our knowledge. Little is known, for example, about why the 'society of great friends' should have fewer schisms than most parties, the most significant being the split by the small Trotskyite 'Balham group' in 1932, and why the purges should have had less impact in the CPGB than in other countries, the most notable being the expulsion of J. T. Murphy. Despite the large corpus of academic work on the subject, many aspects of the study of the CPGB remain shrouded in mystery. Perhaps Glasnost, and the secret CPGB papers spirited away to Moscow, will help illuminate one of the continuing black holes of modern British history. In this sense both the CPGB and the British state have been less than frank in their disclosure of information.

f) The National Council for Civil Liberties

The United Front period after 1935 also is clouded. Whilst the papers on the NUWM provide an interesting glimpse of state attitudes to a CPGB 'satellite' organization during the 'class against class' phase, little has been declassified with regard to the interlocking network of fronts designed to incorporate progressive middle class and working class support within communist influenced bodies. The whole issue of state surveillance and management of the so-called United or People's Front, the recruiting campaign for the International Brigade and in support of republican Spain, the Aid Spain movement, the Labour Research Department, the Russia Today society, the Society for Cultural Relations with the Soviet Union, the Tenant Defence Leagues and the growth of the Left Book Club, are still state secrets.[171] However one set of papers from this period has now been declassified and provides an insight into the attitude of the authorities: it relates to a significant file, in three boxes, on the National Council for Civil Liberties (NCCL), between 1934 (its foundation) and 1941. Two of these are now available, although the box for 1940–1 has been 'temporarily recalled' (one hopes they mean this) to the Home Office. The NCCL was portrayed as a communist front organization, which used middle class progressive opinion in support of CPGB policy and as such its function as a pressure group was officially ignored.

As the discussion of public order in chapter 5 makes clear, this view was accepted across the administration of the National Government and was not just a paranoid view of secret policemen. The file certainly contains evidence in support of such an interpretation, but why the substance of the NCCL's complaints should always be subordinate to its status as an alleged communist front organization is not clearly explained. There is also evidence to suggest that the NCCL was not wasting its time, as both the Home Office and the Commissioner of the Metropolitan Police went out of their way to impress on the forces of law and order the importance of civil liberties. Opposition MPs also were influenced by NCCL arguments.

The declassified material is interesting as it gives an indication of the authorities' attitude towards the alleged methods of CPGB front organizations during the United Front period. The evidence is based on a Special Branch report on the Secretary of the NCCL, Ronald Kidd. This is a potted history of his anti-police criticisms, combined with information designed to show him in an unfavourable light, and to accuse him of organizing disruption at fascist demonstrations.[172] Thus it was emphasized that Kidd had left his wife and child to live with Miss Sylvia Crowther-Smith, who was Treasurer of the NCCL. He had sold his business, the 'Punch and Judy' bookshop, to a communist friend, to concentrate on building up the organization. According to Kidd, he made his decision out of concern at the alleged *agent provocateur* activities of police during unemployment and labour demonstrations.[173] Kidd's correspondence on this theme in the *Weekend Review* (following a critical article, by A. P. Herbert MP, on alleged *agent provocateur* tactics by the police at night clubs), in August 1933, suggested that Kidd formed the NCCL in response to alleged police brutality at NUWM demonstrations and Hunger Marches.

A rather different version is provided in the report. Here the formation of the NCCL is directly related to the increased concern of the CPGB, the NUWM and the ILD about the attention the authorities were devoting to them. The use of the Seditious Meetings Act (1817) and the Justices of the Peace Act (1360) against several communists and members of the NUWM, together with the knowledge that the government intended to introduce a bill to give police greater powers to deal with sedition, led to the establishment of a legal panel of solicitors and barristers, belonging to or sympathetic with the CPGB, to defend arrested party members in court. Gradually references to the panel disappeared from party literature, and after the formation of the NCCL in 1934 the panel was absorbed into it.

According to Special Branch the NCCL owed its existence to the formation of the legal panel, as the CPGB leaders realized that much better results could be obtained if an organization could be established that was ostensibly based on nonparty lines, and was capable of securing the support of Liberal and parliamentary Labour parties, and political, intellectual, pacifist and industrial societies. Thus, according to Special Branch, the CPGB developed the tactic of the Popular Front with regard to the defence of workers' rights a year before it was sanctioned as a tactic by Moscow. Special Branch alleged that following Kidd's application to join the CPGB in 1934, Harry Pollitt, the General Secretary, informed him that he could serve the party more effectively if he remained nominally outside the party, so that the NCCL could pose as a nonpartisan body which defended civil liberties.

The evidence for this view was provided in a typewritten letter intercepted by the authorities and sent to the Home Office by Kell, the Director-General of MI5. The letter was from Kidd, as a member of the Friends of the Soviet Union, to the Secretary of the ILD in February 1934, regretting that he would be unable to attend a meeting of the Revolutionary Writers. He said he saw the proposed NCCL as a propagandist body of intellectuals against fascist or semi-fascist abuses. The Council, he emphasized, was keen to adopt the 'correct party line', and he did not think it would allow much scope to liberals 'for deviation'.[174]

A Home Office minute argued that the difficulty with the NCCL was that it involved two distinct types: communists and agitators who wished to foment trouble, and 'serious citizens of a literary or religious turn' who were worried about threats to civil liberty. To the authorities this latter group was exploited by the former, and they therefore believed that 'it rests with the police and the Home Office to see that in future administration civil liberty is respected as being an essential part of law and order. The Police show great patience and mistakes are surprisingly few.'[175] The rest of a large box, 637 pages long, is devoted to Kidd's participation in the demonstrations against the Incitement to Disaffection Bill in 1934, the attempt to stop the authorities censoring and controlling the distribution and performance of Soviet films, his part in the demonstrations outside labour exchanges, his alleged attempts to organize disruption at fascist meetings in 1935 and 1936, and his participation in the Thurloe Square demonstration.

The alleged methods and function of the NCCL were further examined in an interesting note from Special Branch in March 1938, which assessed the CPGB penetration of the organization. It argued that the CPGB had various secret groups, consisting of middle class or professional people who wished, for confidential reasons, to hide their allegiance to communism. These groups were controlled, not by the District Committees, but by a middle class bureau, set up by the Central Committee of the CPGB. In 1937 the CPGB legal cell came to control the Haldane Society, when Dudley Collard, its chairman, became the secretary of the latter group, and D. N. Pritt, a leading fellow traveller, became a vice-president.

In the NCCL the fraction of the CPGB's legal group worked in conjunction with other fractions, which like it were controlled by the middle class bureau, and so received the same directives. These included doctors, artists, writers, civil servants and journalist groups, but given the nature of the NCCL it was the legal fraction which played the principal role. All the NCCL's executive and subcommittee problems were discussed fully at group meetings beforehand. Although not all members of the Haldane Society or the other groups helping the NCCL were communists, the coordinated work of the fractions, together with their proselytizing zeal, was sufficiently powerful to ensure that NCCL policy on all issues of importance was that of the CPGB.[176] The conspiratorial interpretation did not take account of the issues which the organization investigated, and merely assumed that if it was supported by the NCCL or CPGB it must be a tainted cause and not to be given official weight or sanction. The NCCL's protests were officially disregarded by the authorities because the organization was allegedly controlled by the CPGB, and this in the eyes of the state made its complaints worthless.

5

THE MARCH OF THE BLACKSHIRTS (1923–1939)

Communism was perceived as the major public order and internal security problem for the authorities in the interwar period, but during the 1930s the native form of fascism also was seen as a persistent political irritant. British fascism can be given rather more attention than its significance warrants because the authorities are now less secretive about state management of the British Union of Fascists (BUF) than other forms of political extremism. However, important matters are still kept under wraps, and it appears that politicians, civil servants, intelligence and the security services had very different ideas on how it should be managed. Important clues about government attitudes towards other movements can be gleaned from the released material.

The study of British fascism has benefited from the amendment of the Public Records Act in 1967 which allowed for the release of declassified Cabinet records after 30 years. As a result of public pressure, most notably an unusual alliance between Lady Mosley and left-wing Labour MPs, and the liberal attitude of Leon Brittain as to what could be disclosed, most of the Home Office records pertaining to British fascism have also been released, mainly from series which have a 75- or 100-year closure period. Lady Mosley thought the papers would prove the innocence of Sir Oswald and other members of the BUF with regard to any illegal or dubious behaviour and show their patriotism, whilst Labour MPs wished to demonstrate the links between Conservative politicians and fascism. Not surprisingly, given the retention of some files, neither of these arguments can be fully substantiated. The material now available on British fascism includes Cabinet minutes and papers, the Metropolitan Police Commissioners' Papers and Correspondence (MEPO 2) and numerous Home Office files from the HO 45, 144 and 283 series.[1] Much of this material can now be obtained from the PRO on microfilm.

Although MI5 files on British fascism remain closed, there are eight reports on the BUF from the security service between June 1934 and November 1936 which have been located in the Home Office papers, as well as numerous Special Branch reports.[2] Since 1983 most of the surviving general and personal files on the BUF have been declassified, together with information on smaller fascist organizations and public order in the 1930s. The material that has been withheld, often under Section 3(4) of the Public Records Act of 1958, gives the authorities powers to review its suitability for release at intervals, but in theory could lead to indefinite retention. Much of this classified material relates to internment and the investigation of fascist renegades at the end of the Second World War.

Whilst the reasons for retention are usually not divulged, it is known that these fall into two main categories (the authorities dropped embarrassment as a cause for continuation of classification, following the Wilson Committee report in 1981). These relate to the protection of confidential information, and material that could compromise national security. It is thought that many of the retained files give information about security operations against British fascism.

Some of the retained material for the later 1930s probably also relates to alleged establishment and intelligence connections with the fascist powers. It is known that files have been retained on the Link, an organization designed to promote Anglo-German friendship through cheap travel and cultural exchange, and the Right Club, Archibald Maule Ramsay's secret establishment society which was of particular interest to the authorities during 1939–40. Nothing has been forthcoming about the Anglo-German Fellowship, an influential establishment organization whose social activities appear to have been orchestrated by the German embassy. Also there has been persistent speculation, as well as several best-selling books about, the connections of the Duke and Duchess of Windsor with Nazi Germany, and the rumour and intrigue surrounding Edward VIII's abdication. Some of these authors have had access to intelligence information. One of the most enduring of these stories relates to the collection of much compromising material on these connections at the end of the Second World War.[3]

a) Prologue: The British Fascists

In general most of the establishment was both hostile to British fascism and complacent about its impact on British society in the interwar period. The secret world displayed a more ambivalent attitude. Until the creation of the BUF, native forms of fascism were seen by the authorities as minor public order irritants whose existence was best ignored. Britain's first fascist movement, the British Fascisti, was formed in 1923, although it was renamed the British Fascists (BF) in 1924. It was considered to be politically irrelevant.[4]

The prevailing official image of the BF was that it was a disreputable and irresponsible organization; a Foreign Office minute stated that in Britain the BF were treated with 'derision or contempt'.[5] The Home Office file on the BF portrayed them as a highly eccentric movement surviving on the resources of its founder, Rotha Lintorn Orman, who during the 1920s was allegedly dependent on alcohol and drugs. Even right-wing anti-communists viewed it with suspicion and distaste, and William Joynson-Hicks (Jix), the Home Secretary, threatened to resign as Vice-president of the National Citizens Union if the BF were allowed to work with them in the Organization for the Maintenance of Supplies.[6] Jix objected to the BF vague commitment to the corporate state, which he saw as being against the constitutional and democratic traditions of British parliamentary party politics.

This obscure dispute, which led to a split in the BF and hastened its demise, nevertheless illustrates an important point. If Jix, who was arguably the most reactionary member of any of the interwar Cabinets, could so vehemently oppose an innocuous organization on such grounds, it is clear that the state authorities were very wary of aligning themselves even with patriotic groups who saw themselves as defenders of the social order. No doubt the authorities were worried about the need to ensure that fascists were at all times under the control of the state apparatus, a condition that appeared dubious given the behaviour of Mussolini's fascists in Italy and the rowdyism of fascist–communist confrontation in Britain in the 1920s.

This view was further illustrated in an interesting exchange between the Prime Minister, Ramsay MacDonald, and the head of Special Branch, Wyndham Childs, in 1924. With security suspicions about the reliability of the Labour government, Childs thought it expedient to enquire whether the Cabinet should still receive copies of weekly intelligence reports about the Communist Party (CPGB). MacDonald replied in a flippant manner. He said there was nothing in the report he had seen which those who regularly read left-wing newspapers did not know already, that it would be much improved if Special Branch devoted some attention to the activities of the BF and the origin of the *Patriot* newspaper, and it would be turned into 'a work of art' if it investigated the source of funds behind the *Morning Post*.[7] Childs archly replied that he did not investigate organizations which wished to achieve their aims through the ballot box. He did acknowledge that the BF, although nominally loyal, would use force in certain situations. He said nothing about the Duke of Northumberland, the founder of the *Patriot*, having connections with MI5.[8] Childs continued to send reports to MacDonald, if not the Cabinet, and these concentrated on communist subversion in the Labour movement.

The BF, then, was seen in official circles as essentially a more dotty version of the plethora of middle class pressure groups which emerged after the First World War, who were concerned with the threat to social stability posed by militant trade unions, the rise of Labour and the emergence of the Communist Party (CPGB).[9] The BF represented, on the surface at least, a peculiar mixture of ex-officers of the Colonel Blimp mentality, enthusiastic middle class women often with an ex-suffragette pedigree, a small anti-socialist working class faction, and an alienated youth element who found it difficult to adjust to the post-war world. The fact that these included groups who had been of previous concern to the authorities, as well as a potential hooligan element, meant that they were viewed as a dubious organization by the authorities. Increased clashes with communist and other radical movements in the 1920s, the need for police to look for non-existent arms dumps as a result of information given by the BF, and intervention to sort out power struggles between pocket Mussolinis brought it to the attention of the authorities.[10] The collapse of the BF in the later 1920s meant that it could be safely ignored. Only the conspiratorial right, centred around the *Patriot*, had good words for the BF; and Nesta Webster, for example, thought they had done more for British patriotism than all the other middle class organizations together.

The obvious question to be asked about an organization which was perceived as little more than a political joke in bad taste, was why was there such an aura of secrecy about it? Five subfiles within the main file are withheld under Section 3(4) of the Public Records Act. A clue is provided in the index to the file, which has not been weeded out of the document, that one of these sub-files relates to the activities of Captain Gerrard Strina, who wished to form a branch of the British Fascists in Italy.

Careful scrutiny of Foreign Office correspondence by John Hope has unearthed an important document which illustrates why some aspects of the BF are shrouded in secrecy. This related to a copy of a Home Office memorandum of an interview, about Strina, between Lieutenant-Colonel Carter of Special Branch and the representatives of British Fascists Ltd. The relevant point was that Special Branch was given a list of the Council of the BF in 1926, the most significant being 'Maxwell Knight Esq'. A document discovered in the Australian National Archives refers to Knight as the Chief Intelligence Officer of the organization.[11] Knight had been recruited into MI5 in 1925, and later as head of Section B5b in the later 1930s was responsible for infiltrating agents into extremist organizations.[12] Knight's role was not known in the Home Office in 1926, as Jix gave permission for the document to be sent to the Foreign Office.

This evidence confirmed the extraordinary outburst of Neil Francis Hawkins, Director-General of the BUF, in his last appearance before the Advisory Committee on Internment in 1944. Hawkins, like Quentin Joyce, had allegedly been separated from fellow fascist internees in 1940, because they knew of Knight's past activities, and the authorities did not want the past connections of the chief MI5 interrogator at Brixton Jail exposed. Hawkins claimed that Knight had been Director of Intelligence of the BF in the 1920s, and that he used Hawkins' brother-in-law to spy on him and the BUF administration.[13] Hawkins had been the BF chief negotiator in discussions which resulted in the majority of the movement joining the BUF in 1932. Knight used his links with the BF in anti-fascist operations in the 1930s.

There are also other clues which suggest the authorities used ex-BF personnel for surveillance purposes in the 1930s. An MI5 agent in the BUF, who was connected with the BF, was P. G. Taylor. One of Hawkins' fellow negotiators with the BUF in the merger talks was E. G. Mandeville-Roe, who had journalistic cover, and had been a leading member of the BF and early BUF.[14] Some reports by him appear in the documents sent to the Home Office in 1939 by Neville Laski, from his own private intelligence service, which he ran for the Board of Deputies of British Jews. His brief reports singled out three members of the Nordic League as definite German agents. He appears to have been a trained intelligence officer who acted as an *agent provocateur* in the Anglo-German Fellowship in 1939, advocating a strong pro-Nazi stance.[15] These alleged German agents are also mentioned in other files.[16] An interesting intelligence report observed that two of the longest serving internees, St Barbe Baker and Elwin Wright, lived at the flat of one of these agents.[17]

Aubrey Lees told the Advisory Commission on Internment in 1940 that he thought Mandeville-Roe's behaviour was 'fishy' when he offered to get published anonymously Lees' anti-Jewish views on the Palestine mandate.[18] An MI5 report had inserted 'thought' before Lees 'had discouraged' two of 'our' agents, P. G. Taylor and Mandeville-Roe.[19] Lees also considered that an official government warning about his activities could only have derived from information he had given Mandeville-Roe.

There is also the very strange case of William Joyce. This connection suggested a degree of personal affinity between MI5 and British fascists. In a 'secret minute' in 1936 (a euphemism for an MI5 source, and almost certainly Knight), it was stated that somebody who knew him well in 1934 thought that nothing could have threatened William Joyce's 'basic patriotism'.[20] This was so even though MI5 intercepted, or had sent to it, a wildly optimistic intelligence report that William Joyce sent to Berlin during 1936 about the BUF.[21] It appears that Knight knew William Joyce in the BF and that the latter was aware of his true employment, as evinced by the fact that his brother Quentin Joyce, a relatively inconsequential supporter of fascism, sent Knight his papers when he was interned. It is safe to conclude that Quentin Joyce learned of Knight's role in MI5 from his brother.

b) Mosley, the BUF and British Politics

The hands-off approach to British fascism changed somewhat when Sir Oswald Mosley became a fascist, and after the increased public order problems arising from clashes between the BUF and the communists in 1933. The view of British fascism in Whitehall in the 1930s was almost a uniformly negative one, although there was concern about sympathy for fascism in some sections of the establishment, particularly in the views of the Prince of Wales, who became Edward VIII in 1936. This centred around Mosley's personal, social and economic connections with the aristocracy, big business and the armed services, and the apparently unconnected activities of the German embassy and its agents in London. The information seeping upwards from the secret state about British fascism strengthened the hostility felt towards the personality of Sir Oswald Mosley within high politics in the interwar period.

Mosley was a brilliant political orator and was socially well connected, having married a daughter of Lord Curzon. He possessed a good mind and a commendable social conscience. Unfortunately, as two books on him by his son, Nicholas Mosley, show, he ignored the *Rules of the Game* and went *Beyond the Pale.*[22] Mosley was personally and politically suspect, putting principle before party, and despite basing his personal philosophy on a synthesis of opposing views, he found it difficult in practice to harmonize differing opinions with his own. Hence he engaged in a personal political odyssey in the interwar period across almost the entire spectrum of high politics, before adopting the street corner agitation and low politics of British fascism.

Elected as a Conservative in 1918, his radicalism led him to split from the party and flirt with the Liberals in 1923, before joining Labour. As a junior member of the Labour government in 1929–30, he failed to convert the Cabinet and the Labour Party Conference to his pragmatic programme of action to deal with unemployment. Frustrated, he left the Labour Party, and formed the New Party with six ex-Labour MPs and one ex-Ulster Unionist. With the annihilation of this group at the 1931 election, Mosley became steadily more authoritarian in his attitude, and formed the BUF in October 1932.[23]

Although the BUF grew steadily from October 1932 to a peak membership of about 50,000 in July 1934, this derived more from alienated apolitical elements than from discontented supporters of the 'old gangs' of the parliamentary parties, and the decomposing liberal vote.[24] Although some disillusioned Conservatives were persuaded for a time to support Mosley, as a result of Rothermere's propaganda in the *Daily Mail* between January and July 1934, and in 1939 following the 'Mosley and Peace' campaign, in general Mosley became an increasingly disreputable figure, after the Olympia meeting of 7 June 1934.[25] The fascists received most of the blame for the resultant political violence, a view which was reinforced by the anti-Semitic campaign in the East End of London after October 1935, and the Battle of Cable Street on 4 October 1936. Although the social functions of the January Club in 1934 were successful – where up to 450 members of the aristocracy, the political parties, big business and the armed services attended to hear the fascist case – there was no evidence that they had any lasting impact. In the 1930s Mosley was shunted into the political sidings because of his own political failings, the hostility of the state and negative public opinion.[26]

Although some right-wing Conservatives, including for a time Winston Churchill, admired Mussolini for his firm stand against social unrest and communism in Italy, only a few Tory mavericks, like A. H. Maule Ramsay, Michael Beaumont and Lieutenant-Colonel T. C. R. Moore, were prepared to excuse the BUF's behaviour in parliament. Most supporters of the National Government agreed with Baldwin that 'Tom Mosley was a cad and a wrong un'.[27] They objected to both his political cavortings and his personal lifestyle, which so offended the narrow nonconformist conscience that dominated the politics of the interwar period. Most Conservative opinion at the Olympia meeting blamed Mosley for the violence, and thought he had been deliberately provocative in ejecting interrupters, rather than trying to answer them.[28]

Both Labour and Liberals were hostile to what they perceived as the authoritarian and elitist structure of the BUF. Both objected to fascist stewards at meetings and the paramilitary aspects of Mosley's Blackshirts. Labour politicians considered Mosley a traitor; Dalton called fascists a 'political bad smell',[29] and Attlee thought Mosley was a megalomaniac who was not entirely stable.[30] Morrison argued in the aftermath of Cable Street, that all the political parties in the East End of London wanted the fascists banned.[31] Political pressures also came from the Amalgamated Society of Locomotive Engineers and Firemen, who complained to the Home Office of BUF plans for the suppression of parliament, the imprisonment of opponents and the establishment of a private army.[32] The Labour Party argued that unless the government took action against the BUF the Labour movement would be unable to control the justified anger of extremists, who were already forming anti-fascist organizations such as the Greyshirts.[33]

That such public hostility to British fascism should be expressed by the representatives of the 'old gangs' of British politics was not surprising, given that Mosley's aim was to replace parliamentary government with the corporate state, and to outlaw all political opposition parties to the BUF. However, such negative views expressed from all sides of the House of Commons did not make the administrative problems of regulating fascist activity, and the consequent legal restraints, any easier.

The preferred method for dealing with the BUF was through informal techniques of political management. Tinkering with the common law was viewed as a weapon of last resort by the politicians and the Home Office, as it let out a Pandora's box of problems, encompassing resistance to the restrictions on civil liberties; a dread of special legislation discriminating against, or drawing attention to, specific groups; and limiting the freedom of manoeuvre of the authorities. Hence the pressure applied to the media, whether in the form of polite requests from the government, or more subtle ways of ensuring Sir John Reith's cooperation at the BBC. After the ending of Rothermere's 'Hurrah for the Blackshirts' campaign in the *Daily Mail* in July 1934, it appears that the National Government approached newspaper editors to avoid unnecessary publicity for the BUF. The BBC avoided presentation of extremist views through an unofficial ban which denied both fascists and communists, as well as independent maverick opinions critical of government policy such as Winston Churchill, access to the radio in the 1930s. Indeed, neither Mosley nor the communists were allowed to broadcast until 1968. Newsreel companies were also asked not to film mass demonstrations in the 1930s.[34] Only when such measures were shown to be insufficient in 1936 was the nettle finally grasped and the necessary powers to maintain public order strengthened by the politicians.

c) Public Order in the 1930s

The regulation of public order in the 1930s has proved the most controversial aspect of state management of British fascism in the interwar period. Recent interpretations of the

12 Sir Oswald Mosley addressing a meeting at Royal Albert Hall, 1934

Public Order Act of 1936 have tended to place the fascist disturbances of the 1930s in a wider context, with changes in the law seen primarily as a response to left-wing demonstrations, particularly to the issues raised by unemployment marches, militant trade unionism and communist activities.[35]

The conflict generated between Mosley's Blackshirts and anti-fascists was merely the trigger mechanism for changes in the law, which had been formulated in response to previous concerns. D. S. Lewis, echoing the contemporary criticisms of the National Council for Civil Liberties (NCCL), has gone further and criticized the 'reactionary' and 'regressive' measures passed by the National Government with regard to public order and internal security issues in the 1930s.[36] The release of most of the Home Office public order files now enables us to understand the rationale behind policy making in this area, the prejudices and preconceptions of the authorities and the interpretation of these events by other historians.

It is now clear that although an understanding of public order problems which arose from challenges to the authorities from the political left were of primary importance in comprehending the Public Order Act, they were far from being the only source of concern. The 1936 legislation represented a response to a number of unresolved issues, apart from those presented by left-wing militancy. The issues included whether fascist meetings and processions were designed to intimidate or merely express an opinion in an attempt to convert (whether *Wise* v. *Dunning* (1903) or *Beatty* v. *Gilbanks* (1882) was the relevant case law), if there was a right of 'free born' Englishmen to demonstrate in public places, and whether special protection should be given to specific minority groups who were subject to group libel or physical abuse. Matters pertaining to conflict situations which had arisen as far back as the 'Salvation Army' and Trafalgar Square riots of the 1880s, the Kensitite demonstrations of 1903–9 and the suffragette disturbances of 1906–14, were all dealt with under the bill.[37] The most important aspects of the Act obviously addressed the prevailing public order concerns of the fascist–communist violence in the 1930s, but it was the trigger mechanism, or catalyst, which enabled the reluctant authorities to regulate more general aspects of law and order, not just problems posed by contemporary extremist violence. Together with amendments to the Public Meetings Act (1908) in 1938, it provided the new legal framework for the control of mass political demonstrations.

Although mistakes were obviously made by the authorities, it is a misconception to see the changes in the law solely as unnecessary restriction on civil liberty, or as a conscious or unconscious centralization of power. Although the activities of MI5, Special Branch and the uniformed police in the interwar period obviously heightened the authorities' concern about public order and internal security, there were important countervailing tendencies pulling in the opposite direction. Changes in the law were dependent on political factors, and although the right and security conscious MPs were influenced by such concerns, most politicians viewed the activities of MI5 with some scepticism and distaste. Indeed, the parsimony which affected all government expenditure in the interwar period extended to the security services.[38] The security authorities had neither the resources nor the political clout – except through the influence of Sir Basil Thomson between 1918 and 1922, the receptive ear of Jix as Home Secretary between 1924 and 1929 and the relationship between Sir John Gilmour and the Metropolitan Police Commissioner, Lord Trenchard, between 1931 and 1935 – to be more than a factor in decision making. The fact that there was considerable opposition to all these pressures at the time shows the complexity of the situation.

It appears, too, that the opposition parties in the House of Commons held what was in effect almost a veto power on much of the content and operation of the Public Order Act in the 1930s. At all stages of discussion the Cabinet placed importance on the attitude of Labour and the Liberals to the proposed content of the legislation. The three attempts to bring forward new public order law in 1934 were finally dropped when it became clear that the opposition were lukewarm about the idea.[39] Although they were critical of certain sections of the Act, particularly Clause 3, the opposition nevertheless supported most of the legislation in 1936. Similarly, when Clause 3(3) was invoked in the East End of London in 1937, Labour suggested the time limit for the banning of all political processions, and were consulted and agreed to the extensions of the ban until the Second World War.[40] The Cabinet opposed the extension of the ban outside the East End in 1938. Politicians from all the parliamentary parties were reluctant to limit rights of assembly, and only hesitantly moved to change the law when police powers to manage civil liberties were shown to be inadequate by the Battle of Cable Street on 4 October 1936.

Within Whitehall there were also important administrative forces which counteracted the restrictionist attitude of the security authorities in the 1930s. The permanent officials of the Home Office interpreted the law in a liberal manner and acted as a conservative brake on over-enthusiastic police or security officers. The Home Office officials were suspicious of the Colonial Office influence and military backgrounds of many in the police and security administrations. Always emphasizing the necessity for caution, the officials stressed the need to have sufficient powers to control and discourage fascist–communist violence, whilst at the same time preserving the maximum degree of civil liberty. The Home Office stressed that the police maintained public order and were not interested in the political views expressed at meetings. They upheld the three fundamental liberties we enjoyed in this country – free speech, free association and free assembly – whilst not allowing them to degenerate in to sedition, conspiracy or tumult. What, then, is most interesting is the conflict which arose in Whitehall as a result of the competing views, and pressure from within the administration, which helps to explain the hesitant views of the state to British fascism.[41]

The Home Office was responsible for formulating policy towards the fascists. In the 1930s four very different Home Secretaries, Sir John Gilmour (1932–5), Sir John Simon (1935–7), Sir Samuel Hoare (1937–9) and Sir John Anderson (1939–40), reacted according to the conflicting information and advice they received from the Home Office, the Cabinet, parliament, the Law Officers, the Metropolitan Police Commissioners, the Chief Constables, MI5 and public opinion in general. Of these, Gilmour and Hoare tended to follow the advice of Lord Trenchard and Sir Philip Game, their respective Metropolitan Police Commissioners, whilst Simon was more inclined to be receptive to the arguments of his officials, and Anderson, the personification of the liberal traditions of the Home Office, was prepared to challenge the increased authority of MI5 once war had broken out.

The permanent Home Office officials under Sir Russell Scott (1932–8) and Sir Alexander Maxwell (1938–48) as Undersecretaries of State played an increasingly important role in upholding the liberal traditions of the Home Office. The continuity of policy and personnel was perhaps best demonstrated by the part played by Frank Newsam, deputy to Arthur Dixon in the Police Department and the Home Office mandarin most concerned with law and order issues in the 1930s. Newsam was later knighted and became Permanent Undersecretary (1948–58). The critical reaction of the Home Office Civil Servants, and of Section F, the Police Department under Arthur (later Sir Arthur) Dixon to Lord Trenchard's police reforms, which proposed a graduate entry and accelerated promotion for high flyers, shows that tightened Home Office control over the police was only partly achieved in the interwar period.[42] They had more influence over Game and were later to moderate the impact of Trenchard's radical reforms.[43] The Home Office officials did not wish to increase the powers of the Home Secretary, or to undermine local autonomy. They basically reacted to events and only suggested changes in the common law as a result of political pressure, or the impact of conflict. Even then it was only after painstaking research had been examined. The banning of paramilitary organizations in Section 2 of the Public Order Act was only agreed after a comparative survey of European developments, when it was decided that Swedish legislation should provide the model for Britain.

The Home Office view was developed in response to the pressure applied by the police, particularly the Metropolitan Police Commissioners. Apart from voicing general worries, that various Chief Constables and the local government controlling borough Watch Committees were exceeding their powers in prohibiting or threatening to ban BUF marches and meetings, the Home Office had little control over police policy outside the Metropolis. It was extremely concerned that over-vigilant policing would be challenged successfully in the courts. This was the chief worry embodied in the Home Office response to the assumption of powers by the police, the legality of which they doubted, when Manchester threatened prior to the 1936 legislation to ban a fascist procession if uniform was worn, and Leicester stopped Blackshirt meetings in the marketplace.[44]

The problem for the Home Office was further complicated by the personality of the Metropolitan Police Commissioner, Lord Trenchard. His reforms were introduced over the objections of Home Office officials, and the sometimes fraught relations between them found expression in differences in public order policy as well.[45] Trenchard considered several leading Home Office mandarins to be administrative lightweights.

These problems were shown quite clearly in 1934 in a response to Trenchard's call for the banning of the BUF. The Home Office replied that the same consideration still applied as when General Horwood wished to ban the communists in the 1920s: there was no argument for outlawing extremist beliefs provided the expression of such policies did not break the law. Only if the authorities' management of the situation under existing powers appeared to be threatened could changes in the law be contemplated. So long as public opinion believed we had a fair and efficient government which upheld the law, the state should not attempt to restrict the holding of political beliefs, no matter how obnoxious they appeared to those who held democratic values. Political surveillance of such movements was necessary, but attempts to restrict liberty would drive political expression underground, and create worse problems in the long run.[46]

Trenchard's trenchant views on fascists were somewhat ironic given that the communists accused him of being a closet fascist himself, because of his autocratic style of management and the alleged close connections Mosley had with the RAF, of which the Metropolitan Police Commissioner had been the founder. Trenchard wished to ban fascists because of the public order problems they presented, and the waste of police resources associated with the management of processions and meetings. He particularly wanted to outlaw paramilitary organizations and the wearing of political uniforms. He did not want uniformed stewarding of meetings outside police control, neither did he want the police to be seen as protecting fascists. Trenchard was also concerned that 'respectable' people would appear on CPGB platforms in support of their anti-fascist activity. He believed that police should also be given powers to enter meetings to prevent disturbance.[47] Just before his retirement he began to advocate the view that fascist processions should be banned.

Trenchard's views developed in response to practical problems, after it was made clear to him that restricting the rights of fascists outside the use of emergency powers was not a feasible political or legal option. He was succeeded as Metropolitan Police Commissioner in 1935 by Sir Philip Game, who, as his leading administrator in the RAF, had been personally selected to succeed him. However, although the Home Office officials found him more reasonable to deal with, he was even more anti-fascist than his predecessor. Game wished to outlaw political anti-Semitism and to ban the fascist movement.[48] His experience as Governor-General of New South Wales in the early 1930s, when he had sacked the Prime Minister and experienced problems with fascist demonstrations, gave him the right background for dealing with the troubles in the East End.[49] Whilst maintaining civil relations with the Home Office, he was able to use his personal influence with the Home Secretary, Sir Samuel Hoare, to maintain the ban against the advice of Home Office officials during 1938.[50] He wished to extend the ban to the whole of London, but this move was turned down by the Cabinet after objections by Home Office officials and consultations with the opposition.[51] Hoare had been Trenchard's closest political supporter in the inter-service battles of the 1920s, and the Home Office and Commissioner's files have several congratulatory notes from the Home Secretary relating to Game's efficient and hardline management of fascist disturbances in the 1930s. Problems associated with the alleged partiality of the police in favour of the fascists in the 1930s most certainly did not originate in official policy.

While official attitudes were not pro-fascist, it remained true that police arrested far more anti-fascists than fascists as a result of disturbances in the 1930s, and local magistrates gave communists stiffer sentences. Stephen Cullen has argued from an analysis of police statistics on disorders and public meetings that the concept of the fascist thug is a myth, as political violence resulted from opponents of the BUF trying to break up their meetings. Such an argument, although it no doubt reflects the gut reflex of those engaged at the sharp end of maintaining law and order, ignores the social and political context within which such violence took place. It assumes that fascists did not provoke individuals and groups when it is known that they stood for the closing down of all other political parties, and that they wished to deprive those of Jewish background of their rights of British citizenship.[52]

Although some policemen were cautioned or disciplined in the East End for not arresting blatantly abusive anti-Semitic speakers, Game was forced to admit that the tactics of the fascist speakers kept most of them within the law, which was difficult to enforce.[53] Game complained that attempts to prosecute anti-Semitic speakers foundered on the belief of the Director of Public Prosecutions that proceedings would probably fail, because fascists had developed the technique of criticizing the Jewish people as a whole rather than those present at meetings.[54] Police moved quickly against those who tried to disrupt meetings but were less keen to move against those whose verbal abuse and insults had provoked political violence. Whilst both Sir John Simon and Game repeatedly emphasized the need for the police to be seen to arrest perpetrators of anti-Semitic libels, the vagueness of the law with regard to defamatory speech made it difficult to operate in practice, despite the outlawing of abusive words and behaviour in Section 5 of the Public Order Act in 1936.[55]

The state's hostile perception of British fascism was reinforced by reports from Special Branch and MI5. The former were mainly concerned with the overt behaviour of fascists, and particularly monitored demonstrations and anti-Semitism in the East End of London between 1936 and 1939. Special Branch reports take an interactionist perspective of the violence between fascists and communists in the 1930s, although both fascist and communist violence was portrayed as the work of a criminal or hooligan element, particularly in the East End of London. Official fascist reactions were presented in a more neutral manner. Fascists for the most part obeyed all police requests without question and kept the authorities informed of their plans for processions and meetings. Communists were less accommodating, and complained vigorously about police harassment and infringement of civil rights.

Special Branch tended to assume that all left-wing and radical anti-fascist organizations not explicitly aligned to the Labour Party were communist front organizations that were directly or indirectly controlled by the Comintern in Moscow. They were even suspicious of independent populist nonpolitical anti-fascist groups, such as the Democratic Union and the Legion of Democrats, which were not aligned to respectable law abiding organizations. These were not regarded as genuine movements by Special Branch, but groups run by confidence tricksters, who were mainly concerned with pocketing financial contributions from the public.[56]

The MI5 reports also are very informative with regard to official attitudes to public order. They particularly stress the constitutional implications for Mosley's adherents of supporting the BUF. For MI5, public order disturbances, such as those following the Olympia meeting of 7 June 1934 and the Battle of Cable Street on 4 October 1936, led to publicity and the growth of political extremism in general. Many of the middle and working classes, who were worried about unemployment, were also attracted to fascism by the argument that Mosley was upholding the right of free speech, and was making a stand against 'red violence' and the disruptive tactics of communists and other radicals at political meetings since the war. Similarly, communists could portray their mass demonstrations against the BUF as defending democracy against the threat to constitutional liberties posed by the native form of fascism.

MI5 argued that many of those recruited to fascism were unaware of the central contradiction of the BUF. A party which ostensibly stood for the principle of free speech would, according to its platform, capture power at a general election, then suppress all opposition opinion.[57] Like the communists, the fascists were patently insincere in using civil rights and democratic arguments to harness support. For the fascists, MI5 argued, force, not rule of law, was the basis of political control. Frank Newsam, at the Home Office, used these reports to argue that if economic conditions worsened and people became more concerned about the threat of unemployment, the BUF could contain the 'seeds of mischief'. He believed that fascism strengthened communism, as it encouraged the growth of a united anti-fascist front (under communist influence) which included individuals who in no other circumstances would appear on the same platform as communists. Newsam also disliked the fact that the necessity of protecting fascists against their enemies was being misrepresented by communists and others, who were arguing that the authorities were pro-fascist and that the law was not being administered impartially.[58] There was absolutely no truth in these allegations.

If the first three reports gave some cause for concern in the Home Office and within MI5, this quickly evaporated once it became clear that the withdrawal of Lord Rothermere's support for the BUF in the *Daily Mail* in July 1934 led to the near collapse of the movement. The Chief Constables' returns appended to the MI5 reports give a clear indication of the extent of the decline of the BUF, particularly in the major cities. Notwithstanding this, revisionist views, like those of Gerry Webber and Stephen Cullen, have suggested the BUF made a steady recovery in the later 1930s.

Webber has argued that total membership rose from 17,000 in February 1934 to a peak of 50,000 in July 1934, and then collapsed to 5,000 by October 1935. Then followed a slow recovery to 10,000 in March 1936, 15,500 in November 1936, 16,500 in December 1938 and 22,500 by September 1939.[59] Although some assumptions behind these figures are questionable, the basic pattern is the most plausible that has been suggested.

MI5 argued that the contradictions within the BUF led to a high turnover of membership, and that after an initial surge the Olympia meeting proved a decisive setback for Mosley. This was not due to the communist opposition to the meeting, but to pressure from Conservative MPs, the Conservative press and public opinion, which made Mosley abandon his policy of using Blackshirts to overwhelm interrupters.[60] Whilst adopting the techniques of low politics, Mosley was not prepared to challenge the large body of public opinion which resented the determination of fascists to use unlimited force to eject interrupters from their meetings.[61] MI5 saw the failure of Mosley to make more capital from the East End campaign either as a result of his incapacity, an unwillingness to challenge the law, or as yielding to the threat of new legislation.[62]

The failure of the BUF meant that MI5 began to report to the Home Office at ever lengthening intervals, and after the ninth report in November 1936 the Home Office ceased acquiring them. It still received Special Branch reports, but between July 1934 and 1939 the authorities were mainly concerned with public order issues that arose from opposition to fascism rather than any threat posed by the movement itself.

The attitude of the authorities, then, to fascist-inspired problems of public order was not a simple one. The state recognized that political anti-Semitism was as potent a source of conflict as fascist–communist disturbances, and was equally concerned to defuse this related issue. The Public Order Act took an even-handed approach to this matter as well. If the authorities were nervous, hesitant and often divided about further restricting civil liberties, the same was true of their attitude towards immigration and anti-Semitism. They viewed political liberty as a precious flower which was constantly threatened by issues like unemployment and immigration, issues which could be whipped up by political extremists to influence the electorate against the government. This nervousness about extremism also became manifest during the abdication crisis, when, despite consensus across the political spectrum not to form a 'King's Party' in support of Edward VIII, MI5 became worried about BUF attempts to organize support for the King.[63]

Whilst the authorities trusted the ability of the democratic electorate to see through what they regarded as the false claims of extremists under normal conditions, they became far less confident if the political system seemed to be in crisis. This led to a schizophrenic attitude. In the 1930s the state's reaction to fascist anti-Semitism highlighted the contradiction between political asylum for those fleeing persecution on the Continent, and increasing restrictionist pressures on immigration caused by establishment fears of working class unrest as a result of increased competition for employment and housing.[64] One such alarmist view came from Sir Philip Game, who despite Home Office scepticism expressed the fear that any influx of refugees coming from the Continent might bring the political extremes together; the fascists who had been attacking the Jews for three years, and the communists who might argue that Jewish refugees were taking away gentile employment.[65]

The state also feared any mass reaction to changes in the law which would specifically protect minorities, even against the most vicious forms of racist propaganda. This was made clear in the government response to the *Rex* v. *Leese* case in 1936. Unlike the summary jurisdiction of magistrates' courts used to regulate public order, Leese was indicted on charges of seditious libel and creating a public mischief in September 1936. Leese was 'Director-General' of the Imperial Fascist League, which was Mosley's most significant, if unsuccessful, rival in the 1930s. In February 1936 Leese's newspaper, *The Fascist,* alleged that the Jews practised ritual murder against Christian children. The jury found Leese guilty of the lesser charge, but not guilty of seditious libel.[66] He still went to prison for six months because he refused to pay a small fine.

The Attorney-General was astonished at the verdict and concluded that the jury viewed Leese as a stupid crank with honest convictions who should be found not guilty of the serious charge of seditious libel. The Home Office viewed this as a precedent, and resisted all attempts to include specific clauses with respect to racial incitement in the Public Order Act. Unless it could be proved to have provoked disorder the authorities refused to prosecute even the worst cases of anti-Semitic or racist libel. This proved to be the central issue in three, more blatant transgressions than the Leese case in the following years: Leese was not charged over more detailed accusations expressed in his pamphlet *My Irrelevant Defence*, published in 1937, because a further acquittal might be misunderstood by the public;[67] A. K. Chesterton, following his alleged call to string up Jews on lamp-posts at a Nordic League meeting in 1939, was not prosecuted in order to avoid publicity for the organization, and because of a slight discrepancy in the evidence;[68] and there was no prosecution of Alexander Ratcliffe's *Truth about the Jews*, published by the British Protestant League in 1942, because although it was deplorable, legislation protecting a particular group or person would set a dangerous precedent.[69] Fear of an imagined nativist reaction which could be used by both right and left extremists proved a more potent influence on policy than the need to protect minorities from verbal abuse.[70]

What was also interesting in the state's response to violence and anti-Semitism was the administrative concern of Whitehall to avoid the impression of reacting to pressure from street politics. Whilst proper attention at all times was paid to secure the support of the opposition, particularly the Labour Party, to proposed changes in legislation, care was also taken to encourage a proper distance between Labour and more left-wing opinions, and to avoid any connections between the Home Office and what were deemed CPGB front organizations. With regard to opposing political anti-Semitism, the support of the moderate Board of Deputies of British Jews (BDBJ), as the leaders of Jewish public opinion, was cultivated, while government distanced itself from the militant Jewish People's Congress (JPC). No deputation was allowed from the National Council for Civil Liberties (NCCL) to protest about aspects of the Public Order Bill, on the grounds that such issues had been considered fully in parliamentary debate.

Other reasons were given in a Home Office minute. This argued that both the JPC and the NCCL were alleged to have 'close subterranean connections' with the CPGB, particularly through the NCCL secretary, Ronald Kidd. Although distinguished persons were vice-presidents, and it ostensibly had laudable aims, it vilified the police and alleged that they displayed partiality to fascists in the East End of

London. The BDBJ had also made clear that the JPC was not a body which commanded respect in responsible Jewish quarters. The Home Office pointed out that at the JPC delegate conference one of the speakers argued that fascist violence should be met with counter-violence in the street. Both the NCCL and the JPC appeared to oppose fascism as a political philosophy, and if the government received a deputation from organizations who wished to prevent the lawful propagation of a political creed, the government might be open to misrepresentation.[71]

The hostility towards the NCCL was also shown with regard to its report on the Thurloe Square demonstration in March 1936, when a police charge broke up an anti-fascist demonstration. In spite of 46 complaints listed by the NCCL, Sir Philip Game argued that he had a 'great deal of evidence' on the other side, and then partially contradicted himself by admitting he had only five witnesses, two of whom were police inspectors. Nevertheless, with two MPs and Lord Dawson of Penn, the police had 'quality' on its side. He then accused Kidd of manufacturing the case against the police through rehearsing the evidence given by witnesses at the NCCL enquiry.[72] Game argued against the establishment of an official enquiry in to the events at Thurloe Square because it would affect police morale, encourage the NCCL's 'troublesome activities' and give credibility to an organization with 'no public backing whatever'.

Such attitudes bolstered the argument that Whitehall did not respond to low politics pressure groups, particulary those which could be portrayed as subject to extremist influence. The reality of the situation was somewhat more complicated. The NCCL was fully aware that its direct influence on official circles was counter-productive and that its indirect pressure was much more significant. Both Labour and the Liberals were receptive to some of the arguments about the threat to freedom put forward by the NCCL, so Opposition MPs were cultivated. Whilst political influences originated from a variety of sources, there can be little doubt that the NCCL played an important role in articulating some of the constitutional concerns which affected the Opposition's view of government legislation with regard to public order and internal security in the 1930s. As the government tried to formulate new legislation in these areas with as much consensus as possible, the views of the Opposition were important on such matters, and led to significant changes in proposed legislation. Whilst the NCCL was seen as a communist influenced organization, and its defence of cherished liberties was viewed as hypocritical in some sections of the non-communist left as much as in the Home Office, it nevertheless remained true that it had more influence than its cursory and hostile treatment by Whitehall would suggest.

The denigration of extraparliamentary pressure does not change the fact that the authorities were as concerned to preserve civil liberties as their critics, and that they acted with hesitation and reluctance to alter the law. Indeed, despite prolonged examination of the situation, public order legislation was not introduced after the problems posed by the 1932 hunger march, nor the fascist–communist violence in the spring and summer of 1934. In 1932, Sir Thomas Inskip, the Attorney-General, decided that greater use of existing powers, through binding over to keep the peace, was preferable to new legislation; and in 1934 lack of Opposition support for changes to the law, and the decline of political violence after July 1934, persuaded the politicians to act with caution, as there had been no agreement reached despite three separate attempts by the Home Office to produce a Public Order Bill. It took the Battle of Cable Street and possible worries over the Abdication Crisis in December 1936 to force the government to change the law and bring forward aspects of previously proposed legislation, which was hastily cobbled together in a Cabinet interdepartmental committee, to form the Public Order Act of 1936.

The change in the law was a consequence of Sir Philip Game's inability to ban Mosley's proposed march in the East End of London on 4 October 1936. Game realized in advance that he did not have sufficient police resources to control the proposed massive counter-demonstration. When the Home Office informed him that he had no powers to ban a perfectly legal march, and that it was inadvisable to make a martyr of Mosley and give him publicity, Game used the only legal power at his disposal, and re-routed Mosley's march to the West End of London.[73] This would avoid a confrontation between 1,900 fascists and 100,000 anti-fascists. The Home Office was unsure of police legal powers, because although outside London the chief officers of police often interfered with meetings and processions, in law they had no power to do so, and they only avoided legal setback because no one had challenged their instructions.[74] The Home Office was particularly conscious of the fact that Mosley was litigious, stood up for his rights, had never lost a case in court, and was therefore loath to overreach police powers in its dealings with him. The Home Office also felt that attempts to bind Mosley over to keep the peace, the favoured legal weapon to control mass demonstrations since 1932, would rebound against the authorities and lead to bad publicity, with Mosley claiming he was being unfairly discriminated against. The NCCL wanted Mosley to be bound over, a view the Home Office considered humbug, given the opposition to its use against left-wing processions by the NCCL.

Whether or not the Home Office's views on these matters were the correct interpretation was never tested. Certainly it could be argued that the Home Office was far too cautious in its appreciation of the legal powers of the police. *Thomas* v. *Sawkins* (1935) and *Duncan* v. *Jones* (1936) both appeared to show that police powers were far more extensive than the law officers and the Home Office realized.[75] The former case showed that the courts would support the police if they entered a private meeting where they had reason to believe a breach of the peace was threatened, and the latter that the police had extensive powers to ban meetings in public places, even if they were law abiding and orderly. Both judgements were based on narrow grounds, and police officers were still advised to be cautious in breaking up meetings or demonstrations.

These two judgements illustrated the difficulties the Home Office faced in strengthening the law. The worst of the trouble at the Olympia meeting on 7 June 1934 was caused by the fact that neither the Home Office nor the Metropolitan Police Commissioners thought they had the power to intervene in a private meeting, even though they considered disorder a likely possibility. Indeed, a Special Branch report alleged that the communists had plans to locate the main light switch so that the lights could be cut off at a favourable moment.[76] The Home Office, until *Thomas* v. *Sawkins,* argued that the police could only attend meetings if asked by the organizers under the terms of the Public Meetings Act of 1908, and as Mosley's policy was based on showing that fascists could maintain order at their own meetings, this was unlikely. The changed situation following the fracas at Olympia, and *Thomas* v. *Sawkins,* was implicitly recognized by the government when Gilmour's proposed public order legislation in 1934, which included police powers to enter meetings, did not become part of the Public Order Bill in 1936. The police were now seen to have sufficient powers already.[77]

On the other hand, Section 5, making abusive words and behaviour an offence, was included, although it was already enacted in the Metropolitan Police Act of 1839, which applied only to London, and which had arguably already failed to contain political anti-Semitism in the East End. The extensive control the police already possessed over meetings, suggested in *Duncan* v. *Jones,* also did not become part of the new legislation. The fears expressed over these two judgements were somewhat exaggerated. Although police powers over processions became a main issue of contention in the bill, police interference with meetings did not noticeably increase before the Second World War, except where disorder was threatened. This was shown in the East End of London, where over 1,000 political meetings were held in each of the summer months between 1937 and 1939, with the majority being fascist or anti-fascist, and only a few were interfered with by the authorities.[78] Although there was some continuing political violence, there were no fatalities resulting from fascist–communist violence or anti-Semitic attacks. *Duncan* v. *Jones* does suggest, however, that if Game had had his wish and banned Mosley's march he would have been supported by the courts. The response of the Home Office was partly a liberal rearguard action and partly bureaucratic inertia.

It was indeed political arguments which influenced the

Home Office not to intervene with Mosley's proposed march. Sir John Simon, in an important speech on civil liberties at Spen Valley on 7 October 1936, argued that the essence of British social life was tolerance and that fascism and communism were both intolerant creeds, and were un-British in sentiment and purpose.[79] Newsam, Dixon's deputy in the Home Office Police Department, argued in a Home Office minute that if Game had banned the march Mosley no doubt would have argued that this was a failure of the authorities to maintain order and to ensure facilities for free speech. If fascist processions were to be banned because they might lead to disorder, then the same argument could be used for communist meetings and processions.[80] Behind the inaction of the government lay fear of an imagined sympathetic response by public opinion to extremist claims that the right to free speech was being restricted by the authorities. Only when the police were forced, by their inability to manage the situation at Cable Street, to cave in to popular pressures did the government act. The preservation of public order suddenly necessitated adjustment of the law to enable the authorities to maintain control.

The bill was rushed through in December at the height of the abdication crisis, and just after the 1936 hunger march. Although a large number of amendments were not allowed by the government, the most controversial elements of the bill were debated thoroughly, and in some cases altered.[81] The attempt in Clause 2(4) to enable the statements of any adherent of an organization admissible in evidence for the prosecution of its leaders, was dropped at the Committee stage of the bill, thus denying the evidence of *agents provocateurs*.[82] Newsam argued in a Home Office minute that the chief officer of police should not be allowed to prohibit processions by imposing stringent conditions on individual groups.[83] This was a point which was raised at several stages of the bill in parliament, and was to be the basis of Home Office interpretation of Section 3 of the Act. The Public Order Act was not an anti-fascist bill and it was particularly emphasized that the impression should be given, in fact as well as in theory, that extremists of right and left should be dealt with in an even-handed fashion.[84]

The legislation had three main objectives: the prohibition of political uniforms, the outlawing of paramilitary organizations and the regulation and control of public processions and assemblies. Section 1 made it an offence to wear a political uniform; Section 2 declared it illegal to manage or control a group designed to usurp the function of the police or armed forces; Section 3 gave the police powers to impose conditions on marches, or for the chief of police to approach a local council (or in London the Home Secretary), for an order to ban all political processions in a locality for three months; Section 4 made it illegal to possess an offensive weapon at a public meeting; Section 5 established it as an offence to use threatening, abusive or insulting words with intent to provoke a breach of the peace; and Section 6 enabled chairmen of meetings to ask a constable to take the name and address an offender, who if he refused or provided false information, was liable to arrest.[85] The aim was to increase police powers to regulate public order and prevent disorder, and not to discriminate against any particular creed or party. In practice Sections 1 and 2 had fascists particularly in mind, 5 and 6, communists and other left-wing groups, and 3 and 4, all forms of low politics.

In general the Public Order Act has not been treated kindly by historians. Left-wing critics have complained that in the guise of neutral legislation, prompted by fascist inspired disturbances, the government smuggled in a new law which restricted civil liberties significantly, and which was used by the authorities to discriminate against left-wing groups.[86] Section 5, for example, after being used in the Harworth Colliery dispute, was increasingly applied to radical protests.[87] Revisionists see the public order problems of the 1930s as emanating from a conflict between the two political extremes with the state authorities attempting fairly successfully to regulate and control public order.[88] This view plausibly suggests the rationale behind the policy outlined by the Home Office papers.

It is quite clear that although mistakes were made, state management of public order represented a difficult balancing act. The authorities concluded that both fascism and communism were basically hypocritical creeds, which claimed to be defending democratic rights of free speech, yet ostensibly were totalitarian and arguably controlled by foreign powers. They both emphasized that if they achieved power they would close down all other political parties and silence opposition. This blatant contradiction between ends and means led the Home Office, and more surprisingly MI5, to cast themselves as the true defenders of democracy. The authorities allowed fascists and communists to openly propagate their creed (providing they did not subvert the law of the land) and assumed that public opinion would see through the unrealistic and utopian programmes of political extremists under normal circumstances.

On the other hand, the authorities were nervous that in abnormal conditions extremists could pose political problems. They warned that issues like unemployment and immigration could be used by fascists and communists to destabilize the political system. Hence the state viewed the electorate in a somewhat schizophrenic manner. Whilst they believed in popular fundamental good sense and addiction to democratic values, there was a certain unease about potential social volatility in moments of crisis. There was thus a need for political surveillance of extremist groups, a need to isolate them from contact with potential allies within the state or from respectable society. The best means to achieve this was to convince all sections of the establishment that to associate with either fascists of communists was disreputable and counter-productive; and to deny extremists any publicity in the media. Apart from the support for a time, from January to July 1934, by the maverick Lord Rothermere's *Daily Mail*, this was achieved for the fascists; while the Labour Party displayed consistent hostility to the communists throughout the interwar period, and those who advocated closer links with them risked expulsion, even after the communists' turn to a 'United Front' against fascism and war in 1935.

Within the secret state there was a constant battle between the liberal traditions of the Home Office and the more security conscious police and MI5. With the obvious failure of fascism after July 1934, this expressed itself mainly in public order concerns, with the Home Office determined to maintain as much administrative freedom of manoeuvre and legal flexibility as possible. Whilst this was limited somewhat by the necessary introduction of the Public Order Act, a more complex battleground emerged over the regulation of processions in the East End of London, under the terms of the new legislation, between 1937 and 1939. Whilst Game used his powers to limit the use of loudspeakers, and banned torchlight processions, the Home Office controlled violence through the use of the Public Order Act to outlaw political uniforms and marches in much of the East End after July 1937.[89] It steadfastly resisted Game's attempt to extend the ban to the rest of London after the Bermondsey march in October 1937.[90] Section 3(3) of the Act was seen as an emergency power to be used only sparingly. Indeed, from 1938 the Home Office unsuccessfully opposed the extension of the ban in the East End.[91] A combination of pressures from Game and the Labour Party led to the maintenance of the ban, which was only lifted in 1949. Local councils, particularly Labour controlled ones, also became increasingly hostile to the BUF and imposed bans which prevented the movement from using local government property for meetings. Councils also increasingly interfered with processions and demonstrations, even before the passing of the Public Order Act.

The public order problems associated with British fascism were a nuisance which both politicians and the security authorities managed in the 1930s, despite some disagreements amongst themselves. Fascism and communism were both marginalized in terms of their influence, even if both expanded numerically, as the war clouds loomed in the later 1930s.

d) State Surveillance of British Fascism in the 1930s

The mainly hostile perception of British fascism by the state was both reinforced and placed in perspective by state surveillance in the 1930s. The decision to collect intelligence on British fascism was taken at a conference in the Home

Office on 23 November 1933, attended by Home Office officials, Lord Trenchard, two representatives from MI5 and Superintendent Canning, the head of Special Branch.[92] At this meeting it was decided not to ban political uniforms, but that information should be systematically collected on fascist movements in the United Kingdom. This would mainly be based on monthly reports from Chief Constables, the political surveillance of Special Branch and MI5 agents. The material would be analysed within MI5, whose reports would be sent to the Home Office. In essence this meant the BUF was now placed in the same category as the CPGB, or so-called front organizations, although its threat to both public order and internal security was seen as less dangerous. As a direct result of the increase in political surveillance this entailed, Trenchard expanded Special Branch from 136 to 200 officers in 1934.[93]

Intelligence gathering on British fascism was a fairly competent operation, and it is obvious that the authorities had excellent sources of information. It appears that there were several professional agents operating in the BUF, as well as the usual 'narks' who supplied intelligence titbits for Special Branch. The arguments put forward by Mosley, to the effect that evidence collected by the state was unreliable and tainted, is mainly incorrect for the 1930s, although the BUF had valid reason to be concerned in the 1939–40 period. The bias displayed on the interpretation of such information has to be acknowledged from the outset. Much Special Branch material, for example, highlights the more dubious side of fascist activities, with much stress placed on incompetence and the somewhat seedy aspects of the BUF. Maladministration and petty larceny were alleged to be rife at all levels of the organization, and it was stated that the first leader of the women's section, Lady Makgill, and the deputy leader, Robert Forgan, both left in 1934, partly because they were held responsible for alleged financial irregularities.[94] It was emphasized that Jock Houston, who was alleged to be the originator of the anti-Semitic campaign in the East End, had a criminal record, with a conviction for receiving, and a prison sentence for housebreaking and larceny.[95] Other instances of fascists who had dubious past behaviour include the secretary of one of the Newcastle organizations, who had been convicted of housebreaking, and sundry personages who were expelled from the Brixton branch of the BUF for alleged immoral conduct.[96]

MI5 viewed the BUF as a hybrid organization which contained a 'revolutionary' wing to which Mosley inclined, and a more acceptable group (from MI5's standpoint) of right-wing patriots. The most important input was information from Maxwell Knight and his agents in B5b, which was analysed in B division by F. B. Aiken-Sneath, in 1939–40. Knight himself had been a Director of Intelligence in the BF, and in 1935 another MI5 agent, a 'P. G. Taylor', became head of the Industrial Department and the 'Z' intelligence organization of the BUF.[97] According to information in the Aubrey Lees personal file, his real name was James Hughes, although he was also known as Mcguirk Hughes.[98] His most interesting use of the BUF to aid the security service, if the evidence of the Advisory Commission on internment is any guide, was to use its members as a precursor of the inhouse MI5 unit which Peter Wright allegedly used to bug and burgle his way across London. According to the NCCL's account, and the 1941 internment hearing of J. C. Preen, Taylor persuaded BUF members to steal confidential documents from the house of an alleged communist. Although interrupted by the police the fascists came out of it rather better than Major Vernon, an employee of the Royal Aircraft establishment at Farnborough. He was sacked for having taken confidential aircraft documents, allegedly to work on at home; the fascists, despite being convicted of larceny, were only bound over to keep the peace. It was interesting to note that the Advisory Commission was intrigued by the ambiguity of Preen's action; that he was working both for and against the fascists, and the authorities, at the same time.[99]

Neil Francis Hawkins, the Director-General, argued that Maxwell Knight used his brother-in-law to spy on him in the office, and others have suggested that one of the secretaries in the administration supplied information for MI5.[100] Several leading personages in the BUF not interned in the Second World War also were alleged to have been used by the authorities. D. S. Lewis suggested that 'D', from a non-existent fund raising department, also acted as a mole in the administration. One or more of these agents was presumably the source of a large number of leaks, details of financial expenditure and reports of BUF administration meetings in the 1930s.[101] Thus MI5 were in a perfect position to analyse British fascism, as an agent ran its intelligence network, and had agents perfectly placed to spy on the administration, and Knight himself had controlled the intelligence section of the most important precursor of Mosley's organization.

Nicholas Mosley has also asserted that his father was fully aware that one of his main backers, W. E. D. Allen, was an MI5 agent.[102] John Hope has suggested, given that the declassified MI5 reports seem unaware that Allen was their agent, that he was in fact the principal SIS (MI6) agent in the BUF, a fact supported by his known role as head of station in Ankara during the war. As Mosley already knew about Taylor's activities, it appears that Mosley recognised the extent to which the BUF had been infiltrated.[103] Mosley later claimed that Allen was a Walter Mitty figure, a fantasist, whose information would have been unreliable. MI6 was interested in Mosley as a possible route through which information about Italian fascism and German Nazism could be learned, as well as being interested in the influence of those movements on British fascism. Mosley always maintained there was nothing illegal in BUF activities, and the fact that intelligence agents were deliberately involved in several of the more secret activities, and he knew of the security authorities' interest, suggests Mosley played a complex intelligence game with the authorities.

The effects of state surveillance thus encouraged Mosley's policy of keeping the activities of the BUF within the law. Mosley's assumption that intelligence sources would be unreliable was optimistic, for even if Allen told fanciful stories, his main evidence with regard to covert foreign funding and the commercial radio interests was certainly accurate. Indeed, it was only as war loomed in 1939 that the increasingly feverish imagination of the authorities began to acquire a Walter Mitty complex with regard to British fascism;

Allen split with Mosley in late 1938 and the authorities lost an important source close to Mosley. The toleration of infiltration in the 1930s then backfired, as remaining MI5 agents were alleged to have turned into *agents provocateurs.*

Intelligence activities also probably helped explain the most secretive aspects of BUF activity in the 1930s. Mosley ostensibly stayed aloof from all aspects of administration and finance, whilst at the same time being fully aware of a secret bank account and a byzantine system of accounting which covered up the sources of foreign funding of the BUF before 1937. Mosley was also secretly involved in trying to corner the market in commercial radio franchises (including a highly controversial deal with Hitler), in an attempt to provide funds for the BUF.[104] The fact that Allen was involved in both these operations suggests that Mosley wished to inform the authorities of these operations, whilst organizing them in such a way that it would be impossible to unravel the complexity of such deals. That Allen and Taylor operated for so long near the centre of the BUF suggests there was sophisticated appreciation of the potentialities on both sides. Mosley wished to acquire accurate and early intelligence of what measures were being planned against him by the state. Also, he was well aware that the political views of counter-intelligence officers with regard to communism were much the same as the BUF, and he recognized that some security service personnel were far less anti-fascist than anti-communist. This appears to apply to Maxwell Knight, with whom the Mosleys developed a cordial relationship after the war. It is interesting to note that two intelligence agents wrote perceptive accounts of fascism: W. E. D. Allen had, as 'James Drennan', produced the best contemporary account of the movement; his *BUF, Mosley and British Fascism* had emphasized that the BUF was basically law abiding, and would never use force except against communist violence.[105] E. R. Mandeville-Roe also wrote a book extolling the virtues of the corporate state in Italy.

Amongst the most interesting intelligence reports released on pre-war British fascism has been the material on the miniscule self-proclaimed 'Jew-wise' groups. With the worsening of relations with Germany in the later 1930s the authorities became very interested in the activities of the secret societies established by Archibald H. Maule Ramsay (the Conservative MP for Peebles), the Nordic League and the Right Club. Although MI5 material has not been released, the disclosures of an ex-agent, Joan Miller, has told us something about security service operations against the Right Club in 1940. The Special Branch reports on Nordic League meetings in 1939 and some material from the intelligence service of the BDBJ are now available in the Home Office papers.[106]

This material shows that the authorities used both uniformed officers to take transcripts of proceedings, and infiltrated agents into extremist organizations. Uniformed officers were used as a warning to the participants not to break the law by openly advocating violence or through the use of abusive language against political opponents or the Jews. In both cases speakers at Nordic League meetings sailed close to the wind: Commander Cole said parliament was full of 'dirty corrupt swine', and Captain Elwin Wright that it was a 'blackmailing corrupt body of bastards'.[107] Audience comments allegedly included such reactions as 'Kill the Jews', 'We hate them' and 'Bastards'.[108]

The Special Branch reports were supplemented by material from BDBJ agents. In the later 1930s the national government cooperated closely with the Board of Deputies, as it wished to work closely with the leadership and more conservative elements in the Jewish community, to avoid the accusation that it was doing nothing against fascist anti-Semitism, and to counter the possibility that East End Jews might shift allegiance to either Labour or the CPGB. The BDBJ wished to maintain its non-political stance, whilst at the same time isolating Jewish militants as political extremists. Neville Laski established a Defence Secretary, and his own private intelligence operation, whose results he forwarded to the Home Office in 1939. He employed a recently retired Inspector from Special Branch called Pavey to infiltrate the Nordic League.[109] He also received reports from Mandeville-Roe.[110] Both appeared to have gone on visits to Germany in 1939.

Pavey's interesting report on the Nordic League emphasized

the dilemma for the authorities. The very eccentricity of its extreme anti-Semitism and verbal excesses had to be weighed against the fact that it was preaching to the converted, a coterie of dedicated fanatics, whose numbers at its closed meetings rarely rose above 50, while its attempts to reach a wider audience at public meetings usually flopped, although one such event attracted 600 in 1939. It was considered that any prosecution would give the organization publicity, and given the outcome of *Rex* v. *Leese* (possible acquittal), a signal which might be misunderstood. Given the erratic behaviour of many of its leading members, the authorities decided the best form of control was through state surveillance, and denying the organization publicity. This became even more necessary when Pavey reported that Ramsay had threatened to arm his son against the Jews, for if constitutional methods failed to control Jewish influence, then other means would have to be employed.[111] Pavey's report also pointed out that there were strong connections between the organization and German and Japanese intelligence and close liaison with the German embassy. Moreover, respectable organizations, such as the Liberty Restoration League, and some establishment figures, were connected to the organization. The security authorities regarded the Nordic League as the British branch of the *Nordischer Gesellschaft*, the Nazi international.

The MI5 reports on British fascism are of particular interest because they shed more light on the methods of operation of the security service than any other released material, and show considerable change of emphasis over time. The reports show the main concerns were the size and regional distribution of membership, the funding of the movement, attempted fascist infiltration of the establishment and armed services, the extent of secretive activity by the fascists and the links with Continental fascist powers.[112]

In the 1930s MI5 appeared to have found out little of interest with regard to these matters, except in respect of financial and other links with the fascist powers. This was why the activities of Mosley and other fascists were viewed in a relaxed manner until 1939. Information, presumably from Taylor, suggested that the BUF had established 'cells' on the communist pattern in the Civil Service, the legal profession, banks and in several universities and public schools.[113] The Home Office were particularly interested in this information, and Newsam wrote to Kell, and Sir Russell Scott contacted Sir Warren Fisher, head of the Civil Service, about it, but there was no evidence of further action being taken. Taylor also enquired of Robert Saunders, the District Leader for Dorset West, of the extent of British Union representation in the Whitehead torpedo works at Weymouth.[114] With regard to the infiltration of the armed forces, Theodore Schurch, who was hanged as a traitor in 1946, claimed to have joined the army on the orders of the BUF, but many members who were not interned fought honourably in the armed forces during the war, and BUF official policy was to support the defence of Britain against the threat of invasion, if Britain was attacked and a satisfactory peace had proved impossible to negotiate. MI5 argued that Major Yeats-Brown, the Bengal Lancer and one of the driving forces behind the January Club, a dining club which enabled the BUF to propagandize a broad section of the establishment with fascist ideas, had tried to make contact with younger officers in the services, but there had been no contact with the rank and file.[115] In general MI5 were satisfied that BUF attempts to infiltrate the establishment had proved a damp squib.

It was with regard to financial support and contact with foreign powers that the most interesting information was discovered. Not only has definite proof been found in Italian archives that Mosley did receive significant funds from Mussolini, but several sources within the security apparatus considered they had discovered proof of this, including MI5. W. E. D. Allen, who had been connected with Mosley since the foundation of the New Party, appears to have given details of such links between Mosley and the fascist powers from the early 1930s. Some of this funding appears to have been laundered into bank accounts via a Paris lawyer, Armand Gregoire.[116]

Before October 1935 MI5 reports explicitly stated that the balance of probability was against any such financial leverage, but its sources and Mussolini's invasion of Abyssinia left the security service in no doubt.[117] MI5 now believed that Mosley received £36,000 a year from Mussolini, which was reduced to £1,000 a month in 1936.[118] Chuter Ede, the Labour Home Secretary in 1946, claimed in the House of Commons that Mosley had been funded by Mussolini in the 1930s, and recently discovered Italian sources confirm this fact.[119] MI5 found no evidence with regard to Nazi funding of the BUF, although there is some suggestion in the Goebbels diaries about possible help. A Labour Party research document argued that Mosley had received large contributions from entrepreneurs in the aviation and automobile industries, as well as from W. E. D. Allen and Lord Rothermere in the New Party, and that these had probably continued for a time after the founding of the BUF. MI5 and Special Branch sources found little evidence to suggest there was significant outside funding after 1936. A secret BUF bank account was uncovered by Special Branch during the war. This showed that £224,000 had been laundered into BUF funds between 1933 and 1937 by way of foreign currency transactions.[120] Mosley claimed this represented secret donations by British entrepreneurs, but at least £40,000, and possibly much more, appears to represent Mussolini's contribution, and some may have come from the Nazis. The fact that, despite expanding membership, there were severe financial cutbacks and redundancies in the BUF administration between 1937 and 1939, suggests that both foreign funding and entrepreneurial injections of capital dried up in the late 1930s.

The suspicions aroused over possible Italian subsidies for the BUF convinced the authorities that although the fascists had been successfully marginalized as a political force, Mosley's covert activities still needed surveillance. Information (presumably passed on by the head of the BUF Industrial Department, and MI5 agent, P. G. Taylor) had suggested that in 1934 Mosley and Rothermere had a scheme to self-finance the BUF by using it as a distribution network for cigarette production, and later developing a range of manufacturing, banking, retailing and financial functions. 'New Epoch Products' had a Board of Directors and initial capital of £12,500, but Lord Rothermere changed his mind about a £70,000 grant and the project never got off the ground.[121]

The attempts to disguise the sources of finance through

secret bank accounts, front organizations, covert activity and creative accounting, naturally alerted MI5 to the possibility that Mosley had secret connections with the Nazis, particularly as war approached. The authorities realized that relations between Mosley and the Nazis had been somewhat problematic. MI5 did not find significant evidence of Nazi funding; rather, relations were often strained between the two organizations. Special Branch reported in 1934 that Otto Bene, the Nazi leader in London, regarded Mosley as a political adventurer, and thought Otto Pfister, Alexander Raven Thomson and Ian Hope-Dundas more worthy of support as leaders.[122] MI5 reported that a leading Nazi agent, Colin Ross, had reported to Berlin in 1936 that though Mosley was a fine leader, the BUF was a ramshackle organization.[123] They also knew that Mosley had sacked Otto Pfister after he had been uncovered as a Nazi intelligence agent. MI5 were aware, too, that Mosley avoided any overt contact with the German embassy, known Nazi agents in Britain or the Anglo-German Fellowship.

However, there was knowledge of more covert activity on Mosley's part. By 1939 it was known that Mosley had secretly married Diana Guinness in Berlin at a ceremony attended by Hitler in 1936, despite his passport having expired in 1935. The Advisory Committee on Internment in 1940 were told of a secret deal whereby Hitler was to build a radio transmitter for Mosley in Germany to help him corner the market in commercial radio franchises.[124] This information probably came from MI6, as W. E. D. Allen had been involved in the early negotiations before his split with Mosley in 1938. This secretive behaviour increased the authorities' suspicions once diplomatic relations with Germany deteriorated sharply after March 1939.[125]

Thus in both public order and internal security concerns, British fascism and the activities of Sir Oswald Mosley were seen as minor irritants which needed surveillance. However, they provided the catalyst for important changes in the law with regard to how public disturbances were managed. Although there were continuing doubts about Mosley's covert activities, his lack of impact after 1936, except in the East End of London, meant he could be safely disregarded. His cooperation with the authorities, his social connections and his ostensibly law abiding behaviour meant he could be safely pigeon-holed as a discredited upper class renegade with minimal public support, rather than as a threat to public security. Hence, until the international situation deteriorated after March 1939, the authorities took a complacent attitude to the activities of the BUF. Indeed, some within MI5 sympathized with the militant anti-communism of the fascists, and the authorities were at least as concerned with anti-fascist activities, as with possible fascist subversion.

6

THE SECOND WORLD WAR (1939–1945)

The publication in 1990 of the official history of security and counter-intelligence in the Second World War, together with the release of files in 1986 on the internment of aliens and fascists after 1939, and the beginning of the declassification of Home Office material on the Communist Party of Great Britain (CPGB) between 1939 and 1945, has provided more official papers relating to the themes of this book than any other period.[1] There is also a significant amount of information to be found in Cabinet papers. That is not to say that much does not still remain unclear and that secrecy does not still bedevil a large area. For example, the important minutes and papers of the Home Defence (Security) Executive, and its associated Committee on Communism, have a 50-year closure period, and although under review, many will remain closed. Similarly, the official histories of the Special Operations Executive, the Political Warfare Executive and the British Information Services in America remain to be published, although a start has now been made to review some of the surviving material under the Waldegrave initiative.

It is not just the failure to release material that hinders

research, however. The authorities have actively discouraged ex-members of MI5 or MI6, or others with knowledge of security or intelligence issues, from publishing war memoirs, through the deterrence of threatened legal action. This rests on breach of contract, the need for confidentiality, or even the use of the Official Secrets Act. Even where publication has occurred this has sometimes followed delays caused by government attempts to block the book. Peter Wright was not the first to experience governmental displeasure at disclosure of aspects of the secret world.

Even before the introduction of legislation on government secrecy the authorities had shown displeasure against those who leaked secrets in the nineteenth century. The first intelligence agent to be prosecuted for publishing his war memoirs was the novelist, Compton Mackenzie. The first edition of *Greek Memories* in 1932 still remains a banned book because it gave the names of 14 intelligence agents, disclosed that the passport and visa offices in British embassies abroad were often fronts for the operation of the Secret Intelligence Service, and that the head of the wartime secret service was Sir Mansfield Smith-Cumming, and that he was universally known as 'C'.

Two interesting cases pertaining to the Second World War illustrate that official attitudes have not become more liberal. The posthumous publication of Joan Miller's *One Girl's War* in 1987 told the story of an agent, Miller, working under Maxwell Knight in Section B5b of MI5. She infiltrated the Right Club in 1940, an establishment secret society formed by the anti-Semitic Conservative MP, Archibald Maule Ramsay, and was instrumental in providing evidence which helped convict two of Ramsay's associates, Tyler Kent and Anna Wolkoff, of obtaining secret information. The attempt to stop publication of Miller's book occurred despite the fact that her book did not discuss the most sensitive aspects of the Tyler Kent affair, and after 40 years' hindsight, her memory, not surprisingly, was somewhat defective on matters of detail.[2] Nevertheless, the government tried unsuccessfully to prevent the publication of *One Girl's War* in Dublin in 1987. This attempt failed, but gave the book publicity and boosted its sales.

Other projected works of which the authorities disapproved failed to appear. One example of this was a planned book by Kenneth de Courcy, the Duc de Grantmesnil, who was the intelligence officer of the Imperial Policy Group, and a friend of the Duke of Windsor. In 1959 he announced he was writing a book on the background and history of his journal, *Intelligence Digest.* This book would be controversial and much attacked, and would deal with the activities of de Courcy and his circle during the Abdication Crisis and the Second World War, as well as discuss the origins of *Intelligence Digest* and the naturc of its sources.[3] The book was never published.

However, matters which no doubt would have been discussed in it began to appear in *Intelligence Digest* during 1961. These related to the activities of a 'political correspondent' who had secret discussions with Joseph Kennedy, the American Ambassador, in London in 1940, about the political situation in Europe and the possibility of a peace settlement. These discussions were approved by Lord Halifax and R. A. Butler at the Foreign Office, and appear to have been conducted on the assumption that Churchill's views on the continuation of the war would not prevail because half the Cabinet was opposed to them.[4] Similarly, a 'correspondent' revealed the assumptions behind Chamberlain's policy at Munich, with the failure of Poland and France to give Czechoslovakia military support, and the negative assessments of the Chiefs of Staff.[5] Chamberlain's position at Munich had brought the necessary time to strengthen Britain's defences by the outbreak of war. Such leakages then dried up. The significant details of de Courcy's interesting story have since surfaced in both academic and revisionist histories of the period, yet in the early 1960s they were a state secret which the authorities did not want discussed.[6] In 1963 de Courcy was convicted of fraud – framed, he alleged, as a result of dubious evidence designed to reduce him to silence; framed for political motives which also suited non-political interests.[7]

Whatever the truth behind de Courcy's claims, and it should be pointed out that *Intelligence Digest* developed a conspiratorial interpretation of modern history for a time in the 1960s, it has to be noted that there were secret sessions of the House of Commons and that crucial Cabinet minutes from 1940 have not been released. It is now quite clear that in perhaps the greatest crisis of twentieth-century British political history, there was both significant political paranoia, which developed into a kind of British McCarthyism, and a countervailing grim determination to maintain as much of the fabric of constitutional freedom as possible. These contradictory tensions were both backed by significant public opinion, and it was so-called political extremists who experienced the harshest curtailment of their rights and liberties.

Whilst all the evidence is not yet available for scrutiny, what is clear enough from the available documentation and the account in the official history is the importance of First World War experience in the putting in place of the necessary extension of state powers in the official preparation for war. With regard to internal security, public order and political extremism, the basic structure of limitations on individual liberties, the growth of state control and regulation, the dramatic expansion of the security apparatus, increased political surveillance of public opinion and actual or potential opposition to the war, and the modelling of the Defence Regulations on the Defence of the Realm Act (DORA), were all areas of restriction of normal rights. The Emergency Powers Act of 1920 – which itself was modelled on the DORA regulations, and which gave the government powers to replace the working of the common law with emergency powers if it so desired during a proclaimed period of crisis – was made permanent for the duration of the Second World War. Having said that, there were also other tensions within the state which mirrored First World War problems. There were differences between the Home Office and the security authorities, particularly MI5, over both aliens and fascists, which rumbled on throughout the war, though rather less over conscientious objectors than in the First World War. Difficulties and suspicions also emerged for a time over military powers in 1940. Whilst security was given a much more significant influence in war, the traditional suspicions of liberal politicians and civil servants did not disappear, and whilst many traditional liberties were curtailed, and some British subjects interned for a significant period (as between 1914 and 1918), such limitations were temporary expedients to meet the national emergency.

a) The Phoney War

One major difference between the two world wars was that in 1939 there was little of the euphoria present in 1914. Also, apart from the evacuation of children from London in autumn 1939, the gradual development of shortages of consumer durables and the beginnings of rationing for the civilian population in January 1940, there was little indication that Britain was at war until the spring of 1940. Hitler attacked Poland in 1939 and neither Britain nor France was in a position to provide military aid for that country nor to attack Germany in the west. The feared German bombing offensive also did not materialize in 1939. Thus the first period of the war earned itself the label of the 'phoney war'.

Within the National Government itself appeasement influences had not entirely disappeared with the outbreak of war in September 1939. Some of the main reasons for appeasement were still important between September 1939 and March 1940: the belief that Britain was fighting the wrong enemy, that communism was the greater threat, helped explain the political drift and indecision in this period. Other factors included the Treasury orthodoxy that Britain could not afford a more general conflagration, the unpreparedness of the armed services, and the threat to the unity of the Empire, both in terms of potential Dominion disunity and the impetus it might give to nationalist movements in the colonies.[8]

Suspicion of such continuing influences explained the unwillingness of the Labour Party to accept office under the architect of the disastrous Munich policy, Neville Chamberlain. Whilst the above mentioned undercurrents existed, the parliamentary, aristocratic, pacifist, fascist and communist opposition to the war was small and disunited, and Chamberlain refused to be influenced by it.[9] In spite of these suspicions the Labour Party did come to an agreement with the government and the Liberals not to fight by-elections, but to allow a new representative from the sitting party to be elected unopposed in the unrepresented constituency. Normal politics was suspended for the duration, but the opposition reserved its right to criticize the government for its conduct of the war. This meant in effect that only non-parliamentary groups would challenge the government in by-elections. With the official opposition muted, both communists and fascists had the opportunity to provide an alternative anti-war policy. Although both propagandized such a cause, neither made much of an impact on public opinion, despite the evidence that there was not much public enthusiasm for the war during the phoney war period.

It was not only the obvious security threats posed by German and Austrian aliens and by supposed British fascist fellow travellers which worried the British government and authorities. The Nazi–Soviet pact of 26 August 1939 made war inevitable, but it also raised the spectre either of an unlikely domestic alliance between fascists and communists, or of both being involved in a concerted anti-war campaign leading to demonstrations and civil disobedience. MI5 was obsessed with the CPGB implementing a Leninist policy of 'revolutionary defeatism', and was very conscious of the problem of leakage of information to the enemy from the operations of both Nazi and Soviet agents – after it became obvious following the partition of Poland, the incorporation into the USSR of the Baltic States and the attack on Finland, that there was more to the agreement than the stated non-aggression pact.[10]

The necessary security precautions were complicated by a further problem at the outbreak of the war: the spread to mainland Britain of political terrorism instigated by the Irish Republican Army (IRA). From January 1939 several bomb outrages, some involving loss of life, had occurred in London, Manchester and Coventry. In July 1939 the Prevention of Violence (Temporary Provisions) Act was pushed through parliament; it prohibited the entry of suspected IRA members and gave the authorities powers of expulsion.[11] The Irish in Britain were seen as a potential source of a 'fifth column' in some quarters. Both the British and Irish governments were worried about the potential for a Nazi–IRA alliance at the outbreak of war.

These fears were a harbinger of more restrictions. On 24 August as a response to the worsening international situation the Emergency Powers (Defence) Act was pushed through parliament and Code A of its provisions was brought into operation on 25 August. The more controversial Code B, involving almost unlimited powers of detention and internment of individuals with the potential or intention of aiding the enemy, was instituted on 1 September. These regulations had been drawn up by the War Emergency Legislation subcommittee of the Committee of Imperial Defence (CID) first established in 1924. The preparation of the regulations and the drafting of the bill had been approved in July 1937 by the CID.[12] The regulations were mainly derived from the DORA legislation from the First World War, with suitable amendments. The most important of these was the suspicion of 'internationalist' or 'disinterested' opposition to the war by British nationals rather than by 'persons of hostile origins or association' (enemy aliens resident in Britain).[13] Thus fifth column extremists of fascist, communist or pacifist sympathies were initially seen by the military and security authorities as more of a problem than enemy aliens.

At first the legislation was accepted as a necessary evil, but the Labour Party rapidly became concerned that the executive had been granted too extensive powers over the liberty of the individual.[14] A Liberal campaign, backed by many Labour MPs and the National Council for Civil Liberties (NCCL), led to a prayer being moved in the House of Commons on 31 October by Dingle Foot to annul the Order in Council which had brought Code B of the regulation into force.[15] The Opposition were particularly concerned about DR 18b (powers to detain or impose restrictions on those thought capable of compromising national security), DR 39b(2) (power to censor publication of sensitive material), DR 39e (power to stop meetings and processions), DR 39a and 39b(1) (tightening up of offences attempting disaffection, in the armed forces), DR 88b (power to stop and search vehicles) and DR 88c (power to arrest without warrant). These regulations were thought to undermine the principle of habeas corpus and threaten the liberties of Englishmen.

Whilst in theory this objection was valid, the operation of the powers inherent in such regulations showed the authorities were very cautious about infringing fundamental liberties. The Minister for Home Security (as the Home Secretary became in wartime) in 1939–1940 was Sir John Anderson, probably the greatest single influence on the policy, organization and administration of the Home Office in the twentieth century. His administrative experience gave him a wide knowledge of security issues.[16] As well as his formidable statistical contribution to the structure and organization of government during the war – as Home Secretary, and after October 1940 as Lord President of the Council, where one of his responsibilities was domestic security, and from 1944 as Chancellor of the Exchequer – he proved a fanatical advocate of establishing sufficiently powerful administrative machinery to control potential trouble, whilst being cautious in operating those powers and endeavouring to limit the damage of loss of rights during a national emergency. Whilst the powers assumed during the Second World War were draconian, the practice was tempered by insistence on political control over national security, sensitivity to the wishes of the House of Commons, and resistance to military pressures to curb fundamental rights, even during the dark days of the threatened invasion during the spring and summer of 1940.

Throughout the phoney war the pressure applied by the Opposition before May 1940 was met with a sympathetic response in the Home Office. The authorities agreed that provided the wartime regulations were not compromised little should be done which would affect the morale of the civilian population or organized labour. Indeed, the Home Office was even more liberal than the Opposition with regard to this matter. Whereas Labour and the NCCL's concern for habeas corpus and civil liberties ended abruptly with the rights of British fascists, the Home Office argued that an even-handed approach should be continued for all

13 Sir John Anderson, Minister for Home Security, 1939–40

groups and that only where organizations could be proved to engage in treasonable or illegal activity, through 'acts prejudicial', could action be taken. Thus the outcome of negotiations between the government and the opposition parties in the Home Office following the House of Commons debate on 31 October 1939 led to considerable amendments of provisions to Section B of the Emergency Powers Act in November 1939.[17] Individuals now had to commit acts detrimental to the safety of the realm rather than be thought capable of having the power to do so. Whilst the potential powers of the government over the citizen were safeguarded, the Opposition nevertheless were unhappy that

British fascists were left relatively unmolested by the state – at least to outward appearances.

A further complication was provided by the actions of British fascists and communists. They were both fully aware that in any national emergency they were liable to be made scapegoats of the authorities' fears, irrespective of whether they had committed any illegal act. This no doubt was a powerful factor in the decision of most pro-Nazi or fascist groups to go into voluntary self-liquidation with the approach of war. Thus by September 1939, the Anglo-German Fellowship, the Link, the Imperial Fascist League, the Nordic League, the Militant Christian Patriots and the Right Club had all ostensibly closed down for the duration. Only the British Union soldiered on regardless.[18] With the outbreak of war Mosley issued a statement denouncing the role of Jewish interests in fomenting a war between Britain and Germany, but stated categorically that British Union members should do nothing to impede the war effort.[19] The CPGB more ambiguously (whilst performing theoretical gyrations as a result of the Nazi–Soviet pact) came to oppose the war as an inevitable consequence of imperialist rivalries, and called on British workers to demand social reform and an improvement of living conditions.[20] However they too were careful not to invite precipitate action by the state. Whereas France immediately interned fascists and banned the communist party at the outbreak of war, Britain responded far more slowly.

The pressures from politicians and the actions of those groups under political surveillance suggested a cautious approach to the limitation of civil liberties. The growth of friction between the Home Office and MI5 during the phoney war reinforced this development. The caution arose from the anomalous role, the confused status and accountability, of MI5 within the British constitution, and the fact that the Home Office was more concerned about public order, whilst MI5's main concern was security. As the activities of the security service were not subject to parliamentary scrutiny, in official terms its existence was not even acknowledged, and informal custom rather than agreed binding instruction defined its jurisdiction and accountability, and meant its executive authority was questionable. Against that was the undoubted fact that security concerns had a much higher profile in war than in peace, and this led to a massive growth in the power and influence of the security service. The problem arose of what role a secret institution should have in cases of disagreement on policy with accountable executive authority within the state.

This difficulty was connected with plans set in motion by the Committee of Imperial Defence (CID) preparations for war. With regard to the internment of aliens, the Home Office and MI5 staged a reprise of the debate between the 'frocks' and the 'gowns' during the First World War on this issue. Before the war the Home Office argued for general internment of all enemy aliens on the grounds it would be demanded by public opinion, and necessary as a public order measure for their own protection. MI5, mindful of the First World War experience and the administrative difficulties involved in suddenly interning over 20,000 people, said this would not be necessary and proposed the division of aliens into three categories, with only the most serious security risks to be immediately interned. The experience of the first weeks of war prompted the Home Office and MI5 to reverse their positions. With the failure of public opinion to demand internment, and the realization that most aliens were anti-Nazi or refugees, the Home Office developed a strong commitment to intern as few aliens as possible. This position changed with the fifth column scare, a fact illustrated by the rapid crackdown on anti-Italian rioters in London and the north east. The authorities immediately interned Italian aliens in Britain once Mussolini declared war, as much for their protection as to tighten security; the state saw the necessity for maintaining public order as paramount during the crisis of 1940. MI5, on the other hand, became increasingly concerned about leakage of information and considered aliens as open to possible blackmail by the enemy, or as a possible means by which Nazi agents could be infiltrated into Britain. The Home Office began to accuse MI5 of paranoia, and the latter berated the former for maximizing the security risks.[21]

The debate over aliens and leakage of information to the

enemy led Sir Maurice Hankey, the Minister without Portfolio, to chair an enquiry into both MI5 and the Secret Intelligence Service (SIS or MI6) between December 1939 and April 1940. Although no answer to this problem was forthcoming from Hankey, the immediate need to give security an overriding priority as a consequence of the collapse of Western Europe before the Nazi blitzkrieg in April and May 1940, greatly strengthened MI5's position, despite the sacking of its head.[22]

From the outbreak of the war the authorities were concerned about possible leakages of information to the enemy. This allegedly included gossip picked up by Italian and other waiters in London restaurants, material sent via the diplomatic bags of foreign embassies, contact with the German embassy in Dublin, secret wireless communication, and information obtained and passed directly or indirectly by fascists, communist or IRA sources to the enemy. It was particularly emphasized by the Joint Intelligence Committee that absolute discretion should be operated at all times, and information should only be given on the need to know principle. Of these threats only the IRA's terrorist campaign gave the state the immediate excuse to take strong action against it. Over 100 people were convicted and most were sentenced to long terms of imprisonment – including Brendan Behan, who received three years – and 167 people were expelled from Great Britain under the new powers.[23]

The unease was increased by the suspicion that some within the state did not want war with Germany. During the phoney war the security service became worried about possible probing to obtain a peace settlement. German foreign policy documents captured after 1945, which discuss the attitudes of 'Undersecretary Butler' and 'our friends in the Air Ministry', appear to refer to doubts about the political wisdom of the war which were held in some sections of the establishment during the phoney war period. The latter statement appears to relate to German misinterpretation of intelligence probing before 1939.[24] The Venlo Incident, where MI6 agents were captured by the *Sicherheitsdienst*, the Nazi intelligence organization, attempted to further Chamberlain's covert policy of aiding an imaginary *coup d'état* plot against Hitler, so that a compromise peace could be negotiated with a new German government.[25]

A further complication arose following the creation of a War Cabinet on 3 September 1939. The admission of the Chiefs of Staff and the creation of the Supreme War Council with the French, increased the risk of leakages of classified information. The unwieldy administrative structures raised the possibility of material seeping out, particularly as a key appointment increased the suspicion of the security authorities. The installation of Sir Edmund Ironside as Chief of the Imperial General Staff (CIGS) was resisted in Cabinet on the grounds that he was suspected of being indiscreet, had dubious connections and it was thought his presence would upset the Chiefs of Staff committee.[26] Ironside was contemptuous of politicians, although he admired Chamberlain's handling of the Cabinet in 1939. It appears that he wished to appoint Major-General Fuller as deputy CIGS, which no doubt increased the suspicions of the security authorities.[27] Fuller, an opponent of the war, was a known associate of Sir Oswald Mosley and had been responsible for administrative reforms in the BUF. One of the major unexplained problems is why Fuller was not interned when so many unimportant fascists were. His file has apparently been destroyed. Other important fascists also remained free: A. K. Chesterton, the leading BUF propagandist before 1937, fought in the British army in Somaliland. It is thought that MI5 intercepted his indignant refusal in 1939 to work for German radio.

Similarly, the acceptance of a liaison post with the French by the Duke of Windsor, with access to classified information from the Supreme War Council, also caused concern. The connections and indiscretions of the Duke and Duchess of Windsor provided a considerable source of worry for the authorities. Their private visit to Germany in 1938, and the Duke's peace broadcast at Verdun in May 1939, were also disapproved of by the government. As released German foreign office documents showed after the war, the Duke appears to have been the source of significant leaks of classified material, probably as a result of letters to ex-Kaiser Wilhelm II in Holland, or through his connections with

Charles Bedaux, a man with known Nazi ties who was to die in captivity, imprisoned on suspicion of being a spy.[28]

This complex background led to a policy of caution with regard to the management of political extremism during the phoney war period. The main security activity was increased political surveillance of fascists, communists and pacifists, and the management and monitoring of public opinion. MI5 and Special Branch were particularly concerned about the issues outlined in the first MI5 report on the BUF in April 1934; namely, the threat to public order, the possible existence of secret underground activity, connection with the enemy, contact with the establishment, and links with the armed services.[29] The activities of informers and *agents provocateurs* now became of greater significance, as MI5 argued it was a security risk not to take a stronger line against potential Trojan horses in British society. They were particularly concerned to marginalize fascist and communist anti-war propaganda and to isolate those groups from society.

The authorities also beefed up the existing facilities for the assessment of public opinion. State support for the first mass surveys of attitudes to popular issues, with the use of Tom Harrisson's Mass Observation facilities by the new Ministry of Information and the Home Office, reinforced by the establishment of the Home Office weekly intelligence reports after September 1940, provided a separate source of information to that provided by the security authorities. Such reports signal a confusion and apathy about the war amongst the general public during the phoney war, which was counterbalanced by a general hostile response to political extremism and an increasing suspicion of Mosley and British fascism in particular.[30]

Neither communists nor fascists were able to mount a credible opposition against the war and both did badly in by-elections in 1939–40, despite the electoral truce between the major parties. In the three elections fought by the British Union, they performed pathetically, obtaining less than 2 per cent of the vote in all three constituencies. Whilst the Nazi–Soviet pact did not lead to a marked hostility to the CPGB, the Soviet invasion of Finland led, amongst the British public, to an increased indifference to and suspicion of British communism.

In spite of the evidence that the activities of extremists and anti-war groups were inconsequential, MI5 and Special Branch greatly increased the attention they gave to British fascism and communism. Although not all the information has been released, the authorities appear to have been markedly well informed of the operations, policies, tactics and connections of the BUF and the CPGB. It appears that several agents, including P. G. Taylor, the Intelligence Officer of the BUF, and Harald Kurtz were actively involved in monitoring and possibly encouraging secretive activity on the part of British fascists. This is quite clear from evidence in the personal files of Aubrey Lees and John Beckett,[31] and the information from the minutes of the Home Defence (Security) Executive referring to the case of Sir Barry Domvile.[32] Information had also been given to the authorities by the Board of Deputies of British Jews and the Economic League. Little is known of the details of the infiltration of the CPGB during the war; Olga Gray, who had worked as a secretary for the Friends of the Soviet Union, and in the CPGB headquarters in King Street during the 1930s, had her cover blown by the Percy Glading spy case in 1938.[33] However, the infiltration was extensive, as was illustrated by an MI5 report circulated to the Cabinet in 1943; this contained the cheerful admission that 'The minutes of the meetings of the Central Committee of the Communist Party from September 1939 to the early part of 1940 have come into the hands of the investigating authorities'. These allegedly were taken from the home of the stenographer after a Special Branch raid.[34]

The authorities estimated that the BUF had 8,700 members in May 1940, although this only counted active followers rather than the passive support shown by an increasing number of mainly right-wing middle class ex-Tories. The CPGB was seen as more significant for having 20,000 subscribing members.[35] MI5 warned that, contrary to public perception, the CPGB had not declined as a result of the Nazi–Soviet pact, and what loss there had been was made up by the recruitment of fellow travellers into the party, and by the loss of secret sympathizers in the Labour Party who now openly joined the communists.[36]

What was particularly interesting about the reactions of the state to political extremism in 1939–40 was the increasing convergence of the attitudes of politicians, administrators and the security authorities to the matter. Increasingly, differences were about tactics rather than the ends of policy. In effect the conspiratorial interpretation of MI5 of communism and fascism now became a commonplace within the state outside the Home Office, even if administrators and law officers were fully cognizant of the legal and practical difficulties involved in outlawing these groups. Although the Home Office was completely aware that both the BUF and the CPGB were not actively opposing the war, and that there were significant differences of opinion about it amongst members, in practice the underlying attitude was not dissimilar to the monotonous refrain emanating from Special Branch and MI5, even if civil servants remained suspicious of the increased influence of the security service. This belief implicitly, and sometimes explicitly, emphasized that both the BUF and the CPGB were agents of foreign powers, who owed their primary allegiance to nations either at war with, or hostile to, Great Britain, and were either openly or covertly adopting a 'revolutionary defeatist' line. The actual fact that Mosley asserted that fascists should do nothing to impede the war effort and that members of the BUF were loyally fighting in the armed forces was viewed in a suspicious light. In truth, the security service actually found little evidence of dubious behaviour amongst members although this was seen simply as a tactic to keep the authorities from closing down British fascism. Similarly, the authorities could point to the complete volte-face by the CPGB following the Nazi–Soviet pact, when the successful united front anti-fascism was replaced overnight by the 'imperialist war' theme, as proof the CPGB was run from Moscow. 'Bolshevik discipline' and the recantations of Campbell and Pollitt, who initially voted against the change of policy, were cited as evidence that British communism was totally controlled by the Comintern.

Thus the state was prone to accept the basic assumptions

of the security service assessment of the aims of British fascists and communists. The persistent demands for tighter security from MI5 and Special Branch acted as a corrosive force on the state once it became clear in 1939 that hostilities were not going to be over by Christmas. A conspiratorial interpretation of the activities of British fascists and communists, as well as aliens, became increasingly vocal despite the resistance of the Home Office to such developments.

Special Branch emphasized Mosley's supposed belief that a revolutionary anti-war situation would soon develop which the fascists could either benefit from themselves, or could use their contacts with the armed services to help defeat the communists. This might provide the opportunity for a 'march to power'.[37] Whilst this fantasy lacked credibility, MI5 reported on 'secret meetings' designed to unify the fascist fringe. This related to a supposed agreement on a policy of cooperation between Mosley and Maule Ramsay, at the 'London and Southern Counties anti-Vivisection Society', where members of most of the pro-Nazi groups met to discuss the threat to themselves, given the internment of four fascists at the outbreak of the war. Political surveillance was kept on the British Council for Christian Settlement in Europe, a front for the Duke of Bedford's British People's Party, which attempted to link the fascist fringe to a wider peace movement.[38] According to 'a very reliable informant', some collaboration resulted from these meetings but those present could not agree who should be leader. In another report it was stated that the meetings were designed to secure the greatest possible collaboration and to make preparations for a *coup d'état*.[39] A report by an agent about a wild speech made by T. St Barbe Baker at a joint meeting of Nordic League and BUF members in Maida Vale in October 1939, said that the speech had suggested that the king should abdicate and a ruling council be set up by the Duke of Windsor and General Ironside.[40]

Whilst during the phoney war such reports were treated with scepticism, after the collapse of western Europe politicians readily took such reports at their face value. Sir John Anderson told the committee on Communist activities in January 1941 that the fascists had been interned because they were preparing secret plans which would enable them, in the event of an invasion of this country, either to range themselves on the side of the enemy or, by a coup, to seize power and make terms with them.[41] This was the same Anderson who as Home Secretary argued against the internment of aliens, fascists and communists in May 1940. No material has since come to light suggesting that his original argument against the internment of fascists, communists or aliens on security grounds was false, even if the Tyler Kent affair showed that a very small number of extremists, monitored and perhaps encouraged to break the Defence Regulations by MI5 agents, provided one of the pretexts for the security revolution.[42]

Whereas the security service initially had an uphill task persuading the government of the threat posed by aliens and British fascists, the ingrained suspicion of the CPGB rapidly led the British state to an old, stereotyped interpretation of the complex manoeuvrings of British communists during the phoney war period. The actions of the communists themselves reinforced all the preconceptions of the dominant conspiracy theory which dictated that the CPGB was controlled by the Comintern and acted purely as an agent of the USSR. This proved to be the case even though more subtle minds, like that of Guy Liddell in MI5, pointed out that the initial response of the CPGB to the war suggested that there were significant differences within the party and it should not be associated too closely with the USSR's position. For Liddell, the 'war on two fronts' arguments of the CPGB's General Secretary, Harry Pollitt, in September 1939, was unobjectionable because although he bitterly attacked the 'men of Munich' and the Chamberlain government, he was vehemently anti-Nazi and initially supported the war against Hitler. Although he strongly criticized the government, there was no indication that the CPGB intended to oppose other than by constitutional means. MI5 were only worried about the communists if a revolutionary situation should develop, but in the meantime repressive action would only tend to unite the party and to drive its activities underground, bringing the extreme revolutionary element into the leadership. The CPGB had been damaged by the

Percy Glading case in 1938, when a leading member had been convicted of espionage for the USSR, and MI5 wanted to do nothing which would increase support for the party.[43]

Such relatively sophisticated views were replaced by the perceived forcing of the CPGB to change its line on the war, the removal of Pollitt as General Secretary, and the 'extremists' taking over the leading positions in the party. Thus MI5 emphasized the 'revolutionary defeatist' aims of the CPGB, in its reversion to a Leninist 'imperialist war' interpretation of hostilities, where the logic of the CPGB's leading theoretician, Rajani Palme Dutt – that opposition to imperialist war meant fighting British imperialism, not the enemy's – was adhered to. The authorities could quote from impeccable sources, including the secret minutes of the highest policy making committee in the CPGB, to show how pressure could force leading recalcitrant comrades like Harry Pollitt and J. R. Campbell to accept 'Bolshevik discipline' and recant their opposition to the 'imperialist war' line.

The authorities failed to realize that the divisions in the CPGB represented the clash between those who saw international communism purely as the interest of the Soviet Union, and those who saw British communism as the leader of an anti-fascist crusade. The fact that Stalin refused to give any guidance from Moscow meant the Comintern was reluctant to offer advice until after the notorious treaty of friendship between Germany and the Soviet Union signed on the 28 September. Such stereotyped views dominated the state's attitude towards the CPGB even when British communists became fervent believers in the war against Germany after the Nazi invasion of the Soviet Union in June 1941.[44] The authorities were fully cognizant of the fact that the most important communist trade unionist, Arthur Horner, had abstained on the change of line in September 1939; however, they regarded his recantation in much the same light as those of Pollitt and Campbell, as a good example of 'Bolshevik discipline' in practice. The authorities failed to distinguish, let alone take advantage of, the significant difference between the 'revolutionary pragmatism' of the Popular Frontists in the CPGB and the 'revolutionary defeatism' of Stalin's British henchmen. The blinkered assumption in such an analysis was that Horner's actions showed that he ignored the CPGB line where he thought it conflicted with his anti-fascist beliefs and the interests of South Wales miners.[45] The heresy of Hornerism, and his ability to avoid retribution, should have made the authorities more aware that labour activists did not always adopt bovine obedience to the party line, let alone the commands of Moscow. There appears to have been no attempt at any stage of the CPGB's history for the authorities to probe the differences between the Pollitt, Campbell, Hannington, and Horner revisionist line, and the more doctrinally pure and unrealistic policies of Palme Dutt, Rust and Springhall amongst the leadership. In short, neither the security service nor any other state agency was sophisticated enough to see, let alone attempt to make use of, the very real differences within the CPGB.

It would be difficult to exaggerate the contempt felt by all sections of the establishment, including in particular the Labour Party, for the political gyrations of the CPGB between 1939 and 1941. It is now known that the changing focus of the policies of the CPGB were less of a U-turn than contemporary opinion surmised, and that the anti-war policies could develop naturally from the deep-rooted hostility to the Chamberlain government shown during the united front period before the war.[46] However, damning evidence of Soviet manipulation and control meant the authorities continued to treat the CPGB as a pariah organization.

Although only a small amount of material is available it is quite clear that the state's surveillance of the CPGB was highly successful. The problem lay with the analysis of the obtrusively infiltrated organization. The obsession with the outmoded and almost redundant Comintern obscured the reality that revolution was off the Stalinist agenda, despite the tepid rhetorical revival of 'revolutionary defeatist' slogans. Although politicians and MI5 may have recognized tactical shifts in the outlook of the CPGB – from 'war on two fronts' to 'revolutionary defeatism', to a concentration on economics and social reform issues – its analysis remained unaltered. Dave Springhall, who brought the news of the change of line from Moscow in September 1939, was seen as a particularly dangerous extremist. He became part of the triumvirate who ran the party from 1939 to 41 following the removal of Pollitt, in response to his initial opposition and reluctance to accept the anti-war line. In 1943 Springhall was convicted of espionage for the Soviet Union. In 1939 Special Branch obtained a copy of his notes for secret meetings which stressed the importance of members' struggle against the war on the home front, advocated an end to hostilities against Germany and a stop to aid to Finland, and discussed turning economic grievances in factories into effective strikes. The workers' aim should be industrial disruption, the increased understanding of the link between economic and political activity, and finally the revolution. Successful battles on the home front would encourage the soldier comrades to initiate effective action against the war.[47]

Such arguments also allegedly formed the stock indoctrination which some tutor organizers provided workers' educational classes in 1943, according to the MI5 report circulated at Cabinet. That such material should be taken seriously, given the lack of impact of the CPGB before the change of line in 1941, shows the growth of concern by the authorities. The security service remained set in the rigid patterns of thought and tunnel vision established by Kell, Thomson and Unionist politicians in the aftermath of the First World War. According to such views the underlying reality of British communism was its dependent relationship to the Comintern as a tool of Soviet foreign policy.[48]

Politicians were still prone to outbreaks of revolutionary hysteria: Major Desmond Morton, Churchill's personal representative on the Security Executive, was alarmed by the closing of CPGB branches and their replacement by 'factory units' in 1942, which signalled for him the turn to policies, outlined in the 'official textbooks of the Third International', for the organization of revolution. Churchill earlier had agreed that an expert on Comintern policy should be attached to the MOI.[49] This suggestion was ignored. Sir John Anderson also justified his devious policy banning all political meetings at factory gates in 1941 as due to the fact that the basic revolutionary aims of the CPGB had not altered.[50]

This paranoia had been fed by the political surveillance of the CPGB during the 'imperialist war' period, and was compounded by the inconclusive study by MI5 on the funding of the *Daily Worker.* It was surmised that although the circulation was increasing the repeated calls for funds and the miraculous subscription of the exact amount could only be attributed to considerable topping up from Party funds in 1939–40. This vagueness was all that could be concluded even though the authorities were in possession of the accounts of the *Daily Worker* for much of the period from 1930 to 40.[51]

Such suspicion of fascist and communist activity was magnified by the success of the Nazi blitzkrieg in western Europe in the spring of 1940. The increased use of propaganda which seemed to emanate from such sources led to demands from MI5 to close down extremist newspapers and magazines. The authorities became concerned about the growth of rumours originating from the broadcasts of William Joyce on Radio Hamburg.[52] They became perturbed by more subtle and sophisticated material peddled by the Buro Concordia, which supplied information for the 'New British Broadcasting Service' (NBBS), the 'Workers Challenge' and the 'Christian Peace Movement'.[53] These new radio stations, immediately established after the opening of the blitzkrieg in western Europe and beamed to Britain from the Continent, were designed to appear to be anti-war underground stations operating from within the United Kingdom. Printed material advertising them, together with anti-Semitic sticky-back labels, were distributed in 1940 and greatly alarmed the authorities, as it was interpreted as a means by which a fifth column could be organized. According to information provided by Mrs Eckersley and John Lingshaw, William Joyce was responsible for the collection and editing of the material for the news reviews of these stations.[54] Maule Ramsay asked questions about them in parliament, ensuring that the wavelength of the NBBS was advertised. NBBS broadcasts were clever propaganda and to some it appeared to show knowledge of delicate security information about the lend-lease agreement with the United States, over and above that which appeared in the press.[55] The authorities were concerned about the evidence that so many were evading media censorship by tuning in to English language German radio.

The disquiet felt about the export of fascist and communist literature to Europe was expressed in the recommendation of the Home Policy Committee following discussion in April and May 1940 to ban the export of the British Union's *Action* and the CPGB's *Daily Worker*, and in a letter from Roger Hollis of MI5 to the Ministry of Information (MOI), which argued against the Home Office and MOI view that newspapers sent abroad should not be censored. Hollis argued that a study of German wireless propaganda from the NBBS and the 'Worker's Challenge' showed that the enemy were making good use of fascist and communist lines of thought. Hollis stated that it was interesting to note how closely the NBBS mirrored the *Daily Worker* in agitating for deep shelters. For him, this illustrated how the two extremes were coming together; the communists were adept at skating on thin ice, and if control was relaxed there would be much more criticism of the war effort. Both the fascist and communist press represented the nation as having a dissatisfied majority who were eager for peace and who were held down by a ruthless and unscrupulous ruling class. It was not known abroad that these papers represented an 'irresponsible and malignant minority'.[56]

Such views, in the changed situation in the spring and summer of 1940, overrode the defence of traditional liberties by the Home Office and MOI, and both *Action* and the *Daily Worker* were banned from sale overseas.[57] The Home Defence (Security) Executive successfully resisted attempts to remove the ban.[58] They also showed interest in the contents of NBBS broadcasts, and a letter from Lord Swinton to the MOI alluded to two NBBS broadcasts which advocated violence against 'war mongers'.[59] It is quite clear that the real purpose of the ban was to stop the Germans beaming British fascist or communist propaganda back to Britain to reach a wider audience, thus getting round the unofficial government blackout on extremist propaganda.

b) The Tyler Kent Affair

The Nazi invasion of western Europe led inexorably to the downfall of the Chamberlain government and his replacement by Churchill as Prime Minister on 10 May 1940.[60] The creation of the new coalition, with two of the initial five members of the new War Cabinet being Attlee and Greenwood from the Labour Party, ensured much-needed support for the refusal of Churchill to countenance peace proposals. There have been persistent rumours that the political price of Labour's support for the government was the internment of Mosley and leading fascists, but whatever the truth behind that story, the security revolution which was inaugurated by the new government represented more an *ad hoc* response to the severe crisis which confronted the nation in the spring of 1940, rather than a preconceived plan.[61] National security became of seminal concern, and MI5, backed by the military, argued that given the supposed role of a 'fifth column' of fascist sympathizers in Nazi victories, it would be expedient to intern all aliens and suspect persons. The Home Office in addition to its concern about civil liberties, was also becoming concerned about the evidence of increased hostility to the British Union and that preventive detention might be necessary to protect the fascists from the wrath of public opinion.

This pressure had been building up before the fall of the Chamberlain government, and the Joint Intelligence Committee had already argued on 2 May 1940 that it was likely that the Nazis had a fifth column of aliens, fascists, communists and pacifists in place ready to support them in the event of an invasion.[62] On 10 May, after a rapidly convened conference involving MI5, the War Office and the Home Office, the Home Secretary authorized the internment of all male enemy aliens in the east and south-east coastal area from Nairn to Hampshire, and all other aliens who stayed were made to report daily to the police. This draconian action appears to have been influenced not only by the collaborationist activities of Vidkun Quisling's Nasjonal Samling in Norway, which attempted to seize power following the Nazi invasion, but also by an anonymous letter, allegedly from a recent German refugee, who warned of an imminent airborne invasion and sabotage attacks in the south-east; a fortnight later the authorities recognized the handwriting as belonging to a British subject with a criminal record.

Having been forced by events to give in to security pressures, the Home Office dug its heels in to prevent further erosion of civil liberties. On 11 May MI5 applied pressure for the detention of 500 leading members of the British Union and on 16 May produced a contingency plan for the detention of 39 leading members of the CPGB. The Home Secretary declined to take action.[63] However, the invasion of Holland, and the fifth column scare orchestrated by the *Daily Mail* and bolstered by the Dutch royal family's information about the Nazi invasion, produced further pressure. Sir Neville Bland, the British Ambassador at the Hague, informed the Foreign Office that, given what had happened in Holland, even 'the paltriest [German] kitchen maid' was a danger to the British state, that all enemy aliens should be interned and that all police should be armed. Following a Cabinet meeting of 15 May the Home Office issued instructions for the internment of all remaining male enemy aliens in Category B; a committee was also set up to see what further measures were necessary. A memorandum was circulated on 17 May outlining the steps already taken. It also argued that further restrictions were unnecessary at this time; the internment of 64,000 enemy aliens in Category C would be popular, but there would soon be a reaction against it; indeed, there was no evidence of fifth column activity in Britain and, rather, that most of the enemy aliens were refugees from Nazism, and there was no indication that members of the BUF would assist the enemy or that the CPGB had been instructed to take action to aid a Nazi victory.[64] Strong objections were raised against this view in the War Cabinet but no immediate decisions were taken.

However, further pressure from the military, the advice of Chief Constables and the rapidly deteriorating military situation following the successful Nazi blitzkreig in France, led to another meeting between Sir John Anderson and MI5 on 21 May, where the Home Secretary still maintained his stand against further restrictions on civil liberties. It was at this point that the Tyler Kent affair was to tip the precarious balance, and to set events in train which resulted in what Churchill was later to call the 'witchfinding' atmosphere which triggered the security revolution.

The Tyler Kent affair was a real breach of national security, and was uncovered by three agents working in the Right Club, Joan Miller, Marjorie Amor and Helene Louise de Munck.[65] During 1939 MI5 had become concerned about the activities of Maule Ramsay MP and his secret societies, the Nordic League and Right Club. His obsessional anti-Semitism, his group of admirers with known Nazi contacts and his links with the establishment and armed services set the alarm bells ringing in MI5, and close political surveillance was maintained. Although most of the material on Ramsay, the Right Club and the Tyler Kent affair is still classified, enough information has reached the public domain to judge its historical significance.

The Tyler Kent affair started with the interception of secret correspondence between Winston Churchill and President Roosevelt during the phoney war period.[66] Kent was a cypher clerk at the American embassy who kept copies of the material he coded. When Special Branch raided his flat on 20 May 1940 they allegedly discovered 1,929 photographs of items.[67] His isolationist sympathies led him to show copies of the correspondence to Anna Wolkoff, an anti-Semitic and anti-war member of the Right Club who had then passed photocopies to Ramsay.[68] MI5 were concerned because Wolkoff was known to have extensive connections through the Right Club, the Russian tea rooms owned by her father, and other social contacts, which included being a dressmaker for the Duchess of Windsor.[69] The authorities also discovered the 'Red book', the secret list of 241 members of the Right Club in the possession of Kent, given to him for safe keeping by Ramsay. It is interesting to note that apart from the coterie of active members who associated with Anna Wolkoff, few members of the Right Club were interned. A Home Office minute argued that it would be wrong to publish the names of the members because many of them were 'simple minded' people who were unaware of the activities of the leaders. No doubt these included several members of parliament and peers of the realm named in the Red book. Another minute suggested that mere entry of a name in a book was not evidence of membership.[70] It is interesting to note that 'simple minded' members of the BUF, none of whose leaders was ever charged with a serious offence, were not given the benefit of such doubts when it came to the internment of hundreds associated with the movement.

Some of this material was alleged to have found its way to the Nazis via the Italian embassy as a result of Wolkoff's meetings with the Count del Monte. It appears that she may have been set up, by being provided with some innocuous information (which involved an MI5 agent) to send to William Joyce. Wolkoff was suspected of providing the Germans with details of the Allied plan to capture Narvik, in preparation for cutting off German iron ore supplies from northern Sweden. Whether this made Wolkoff a dangerous Nazi agent, or implies she was compromised in an *agent provocateur* operation manipulated by Maxwell Knight, was not clear. It does seem, however, that she was made a scapegoat, or carried the can, for the security leaks within the establishment in 1940. There appear to be at least two other claims about how the Germans discovered in advance the details of the Narvik operation, apart from the coincidence explanation of simultaneous invasion.[71] The evidence on Wolkoff's guilt is a little obscure, as it appears she was convicted on technical issues. Mrs Tyler Kent apparently sent many letters to the British authorities which alleged various misdeeds by Wolkoff at the expense of her son. However Tyler Kent's recollections of the contents of the Roosevelt–Churchill telegrams appears not to be wholly reliable, and such claims have to be viewed with some scepticism.

The discovery of a breach of security added fuel to the security mania that was enveloping Whitehall. The security service now used its influence to demand action against the possibility that a conspiracy was being hatched under German influence. Whilst the evidence for this was farfetched, the actions of Hitler and the Nazis gave credence to the belief that that indeed was what they hoped was happening.

German Foreign Office documents from the autumn of 1939 suggest that a possible 'fronde' against the war was being formed around the Duke of Windsor.[72] He supported the idea of a compromise peace, was annoyed by the relatively junior post offered him in the war and was angered by the refusal of the establishment to grant a royal title to his wife. Both the Duke and Duchess of Windsor were considered to be pro-Nazi, resentful and indiscreet. Although there is no evidence to suggest that Windsor acted improperly, either during the Abdication Crisis in 1936 or in 1940, the authorities were right to be alarmed. Churchill had to use leverage to get Windsor out of Europe, even going so far as to send Sir Walter Monckton to Portugal to persuade him to go to the Bahamas. After the Nazi blitzkrieg on western Europe, it was imperative that Windsor should be out of harm's way. This included keeping him out of Britain.

It is with this background that the MI5 reports of fascist secret meetings and the Tyler Kent affair struck a responsive nerve in government. Whilst there is no evidence of connection between high politics and suggested low politics intrigue, rumour and innuendo in the crisis of spring 1940 made it sound eminently plausible. The 'most secret' Cabinet minute on the Tyler Kent affair makes it quite clear that Ramsay and Mosley were supposedly 'in relations', and this became one of the reasons behind the decision for the internment of individuals from across the fascist fringe, not just the Right Club.[73] The fear of sabotage and the threat of a fifth column of fascists, communists and aliens, and the public order concerns of needing to protect fascists from public opinion, may have necessitated internment, but the authorities were equally concerned about security links.

Indeed, 22 May 1940, when the Cabinet decided to arrest Ramsay and to intern Mosley and 25 leading fascists, saw the victory of the security hawks.[74] On the same day the Defence Regulations were amended to allow for the internment of fascists under DR 18b(1a), to enable state direction of labour and, under DR 58a, to give the authorities powers to suppress organizations which had associations with the enemy or were under foreign influence or control.[75] In effect, powers were put in place which enabled the authorities to intern members of the BUF, or those guilty of the extremely vague accusation that they were capable of 'acts prejudicial' or had 'hostile associations'. This was clearly aimed at communists as well, as was Essential Works Order 1305, which outlawed strikes through the establishment of a compulsory arbitration service to resolve disputes.

What appears to have been behind government action was the fear of the emergence of a fifth column, orchestrated by Joyce's propaganda beamed from Europe. There was also the fear of a possible coup to replace George VI by the Duke of Windsor, and leading to the establishment of a peace government perhaps under his leadership, with Lloyd George or possibly Sir Samuel Hoare acting as peacemakers.

Alternatively, there was a scenario envisaged according to which after a successful invasion Hitler would put Windsor back on the throne with Lloyd George or Mosley as his Prime Minister. One suggestion was that Mosley would be gauleiter of England and Ramsay of Scotland. Indeed Ramsay had allegedly said at his Advisory Committee hearing that 'Scotland' had been offered to him by Mosley, 'in certain circumstances'.[76] There is little evidence for any of this, but these appear to be the most plausible rumours which undoubtedly influenced government in 1940. It should be emphasized that all those concerned have vehemently denied any illegal or dubious activity and have argued that all their actions were motivated by patriotic concerns. Mosley stated that he would rather die fighting for his country than be a quisling, and that he would have been killed by the security service if Britain had been invaded.[77] Certainly the mass internment of fascists, their interrogation under the direction of Maxwell Knight, and the appearance of most of them before the Advisory Commission on Internment, appear to have shed remarkably little light on these rumours. Nobody was ever charged with offences connected with such activity. This leads one to the conclusion that such ideas represented feverish fantasies of Nazi plans rather than the emergence of a significant, coherent peace movement in Britain, and that this latter possibility was prevented by the precipitate actions of the security authorities.

c) The Security Revolution

The pressures being placed on the new government by the threat of invasion, the fifth column scare, the Tyler Kent affair and alleged leakages of information to the enemy, led to the security revolution and the formation of the Home Defence Executive and the Home Defence (Security) Executive (HD(S)E), on 28 May. The HD(S)E was a coordinating body, which despite its name had no executive powers, and was designed to iron out duplication between the various intelligence and security bodies and prevent overlapping with regard to domestic surveillance. Its remit included espionage, sabotage, subversive activities, censorship and the internment and other restriction of aliens. Its name was shortened to Security Executive (SE) in October 1941 to prevent confusion.

The creation of the HD(S)E led directly to the reorganization of MI5 after the enforced retirement of Kell and his deputy, Holt-Wilson, on 11 June 1940. Under the direction of the new head of the HD(S)E, the first Earl of Swinton (Sir Philip Cunliffe Lister), there was an extensive overhaul of its administration and function. After much argument and debate over several months it was decided that MI5 was to retain its independence under the almost nominal responsibility of the Home Office, with a new Director-General, Sir David Petrie, a retired Indian Police officer. After some acrimony Swinton forced the overburdened B division to divest some of its work to two new divisions to cover aliens control and subversion under Deputy Directors; F division was in future to monitor the activity of British fascists and communists. Whilst Swinton's role in reorganization was to be resisted strongly and was far from smooth, he was to prove a powerful influence in maintaining the independence of MI5.[78]

The establishment of new executive institutional quangos and the higher profiles of the military and MI5 in security policy created increased tension between politicians and the security authorities. The first major problem arose over the key appointment of Commander in Chief (Home Forces) in 1940. Churchill wanted Lord Trenchard to come out of retirement but was dismayed by the dictatorial powers he would insist on accumulating if appointed; changing his mind, he was relieved that Ironside volunteered for the post instead.[79] However, Ironside quickly fell foul of both security objections and a renewed civil liberties clamour which seriously embarrassed Sir John Anderson, the Home Secretary. Ironside became the victim of a 'whispering campaign', and he went three months after appointment.[80] The military obsession with security had led Ironside to suggest that aerodromes were being prepared for the German invasion.[81] Major-General Liardet, in charge of defensive preparations in Kent, even went so far as to suggest that there were large numbers of disloyal British subjects in his area who should be moved out of the county and the aliens restriction zone.[82]

It was understandable that Labour suspicions of 'brass hats' should be aroused by such beliefs, and be worried about the almost unlimited powers that were planned for military regional commissioners in the event of an invasion. Churchill, too, although a security hawk, never wavered in his belief that military force should always be subordinate to political power. Fortunately, Sir Alan Brooke, Ironside's successor, organized the necessary military and security preparations with the minimum of political fuss, and had no pretensions to become a military Mussolini. The Home Defence Executive and its military districts worked efficiently.

The unclear division of powers between political and military supervision of national defence was to lead to an on going battle between the Home Office, the SE and MI5 for control over the management of internal security and political extremism in Britain during the war. Indeed, it can be argued that the state itself was guilty of political extremism in its flagrant breach of the civil liberties of some British citizens and other minorities. Mass internment under the Royal Prerogative, of 22,000 German and Austrian aliens, and 4,000 Italians in the summer of 1940, the vast majority of whom were anti-fascist, comes under this category. Many refugees who had come to Britain to escape Nazi persecution were also interned, as were some neutrals under Article 12(5A) of the Aliens Order of 1920 (as amended in 1940).

Whilst causing much hardship, such draconian measures did check Nazi infiltration.

In spite of the intense pressures and dire military situation the Home Office resisted internment for as long as practical, and almost immediately began to argue for the release of the majority of internees once the threat of invasion receded after September 1940. It was not until 21 June, four days after the French sued for an armistice, that the Home Office agreed to the internment of all enemy aliens as fast as accommodation could be provided.[83] The decision to intern 747 British fascists without charge or trial, all of whom were British citizens, represented a significant departure from legal precedent and the norms of British justice. Although the majority of these and many of the aliens were released later in 1940 or in 1941, several hundred were to be released at varying times between 1942 and 1944, and 15 were not released until April 1945. None were ever charged with having committed an offence, and as such they could not be pardoned or receive compensation. Several died as a consequence of incarceration, more suffered temporary or permanent health problems, and all were smeared as potential traitors, through a supposed guilt by association, as having been members of fascist associations, in most cases the BUF.[84] In July 1940 the BUF was closed down by the authorities and was never to be revived. Of the nearly 2,000 individuals interned under DR 18(b) nearly half were associated with British fascist organizations, and the vast majority of the rest were presumed to be in sympathy with, or to support, the enemy. Interestingly, few communists were interned during the war, despite the concern felt by the authorites about the activities of the CPGB. The best defence of government policy was that it was far more liberal than in France, which had interned fascists and banned communists in 1939, and the Home Office strenuously resisted the security hawks until overwhelmed by events in May and June 1940.

Perhaps the most interesting problem for the historian is to explain why aliens and fascists were interned but communists remained at liberty. The argument that national or assumed ideological similarity would, from the authorities' standpoint, make them disposed to detain those with a presumed sympathy with the enemy, ignores the fact that the communists openly opposed the war to a much greater degree than fascist or alien organizations. Whilst public opinion and the security authorities directed attention to a preventive move against the organization of non-existent fifth column activities, the increasingly critical communist propaganda was treated with more circumspection.

Indeed, on 21 May 1940, the day before Mosley was interned, a Home Office memorandum by A. S. Hutchinson admitted that there was more of a case to ban the communist *Daily Worker* than the fascist *Action*, as the anti-war message of the former was far more blatant. He argued that both nevertheless should be closed, as the lack of explicit objections to *Action* did not alter the fact that there was an implicit anti-war hidden agenda in the British Union's propaganda. Unfortunately, the crisis situation meant the 'leisurely procedure' of warning the newspapers under DR 2C was no longer appropriate, and so a more severe power was introduced, DR 2D, which allowed the authorities to seize printing presses.[85] Although *Action* was soon closed down, even though the *Daily Worker* became less critical for a time, it was still more hostile to the authorities than the fascist press had ever been.

It survived until the authorities closed it down in January 1941 following its campaign for the replacement of Churchill's Cabinet by a 'People's Government' that would represent working class interests and demand peace. The victory of such a government would give German workers the incentive to rise up against Hitler and demand similar reforms in Germany. Perhaps not surprisingly the authorities viewed this as a remote possibility and somewhat naive. From their perspective this was crude defeatist propaganda which served the interests of Moscow rather than Britain, and such material had to be stopped immediately.

There were in fact several reasons why communists were treated differently from fascists. To begin with, communists were more strategically placed to create a nuisance if their rights were infringed. Their conspicuous role in the trade unions, and in the re-emergence of an important shop stewards movement in the engineering industry during the 1930s, meant their influence in the crucial aeroplane manufacturing centres had to be taken into account.[86] Whereas fascists became increasingly unpopular in 1939–40, the ability of communists to latch on to and foment popular grievances – such as insufficient and ineffective air-raid precautions, the spotter system in factories, rationing and demands for the rich to pay for the cost of the war – meant the authorities had to be careful about precipitate action. Whilst the communist U-turn over support for the war in September 1939 lost them credibility, and public opinion saw the invasion of Finland by the Soviet Union as a cynical and hostile move, the authorities feared that any precipitate move against the CPGB could create problems with the labour movement, particularly in vital war production industries.

The state also knew from the flow of information from the various intelligence bodies monitoring public opinion that although the CPGB's propaganda was playing on popular grievances it was having little effect. Whilst people were worried about safety precautions, public opinion was often hostile to the CPGB's attempts to create resentment; hence the ejection of a Hackney communist from a shelter when he tried to address the occupants in September 1940. Whilst the CPGB certainly used popular grievances to foment discontent, as in their campaigns in the Tilbury shelter in Stepney, and amongst Chiswick housewives, the authorities were well aware that Ministry of Home Security intelligence reports were telling them that criticism represented real popular grievance rather than propaganda manufactured by extremists.[87] From its own members in the rapidly growing government bureaucracy – and, from late 1940, information from the Soviet agent, Anthony Blunt in MI5 – the CPGB often knew in advance the changing mood of the authorities to their actions. Hence a complex cat and mouse game developed before June 1941; with the authorities prepared to act if necessary against the CPGB if they overstepped the mark, but preferring not to do so, whilst the communists gingerly probed the boundaries of acceptable criticism at any given moment of time. After the Nazi invasion of the Soviet Union the situation subtly altered, even if the traditional suspicions remained unchanged: yesterday's suspected enemy ugly duckling now became an unwanted and embarrassing swan whose Soviet super-patriotism made an uncomfortable ally for the government, and was to remain unacknowledged as far as possible.

The reluctance of the state to alter its traditional hostility to the CPGB was reinforced by the more critical attitude adopted by the communists between June 1940 and the invasion of the Soviet Union. Following the fall of France the party risked the suppression of the *Daily Worker* and the arrest of its leading members by proceeding with a concerted propaganda campaign for a 'People's Government', the arming of the workers, the conscription of wealth and the establishment of an alliance with the Soviet Union. After a discussion in Cabinet in July 1940, the government decided to suppress a pamphlet, *The People Must Act*, to warn the *Daily Worker* that it would be closed down if it continued its irresponsible criticism, and to remit the problem to the Security Executive.[88]

The HD(S)E concluded that the danger from CPGB activity was not acute in July 1940 and that repressive measures risked dividing public opinion. MI5 now began to argue that it was necessary to make a clear distinction between fascists and communists; the former were interned because they might directly aid the enemy, whilst the CPGB concentrated on propaganda, and showed no sign of assistance to the enemy if there was an invasion. However, the HD(S)E was concerned about the effects of communist propaganda and suggested a new defence regulation which would make it an offence to subvert duly constituted authority. This was vigorously opposed by the Home Office and the Law Officers, who argued that it would undermine fundamental English liberties, would be strongly resisted in parliament and would bring duly constituted authority into disrepute.[89] The proposal was dropped, although the boundary between criticism and subversion proved problematic in the continuing monitoring of the CPGB by the authorities.

Whilst 750 fascists had been interned, and the British Union itself proscribed on 10 July 1940, by DR 18b (AA), few communists were detained under the defence regulations. Two leading members in South Wales, T. E. Nicholas, and his son Islwyn, were interned between July and October 1940 for acts prejudicial to the public safety and the defence of the realm. It was alleged that they tried to impede recruitment to the armed forces. They were released after pressure from the South Wales Miners Federation and the NCCL.

John Mason, a Sheffield shop steward, was interned following a decision taken after consultation between MI5 and the Ministry of Labour, who deemed that he had been concerned in 'acts prejudicial'. After an appeal to the Advisory Committee, continued detention was recommended. The Amalgamated Engineering Union, the CPGB and the National Council for Civil Liberties protested vigorously, but a meeting at the Home Office failed to persuade the authorities that Mason could be released. Only after William Gallagher, the communist MP, had given assurances to the Home Office that Mason would not engage in future with activities that would impede the war effort, and that the CPGB would not exploit his release, was the case referred back to the Advisory Committee, and he was released on 7 June 1941. The case highlighted the authorities' determination to warn the CPGB that they would not tolerate any attempt to hinder war production.[90]

It also acted as a warning that there were strict limits that the state would accept in terms of criticism of duly constituted authority. Hence the continued probing of the boundaries in the CPGB's struggle against the state. In September 1940, the Home Office worried about a CPGB air raid precaution pamphlet, *You have taken things into your own hands,* and a poster *They need not have died.* The Home Secretary's immediate response, in a handwritten minute, was 'This conspiracy must be met with the most resolute action. All the resources of the law are to be used.'[91] His anger was directed at the criticism of the state air raid precautions, the inadequacy of the Anderson shelter to protect workers, and its advocacy of civil disobedience through encouraging mass occupation of the underground in London, if the authorities would not provide the safer, and more expensive, Haldane shelter. The accompanying Special Branch report which outlined how the pamphlets were seized provided an interesting example of the cloak and dagger mentality which determined attitudes on both sides at this time.

The raid on the London District Committee of the CPGB's printing works on 19 September 1940 led to the battering down of a locked door, the putting out of a fire where communists were burning leaflets, the prevention by a police officer of Alfred Grandjean flushing a notebook down the toilet, and the prevention of Edward Bramley surreptitiously passing a note to Mary Stanton asking her to hide a list of the leaders of communist cells in factories and the professions to whom the pamphlets were to be sent.[92] The details of the raid were sent to the Director of Public Prosecutions, the Attorney-General and the Home Secretary, who decided it would not be advisable to prosecute under the Defence Regulations.

Consideration was given to interning Bramley and Pat Devine, or the whole District Committee, or the editorial Board of the *Daily Worker*, but this was considered not advisable.[93] The Law Officers, with the lawyers' cell of the CPGB in mind, thought that much of the criticism could be seen as a matter of opinion rather than an error of fact, and that a skilful lawyer could put up a strong defence which might embarrass the government.[94]

Further consideration was given to interning Ted Bramley in December 1940, as a result of his inflammatory speeches in support of the People's Convention. The Home Office strongly advised the Home Secretary that DR 18b was not designed to restrict freedom of speech, and that providing it did not lead to acts prejudicial, there would be parliamentary opposition to such a move.[95] More thought was also given to interning communists by the Cabinet Committee on Communist Activities established in January 1941. But it was decided that this action might produce industrial disruption, by driving the CPGB underground, and be counterproductive in the long run. The closing down of the *Daily Worker* in January 1941 had greatly weakened its ability to transmit its propaganda.[96]

This was sound advice, for the Convention movement was an attempt to keep radical criticism of government social policy at the forefront of public attention, although it did not directly attack the war. The People's Convention was an attempt to continue the Popular Front in wartime conditions. Although the failure to develop alliances with groups not immediately under communist influence or control weakened its appeal; and a mixture of firm state and Labour Party hostility towards it, and timorous leadership from the CPGB, meant it remained on the fringe of political life in 1941.

Much to the annoyance of Palme Dutt, the CPGB transferred all its propaganda activities to the campaign for a second front, and to Anglo-Soviet committees after the Nazi invasion of Russia. After the People's Convention and the closing down of the *Daily Worker*, the CPGB was busy making arrangements to go underground if necessary. Whilst Ernest Bevin favoured internment of communist intellectuals, the prevailing view was that more restrictions on freedom of speech smacked of Gestapo methods. Swinton's argument, despite disagreement in the SE, that fascists would have left British Union if it had been declared illegal before members had been interned, represented an additional reason why the authorities failed to act; fascists were more secretive in their actions than communists, and many ordinary members of the CPGB, like those in the British Union, were patriotic.[97]

d) Internment

The decision to intern enemy aliens and fascists in response to a fifth column scare created a greater departure from the principles of British law than in the First World War. Whilst it took a much greater crisis to put such illiberal legislation in place, DR 18(b) was used for preventive purposes rather than as a response to actual disturbances. In the First World War internment of British citizens was used mainly as a response to rebellion and civil disobedience in Ireland. Denying British fascists and others their basic civil rights was an option followed by the authorities which was popular with public opinion, and as events would also prove to be sanctioned by the law, the machinery evolved to process the administration of internment represented a delicate balance between security, administrative convenience and individual liberty.[98] Under the emergencey regulations all internees were given the right of appeal to an Advisory committee.[99] This had been set up by the Defence Regulations on the model of the First World War experience, and its function was to advise the Home Secretary on detention or other restrictions on individuals under DR 18(b), and the internment and repatriation of enemy aliens under the Royal Prerogative (until June 7 1940).

The first chairman of the committee, Sir Walter Monckton, was almost immediately replaced by Norman Birkett KC. With mass internment of fascists, four separate tribunals were used to deal with the large number of appeals, whose results often took six months to process. At the first meeting on 21 September 1939 it was decided that appellants should present their appeals in person and not be legally represented. After the committee reviewed the case, it passed its recommendation regarding the detainee to MI5, who then sent their comments with the report to the Home Secretary. He was responsible for taking the final decision on whether the detention order should be extended.

The released material on the Advisory Committee shows quite clearly that the government was determined to maximize the degree of criticism permissible under wartime conditions whilst granting itself the necessary powers to impose a security blanket if a crisis occurred. The fact that only 12 aliens and native British subjects were interned before the revision of DR 18b on 23 November 1939 suggests that the government was reluctant to use its powers.[100]

Before the acceleration of internment in March 1940, British fascists were not harassed by the authorities. Although the Crowl/Duvivier case and the internment of Edward Whinfield led to a Special Branch raid on BUF headquarters, the authorities failed to show that either of them was acting under the orders of Mosley.[101] The former were expelled from the BUF after being found guilty of attempting to send naval information to the Germans, and the latter was held after a visit to Switzerland. The direct evidence of illegal activity at this time was very thin. Hinsley and Simkins list only ten minor infringements of the Defence Regulations by sometime members of the British Union of Fascists during the war.[102]

Fascists claim that internment was carried out indiscriminately after 22 May 1940, and insofar as there were suspect persons in the organization the wrong people were arrested. A police source who attended MI5 conferences in London claimed the arrests were uniform.[103] However, during the autumn of 1940 over 60 per cent of the DR 18b internees were released, and the often appalling conditions suffered in Brixton, Stafford and Liverpool gaols, and the two internment camps at Ascot and York, rapidly improved. Those who remained interned were then moved to a council housing estate in Huyton, Lancashire, before the bulk of them were transferred to the Isle of Man. Here they settled in two sexually segregated camps. The rapid diminution of the number of internees corresponded to declining security problems and administrative concerns. Plans to ship many of the detainees to the Empire were scuppered, not only by the *Arandora Star* disaster (when Italian internees were drowned after being sunk by a U-boat submarine during removal to Canada), but also by the law officers, who declared that the government had neither the authority to ship British subjects overseas against their will and without trial, nor power of jurisdiction over an internee once he had landed on the shore of a self-governing Dominion.

By mid-1941, over 500 of the remaining 671 DR 18b internees were in the Isle of Man camps. Of the remainder, 44, including Sir Oswald Mosley and the other leaders of the BUF, were in Brixton prison, and 24 women were in Holloway. Some 18 of the Isle of Man internees were later sent to Walton gaol for disciplinary reasons after a riot following the recapture of escaped internees.[104] The leadership were not sent to the Isle of Man because the authorities felt it could strengthen the detainees' fascist attitudes.[105] During 1943 and 1944 many of the more serious cases, as they were termed – including Mosley, Domvile, Ramsay, John Beckett and Mrs Nicholson – were released.[106] Worries about the deteriorating health of some of the internees appear to have been the most important factor in these decisions. The authorities were particularly concerned that political prisoners should not become martyrs. At least two DR 18b internees attempted hunger strikes, but forced feeding or the threat of it ended the problem.[107]

Political considerations were also important in the decision to continue detention or to release the most important detainees after 1940. Fascists complained that the Advisory Committee was little more than a public relations exercise whose legal basis was extremely dubious. The Committee accepted evidence from MI5 without evaluating the sources, failed to allow for legal representation of the accused and recommended continued internment for individuals even though no evidence had been produced that any crime had been committed. The legal procedure of the Advisory Committee was doubtful and more ritualistic than judicial. The cosy nature of the Mosley hearing, for example, was demonstrated by the agreement of Birkett and Mosley in naming William Joyce as Lord Haw-Haw even though doubts have since been expressed about his identity, although Joyce was undoubtedly the organizer of enemy propaganda beamed at Britain.[108]

No attempt was made to question Mosley about possible British Union involvement in the New British Broadcasting Service (NBBS) propaganda, and the Advisory Committee failed to question the political judgement of Mosley and his wife in negotiating with Hitler to build a wireless transmitter when diplomatic relations between Britain and Germany were deteriorating so rapidly after March 1939. Moreover, the Advisory Committee learned in advance the nature of Mosley's defence from a 'very secret and delicate source'.[109] This suggested that Mosley's cell had been bugged by MI5. The fact that the Advisory Committee accepted secret information from what was in fact the prosecution, made the irregular legal basis of the interrogation even more suspect.

The large number of retained personal files of DR 18b internees suggests that the Advisory Committee was told about delicate intelligence operations orchestrated by MI5. Mosley also complained about dubious treatment meted out to fascists at the Latchmere House interrogation centre on Ham Common, in August and September 1940.[110] These complaints were later expanded by Raven Thomson, J. L. Battersby and others after the war.[111] The allegations included the use of hidden microphones, 'Gestapo' techniques of psychological warfare and a semi-starvation regime. One internee, Charlie Watts, purportedly responded by telling the tribunal, 'Hail Mosley, **** 'em all'.[112] At the end of a gruelling five-week ordeal Raven Thomson had lost two stones in weight.

The complaints of the internees and the failure to charge any of them with a serious crime suggest that despite intimidation and penetrating surveillance since 1934 little of substance could be found to incriminate either individual members or the official leadership of the organization. Indeed, it appears that the surveillants were at least as guilty of dubious behaviour as those under surveillance. As well as the use of *agents provocateurs,* stool pigeons in internment camps, intimidation and microphones, there was also evidence of intercepted mail in an MI5 report on the Imperial Fascist League.[113]

The released minutes of the Home Defence (Security) Executive conference from 15 October, 31 October and 6 November 1940 suggest that the internment of British fascists led to a significant battle for the control of security which was used by the Home Office to maintain civilian oversight over the procedures. The opportunity arose from the disagreement between MI5 and the Advisory Committee over 111 of the 317 cases which had then been heard. Although MI5 had dropped their objections with relation to 96 of these after a conference, they were not prepared to drop their objections to the release of the other 15.[114] A Home Office minute stated that it had been agreed, with MI5 dissenting, that subject to special circumstances the Home Secretary should be advised to accept the recommendations of the Advisory Committee, that the armed services should have the right to refuse the employment of ex-internees, that all those released should not engage in political activities during the war and that in special cases orders imposing restrictions on individuals should be invoked.[115]

This represented a significant victory for the Home Office and an advance of its political control of national security. With the defeat in Cabinet of Sir John Anderson's reluctance to impose blanket internment measures on aliens and fascists, the insistence by the Advisory Committee that as many internees should be released as quickly as possible and that MI5 should have no effective veto on who was released, quickly restored Home Office control. Thus the backwash of the fifth column scare and the Tyler Kent case were minimized. Sir John Anderson and Herbert Morrison, the two Home Secretaries concerned, accepted 400 of the 455 recommendations for release by the Advisory Committee, 87 per cent of the total, by February 1941.[116] The Cabinet accepted that there would be problems in parliament if most of the conclusions of the Advisory Committee were not accepted.

The significance of this victory for the more liberal view of the Home Office was reinforced by the evidence that in war time conditions the case law, based on the important *Liversidge* v. *Anderson* (3 November 1942) upheld the suspension of habeas corpus and enabled the Home Secretary, acting on the advice of the relevant authorities, to intern those who, in good faith, were seen as dangerous to the security of the realm. This emphasized the importance of the Advisory Committee, who were sometimes unimpressed with evidence used to justify internment, and acted as a buffer between MI5 and continued detention. The case of Ben Greene illustrated that MI5 sometimes cut corners to obtain conviction, when its agent Harald Kurtz was proved to have given false evidence.[117] Evidence from Kurtz was also viewed as suspect by Morrison when reviewing the case of John Beckett in 1942.[118] The infiltration by the authorities of the new religion of the obviously mentally ill Thomas St Barbe Baker in the Isle of Man internment camp was another example of security going over the top.[119] In this bizarre cult, where a few fellow internees were converted, Hitler was viewed as God and Baker's son was deemed to possess miraculous powers.

Whilst fascists viewed the independence of the Advisory Committee with some scepticism, others could point to its valiant battle to limit the damage inflicted on civil liberties and the rule of law in the grave national emergency of 1940, and stand up to MI5 pressures. Certainly proscription and internment were an ironic fate for members of a political party which had announced that it would silence all organized opposition to itself if it ever gained power, and that it would have set up similar bodies to decide whether Jews were patriotic Englishmen or not.[120] Internment was 'in the highest degree odious', particularly as most of its victims – aliens, fascists and other Britains deemed pro-Nazi – were never compensated, and some suffered permanently from physical illness or mental traumas induced by the experience. In some cases there were alleged suicides.[121] Although the fifth column crisis made the paranoia of the authorities understandable, and the state provided checks and balances to ensure that internment was managed as humanely as possible, its necessity still leaves a nasty taste in the mouth.

e) Stealing the Thunder of the Left

After the Nazi invasion of the Soviet Union in June 1941 the state became increasingly concerned about the domestic implications of favourable public opinion to the new alliance with communist Russia. Whilst internment and proscription made the BUF (or British Union, as it had been called since 1937) as extinct as the dodo, the 'favourable reference to the devil' in 1941 became 'the sword of Honour' in 1942, as British public opinion rallied to the resistance of the Soviets at Stalingrad and began to demand a second front to give tangible aid to our valiant comrades in the fight against Nazism. This was reflected in government by the more favourable view of Soviet Russia taken by Sir Alexander Cadogan and the Foreign Office, and was bolstered by the signing of the ten-year Anglo-Soviet treaty in 1942. Although R. A. Butler, as the junior minister in July 1940, was one of the leading appeasers, his belief that the Home Office had 'misinterpreted' the attitude of the CPGB by turning them into 'pariah dogs' in 1940–1 found greater political support.[122] The domestic implication of this was a new lease of life for the CPGB. This prompted the security service to exhibit great concern with reference to the activities of British communists, as they remained unconvinced that the revolutionary agenda of either the Soviet Union or CPGB had changed.

The problem was no longer defeatism or anti-war propaganda but their opposite. The CPGB, almost overnight, suddenly became more anti-Nazi than Churchill, and their unconditional support for total victory and the interests of the Soviet Union was unimpeachable. Yet MI5 had a long memory and assumed that neither the Russian Bear nor the CPGB had blunted their claws; even after the Comintern had been closed down in 1943, few in government outside the Foreign Office, and even fewer in the secret state, thought the communist ideology had fundamentally changed; the old revolutionary agenda was still seen as the ultimate aim both of the Soviets and the CPGB.

There are still doubts about the exact size of CPGB membership in 1941, with both MI5 sources and the official published statistics suggesting a fall before June, but recent academic interpretations argue strongly for a recovery in the period before the Nazi invasion of the Soviet Union. The evidence for the rest of the war suggested rapid growth which slowly declined after 1942.[123] The membership figures rose from 15,000 in June 1941 to 23,000 by December. Between January and March 1942 numbers more than doubled and had risen to 64,000 by the end of 1942. In April 1942 there were estimated to be more than 1,000 factory groups. Although membership figures fell to 50,000 in 1943 and never reached the 1942 figure again during the war, the concern of the authorities was shown by the increased political surveillance of communist activities. These figures need to be contrasted with the decline in individual membership of the Labour Party as a result of the electoral truce during the war: from 400,000 in 1939 to 219,000 in 1942.

The concern of the authorities was demonstrated by the circulation in Cabinet of a MI5 report sent by the SE in October 1941, soon after the German invasion of the Soviet Union. This underscored that both the CPGB and the Soviets had not changed their objectives (namely, a revolutionary takeover of power), merely that the necessity of the anti-Hitler alliance had forced the communists to revert to the tactics of the popular front rather than class against class. Particular emphasis was placed on the build up of a communist shop stewards' movement whose aim was 'dual power' and rank and file undermining of the official trade union leadership. What is interesting about this document, apart from the monotonous revolutionary line taken by MI5, is that it fails to see that the revolutionary pragmatism of the rapidly reinstated Harry Pollitt and Johnny Campbell in the CPGB made trade union loyalty a higher priority than the now discredited revolutionary defeatist line, and that the establishment of Joint Production Committees was to be first and foremost a contribution to winning the war rather than the instrument for establishing workers' control.[124]

Whilst the SE papers are not due for release until 1996, it is known that a special Committee on Communism was established under Alfred Wall, the trade union representative on the executive, which met weekly for much of 1941 and fortnightly thereafter until the end of the war. In 1943, the Cabinet regretfully decided not to publish two MI5 reports which the Home Secretary brought to Cabinet on the activities of the CPGB and the British Union during the war. Whilst MI5 wished to publish the minutes of the CPGB's political bureau in September 1939, and the evidence of continued educational subversion in the armed forces by communist educational tutors, both the Home and Foreign Offices thought this could unnecessarily aggravate relations with the Soviet Union. The Cabinet was also worried that Mosley might institute legal proceedings, and this could compromise some of the sources of such information.[125] The intention obviously was to influence the Labour Party to reject the renewed application of the CPGB to affiliate. The concern of the government that disclosure of such information should even be considered shows the extent of the authorities' fears.

Such views show that political considerations were dominant in the policy adopted toward the CPGB. The government were concerned that industrial production should not be threatened and that Labour politicians and right-wing trade union leaders should maintain both the political and moral leadership of organized labour. The SE was particularly concerned about the revival of CPGB attempts to affiliate to the Labour Party and the policy of infiltration they were practising. The SE were relieved when Home Office Intelligence reports suggested that the banning of the *Daily Worker* had led to a mainly disinterested reaction from public opinion, although the left vociferously objected. The authorities were concerned with distancing the Labour leadership from its left-wing adherents, and wished to do as little as possible to inflame trade union unrest. Swinton told the SE on 10 December 1941 that the government should do nothing to lessen the embarrassment of the CPGB as a result of strikes caused by Trotskyist organizations. Joint Production Committees (JPC) were seen as a useful method of harnessing the radical leadership of communist shopstewards – who, after June 1941, were enthusiastic supporters of the war effort – to the task of maximizing production and increased efficiency.[126] Whilst the CPGB had reorganized itself in industry, with the administrative emphasis on the old Bolshevik factory group as the main focus of its organization, to make it more difficult for the authorities to persecute its activities, greater participation in management decisions incorporated CPGB shop stewards in to the unaccustomed role of encouraging maximum output. The induced Stakhanovite mentality led communist shopstewards to criticize inefficient managements for production bottlenecks, and to blame Trotskyists for industrial unrest.

The authorities were well aware that communists were no longer the instigators or developers of industrial disputes; the harsh regulation 1AA, which forbade strikes, was to be used against Trotskyists instead. Following strikes in Barrow and growing discontent amongst engineering apprentice workers and women dilutees in 1944, three of the Trotskyist leaders were imprisoned, and after serving some of their sentence, released on appeal. The Department of Labour was well aware that Trotskyists did not cause strikes, but they fanned the flames once they had started. Trotskyists were prosecuted as scapegoats; a warning that the authorities were not going to tolerate industrial discontent in the closing stages of the war. Interestingly, they were charged under the defence regulations; the state was not going to risk sympathy action on behalf of radical socialists by interning them without trial. None the less, the state remained forever suspicious of communist intentions. The *New Propellor*, the organ of the communist shop stewards, despite the new line after June 1941, was not to be allowed more paper for printing in November 1941 because of its history of mischief making in British factories.

Class collaboration rather than class conflict was now the order of the day, but old habits died hard and capitalists still bore the brunt of CPGB criticism. Now Coventry shop stewards, who blamed big business and its war policy for the destruction of the city in November 1940 (in a pamphlet which did not mention the role of the Nazis in the decision to bomb Coventry), after June 1941 began to criticize management for inefficiency. This was supposedly caused by management's secret desire to come to a peace agreement with the enemy, leaving them free to destroy the Soviet Union.[127] With friends like this, the authorities' concern was to isolate the influence of the CPGB and to 'steal the thunder of the left'.[128]

This proved to be one of the chief functions of the Ministry of Information after June 1941. Regional Information Officers (RIOs) were to take over all independent attempts by the CPGB to start campaigns in support of Soviet Russia. This was tacitly approved by the Soviets, whose chief priority was the establishment of the second front, rather than establishing the influence of the CPGB. Whilst the 'all-in' Anglo-Soviet Committees created very peculiar anti-Nazi alliances of Conservatives, Liberals and Communists, and often forced the Labour Party to turn a blind eye to its policy of refusing to appear on the same platform as the CPGB, Home Intelligence reports were reassuring and not alarmist. The relative scarcity of reference to communism in the reports suggests that either security measures were effective in discouraging subversion, or not really necessary. Ordinary workers were often as cynical as the authorities with regard to the chameleon-like behaviour of the CPGB in the war. One report suggested that those seen as most vociferous for war production in the autumn of 1941 were those very people who did their best to slow down war production after the non-aggression pact in August 1939.[129]

Similarly the RIOs reported very mixed reactions to the communist demand to open a second front immediately in the west.[130] It appeared that the authorities' fears of the British worker being attracted to the native form of communism as a result of Soviet successes was not justified, despite the success of Harry Pollitt's oratory at mass meetings designed to put pressure on the government to institute a second front in Europe in 1942–3.

This was most clearly shown in the great surge of public hostility to Mosley's release in 1943. This event witnessed one of the great ironies of wartime politics. The left demanded infringement of civil liberties without due process, whilst the government valiantly defended its release of Mosley. Harold Nicholson and 38 others resigned from the NCCL on the grounds that they thought it illogical that such a body could support a belief that citizens could be kept in prison without trial.[131] The Transport and General Workers Union and the TUC argued that the release of Mosley would reduce civilian morale.[132]

At least 21 anti-Mosley meetings were reported to the authorities in London in the month following his release, most of them organized by the CPGB.[133] Initially the RIOs reported 'There could hardly have been more commotion if Hitler had been turned loose'.[134] A week later, however, the authorities argued that it was no more than a 'storm in a teacup'.[135] The communists, after protesting the release of Mosley, decided that winning the war was a higher priority than disrupting production in an attempt to reintern Mosley.

Even the influence of Browderism on the CPGB was interpreted in a cynical fashion by the authorities. In the United States the Communist Party dissolved itself and told members to work for the maintenance of a progressive coalition and a New Deal policy which would support continued US–Soviet cooperation after the war. Although the CPGB did not go to the same extreme lengths in an attempt to ingratiate itself with the authorities, it did press for a continuance of the wartime coalition and the maintenance of friendly relations with the USSR, thus providing the political space for the Labour Party to reap all the electoral benefits in 1945 from the public suspicion of the economic and social programme of the Conservatives. Slavish adherence to Stalin's interests once again was to rebound in 1945, when the CPGB failed to reap the benefits of its wartime role since 1941.

The smug cynicism of the state and security services towards British communism during the war we now know represented a great intelligence disaster. This arose from the basic prejudices and preconceptions about communism by the establishment. The state and security service were obsessed with the bogeyman of international revolution, the belief that the CPGB was the main source of Soviet espionage by British citizens. Because of the proletarian nature of the phenonemon, insufficient attention was given to the problem of infiltration within the upper classes and the higher echelons of government. This was both a political and a security error: the ingrained assumption across government was that although undergraduates at universities may for a time be influenced by communist and united front propaganda, when they came in contact with the real world they reverted to their social class loyalties and behaved like patriotic Englishmen.

Whilst MI5, with its old school tie recruiting methods up to 1939, was more aware of the problem than most within the state and cannot be held solely responsible for Soviet penetration, the exigencies of war led to a loosening of vetting procedures for applicants for state employment. Still influenced by the myth of the revolutionary Comintern, the security service failed to realize the extent of the sophistication of the Soviet NKVD and the GRU, or that the Stalinist agenda with its emphasis on 'socialism in one country' and the Soviet national interest had significantly altered communist priorities. One authority has compared the performance of Soviet intelligence and British counter-intelligence during the war as a contest between Manchester United and the Corinthian Casuals during the decline of amateurism.[136] This was not the entire story: British counter-intelligence proved itself as adept at deception as any Soviet operation with its use of the XX Committee to provide imaginary intelligence to the Nazis through controlled agents during the Second World War and the Ultra secret was never uncovered by the enemy.[137] On the other hand, the much higher priority given to anti-fascist operations meant that the defences against a new type of Soviet mole were lowered. That the most experienced counter-intelligence officer in MI5, Guy Liddell, should have been so friendly with Soviet spies such as Anthony Blunt and Guy Burgess during the Second World War, speaks volumes about the very serious failure of one aspect of British counter-intelligence.[138]

This was the basic error of the authorities. Whilst the security revolution of 1940 had effectively tightened the state's defences against Nazi subversion and the activities of the British Communist Party, it failed with the main thrust of the Soviet effort. The crushing of British fascism emasculated the putative peace policy of some establishment groups, but the large bureaucratic apparatus designed to monitor the activities of the CPGB missed the point entirely. Whilst it is quite clear that CPGB headquarters in King Street was infiltrated by MI5 agents, and that the Security Executive established a Committee on Communism which met more frequently than the main body, this merely reinforced the blinkered approach of the authorities.

These developments overlooked the fact that since at least the General Strike in 1926 the CPGB had not been at the forefront of the Soviet intelligence effort in Britain. MI5 were well aware of the subtlety of method and the resources of the NKVD but were unable to adjust their stereotyped view of the nature of Soviet operations in Britain. The authorities assumed that close surveillance and tightening up of security had forced the CPGB to become law abiding to prevent proscription, and that this had been accepted by the Comintern and their Soviet masters.

The war transformed the all-pervading obsession with communism. Now anti-Nazi operations became the dominant theme and the rapid expansion of both MI5 and MI6 opened the closed world of the secret services to new influences. Some of the best brains of British academe were grafted somewhat uneasily into the system to play the great game. Now the failure of imagination and resources in the 1930s came home to roost. The inadequate monitoring of communist influence in the universities now enabled the rapid Soviet infiltration of the secret world. Agents such as Blunt, Burgess, Philby, Maclean and Cairncross were to provide the Soviets with details of MI5, MI6 and Special Operations Executive (SOE) as well as crucial government policy decisions, including Cabinet minutes, especially from the Foreign Office but also those of the Security Executive – Donald Maclean was one of the Foreign Office representatives at the 15 October 1941 meeting.[139] Whilst a cautious interpretation of Soviet infiltration must be observed, as the Soviets appear to have disregarded both the leaks sent to them by the British government in June 1941, and unofficially by 'Stalin's Englishmen', nevertheless the political damage of illegally gained material was immense. There was a problem too at Moscow centre of interpretation; Stalin gave too much credence to the gossip transmitted from Philby about the significance of the bizarre flight of Rudolf Hess, the Nazi deputy leader, to Britain prior to the invasion of the Soviet Union, for example.

Espionage was of equal importance to political and intelligence subversion, and provided the Soviets with secret material including Ultra intercepts, Treasury documents outlining Britain's economic weakness, allied policy in the Far East, German troop movements on the Eastern Front, and information on atomic research in the USA. With Philby rising to head the anti-communist section of MI6, and Blunt and Burgess acting as leeches on Guy Liddell, the head of counter-intelligence in MI5, very grave damage was inflicted whose importance became manifest in the Cold War. Similarly, Soviet infiltration of the scientific community, and the use they made of secret and open exchanges of material, particularly with relation to espionage of the atomic bomb, was undetected until too late. MI5 also failed to appreciate the extent or importance of Soviet infiltration of the governments in exile in London.[140]

Such a catalogue of errors needs to be remembered when reading the official history of British counter-intelligence during the war – most of these problems are not even mentioned let alone assessed. Whilst useful information is given on the surveillance of the CPGB, and its espionage activities exposed (there is credible evidence which supports the jaundiced cold-war views of ex-communist Douglas Hyde),[141] a one-sided view of the performance of MI5 results.[141] It is of course a bonus to have the undoubted successes of most aspects of anti-Nazi counter-intelligence and deception operations given their due weight, but the inability to take the sins of omission properly into account means that official secrecy has reduced its historical value.

Earlier concern with and surveillance of communist influence at Cambridge and other universities lapsed. Even the security successes reinforced the traditional interpretation rather than uncovering new Soviet methods. The discovery of John King as a spy in the Foreign Office in 1939 strengthened existing stereotypes of the lower class origins of Soviet spies. The imprisonment of Douglas Frank (Dave) Springhall, national organizer of the CPGB, for obtaining details of the jet engine from an Air Ministry clerk, and Captain Ormond Uren for giving Springhall a description of SOE headquarters, appeared to confirm the key role of the party in Soviet British espionage.

As a direct result Springhall was expelled from the CPGB. It was decided that in future no prominent member should engage in spying activities and that the CPGB interview room in London, under the cover of the Workers' Musical Association, should be closed down, together with the organization which contacted the armed forces and the undercover groups amongst junior civil servants. News that secret work was being ended was disseminated throughout the party.[142] Whilst the Security Executive had recommended in 1942 that all new entrants to sensitive areas should be vetted, and that MI5 should advise on whether known communists could be used in secret work, the pressures of war meant that security considerations were often not properly applied.

The death sentence carried out on Thomas Armstrong for taking Comintern policy too literally during the Nazi–Soviet pact period, for giving details of British convoy movements in the north Atlantic to the enemy, also was interpreted within a rigid framework. Even the CPGB's expulsion of Tom Driberg, an MI5 double agent, after he was discovered by Blunt, failed to alert the authorities. Thus Stalin's disbanding of the Comintern in 1943 not only pleased Roosevelt and Churchill, and enabled the Soviets to close down a redundant institution, but also showed that new forms of political and industrial espionage were being operated by the soviets independent of old traditional networks.

7

THE COLD WAR (1945–1989)

After 1945 the official sources for a study such as this begin to dry up. What declassified information there is needs to be supplemented by other material in the public domain. This inevitably places a reliance on matters that the authorities are happy to inform us about, mainly the official viewpoint given in parliamentary papers and debates. Theoretically the 30-year rule should provide us with a reasonable number of Cabinet papers touching on internal security, public order and political extremism up until 1962; the practice has been but a small amount, perhaps accounted for by the languid 'You have never had it so good' complacency of the Conservative administrations of the 1950s. The almost total dearth of Home Office material has not helped. It remains to be seen how far the desire of John Major, the Prime Minister at the time of writing, for more open government will lead to more file releases relating to this area. The cautious approach of the authorities, and the continuing secrecy based on the importance in the government's eyes of the principle of confidentiality (with regard to the donation of funds to the Conservative Party, for example), suggests that with resource restraint and the time consuming and intricate process of declassification, progress will be slow.

To a considerable degree this attitude is understandable. Between 1945 and 1989 the Cold War had divided Europe into two armed camps based on ideological divisions between capitalist and communist systems. It was therefore not surprising that even given the collapse of communism in Europe between 1989 and 1991 (including the Communist Party of Great Britain (CPGB)), the realization that an alliance of Soviet and nationalist elements had developed in Russia, and perhaps in other areas of the Commonwealth of Independent States (CIS), together with the weak position of President Yeltsin and his reliance on the military to crush the attempted coup by the parliamentary opposition in the autumn of 1993, meant that the authorities would remain cautious. The fear that Balkanization could turn nationalist rivalries into shooting wars (as in former Yugoslavia), and the fact that some of the unstable states in the CIS possess nuclear weapons, increased the reluctance of the British authorities to pierce the mask of secrecy surrounding political surveillance and the management of political extremism, which for most of the period since 1945 centred on the CPGB and other Marxist groups. National security has much greater force as a plausible excuse for classifying files for post-1945 material than for information before the divide of the Second World War.

Similarly, the necessity of protecting sources of information and the security of intelligence personnel were also unanswerable arguments with regard to recent operations. Against that, the suspicion that justified worries about the lack of accountability of secret organs of government to parliamentary or independent scrutiny led to abuses of power persisted. This was both with regard to worries about civil liberties, doubtful behaviour on the part of elements in the security service, and the extension of political surveillance to pressure groups such as the Campaign for Nuclear Disarmament (CND) and has led to much continuing controversy over the role of the authorities in such areas. The Cold War was used as an important justification for such activities.

It is for these reasons that study of the impact of the Cold War must necessarily be truncated and will be less informative than previous chapters. Where there is a reasonable amount of material – on the transition from anti-fascist to anti-communist phobias, and the origins of the Cold War –

the issues will be more fully discussed. In other areas where there is little material, but where there has been much public concern or controversy relating to the effects of Soviet infiltration into government and the security and intelligence services, the issue will be covered mainly through an analysis of the Peter Wright affair. Finally, the Cold War itself will be placed in context and an explanation offered as to why the American anti-communist phobia, McCarthyism, was less of a factor in British post-war politics, although the issue led to problems in the closed secret world of the intelligence and security communities, problems whose implications were fiercely resisted by politicians and throughout Whitehall.

a) The Aftermath of War

The cessation of hostilities in 1945 and the total destruction of Nazism left several loose ends to tie up with regard to anti-fascist activities. One of the most interesting was the fate of the Channel Islands. This was the one part of the British Isles which had suffered German occupation during the war, from July 1940 to April 1945. The Channel Islands were the last remaining territorial reminder of the Norman Conquest, British islands off the coast of northern France which had evolved a traditional degree of self-government and administration under the control of the Bailiff (in Jersey and Guernsey) and his leading officers, the Jurat and Attorney-General, or the Judge (Alderney). The elected states of Jersey and Guernsey had turned the islands into free ports and tax havens, and imposed financial restrictions on immigration. This system was regulated by a paternalist department in the Home Office whose principal concern was to oversee efficient management of local self-government and to do as little as possible to alienate the political class in the islands. The trauma of 1940, and the subsequent growth in the islands of a feeling of neglect by the British government, led the Home Office to a determination to revert to normal practice in 1945, and to avoid as far as possible constitutional change or political reform once the islands had been reoccupied in that year.[1]

The government papers relating to this occupation, many of which were not due for release until 2045, have now been opened as a result of public pressure, although 7 of the 33 files have been retained, mainly under Section 5.1 of the Public Records Act of 1958. This implies that issues of personal sensitivity were involved, presumably with relation to the alleged activities of individuals under the occupation. Whilst 'collaborationism' remains a delicate matter, the files contain little which throws much light on the dark secret discovered recently off the cliffs of Alderney: the skeletal remains of what appears to be the inmates of the concentration camp established on the island. The papers do, however, contain interesting information on government attitudes towards the administration of the islands during the war, and intelligence reports of conditions under the German occupation.

What is particularly noticeable is the concern of the Home Office to be as fair as possible to the islanders and their administration. Unlike the aftermath of war in Italy and France, there was no witch hunt to punish those who were seen as traitors. In France somewhere between 10,000 and 20,000 alleged collaborators were executed at the end of the war.[2] There were none in Jersey, although James Gilbert received a short prison sentence for broadcasting on German radio from Berlin, after volunteering his services for an international peace movement in 1940. John Lingshaw was also sent from Jersey by the Germans to work with William Joyce on German radio, and was interviewed by Special Branch after the war.[3] The Home Office convinced itself as a result of its enquiries that both the administration and the population had behaved in an understandable if not heroic fashion in the war, and swept the matter under the carpet. The difficult position of the island authorities was emphasized and their generally cooperative behaviour towards the occupying forces was deemed to have minimized the risk of German reprisals against the islanders. Indeed, the Bailiffs of both Jersey and Guernsey during the war received knighthoods for their services, despite considerable criticism of their behaviour during and after hostilities.

The attitude of the Home Office was determined by a

number of factors. It was generally supportive of the authorities and saw criticism of them as often unfair given the difficulty of their task. The Home Office also was determined not to be seen as undermining the position of the ruling bodies of Jersey and Guernsey, as they did not wish to alter the self-governing status of the Channel Islands, or to increase Home Office responsibility for them.[4] It was recognized that the sudden British evacuation in June 1940 had left the Channel Islands defenceless, particularly as there had been insufficient time to evacuate all those who wished to leave.[5] Even so, boats from the Channel Islands had already performed valiantly in evacuating British troops from Normandy. Sir Alexander Maxwell, in the Home Office, had instructed the Bailiffs and the other Crown officials to stay in their posts for the duration of the German occupation.[6]

Lord Justice du Parcq informed Sir Frank Newsam in 1945 that although mistakes were made, Jurat Leale, the effective administrative functionary in Guernsey, had made an 'excellent apologia' justifying his actions, and he wished that Mr Coutanche, the Bailiff in Jersey, would do the same.[7] This response was confirmed by an internal investigation by the Home Office which argued that Leale, and his Attorney-Generals, Sherwill and Martell, had performed an extremely difficult task reasonably well.[8] Leale revealed that the Germans, presumably not well pleased by the discovery that half the population had been evacuated to England, had to be talked out of a threat to shoot 20 of the leading citizens of Guernsey on the pretext that British soldiers were being hidden by the population.[9] Leale argued that it was threats like this which persuaded him that cooperation with the Germans would create the minimum friction and would safeguard the civilian population from reprisals from the occupying force. According to the Home Office report the attitude of the Guernsey population to the invader was generally negative and the worst charge that could be levelled against them was, in the words of a German officer, that they were 'obsequious peasants'.[10]

General Hurd's report on Jersey commented on the fact that the Channel Islands were the sole territory administered by the Germans where there was no resistance movement towards the invader.[11] However, the Home Office realized that any organized opposition would have been suicidal in small flat islands bereft of mountainous or wooded terrain, and that Coutanche had a better chance of keeping two British agents hidden if he seemed to cooperate with the Germans. They also realized that the British government was as unpopular as the Germans in Jersey in 1944–5. The failure to reconquer the islands until ten months after D-Day led to siege conditions on Jersey and a severe reduction of inadequate rations for the islands cut off from Continental Europe and the United Kingdom. Bailiff Coutanche, in a report smuggled out to the Home Office in November 1944, complained of the very grave situation facing the island. The courier said there was much 'bitterness of feeling' about the lack of relief of the Channel Islands and inhabitants had lost their confidence in the British government. Such intelligence was given an A rating, as being a very reliable source, by the Home Office.[12] These views reinforced feelings that they had been deserted in 1940 and that the failure to raise morale through special broadcasts by the BBC World Service, or the dropping of leaflets, confirmed this neglect.[13]

Thus the British government took fully into account the circumstances of the occupation. The lack of a more positive response to aid the islanders during the war was explained by the same arguments as the local administrators used in their policy of cooperation with the occupying force: they wished to do nothing which would encourage German retaliation against the islanders. Such appeasement was sometimes taken to excessive lengths by the representatives of the Home Office in the Channel Islands. Although the Guernsey police were described as patriotic from a British point of view, they cooperated in the roundup of non-Channel Islands residents who were sent to German internment camps on the Continent in 1942. Over 2,000 were sent to France from the Channel Islands, and the Home Office threatened to take the issue to the War Crimes tribunal. Even more seriously, papers released in Guernsey show that Victor Carey, the Bailiff, informed the Germans that he 'had the honour' of ethnically cleansing the island of nonresident

Jews, as three foreigners were sent to an internment camp in Nancy in France en route to Auschwitz.[14] It was also suggested that the Guernsey administration encouraged their fellow subjects to denounce those who infringed German laws.[15]

It was not only the administrators who were accused of becoming too cooperative with the Germans. Some women in both Jersey and Guernsey were alleged to be consorting too freely with the master race. A campaign to smear so called 'Jerrybags' was aimed at those who became too friendly; certainly there appears to have been an increase in the number of illegitimate births. In Guernsey an informer alleged that the 'Guernsey Underground Barbers' (a parody of the Glass Utilization Board, a major employer) conducted reprisals against women who fraternized with the invaders.[16] The Germans were well-disciplined and were congratulated for their behaviour by the authorities. Jurat Leale wrote a memorandum on the German Occupation which was praised by Sir Frank Newsam for its 'far seeing fair mindedness'.[17] Doubtless he had the vindictive attitude of the coupon election in mind, and still felt it should not be published because, despite its balanced approach, it was too advanced for public opinion in 1945.

The authorities were aware of the more sinister aspects of the German occupation. Not only did informants and escapees provide military intelligence with details of German fortifications, they also informed MI19 of conditions in Alderney. In 1940 the entire population of the island was evacuated.[18] The Germans established a concentration camp there where they employed forced labour. Jews were made to wear the yellow star and an informant told the authorities that he had seen two political prisoners killed for minor misdemeanours while working. French and British workers were given slightly inferior rations compared to German soldiers, but much better than those given to political prisoners or Jews. It was also alleged that six Jersey women who serviced a brothel for German troops had to be sent home with VD.[19]

If a complex, fair minded and supportive attitude was taken to the plight of the Channel Islanders, with full recognition and understanding of their difficult plight in the war, and substantial economic help after the retaking of the islands in 1945, then the same sympathy was not extended to the tiny British fifth column who had aided and abetted the Nazis during the war. This related to so-called renegades who had actively volunteered to help the enemy during hostilities. Three traitors were hung after judicial proceedings in British courts in 1945: William Joyce, John Amery and Theodore Schurch. Whilst official papers are still retained, we know that Joyce committed 'radio treason', Amery was the chief recruiter for the Legion of Saint George, a small unit of British prisoner-of-war volunteers who fought on the eastern front for the Germans against Soviet communism, and Schurch collaborated with both Italian and Nazi intelligence.[20] All three had been ex-members of the British Union of Fascists for varying periods of time. The case against Joyce in particular was controversial. His American citizenship, despite his use of a British passport, gave him plausible grounds for arguing that he had not committed treason against the King and the British state.

Although there were several other death sentences, these were commuted at the beginning of 1946. From the renegade files that have been released, and judging from what is known about the others, it appears that in contrast to the rest of Europe there was not an orgy of revenge against alleged Nazi collaboration. Of the 100 or so who had worked voluntarily or been forced to work on German radio, most appear to have been given minimal sentences, or were released without charge.[21] Similarly even the more serious cases who joined the Legion of Saint George appear to have been released by Elizabeth II's coronation in 1953. In spite of the almost daily release of details of Nazi atrocities in the aftermath of war, the British government was determined not to repeat the mistakes of 1918. Nazism and fascism were militarily obliterated, and their remnants driven underground in Europe in 1945; it was felt that sensible people would never again be attracted by such a horrific political idea, and that revenge caused resentment and the seeds of potential future conflict. The official British line on retribution against fascists and collaborators was to make a few examples of enforced punishments and then to rapidly forget the whole episode.

The new Labour government in 1945 dutifully followed pre-existing Home Office practice in its attitude towards British fascism. Although the Labour party, unlike many of its social democratic counterparts in Europe, had remained militantly anti-Nazi throughout the war, its attitude towards fascism and political extremism was an area of agreement with the Churchill coalition and Whitehall administrative practice.[22] The coalition broke up as a result of disagreements and festering wartime political tensions over political and social issues; on the main subject matter of this book there proved to be continuity of policy.[23] Thus when the new administration set up a committee on fascism it was relieved to find that a specially commissioned opinion poll indicated that there was by no means a unanimous public demand for the continued political suppression of Sir Oswald Mosley.[24]

The Home Secretary, James Chuter Ede, also informed the Cabinet that fascism should not be outlawed as a political creed and that the government should adhere to a traditional policy of maintaining freedom of speech. This had served Britain well in the past. Such a policy did not lead to an unmanageable growth of fascism before the war even when conditions were more favourable to its development. If fascism was made illegal, those who were denied the means of political expression could resort to violence. The danger of this was not so much the violence of a small minority, but that it may evoke some public sympathy if these rights were infringed. However, Chuter Ede argued, the chief officers of police should make it clear to their constables to suppress any attempts by the fascists or other factions to bring disorder into politics.[25] It was also clear that any extensive political surveillance of any possible revival of fascism was monitored by the Labour government – according to a note in the general file on the Imperial Fascist League, a weekly bulletin on fascism circulated in the Home Office for some time after 1945. Chief Constables were asked in March 1948 to report to the Home Office of any Union Movement meetings and to monitor public order in the vicinity. A copy of any such report was also to be sent to MI5.[26]

The authorities then appear to have established the necessary machinery for the political surveillance of neofascist extremism and would have been prepared to increase the power of the state if the resurrection of Mosley's political career had struck any chords outside areas of East and North London. It was assumed, however, that the problem would not arise, as it was concluded that fascism had become disreputable, and that Mosley would be forever so tarred by association with such a creed that any further infringement of civil liberties would be unwise. In this the authorities were undoubtedly correct. Problems then developed amongst radical elements, some linked to the CPGB, who assumed such a policy of benign neglect was pandering to fascism. The 43 Group, formed during the war, was quick to oppose the reemergence of some of Mosley's henchmen, like Jeffrey Hamm and Alf Flockhart in Dalston and elsewhere in London, and it was such public order problems in 1947 and 1948 which delayed the lifting of the embargo on political marches in much of London, which had been renewed every three months since 1937.

Whilst nothing on Mosley's political activities after 1945 has been released, there are indications that the authorities began to adopt a more ambiguous attitude towards some fascist groups as the Cold War developed. Although at the levels of the government and in Whitehall there is no change in official hostility and watchful benign neglect of neofascist groups, and the recognition that Nazism was viewed by public opinion as deranged lunacy, there is now a significant amount of information in the public domain which suggests the British were involved in the recruitment of emigré Nazi collaborators in anti-Soviet operations in the 1940s and 1950s. Although there is no evidence which directly shows collusion between British fascists and the state, there is a growing body of material, mainly emanating from sources in the United States, which suggests that the most secret agencies of government were actively recruiting nationalist collaborators in Displaced Persons (DP) camps, many of whom had been implicated in Nazi atrocities in the war, but who were militantly anti-communist.[27] There are also grounds for believing that ex-fascists, and some anti-communist right-wing elements, were used by British intelligence to help organize emigré groups in what ultimately became suicidal missions aimed at sabotaging and undermining communist regimes in the Soviet Union and eastern Europe. Soviet infiltration into the emigré networks, and the fact that Kim Philby oversaw the operation from the British end, ensured its failure.[28] The creation of the Anti-Bolshevik Bloc of Nations (ABN), an alliance of nationalist anti-communist and often ex-Nazi elements from central and eastern Europe and recruited from the DP camps, was to provide the cannon fodder for a disastrous Cold War operation.

The ABN held an interesting 'religious' conference in Edinburgh in 1950 at wich were present some of the more notorious nazi collaborators from the Ukrainian Nationalists (OUN), the Bandera faction, the Belorussian Belarus Brigade, and other assorted anti-communist groups from Poland, the Baltic states and Yugoslavia. This was organized by the Scottish League for European Freedom, whose president was the Earl of Mansfield, and whose most active committee members appeared to be the ex-fascist Major-General 'Boney' Fuller and Lord Ironside. This organization was deemed to be 'notorious' by the Foreign Office, and some of its leading members 'irresponsible'.[29] John Stewart for the League wrote to the American State Department to complain about the 'totally unjust accusation' that such dedicated anti-communist nationalists in the ABN were Nazi collaborators.[30] It was clear that the busing in of the emigrés for the Edinburgh conference must have been heavily subsidized, and as the Foreign Office refused to acknowledge the existence of the ABN, it is clear that British and American intelligence sources were probably involved. The Soviet infiltrated ABN was 'sold' to the Americans in 1949–50, so it was not surprising that their operations went so disastrously wrong under American tutelage in the 1950s.[31] The chaos in central Europe after the war, and the more conscious anti-communist recruitment operation in DP camps at the end of hostilities, led to later discoveries that Nazi collaborators had settled in Britain and the United States as well as in other countries. Whereas the Foreign Office seemed well informed about Nazi collaborators in the OUN and the ABN, the failure to declassify some of the subfiles and the dubious view taken of the SLEF suggests the telescope was being applied to a Nelsonian blind eye.[32]

b) 'A Tightly Knit Group of Politically Motivated Men'

If there was a transition from fascism to communism as the main enemy of the democratic state after 1945 it was the onset of the Cold War which explained this development.[33] Although the origins of this conflict do not directly concern us, as they derived from perceived global strategic, military and political factors, the implications for domestic politics need some elaboration. This is necessary for two reasons: firstly, a pragmatic appraisal of Soviet motives was transformed into a reactivation of the conspiracy theory outlined in chapter 4, and put on the political backburner since 1941; and secondly, the election, with an overall majority of 148 seats in July 1945, of a radical reforming Labour government dedicated to democratic socialist ideals, was to prove beyond any shadow of doubt that a Labour government was as anti-communist as any Conservative administration.[34]

The British electorate was determined to erase the memory of mass unemployment in the interwar period, to avoid disillusionment from the failure to reform society in 1918, and to forget the failure of Chamberlain's appeasement policies, for all of which they blamed the Conservatives. As a result the change in perception in Whitehall about the Soviet threat was ahead of public opinion and the new Labour government had to proceed carefully before coming into the open about its new fears about the Red Army spearheading an export drive for Russian communism in Europe. Whitehall changed its mind about the trustworthiness of Stalin following the failure of the allies to agree about the government of Germany after the war, the blatant Soviet manipulation of elections and the repressive activities of the NKVD in Poland in 1945–6. The British public, influenced by the pro-Soviet editorial writings of E. H. Carr and

Barrington Ward in *The Times*, and by the popular journalism of the Beaverbrook press, did not become reconciled to a Cold War mentality until 1948.

In much of the rest of Europe the necessity of having to come to terms with Nazi domination had divided social democracy. The exploits of the Red Army and the coherent, united and often heroic resistance of national parties to German domination since 1941, had led to communism emerging as a leading political force in Europe. The communists were the largest party in Czechoslovakia before they seized power in 1948, and remained the most important opposition in both France and Italy until the 1980s.[35] Compared to these the CPGB remained insignificant. It gained only two seats in the 1945 election – Willie Gallagher in West Fife, and Phil Piratin at Mile End – and two London County Councillors in 1946. Although several left-wing Labour and Independent Labour Party MPs were clearly pro-Soviet and anti-American, they had little or no influence on policy. By the 1950 general election the effects of the Cold War had led to the collapse of support for the CPGB and it had become, in the words of Kenneth Morgan, 'feeble in the extreme'.[36]

Of its one hundred candidates in the 1950 general election, all lost, and 97 of them lost their deposits. Between them they gained 0.3 per cent of the vote, and most of the fellow-travelling left-wing Labour MPs were also heavily defeated. The official membership of the CPGB fell from 45,435 to 38,853, the *Daily Worker*'s readership slumped. After 1948 the party became little more than a narrow sect mouthing similar slogans to the 'class against class' period from 1928 to 1933, and it reverted to its isolated pariah status on the far left of British politics. The effects of partial deStalinization in the Soviet Union, with Khrushchev's secret speech, followed by the crushing of the Hungarian reforms in 1956 (which showed the leopard had not changed its spots), created a further crisis for the CPGB. Not only did it lose 20 per cent of its declining membership, but the 'new left' of ex-communists and independent Marxists which developed from the split was to become the main source of left-wing protest against continued injustice in British society. The

CPGB became an insignificant voice on the margins of British politics from 1956. Even the Soviet Union had already recognized the failure of British communism; the CPGB, regarded as one of the vanguard parties in the 1920s by the Communist International, was not allowed to join its successor, Cominform, in 1947.[37]

The weak performance of the CPGB reflected its own inadequacies, and the hostile perception by public opinion of Soviet actions and the spread of communism – particularly in subverting democratic processes in eastern Europe (most notably in Poland, Hungary and Czechoslovakia between 1944 and 1948), the Berlin blockade, the 'loss' of China, the explosion of a Soviet atomic bomb in 1949, and the Korean War in 1950.[38] Whereas British communism had benefited from its role of chief unofficial drum beater for the exploits of the Red Army after 1941, its perceived slavish adherence to Stalinist direction and control meant it lost a real opportunity to seize the moment and campaign after 1941 for radical economic and social policies.

Ironically, its campaign for social reform and working class rights before 1941 plugged the CPGB into a groundswell of public discontent about the need to change the nature of class society in Britain. Its obsession with doing nothing to undermine the war effort after 1941 meant the Labour Party were the beneficiaries of the desire for change. With their experience of government since 1940, their impeccable anti-Nazi credentials, and their commitment to reform and full employment, Labour were in tune with public opinion which did not wish to continue the coalition and rejected Conservative policies.[39] The CPGB's espousal of a variant of American Browderism, the continuance of the wartime coalition committed to progressive policies, was decisively rejected by the electorate in 1945, and by the Labour Party in the same year, when conference, as a result of the Union bloc vote, disallowed the proposal for the CPGB to affiliate to the party.

With the onset of the Cold War this decision was made permanent and a wide range of infiltrated organizations were proscribed. The lurch to the extreme left by the CPGB in 1948 – given recent wild oscillations in policy from anti-fascism, to anti-imperialism, to anti-Nazism, and back to calling the Labour party 'social fascists' again – was interpreted as merely highlighting the ultimate dependence of the CPGB to the dictates of its wire-pullers in Moscow. It also represented a domestic response to the failure of its policy of entry into the Labour Party, and the increasing hostility towards it.

The move to isolate the CPGB reflected both the traditional scepticism and hostility of the Labour Party towards the organization, and the deteriorating international situation. Such suspicion had been reinforced by the entirely opportunistic policies adopted towards the war both by the Soviet Union and the CPGB. It appears also that Whitehall encouraged and applauded the obvious moves undertaken by the new Labour government to isolate extremists, and to be suspicious of the motives and actions of the Soviet Union.

The emergence of a Cold War mentality was a reaction to the vacuum of power in central Europe caused by the rapid rundown of American troops after VE day, the sudden ending of Lend-Lease and the wartime atomic partnership, the difficult economic negotiations with the USA on a new loan in March 1946, and the fear of American withdrawal into isolation, combined with what were perceived as Soviet hostile intentions in Europe. Released government records seem to suggest that the emergence of a Cold War mentality represented the convergence of influential political hostility towards the actions of Soviet policy by Ernest Bevin in the Foreign Office, in which he was briefed and fully supported by the new Russia Committee set up in the department, and by the Chiefs of Staff. Officials like Sir Orme Sargent, the Permament Undersecretary who had opposed appeasement in the 1930s, Christopher Warner and Robin Hankey, two successive heads of the Northern Department, and Frank Roberts put the relatively harmonious wartime relationship into an icier compartment after 1945. What was particularly interesting was the extremely skilful strategic and working relationship between the forceful trade unionist, Ernest Bevin, and the conservative foreign office civil servants, particularly their manipulation of both British public opinion, and the role they played in convincing the Americans to oppose Soviet expansionism.

There was a convergence of political and administrative influence with relation to Soviet actions; it led to greater significance being accorded the monotonous drone of the Red Menace stereotype of Soviet Bolshevism being constantly fed into departmental papers by MI5, and the rather more pragmatic arguments of Sir Robert Bruce Lockhart, whose work at the Political Warfare Executive (PWE) impressed on his friend Sir Orme Sargent the necessity to be firm with Stalin. Lockhart argued against the Chiefs of Staff worst case scenario view, and held that the Red Army was overstretched, under-resourced and technologically deficient. Stalin respected power and not appeasement; he may have had more divisions than the Pope, but the only way to deal with him was to call his bluff.

The main resistance to the emergence of a Cold War mentality was provided by the Prime Minister, Clement Attlee, who wished to retain the wartime alliance, and feared the ruinous economic consequence of further hostility. To summarize a complex story, it may be concluded that although there was agreement by all the principal parties of the necessity for the production of an atomic bomb to maintain Britain's place at the top table, Attlee's reluctance to support the anti-Soviet line and wish to cut British commitments in the Middle East, was only altered by the threatened resignation of the Chiefs of Staff (COS) in 1947.

The chill blast from the east was greatly influenced by the chargé d'affaires at the British embassy in Moscow, Frank Roberts, who wrote three letters on Anglo-Soviet relations which became the British equivalent of the famous telegram by 'X' (George Kennan) which was so influential in the emergence of the Truman Doctrine in 1947, the policy of containment against international communism. In the letters Roberts warned of the dangers of a modern equivalent of the sixteenth-century wars of religion breaking out between Soviet communism, western social democracy and the American version of capitalism.[40] To Roberts the Anglo-Soviet ten-year treaty signed in 1942 was now a dead letter. Although he carefully noted that national security rather than international revolution now represented the rationale behind Moscow's actions, the Soviets still used national communist parties, fellow travellers and sympathetic liberals to form a 'fifth column' to spy and act as agents of influence for their own interests.[41] The leakage of atomic secrets to the Soviet Union, and the recent Canadian spy case in 1946 was a good example of this. By 1947 the Soviet need for a new security argument had been downgraded; their actions were now viewed through the prism of the revolutionary goals of Leninist ideology.

The fears of the Foreign Office were more than reinforced by the COS. It appears that part of the fear of the Soviets was explained by the fact that British Intelligence had little reliable information on the Soviet order of battle in the post-war period. The failure of sigint to break the Soviet one-time pad codes after the war meant there was no equivalent of the Ultra secret to assess accurately the intentions of Stalin. Richard Aldrich and Michael Coleman have argued, from a JIC document discovered in the India Office library, that the military only had accurate intelligence on the capabilities of the Soviet air force and Red Army troop dispositions in south-east Europe. The fact that a worst case scenario was therefore adopted as the basis of policy meant that the alleged 70 or 75 combat ready divisions of the Red Army in central and eastern Europe loomed large in discussions of the Soviet threat. This tended to drown out voices which suggested that the Soviet threat was a paper tiger; that it was war weary and lacked modern equipment and the atomic bomb (until 1949).

What is noticeable in released government records is a process of convergence of the interests and policies of the Labour government and the Whitehall administration. A mixture of economic reality, profound suspicion of Soviet and CPGB motives, and a commitment to democracy and social reform, or 'Labourism' as it has been called by its critics, meant Ernest Bevin, the Foreign Secretary, and James Chuter Ede, the Home Secretary, could work in harmony with the Civil Service. There was a mutual shared interest in accepting American aid and hegemony, such as the Marshall plan, and opposing Soviet imperialism and political subversion.[42] Whilst it is not clear how far Whitehall or Labour ministers were aware of all the secret activities of the security and intelligence communities, it was obvious that there was little dispute about ends – although the means were sometimes covered up to ensure that the plausibility of denials of government complicity when embarrassing incidents surfaced, and that Soviet claims of British intelligence complicity in the secret activities of the Cold War could be dismissed as propaganda.[43]

There appears to be continuing controversy over Bevin's role as the leading manipulator of the Cold War: Alan Bullock stressed his commitment to defending democratic socialist values whilst Weiler criticizes the missed opportunity of a socialist 'Third Force' emerging under a British leadership which was independent of the two superpowers. Perhaps the most wide-ranging exposition of Bevin's anti-communism was expressed in his rather luridly entitled paper to the Cabinet, 'The Threat to Western Civilization'. In this he called for a new alliance of all the democratic states against the Soviet Union, in order to prevent the collapse of organized society and protect civilization against a form of communist *lebensraum* and the threat of world dictatorship. This would be established by military means or by democratic states being swamped by Soviet methods of infiltration. It was such argument which highlighted Bevin's important role in the politics of the foundation of NATO in 1948.

The Labour Party (despite its suspicion of Whitehall manipulation) established a new semi-secret propaganda vehicle, the Information Research Department (IRD), whose chief function was to disseminate anti-communist information. This 'Third Force' propaganda was aimed at opposing communism abroad, in the colonies, and at home. Its function was similar to that of the PWE during the war. Some historians influenced by the revisionist and post-revisionist view of the Cold War – for example, Peter Weiler – interpret its effects in Gramscian terms; he developed a complex and sophisticated argument to suggest the incorporation of the labour movement into the hegemonic values and ideology of the state.[44] However the process was more double edged; the triumph of Labourism saw the state itself accept the need for welfare reforms, the nationalization of key industries and Keynesian economic management. It was more a symbiotic and dialectical relationship – 'Butskellism', as politicians and political commentators later called it – rather than a manipulative conspiracy on the part of the establishment.

There is considerable value in Weiler's analysis, however: the discussion of the TUC's role in colonial economic management, the rise and fall of the World Federation of Trade Unions, the propaganda of the IRD, and the illuminating survey of the causes of industrial unrest in the 1940s help place the study of the Cold War in a wider context. But Weiler's argument needs to be criticized because he overstates his case. Whilst the heroism of the Red Army in the war was universally admired, the Soviet purges of the 1930s and the cynicism of the Nazi–Soviet pact came to be universally detested by democratic socialists. Some aspects of the anti-fascist United Front campaign and the Aid for Spain movement were genuinely popular before the war; but the inference that there was a broad left alliance which was subverted by elites in the Labour Party and the union bureaucracy is an exaggeration. It was the generosity of the Marshall Plan, (even if it was generally hoped and assumed its terms would be rejected by the USSR) and the actions of the Soviet Union, rather than the effects of anti-communist propaganda or a semi-conspiratorial incorporation of the Labour movement bureaucracy into the structure of the capitalist state, which ultimately accounted for the line-up of forces in the Cold War.

It was clear that if the Labour Party in 1945 had come to terms with Whitehall and the establishment, it still, for understandable historical reasons, was very suspicious of MI5 and MI6. Although the appointment of Sir Percy Sillitoe, the Chief Constable of Kent, to become head of MI5 in 1945, arose because he was the most successful of the applicants for the post, it was an appointment which also initially pleased the Labour government because he stressed the importance of the need to protect the security of Britain's democratic institutions. Whilst this appointment was resented in MI5 there was little sign of anti-government plots by the intelligence or security communities during the third Labour government. In retrospect, the appointment of Sillitoe may have been fortunate: although it was not regarded as a successful appointment, the recruiting of an inhouse candidate such as Guy Liddell, the head of B Division in the war, could have created worse problems; he was to be severely embarrassed by the defections of the two Foreign Office diplomats, Burgess and Maclean, in 1951, given his contact with the former and close working relationship with Burgess's friend and fellow Soviet spy, Anthony Blunt, during the Second World War.

The British state was to exhibit a split personality with regard to the Cold War. It combined the political hostility of the establishment towards communism, Whitehall's delicate balancing act of maintaining freedom of expression and maximum possible civil liberties, with secretive administrative procedures and the conspiracy mentality of the security service and British intelligence. As in wartime, the main domestic concern was with the role of communism in industry, particularly the activities of CPGB shop stewards in the docks and engineering and electricity industries. The problems of transition to a peacetime economy and the commitment to full employment created tensions, resentment and frustrated rising expectations amongst the workforce in several key industries. The support of the TUC for necessary measures of economic retrenchment and continued rationing meant the incorporation of organized labour into the state apparatus, and left a vacuum within which growing industrial discontent festered.

The CPGB used such unrest to highlight workers' disillusionment and to establish an industrial campaign based on an unofficial shop stewards' movement in the docks, the power stations and engineering industries. Whilst the CPGB no doubt saw such activity as the first stage in a political campaign to undermine Britain's anti-Soviet participation in the Cold War, it was based on an economism strategy of defending workers' rights. The authorities, however, portrayed such activity as a Cold War conspiracy. For George Isaacs, the Minister of Labour, industrial disruption in the docks in

1949 was an 'old and deliberate' plan fomented by communists.[45] The Cabinet worried that the 'good hearted dockers had been duped by communist lies'.[46] For Sir John Anderson, the Chairman of the Port of London Authority in 1950, the communists were doing their best to exploit the situation in the docks.[47] Hugh Gaitskell, the Minister for Fuel and Power, argued that the strike in the electricity generating power stations in 1950 had been instigated by communist shop stewards and acted as a rehearsal for further confrontation. A minute from Sir Edward Bridges, the Cabinet Secretary, pointed out that there could be no question of interfering in industrial disputes between the British electricity authorities and their employees, even if the confrontation had been engineered from political motives.[48]

The 'red scare' atmosphere of 1949–50 was nevertheless strictly limited to manipulable proportions. The support of the TUC for the Labour government, and the frequent use the authorities made of the secret state infrastructure for monitoring and managing strikes, ensured a firm response to Labour unrest. Almost the first act of the new administration in July 1945 was to set in motion the administrative machinery, from the initiative of Sir Alexander Maxwell, Permanent Undersecretary at the Home Office, that led to the re-establishment of the old Supply and Transport Committee as the Industrial Emergencies Committee, which was reconstituted as the Emergencies Committee in 1947.[49] There is evidence as well that the Joint Intelligence Committee (JIC) had taken over by 1948 the coordinating function developed by the Security Executive during the war with regard to counter-intelligence. The management of the JIC was transferred to the Cabinet Office from the Chiefs of Staff in 1957. The Cabinet Secretary is Chairman of the Permanent Undersecretaries Committee on Intelligence Services, who work closely with the Coordinator of Intelligence and Security in the Cabinet Office.

In 1950 there was a revival of prosecutions under Order 1305, one of the wartime emergency measures which had been extended into the first years of peace. This draconian legislation enforced compulsory arbitration and prohibited strikes and lockouts, and was used against unofficial strikers who defied their leadership in the Gas industry (ten in

October 1950) and the docks (seven in February 1951).[50] Although after a row it was replaced by Order 1376, which retained compulsory arbitration whilst dropping sanctions against unofficial strikers, it nevertheless illustrated the government's resolve to be tough on industrial unrest.

As well as using emergency powers, secret planning and the law, the government also availed itself of the military to aid the civil power in containing emergencies in this period. On 18 different occasions between 1945 and 1951 the government sent up to 20,000 troops to act as blackleg labour during disputes.[51] One of these, the dock strike of 1949, has been analysed by Peter Weiler.[52]

Whilst understating the role played by Jack Dash and communist shop stewards, he showed that there was far more to the strike than an alleged CPGB conspiracy to subvert the state. The strike, or more correctly the lockout, represented an attempt by British dockers to 'black' Canadian ships, in protest at the dual unionism of the Seafarers International Union, who with American Federation of Labour backing were poaching members from the communist-led Canadian Seaman's Union, whom the employers wished to undermine. The dispute was at its root a Cold War creation – but the destroyer of deals and subverter of legally binding contracts were not the communists but the Canadian employers and those militant Cold War warriors, the American Federation of Labour. The CPGB also gained support from the men for their outspoken criticism of the Dock Labour Scheme, which although it was an improvement on the degrading casual dock labour prevalent before the war, still created resentment and frustrations. The men objected to the lack of guaranteed daily employment, and the paternal despotism of Lord Ammon, the Chairman of the Port of London Authority after the war. Dockers felt that the incorporation of trade union leaders into the management of the docks left them without an official voice with which to protest against the continuing inadequacies of the scheme; a role which the CPGB shop stewards were only too happy to fill. The fact that some London dockers were out for ten weeks during the dispute was indicative of shared grievances, not communist wool being pulled over dockers' eyes.

The London Dock Strike of 1949 must stand as an example

of a general trend after 1945; the tendency to blame industrial unrest on unofficial elements influenced by extremist Marxist ideology. The development between 1945 and 1979 of an understanding between management and labour, if not the creation of a corporate state, led the Labour Party and the TUC to influence and be influenced by changing establishment values. As a result, industrial unrest since 1945 has been blamed on outsiders and unrepresentative minorities, either communists or Trotskyists.[53] In 1966 Harold Wilson, presumably well briefed by 'senior people responsible for these matters' and 'one of the operators in the field', blamed the seamen's strike on a communist conspiracy, a 'tightly knit group of politically motivated men'. Recent disclosures from Soviet archives suggest that CPGB industrial militancy was partly funded from Moscow until recently. In the 1970s not only were CPGB shop stewards in engineering, transport and automobile industries blamed for the 'British disease' of unofficial strikes, but a new generation of Trotskyists, in three different factions, were increasingly allegedly involved in fomenting industrial discontent within a growing corporate state.[54] Mrs Thatcher of course ended the era of trying to resolve such disputes through cosy tea parties and beer and sandwiches at 10 Downing Street for trade union leaders, even if the shop stewards' movement had always been suspicious of such forms of collective bargaining. Her anti-communism and attacks on militant industrial extremism were no less strident, and were more effective, than those of her predecessors in the corporatist tradition.

Whilst the dock strike of 1949 provides a graphic example of Cold War security paranoia, the peak of anti-Soviet suspicion was not reached until the Korean War, which threatened to turn the Cold War into a hot one. A splendid example of this obsession has surfaced in declassified Cabinet papers; this relates to an informal meeting of ministers chaired by the Prime Minister in October 1950 to see what could be done about the projected World Peace Congress to be held in Sheffield.

According to Chuter Ede, the Home Secretary, no powers existed to ban the Congress, but entry to the United Kingdom could be barred to delegates whom the security authorities deemed undesirable visitors. Special Branch and MI5 had been instructed to keep a careful watch on the Congress. An annex to the minutes included an MI5 report on the World Peace Committee; this stated that the organization was closely connected with communist controlled international bodies, and that it was under the direction of Cominform, which had instructed its affiliated organizations to engage in sabotage and subversion against the Western World. One of the leading organizations in the Congress was the World Federation of Trade Unions, whose General Secretary had instructed members to refuse to produce armaments in all capitalist countries. The penetration of the armed forces was the task of the World Federation of Democratic Youth, and the World Federation of Scientific Workers had transparent intelligence and sabotage interests. The report concluded that the aim of the Peace Congress was not merely to build up pacifist sentiments in Britain, but also to foment industrial unrest, to encourage the evasion of military service, work for the end of rearmament, and paralyse transport and communications in western Europe.

The Attlee administration laid many of the old security ghosts to rest. But complaints of a revival of such fears arose when the Labour Party moved leftwards with the election of Harold Wilson as leader. Most notably, it appears that certain elements in the security service continued their suspicions of the left of the Labour Party, and of their links with extremist elements in British society and the Soviet Union. Whilst much of this rumour can be described as plausible conjecture, one aspect of the Peter Wright affair has highlighted the continuing poor relations between the left in British politics and the security service. This was brought to public attention by the revelations of an ex-MI5 officer, Cathy Massiter, who alleged that amongst her duties were telephonic eavesdropping operations against leading officials of the National Council for Civil Liberties and the Campaign for Nuclear Disarmament. It appears also that Peter Wright was involved in a disreputable campaign to undermine the last Wilson administration.[55]

Ironically, Wilson was as punctilious about secrecy as any

Conservative prime minister; hence the unsuccessful attempt to stop the Crossman Diaries breaking the confidentiality of Cabinet deliberations in 1975, and his terse, uninformative one-page chapter on 'The Prime Minister and National Security' in *The Governance of Britain*. The administration of his Labour successor, Jim Callaghan, was equally protective of the secrets of government; thus the ABC trial in 1977, with its notorious attempt to prove that the intelligence research of the jounalist Duncan Campbell was prejudicial to the interests of national security and of use to an enemy, despite the fact that the Defence proved his evidence was derived from publicly available material. Although all three defendants were found guilty of charges relating to Section 2 of the Official Secrets Act, the original serious charges were dropped and the case was widely seen as a defeat for the government.

David Leigh's dissection of the whole 'Wilson plot' suggests it was a combination of dissident noises made by some British and American intelligence and security officers, and Wilson's own understandable reaction to the episode. Wright alleged that Cecil King, who wished to bring down the Wilson administration in 1968, and replace it with a coalition led by Lord Mountbatten, had already informed MI5 that he would plant a leak discrediting Wilson. What the whole episode illustrated was that the validity of MI5 evidence when used for such purposes appeared no more reliable in the 1970s than it did in the 1920s.[56] Wilson's 'disloyalty' was a figment of the imagination and a 'dirty trick' perpetrated by a rogue element, or elements, in the security service. The origins of such a bizarre story and nasty smear were a misinterpretation of Wilson's trade missions to the Soviet Union in 1947–8, when in retrospect he could have been said to have made a mistake in selling jet engines to the Soviets as Minister for Overseas Trade, but there is absolutely nothing to suggest that such a deal was anything more than a contribution to help lessen the appalling trade deficit. More recently, arms sales to Iraq have shown the dilemma for ministers in maximizing exports whilst (arguably, in retrospect) inadvertently helping to undermine Britain's strategic interests.

Indeed, whilst a post-Cold War problem, nevertheless

the Inquiry by Lord Justice Sir Richard Scott in 1994 has highlighted the difficulties of necessary secrecy in government with regard to intelligence and security matters. The key issues in this case have been whether Public Interest Immunity Certificates should be placed on all government documents preventing their use in the Matrix Churchill trial unless directed by the judge. These documents showed quite clearly that MI6 was kept informed about both the dealings of Matrix Churchill and Saddam Hussein's government and other intelligence related material gleaned from such contact. What the Inquiry uncovered included details of meetings of ministers changing the rules for the granting of export licences to Iraq, without informing Parliament of such alterations; the insistence by the Attorney General, Sir Nicholas Lyell, that it was the duty of all ministers to sign Public Immunity Certificates for all documents, despite the objections of some, and particularly Michael Heseltine, the President of the Board of Trade, about whether such behaviour could be construed as a cover-up; and the failure of the Attorney General's offiice to inform the Judge officially about this worry.

c) The Battle of the Books

Whilst some government records have been released with regard to Cold War industrial confrontation, the activities of MI5 and MI6 have remained hidden by official secrecy since 1945. The Maxwell Fyfe directive of 1952, which outlined the theory of the operation of the security service, provided no supervisory machinery to ensure that its terms were carried out. In fact, the Home Office, although nominally responsible, has no knowledge of its operations. However, certain matters have been drawn to public attention by the actions of certain ex- or retired officers of the two services, by investigative journalists and by planted stories which the authorities wish to leak into the public domain. Without doubt the discovery of Soviet infiltration into the government machinery, which affected in particular the Foreign Office and the security and intelligence services – not only with the loss of secrets, but also with the attempt to cover up what had happened – inflicted lasting damage. This reached an explosive climax in 1987 with the Peter Wright affair, the one employee of the secret state whose name will be mentioned in this section, who was not or has not been investigated as a possible traitor. Fortunately disclosures from Soviet and American archives have enabled a more informed debate on this matter.

The issue was indeed a complex one. The authorities reduced it to the need to protect secret sources and to convince allies, unsuccessfully as it turned out, that the damage was relatively minimal. Critics argued for the need for more open government, a British Freedom of Information Act, and to make the security and intelligence communities more accountable to parliamentary or government oversight or scrutiny.

The problem of Soviet espionage became a pressing matter after the disclosures of the Soviet defector Gouzenko and the discovery of espionage rings in the American government in 1948, exposed before Congressional committees by two ex-communists, Whittaker Chambers and Elizabeth Bentley. The matter became more serious when it became clear that after Gouzenko's information and the breakthrough with interpreting Soviet radio intercepts, in Operation Bride or Venona, that there had been significant leakage of atomic secrets to the Soviet Union, and that the evidence pointed to British sources. Technical information had been given by two British scientists working on the 'Manhattan Project' during the war, Klaus Fuchs and Allen Nunn May, and strategic and political secrets were given by what appeared to be an agent working in the British embassy in Washington.[57] A British version of the Truman Loyalty Security Programme was introduced into the Civil Service between 1948 and 1955; of the 135 civil servants investigated as security risks, 24 resigned, 25 were dismissed and 86 were transferred to other positions without security requirements.[58]

The matter became more serious when, after information from the Federal Bureau of Investigation (FBI), a laborious investigation concluded that Donald Maclean, the head of the American Department at the Foreign Office in 1951,

14 Cabinet Secretary Sir Robert Armstrong arrives in Heathrow from Australia, where he was giving evidence in the Government bid to suppress the memoirs of former MI5 officer Peter Wright, 1986

was a spy. Before he could be challenged he defected with another Foreign Office diplomat, Guy Burgess, to Moscow in May 1951. Maclean had served at the British embassy in Washington from May 1944 to September 1948, a longer posting than any other diplomat in the 1940s apart from the wartime ambassador, Lord Halifax. For most of that period he had been a First Secretary and privy to all the secrets of the embassy, including atomic secrets – a point well known to the Americans. Burgess had been a Second Secretary at the embassy from August 1950 until April 1951. Following this disaster, and partly as a result of American pressure, positive vetting was introduced in 1952 for British government appointments.[59]

Although hushed up at the time, the strong circumstantial evidence that the agents had been tipped off by a third party highlighted justifiable fears that there was concerted Soviet espionage at the heart of government and significant infiltration into the administration. The available evidence suggests that the Cabinet tried to defuse the matter: a formal enquiry was set up which would emphasize the standards of behaviour expected in the Foreign Service.[60] The publication of an accusation from a Soviet defector, Petrov, that Burgess and Maclean were long-term Soviet spies, led to the publication of a White Paper on the two missing diplomats on 23 September 1955. This for the first time acknowledged that Maclean was being investigated prior to his disappearance as a possible Soviet spy, and that he had been alerted and fled the country.[61] This led to pressure for a formal enquiry which was resisted by government.

The Foreign Secretary, Harold Macmillan, argued that such an inquest should be directed at securing national interests in the future rather than muckraking the past. Not only was it necessary to protect the security of government documents, but the inquest should also examine the role of communist trade union leaders and their access to secret establishments.[62] The government was determined to resist a public enquiry of any kind in order to maintain secrecy; the opposition's demand for an enquiry by Privy Councillors was not allowed on the grounds that positive vetting had already been introduced and there had already been a comprehensive reorganization of the Foreign Office.[63] The Americans were never taken in by what they saw as a cover-up: both American and British sources have suggested that both Foreign Office and MI5 files were doctored and sanitized to fit in with the official version. In a paper submitted to Cabinet Macmillan argued that strengthening security would imply an increase in executive power, an infringement of civil liberty and a weakening of the English common law.[64]

The problem with this classic liberal objection to increased security was demonstrated in November 1955 when Macmillan announced in the House of Commons that there was no evidence that Harold 'Kim' Philby was the 'third man'. This response to a parliamentary question led to Philby's re-employment by MI6 (he was sacked in 1951 after the Americans said he would not be allowed back into the USA) as an agent in Beirut. In 1963, after a partial confession to an MI6 colleague, Philby fled to Moscow and became the 'spy of the century'.

The continuing suspicion of a cover-up kept alive public interest in the issue; the 'Battle of the Books' was the outcome. On one level this was the hunt for the third (Philby), fourth (Blunt) and fifth man (Cairncross, after a lot of false accusations) of the 'ring of five' or the 'magnificent five' KGB agents in the British establishment, mentioned in a partially decrypted Soviet wireless intercept.[65] It also relates to the search for the alleged super-mole 'Elli' (now revealed by Oleg Gordievsky to have been Leo Long), which suggested that Peter Wright and the Fluency Committee, a joint MI5 and MI6 operation in the 1970s set up to investigate Soviet penetration, was barking up the wrong tree.[66] Much of the literary genre resulting from leaks about such activity, and the escalating costs of the increasingly technologically sophisticated intelligence and counter-intelligence activities, was rubbished by James Rusbridger in *The Intelligence Game*, a less than reverent and accurate view of the secret world.[67]

Wright's deepening obsession that Sir Roger Hollis, Director-General of MI5, was a Soviet spy eventually led him to collaborate with Chapman Pincher, by providing information for *Their Trade is Treachery*; and later to write his own memoirs, the infamous *Spycatcher*. Others involved in the Fluency Committee saw Hollis' deputy, Graham Mitchell, as the more likely candidate, a conclusion that was suggested also by Nigel West on the grounds that he was the author of the inadequate White Paper in 1955.[68] Other investigators, including John Costello, took up the suggestion that Guy Liddell was a better candidate given the evidence.[69] The opening of KGB and other Soviet archives has provided no evidence of the existence of such a spy: nevertheless, the concerns of the intelligence and security communities is readily understandable. Whilst there were false accusations and suspicions, there were also very real spies. The 'wilderness of mirrors' resulted: it was difficult to distinguish between truth and falsehood given the problems in supplying evidence which would stand up to scrutiny in a court of law. The secrecy involved was highlighted by the Profumo affair in 1963. Lord Denning's report was the first time the existence of MI5 was officially acknowledged by name; although it failed to develop the point that Dr Stephen Ward, who committed suicide after being found guilty at his trial, saw himself as monitoring the liaisons for MI5 between John Profumo, the Soviet attaché Ivanov, and the 'showgirls', Christine Keeler and Mandy Rice-Davies.

Indeed, such arguments were developed by Anthony Summers and Stephen Dorril in their lurid and conspiratorial interpretation of the Profumo affair. They argued that MI5 conducted a classical 'Honeytrap' operation designed to compromise Ivanov to persuade him to become a double agent. Released Cabinet papers show this was not the story uncovered by the Lord Chancellor, Lord Dilhorne, who prepared a report on the matter for the Cabinet in June 1963. Dilhorne was told that MI5 had warned the Prime Minister's Office of Profumo's undesirable acquaintance with Stephen Ward, and the Cabinet Secretary, Sir Norman Brook had suggested to Profumo that he terminate this relationship in August 1961.[70] Brook had not told Harold Macmillan of this meeting, nor had MI5 given him any information about Profumo's association with Christine Keeler, or of any links with Ivanov. Profumo told the House of Commons on 22 March 1963 that he terminated his relationship with

Christine Keeler in December 1961, but this contradicted his earlier statement to Brook's successor as Cabinet Secretary, Sir Burke Trend, that he had ended his association with her immediately after the meeting with Brook. This discrepancy was explained by faulty memory. The most important conclusion from the Lord Chancellor's report was that there was no evidence of a breach of security despite Profumo's misleading information to Parliament and Christine Keeler's relationship with both Profumo and Ivanov.[71] This conclusion was also confirmed in the Judicial Enquiry of Lord Denning, which had access to all the relevant papers, and who stated on their (perhaps partial) declassification in 1994 that any retained material probably related to unsubstantiated rumours about further sexual impropriety by other politicians.

Although press reports suggest that only two-thirds of the documentation has been released, in retrospect the most interesting aspect of this somewhat sordid episode was the resignation of Harold Macmillan as Prime Minister in the autumn of 1963. Whilst there is no direct evidence that this was due to the Profumo Affair, the long succession of security leaks and evidence of espionage certainly sapped Macmillan's belief in the high degree of trust necessary for government service. The Lonsdale and Vassall cases, the exposure of the damage to Western security from the activities of the MI6 officer, George Blake, and the defection of Kim Philby showed that there were serious problems of morale and conduct near the centre of government service. Profumo had been a protégé of Macmillan, and had betrayed his trust; suddenly the old certainties about the high morality and accepted conventions of government service were being undermined. Given his own sense of betrayal in his private life, the undermining of the belief in the high standards of behaviour in government was undoubtedly a factor in Macmillan's decision to resign. For our theme this was perhaps unfortunate; none of 'Supermac's' successors showed as sophisticated an appreciation of the difficulties of maintaining security in a free society. The striving for high standards in public life depended on the assumption of mutual trust. Macmillan believed that only through the

15 Peter Wright arrives at the Supreme Court in Sydney, Australia, 1986

acceptance of the highest possible standards of behaviour in public service could the espionage threat be kept under control in a free society. For him, the Radcliffe report, 'Security Procedures in the Public Service', admirably outlined the difficulties involved in living up to this high ideal.[72]

Whilst this aspect of the battle of the books surfaced in the 1980s, it originated in the bitter divisions within the security and intelligence communities which developed in the 1970s as a response to Soviet penetration. This only gradually became public knowledge in the aftermath of the revival of interest following the naming of Sir Anthony Blunt, the surveyor of the Queen's pictures, as a Soviet spy, the so-called fourth man, by the Prime Minister, Mrs Thatcher, in 1979. This intervention arose from the publication of Andrew Boyle's *The Climate of Treason,* which made pointed reference to the dubious behaviour of 'Maurice', a thinly veiled allusion to Blunt's role.[73] Mrs Thatcher's disclosure of this most notorious skeleton in the Prime Ministerial cupboard breached the secrecy which had surrounded the immunity deal which Blunt had forced out of the authorities before he confessed in 1964.[74] It was perhaps somewhat surprising that Peter Wright's defence in the *Spycatcher* trial failed to utilize this breach of confidentiality by the Prime Minister – although few outside the secret state at the time thought that the need to protect this particular source overrode the duty to deny Sir Anthony Blunt the opportunity to lie in a court of law if he sued Boyle, as he would have to do to protect his reputation. As Mrs Thatcher had not been responsible for the immunity deal she felt that, given the situation, she needed to expose the possible hypocrisy involved. Most commentators, then and now, thought she made the correct decision.

One of the debriefers of Blunt in the MI5 operation after the immunity deal was Peter Wright. He was the first scientist employed by the security service in that function, and he worked for the organization in various capacities between 1955 and 1976, as a scientific officer, a counter-intelligence officer and a personal assistant to the Director-General.[75] Wright possessed a sharp intelligence and a good practical innovative scientific mind which enabled him to produce some ingenious improvised inventions, mainly involving wireless technology with which to combat Soviet spying. Whilst his work was successful in this sphere, he was less impressive when he transferred into counter-espionage. He was also an outsider, whose qualities were not fully appreciated by the establishment, and he developed a grievance against the service. This related to inadequate pension arrangements, which forced him to resign his job in the Civil Service and to apply to join MI5 from outside employment, thereby forfeiting his previous entitlements. Whilst this anomaly harked back to the interwar tradition of underfunding, personal recruitment methods and the supposed private income of gentleman spies, Wright was understandably aggrieved. By making a fuss about it Wright ensured that more adequate arrangements were made for his successors, but his pension entitlements were never improved when in service. In political terms Wright appears to have held views to the right of Mrs Thatcher, whom he admired; he was intensely patriotic, and whilst he and his family suffered severely from the unemployment of his gifted father during the depression, he was proud of his response to such adversity. He became a patriot and worked his way up from the bottom, whilst Blunt, with far more personal advantages, used the depression as an excuse to become a spy.

Wright's counter-espionage work and his membership of the Fluency Committee, set up as a joint MI5–MI6 operation to review the problem of Soviet penetration of British security, led to his strong belief that Sir Roger Hollis, the Director General of MI5 from 1965 to 1972, was a Soviet spy. Wright in his retirement emigrated to Tasmania and became an Australian citizen. After the Blunt revelations Wright was sent a ticket to fly back to England. Wright provided Lord Rothschild with an independent list of his achievements for MI5; he was introduced to Chapman Pincher, the investigative journalist specializing in defence and security matters, with a reputation for relaying off-the-record planted leaks from the state accurately and discreetly. Rothschild, the one establishment insider who fully appreciated Wright's abilities, needed support from a member of the security service against unjustified smears to his reputation. He wished to deny, in the strongest possible terms, that he was the 'fifth man'; his long friendship with Blunt was a social and not a political connection.

He was also worried that Wright had 'gone bad', and that he could do lasting damage if he published independently the details of the great mole hunt in the 1970s outside the jurisdiction of the Official Secrets Act. By bringing together Pincher and Wright, Rothschild perhaps wished either to convince the latter that investigative journalists were already interested in the Hollis story and there was no need for unauthorized leaks or, if Wright gave information to Pincher, that the story might be published and its leading claims denied by the authorities as nothing more than journalistic speculation. In fact he collaborated with Pincher, and the publishers, Sidgwick and Jackson, paid Wright half the considerable royalties of *Their Trade is Treachery*.[76]

The British government did not stop the publication of *Their Trade is Treachery* in 1981, and had only insisted on minor amendments to Nigel West's history, *MI5 1945–72: A Matter of Trust* in 1982. This provided one of the main planks in Wright's defence when the government tried to stop the publication of *Spycatcher* in Australia, in a renowned court case in Sydney in November and December 1986.[74] To the uninitiated the sometimes bizarre proceedings of the case appear incomprehensible, but most of the issues involved have been given an interesting explanation by Chapman Pincher in his account of the affair.[78] Although his characterization of Wright's motives is somewhat one-sided, Pincher outlines the most plausible interpretation of how too much secrecy undermined the government's case, both with regard to the publication of *Their Trade is Treachery* in 1981, and by the clear lack of knowledge of some of the elementary facts displayed by the Cabinet Secretary, which allowed his credibility to be so severely damaged at the trial by Wright's solicitor, Malcolm Turnbull.[79] By showing precisely how the misunderstandings arose, Pincher has helped restore the reputations of Sir Robert Armstrong and the Attorney-General Lord Havers. It was because of strict adherence to the 'need to know' principle that Sir Robert Armstrong inadvertently ventured false information about Havers' role in the affair. Havers was not in fact a member of the group who discussed *Their Trade is Treachery* and, as he was not informed about it, he was obviously not responsible for the failure to interfere in its publication.

The British government sought a permanent injunction on *Spycatcher* and argued that Wright had a lifelong duty of confidentiality, through a contractual obligation, not to disclose the secrets he was party to. As he was now domiciled in Australia he was beyond the reach of British criminal law, so the British government tried to stop publication through a civil case. Wright's defence was that he had not disclosed any information that had not become public knowledge through previous publication, and where this was not the case, the material was obsolete, given the transistor revolution in radio communications. If he had wanted to he could have breached national security by discussing his work in Northern Ireland, or on spy satellites, but had chosen not to do so. This argument had plausibility with regard to anti-Soviet operations, but it could be objected, as with the disclosure in the 1970s of the Ultra secret of the breaking of German codes in the Second World War, that this technology was not obsolete in third world countries – in fact the suspicion remains that such countries were encouraged by British intelligence to purchase Enigma machines after the war. The government claim that they objected to everything Wright wrote, rather than to specifics, and that if *Spycatcher* was published it would undermine confidence amongst sources and intelligence cooperation with allies, was countered by the claim that all Wright wanted was to have his book vetted in the same way in which CIA agents had their memoirs assessed. If Britain's most important ally allowed its secret service agents to discuss their work in a responsible fashion, then why could not British intelligence and security officers?

Turnbull made much of the anomaly of the failure of the government to stop *Their Trade is Treachery* and the lifting of the injunction on *A Matter of Trust* after a settlement had been negotiated on specific deletions. In fact, *Their Trade is Treachery* was allowed to be published because the government wished to disguise the fact that the authorities had obtained a copy before publication and circulated it in relevant government circles. The copy was obtained from an entirely legitimate source: the third party whom Chapman Pincher refers to as 'the Arbiter', who was asked his opinion whether the book could be published. He had secretly sent a copy to Sir Arthur Franks, the head of MI6, to ascertain whether there were security objections to its publication. Copies were then sent to other interested parties in government. As no complaints were forthcoming from Franks, the Arbiter raised no objection to the plan for publication. Sir Robert Armstrong admitted in Sydney that the letter to Sidgwick and Jackson asking for a pre-publication copy so that Mrs Thatcher could answer questions in the House of Commons was intended to disguise the fact that the authorities had already seen the contents of the book via the Arbiter–Franks link. As Sir Robert Armstrong did not need to know either the source of the document, or that the intermediary enquired if there were security objections to publication, his embarrassment for being 'economical with the truth' was made obvious to all in Sydney. Mrs Thatcher silenced the storm in a teacup on publication of *Their Trade is Treachery* by announcing that the Trend Report had investigated the allegations and had exonerated Hollis.

Mrs Thatcher's statement did not silence Wright. He knew that all the Trend Report concluded was that there was no smoking-gun evidence that Hollis was a Soviet spy, and that he had not been put above suspicion. He was concerned that there was still a Soviet mole operating in the security service, given the Geoffrey Prime case in 1981, when a GCHQ employee was convicted of betraying British and American communications secrets to the USSR, and the Michael Bettaney case in 1984, when information (from Oleg Gordievsky) led to the arrest of the MI5 officer before he could commit any damage.[80] Having fallen out with Pincher, Wright was determined to publish his account of the recent history of MI5. His eventual manuscript, and its reworking to make it more readable, with the help of Paul Greengrass, was to produce confrontation with the British government. Greengrass had produced a documentary shown on the ITV network in 1984 in which Wright had reiterated his claims against Hollis. This too had not been stopped by the authorities.

In retrospect it was difficult to see what all the fuss was about. There is nothing in either Pincher's or Wright's account which gives credibility to the accusation. There is no evidence Hollis gave information to the Soviet Union, nor that he was an agent of influence for them in the security service. The material presented by W. J. West in his book *The Truth about Roger Hollis* is very thin and highly circumstantial if it is to be construed as a case against him.[81] More convincing are the arguments denying he was a Soviet spy which are presented by Anthony Glees using Hollis' own papers, and in Sheila Kerr's analysis of his opposition to the Anglo-Soviet treaty in 1942.[82] The picture presented is one of Hollis and his deputy Graham Mitchell, both investigated as possible Soviet moles in Operation Drat and Operation Peters, as being supporters of positive vetting who tried to maintain secrecy in a relatively open society by non-totalitarian means. Certainly Oleg Gordievsky's evidence suggests that the KGB were highly satisfied about the chaos caused by the hunt for what now seems to have been a non-existent mole.[83] The reported revelations from the Soviet archives since 1989 appear to confirm this interpretation.

The conditions under which Wright wrote *Spycatcher* also suggest that it must be treated very sceptically as a source. Although he obviously possessed a good memory for detail there are historical and factual errors in the text: for example, the Arcos raid took place in 1927 not 1928. Similarly, there have been complaints that Wright misinterpreted events and ascribed views to individuals that they did not hold. He has also been accused of lying – for example, the claim that Lord Rothschild sent him a first class ticket to travel to England when it was proved that Rothschild sent him an economy class one. In short, most MI5 and other intelligence officers closed ranks against Wright and accused him of being a four-letter-word man for exposing the secrets, or at least the dirty washing, of the service. Whatever the justification for this response there was little in *Spycatcher* that was new. Other ex-intelligence officers were keen to publish memoirs: Anthony Cavendish, an ex-MI6 employee, sent his reminiscences as an ingenious Christmas Card to friends.[84] The most controversial claims by Wright, presented in a ripping yarn, 'Boy's Own' style, was that he was involved in dubious operations which 'bugged and burgled' their way across London; one such incident was Operation Party Piece, in which the entire CPGB secret membership files were 'borrowed' for a weekend from a flat in Mayfair and photocopied. In all, 55,000 items were allegedly added to MI5's collection.[85]

The attempt to stop the publication of *Spycatcher* led to precisely the opposite effect of that intended. The defeat in the Sydney court and the failure to maintain the injunction until the legal processes had been exhausted in Australia ensured it would become a bestseller. The publication in Australia, and almost simultaneously in the USA, opened the floodgates, and the British government was reluctantly forced to retreat. In Britain the government fought the attempt to publish the book for as long as possible, and obtained injunctions against the *Sunday Times* and other newspapers serializing its contents or reporting information obtained from it. Only after the loss of the last appeal to the highest court in Australia, and the failure to be allowed to pursue Wright for the royalties of *Spycatcher*, was the case finally conceded. Ironically, publication made good the pension grievance of the author. It was significant, too, that Mrs Thatcher's unreflective memoirs made no mention of the Peter Wright affair and said little about her own attitude to secrecy, and the absurd lengths she was prepared to take it with regard to protecting the principle of confidentiality.[86]

In other respects the dispute was a disaster for those who believe that the lack of accountability of the security and intelligence communities has made them 'too secret too long'.[87] The passing of a new Official Secrets Act in 1989, whilst rectifying Section 2 of the 1911 legislation (which potentially made Civil Service dinner menus a state secret) and the Security Service Act which updated the Maxwell Fyfe guidelines, produced a blanket ban on the publication of all unauthorized information, and imposed a contractual obligation of confidentiality on all state employees.[88] This means in effect that all future books on the secret state, including this one, will have to rely on declassified information in the public domain, and what can legitimately be inferred from private sources. This issue will be returned to in the conclusion, but there can be little doubt that whatever his motives, Peter Wright's stirring up of the hornets' nest had the net result of producing more, not less, secrecy.

d) A British McCarthyism?

It is clear from a study of the impact of the Cold War that there has been a less pronounced response to the issue in British society than in other Western countries. This has been the case in nations where communism has been a powerful opposition force, as in Italy; and where, like Britain, it was a political irrelevance, such as in the USA. In Italy there have been right-wing conspiracies within the state since 1945 to subvert what has been seen as a corrupt and weak democratic form of government which has been unable to manage the threats posed at various times by communism, political terrorism and organized crime.[89] In the United States subversion in the Cold War years of the 1950s has been conceived as emanating from a secret conspiracy, whose aim has supposedly been to undermine democracy by liberal elites and by leakage of secrets to the Soviet Union. The phenomenon of McCarthyism, of a populist anti-communism which led to the blacklisting and sacking of many who were or had been associated with the Communist Party of America, was a highly illiberal interlude in a nation purportedly dedicated through its constitution to liberty and political freedom.[90] The purge in Britain was much milder – those judged security risks were for the most part transferred to less sensitive work.

16 A demonstration by Mosley's followers in Dalston, East London, 1948

Somewhat ironically the failure of Goronwy Rees to get the British authorities to believe his claims about Soviet spy rings shows, in retrospect, that the establishment was unwilling to face up to the fact that infiltration was a serious problem, and that unsubstantiated accusations and McCarthyite smears were seen as a greater evil than the possibility of renegade upper class treason. The problem was that Rees' claims were more than justified, whatever the doubts about him personally. A close friend of Blunt and Burgess in the 1930s, he appears to have been approached by Soviet intelligence. Whether or not he was ever part of the ring himself, he knew what was going on. Attempting to put his story in the public domain through revelations in *The People* in 1956 was at least part of the reason why he was forced to resign later as Principal of the University of Aberystwyth. Yet the evidence appeared to point to the conclusion that Britain was more in need of draconian action on security matters than the United States. The discovery of espionage in the early years of the Cold War suggested that the main leakages of information to the Soviet Union came from British rather than American sources.[91]

It was Labour, the 'People's party', rather than the traditional Conservative's Blimpish views on communism that can more justifiably be compared to some of the more sinister aspects of McCarthyism. Whilst Senator Joe McCarthy's oratorical style and powers of invention were aspects not copied by Labour, the use of blacklisting and proscription were similar. In fact, from the 1930s to the 1980s Labour expelled members for associating themselves with alleged communist front organizations, and other suspicious radical and Marxist groups. These were deemed to be proscribed organizations. The Conservatives obviously saw the Soviet Union, and their agent in this country, the CPGB, as the principal enemy of the state for much of the period 1917–89, apart from 1941–5. The Conservatives' ingrained dislike of populism and suspicion of American culture and values meant they were loath to imitate the practices of American anti-communist politics, no matter how much they sympathized with the sentiments behind it.

It is now quite clear that there was a tension in government between the determination to maintain civil liberties in a free society and the need for tighter security. Whilst this remains a highly sensitive area, it appears that the authorities have erected a wall of secrecy around this issue and endeavoured to permit as little information as possible escaping into the public domain. Their rationale has been: If the public knew nothing about the issue then McCarthy-type demands for purging innocent victims would not arise. Whilst it has failed to stop continuing conjecture it would appear that the historical record presents a plausible line for future enquiry. The denigration by the establishment of McCarthyism in all its forms as a disreputable form of politics, was a conscious decision to maintain civility in public life. Positive vetting and the tightening up of bureaucratic security procedures were all that was considered necessary to prevent subversion. Anything more drastic was considered a worse undermining of liberty than the threat of subversion; the cure would be worse than the disease.

What the isolating of McCarthyite pressures to elements in the security services signified was the determination of politicians and administrators to maintain the liberal structure of political discourse and parliamentary traditions. The isolation tactic appeared to contain a number of elements: an administrative commitment to as great a degree of political freedom within the law as possible, and to restrict the influence and nature of the regrettable necessity for a political police and security service, together with a reluctance to acknowledge the extent of political surveillance; an establishment distaste for American methods and political culture which remained despite the appreciation of, and close alliance with, American internationalism, and its vigorous defence of the free world; and a profound belief in the administrative virtues of secrecy, which in the hands of a dedicated, reliable and trustworthy elite had created an efficient government machine which had strengthened democracy and the rule of law in Britain. The fact that a few renegades had caused damage to the machinery of government and its reputation by betraying some of its deepest secrets to enemies of the nation should not be allowed to justify the throwing out of the baby with the bathwater.

Piecemeal tinkering, and excision of the rotten elements, was the response of the state machine. The peculiar fundamental values of liberty and secrecy were to be maintained at all costs, even if the intractable problem of terrorism in Ireland was to necessitate a very different approach to events on the other side of the Irish sea.

8

PUSHING AND SHOVING (1958–1994)

The political history of mainland Britain since 1945 has presented a picture of relative stability compared with many European states. Whilst the Irish dimension created problems from 1969 onward, in England political terrorism and public disorder have otherwise been a manageable phenomenon for the authorities. The main difficulties for the state involved public order, particularly regulating the power of trade unions, and the impact of secondary picketing; demonstrations and riots protesting about inner city deprivation, and racial violence aimed at ethnic minorities; and civil disobedience from elements in the Campaign for Nuclear Disarmament (CND), most notably from the Committee of One Hundred, protesting against Britain remaining a nuclear power. In the 1980s the Greenham Common women's peace camp provided a permanent protest against both nuclear weapons and American cruise missiles being stationed in Britain. Although there have been periods of crisis, the political system has never broken down. This chapter will assess the response of the state, as far as it can be ascertained, to challenges to its authority since the Second World War.

In general it can be argued that most pressure groups have worked within the political system during this period. In mainland Britain minorities from the left and right have for the most part expressed their viewpoint in constitutional terms, and not developed underground conspiracies, direct action or political violence. There have been exceptions of course; nevertheless, the resort to terrorism and political violence by some anarchists, and more organized groups like the 'Angry Brigade', the 'Sons of Glendower', the 'Tartan Army' or elements within the 'Animal Liberation Front' and the Green movement, have presented minor problems for the authorities compared to the operations of the Provisional Irish Republican Army (IRA). Ethnic conflict provoked by clashes between neo-fascists and anti-fascists, as well as a hooligan element, and by Black Power movements also caused minor difficulties for the authorities in the 1960s and 1970s. There has also been a rural aspect of political protest: hunt saboteurs have attempted to disrupt country life with increasing frequency since the 1970s, and environmental groups like those at Twyford Down have caused problems for the authorities through acts of civil disobedience. Most of the expression of opposition to the activities of the state or hostility to minority opinion has been expressed in legal form, however; many of the demonstrations of CND since the 1950s, the anti-Vietnam protests of 1965–8, or the Anti-Nazi League in the 1970s against the National Front, spring immediately to mind.

What problems arose from such demonstrations usually amounted to little more than minor infractions of the Public Order Act. It was also quite clear that there has been extensive political surveillance by the state of both left- and right-wing groups in British society despite frequent denials by the authorities. Although political consensus broke down in 1979, the defeat and then collapse of the left in the 1980s in both the industrial and political spheres, and the failure of sustained constitutional or underground nationalist opposition to the authorities to become manifest in England, Scotland or Wales, has arguably made the security aspects of the secret state redundant if a solution could be found to the very different matter of IRA violence.

The activities of the Tartan Army in Scotland in the mid-1970s, when 52 'terrorists' were imprisoned for a period of 286 years in jail, and it was alleged that there was a 24-hour political surveillance of members of the organization by Special Branch for 15 months; and the arson attacks against English holiday homes in Wales in the 1980s, were exceptions to this lack of nationalist terrorist extremism on the mainland.[1] Moreover, Britain has not been immune to problems of international terrorism, as the Lockerbie tragedy demonstrated in 1992, when a Pan American Airways jumbo jet was blown up in mid air, although this resulted more from a failure in German rather than British security. The activities of the Provos and the Irish National Liberation Army (INLA) in Northern Ireland and on mainland Britain was an altogether more intractable problem.

a) 'You have never had it so good'

Harold Macmillan's famous aphorism summed up the political mood of the 1950s; for our purposes it can stand as a totem for the degree of political consensus which operated in British politics after the war, and particularly between 1945 and 1979, the era of what has been termed 'Butskellism'. This encompassed a shared commitment by both government and opposition to Keynesian methods of demand management and the maintenance of full employment, the welfare state, varying degrees of corporatism, acceptance of a new world order based on freer trade and American hegemony, the granting of independence to former colonies and the creation of the British Commonwealth, anti-communism, and (from the 1970s) a commitment to join and then influence the European (Economic) Community.

Of course there were significant differences between Conservative and Labour administrations during this period, most notably in domestic politics over nationalized industries, the size of the public sector and role of government in the management of the economy. The point was, however, that the Second World War marked a watershed in British history: after 1945 the role of the state in both economic and social management was markedly increased and this was tacitly accepted by parliamentary opinion of virtually all complexions; even the advent of 'Selsdon man', the symbol of the initial challenge to the corporatism and welfare state consensus of British politics since 1945, appeared to have been rejected by the electorate in 1974. Right-wing Conservatives who rejected welfarism and corporatism, and left-wing Labour MPs who wanted more statism, were isolated from the political consensus dedicated to the mixed economy.[2]

The Whitehall administration also accepted the political implications of change in the nature of the state and behaved accordingly. This represented the reaction of a non-political Civil Service, which although possessed of a fetish for bureaucratic secrecy, nevertheless was willing to adapt its liberal traditions. This made it responsive, even in its higher echelons, to a sea change in public opinion. What was notable in the two Attlee administrations from 1945 to 1951 was not only the transformation of reformist democratic socialism into an ossified administrative centralism, but the extent to which Whitehall accepted the new order whilst moulding such necessary economic and social change in the light of its own traditions. This was only a partial brave new world, however; and the most successful harmonization of political and administrative direction was to occur (somewhat surprisingly) in the Foreign Office. Sir Edward Bridges, the Cabinet Secretary, failed in his attempt to persuade his mandarin colleagues to adopt a more leading role in developing new interventionist strategies in the economy and society after the war.[3] The British Civil Service did not play such a dynamic role in the development of post-war economy and society as, for example, its French counterparts. Similarly, the Fulton report 1966, which criticized the Civil Service for its lack of leadership in attempts to modernize the British State, was pigeon-holed by government. The changing nature of the British state led to Whitehall adaptations to reflect the new reality; the preference of most administrators was a return to normality. The British form of corporatism was to reflect this; politicians, rather than administrators, were to define policy. The mandarins were to remain servants rather than become interventionist managers themselves.

Whilst economic controls were progressively deregulated by the Churchill administration between 1951 and 1955, little was done to undermine the social consensus; the welfare state was tinkered with at the margin but the principle remained sacrosanct. Consensus and relative industrial harmony were maintained by lubrication from the 'oil can' of the Minister of Labour, Sir Walter Monckton. The corporate tradition ensured that Labour was placated; Keynesian economic management ensured 'full employment', albeit at the cost of modest inflation. Reformism in Britain meant not only the dilution of socialist ideals by the state, but also realization by the administration of the necessity for change.

The era of Butskellism, despite slow growth and relative economic decline, threw up few challenges to the two-party structure. Although there was public discontent and social frustration at times, there was little evidence of public hostility to the political system. Extremism made little headway in this era, despite rumblings from continental Europe which found mild echoes in Britain in 1968. Insofar as there were signs of political change it was with relation to attempts to restructure the centre of British politics: 'Orpington Man', so named after a famous by-election victory, heralded the start of many revivals for the political centre from the 1970s onwards – initially with the Liberals under Jo Grimond and Jeremy Thorpe, then with the Liberal–Social Democratic Party alliance in the 1983 and 1987 elections under David Steel and David Owen, and from then with the Liberal Democrats led by Paddy Ashdown.

To date this has signalled little more than means by which the electorate, particularly in the relatively prosperous regions south and east of the Humber–Severn line, could advertise mid-term blues with the two-party system, as the voters for the most part reverted to type at the succeeding general election. The political centre, to use the Gramscian jargon, has failed so far to create a new 'historic bloc' to break the mould of British politics.[4] Insofar as the two-party system is in crisis, it has been due to the lack of credibility of the Labour Party in the 1980s, and the emergence of a right-wing populism, embodied in 'Essex Man', which ensured the victory of Mrs Thatcher in the general elections of 1983 and 1987, and John Major in 1992.

For those who objected to the political consensus, revolutionizing the framework of British politics proved a frustrating experience. The great British public proved relatively immune to the simplification of political issues to single causes, and pressure groups found that even when they made headway in converting either of the two major parties to policies outside the political consensus, the knee-jerk reflex of the system was to lead to yet another third party revival. Thus issues like immigration controls and nuclear disarmament created a bee sting effect within the political system.

Keeping as many foreign immigrants as possible out of Britain was adopted as a consensus policy by the Conservatives and Labour in the 1960s partly to check the growth of a Tory populist radical right following the 'rivers of blood' speech of Enoch Powell, and of extremist nationalist groups like the National Front. Similarly, the battles over nuclear disarmament in the Labour Party in the 1960s and the 1980s led to swift counter-measures from its executive to maintain the political consensus, despite the election to the leadership of two nuclear disarmers, Michael Foot in 1980 and Neil Kinnock in 1984. Thatcherism rewrote the rules of the political game, not left- or right-wing extremism. It was changes in high politics, not the street corner tradition, which partially restructured British politics.[5]

The secret state appears to have had little direct influence on national politics since 1945. As I argued in the previous chapter, Peter Wright and perhaps a very small minority of officers have expended energy in muddying political waters from time to time. There certainly have been leaks from the government machine, and though many of these have been planted stories to test political and public reaction, some at least have been unofficial and have originated from elements in intelligence and security, or from civil servants like Clive Ponting or Sarah Tisdall wishing for information to be in the public domain. There is no doubt, however, that the management of the security and secret service have been servants to, rather than destabilizers of, the political system, and have had far less disruptive impact on national politics than their equivalents in other democratic states in Europe like Italy and France, and certainly less influence than in authoritarian regimes like Spain between 1945 and 1975, or the communist states of eastern Europe until 1990.[6]

Although little of relevance has been released with regard to the state management of low politics and public order, enough has been leaked into the public domain to suggest some tentative conclusions with regard to the authorities' treatment of extremism. In general terms it may be concluded that there is an important element of continuity in the attitude of the state towards civil liberties and political surveillance compared with the interwar period. Whereas a tougher response to internal security and a greater emphasis on efficiency and the rationalization of resources can be detected in Conservative administrations since 1979, Labour and the 'one nation' Conservative administrations of Churchill, Eden, Macmillan, Home and Heath since 1945 have been more tolerant of civil disobedience and political dissent. Significant changes since the interwar period have included improved technology and more centralized administration, which have enabled the authorities to monitor and control unrest and the growth of extremism. This has meant not only more sophisticated methods of political surveillance, but also more international cooperation and pooling of sigint knowledge between the signatories of the UK–USA agreement in 1947, which was extended to include Canada, Australia and New Zealand.[7] This has been applied to security as well as intelligence matters.

Although the British tradition of local control by police authorities is still intact, the increased bypassing of Watch Committees through Home Office coordination with Chief Constables has led to several clashes between central and local government, particularly between Conservative administrations and Labour controlled authorities. The ambiguity of the wording of the Police Act (1964), which made the Chief Officers of police responsible for operational matters, and gave the Home Secretary powers to veto decisions of appointment by the local Police Committees, ensured that the long-run trends towards greater centralization, more coordinated planning and protecting the independence of the constabulary would continue. This reinforced the trend of the existing case law.

The two leading decisions emphasized different aspects of this. In *Fisher* v. *Oldham Corporation* (1930) it was held that the constable was not the servant of any organ of government.[8] According to Lord Denning in *Rex* v. *Metropolitan Police Commissioner*, ex parte *Blackburn* (1968) the constable's authority 'is original, not delegated, and is exercised at his own discretion, by virtue of his office'. The formation of a more centralized bureaucracy to improve police coordination has had much the same effect. The establishment of Police Support Units (PSU) and Special Patrol Groups (SPG), the establishment of the National Reporting Centre, the creation of a Special Branch in most of the police authorities, the availability of more sophisticated equipment for dealing with public disorder (like riot shields and NATO helmets), the closing of loopholes in the law and the outlawing of most forms of secondary picketing, have decisively shifted the advantage in confrontation with the authorities to the forces of law and order.[9] Yet the commitment to allowing legal forms of political dissent and to maintaining civil liberties is as much a part of Thatcherism as to more tolerant approaches to the problem. There is, however, a continuing tension between the demand for an efficient administration of law and order, suggestive of a greater degree of centralization, and the local traditions of British policing.

This contradiction was illustrated by the furore over the Police and Magistrates Court Act (1994) when House of Lords opposition forced the Major administration to back down over important elements in the bill. The considerable part played in this by Lord Whitelaw, that key loyalist to Mrs Thatcher, despite his patrician credentials and instinctive sympathies for 'one nation Toryism' and the 'wets', showed that the 'new right' political agenda for speeding up the long-term trends towards the creation of a national police force under centralized direction was being strongly opposed by a broad spectrum of Conservative opinion, as well as by the Opposition. In particular, proposals for the government to be given powers to appoint the Chairmen of Police Committees, and for elected local government representation to be reduced to a minority, were withdrawn. The Act also pointed to the key role of the Magistrates Clerk, as a link between Whitehall and the local justice system, a back-door association which the Home Office had used since before the First World War.

Whilst Thatcherism has led to an emphasis on efficient administrative control with the operations of forces under central government initiative (often at one remove, creating the illusion of no political involvement), it would be misleading to over-emphasize the move to more authoritarian methods, or to make analogies with the 'Prussian' model. If Majorism is Thatcherism with a human face, then the Sheehy Commission's attempts in 1993 to end many of the special privileges of the police are more suggestive of longer continuities in the Conservative tradition; the subordination of even the maintenance of law and order to the need for parsimony in public expenditure, and an insistence on the operation of a free market and a level playing field for all, with no protected priveleges for even those whose duty it is to uphold the rule of law in the system. The failure to implement the most radical proposals illustrated the only partial acceptance of such recommendations.

Equally, the increasing sophistication of political surveillance techniques – from Peter Wright's ingenious Heath Robinson gadgets for snooping, through the transistor revolution, satellite surveillance, the activities of GCHQ, to the controversy on the bugging of the royal family – suggests that the technological revolution in the secret state, and the facilities for intercepting mail, have made the question of who controls the secret policemen more urgent. Perhaps the recent tentative steps to make MI5 and MI6 more accountable, what might be called a charm offensive by the state, will make the secret and security services less privileged. The Director-General of MI5, Stella Rimington, gave an impressive 1994 Dimbleby lecture which explained the role of a security service in the defence of British democracy.

We are constantly being reminded that the operations of MI5, Special Branch and the government's ears on the world at Cheltenham, GCHQ, are subject to the laws of the land. But there has been no adequate accountability for these organizations, although it is known that John Major is in favour of greater oversight. There are indeed plans for a relative degree of parliamentary oversight of the secret and security services, although how far this will silence critics of the privileged world of spies and secret policemen is more debatable. Periodic noises have been made by governments, including the present one, about looking into the possibility of Privy Councillors or other representatives of the great and good being kept informed about the operations of the secret state. As the government always denies any knowledge of what has allegedly taken place when concern is expressed about the reputed actions of the security service, there is, not surprisingly, considerable scepticism still expressed about the activities of the more secret areas of the state. Even if these organizations are such models of legal rectitude as the authorities claim, there is still considerable room for doubt about operations which have been subcontracted out to private operatives so that dubious operations can be made deniable. A classic case of this genre appears to have come to light when a headless Buster Crabb was discovered after unsuccessfully trying to photograph the Russian warship transporting Khruschev and Bulganin to Britain in 1956. Private organizations and individuals were used for surveillance operations against communist and Soviet targets after 1918. Such practices are now firmly denied by MI5.

There are other obvious continuities from the interwar period: most notably in the attitude of the political parties to the infiltration of allegedly extremist elements into their organizations. Thus the Conservatives have been keen to expel or discourage fascists or extreme nationalists, including National Front members, from the party once uncovered; there have been several purges of such individuals, particularly from associated right-wing organizations like the Monday Club, and hostility has been shown to those within the party who advocate compulsory repatriation of coloured

17 The Battle of Orgreave: pickets swarm up trees to keep an eye on mounted police deployed near the Orgreave Coking Plant

immigrants. Powellism, or at least his policy with regard to ethnic relations, was decisively rejected by the Heath government, and Enoch Powell left the Conservative Party to join the Ulster Unionists.

More significant perhaps has been the Labour Party's response to 'entrism' by Trotskyist and other ultra-left groups. Unlike MI5, since 1945 Labour has been much more concerned about the activities of 'Trots' than it has with the CPGB. What is of particular interest is that despite the leftward shift in the leadership since the war, including those initially tolerant of dissent like Harold Wilson (leader 1963–76), and pronounced civil libertarians like Michael Foot (1980–3) and Neil Kinnock (1983–92), 'witch hunts' and 'McCarthyite' purges against Trotskyists have become a significant feature of the internal politics of the Labour Party.

This signals the concern of the effect of both 'raiding party' and 'deep entrist' tactics of different Trotskyist groups to a reformist bureaucracy which has always had problems in retaining the allegiance of young idealists who have proved themselves prone to the attractions of the ideas of utopian revolutionaries. Disciplinary action has also been opposed by those who see the Labour Party as a broad catholic opposition to the alleged evils of capitalism, and welcome the committed support of radicals and revolutionaries.

Again there is an element of continuity in this response; The Labour leadership objects to the party being within a party allegiance of members of such organizations, and is suspicious of the Popular Frontism of organizations like CND and the Anti-Nazi League (ANL), both of which were considered to have had varying degrees of influence exerted on them by other political organizations. In this sense Trotskyism since 1945 has replaced the CPGB of the interwar period as the bogeyman on the left of the party.

This has been the case even though the extreme factionalism of Trotskyism has somewhat diminished its appeal. The history of post-war Trotskyism is a study of the 57 varieties of idealist socialism which to those not enamoured by the attractions of revolutionary Marxism appeared to span a spectrum from a utopian form of direct democracy to a fanaticism which had little contact with the problems of the real world. Broadly speaking, the various factions in the Revolutionary Communist Party (RCP) split in 1949; this appeared to be the upshot of a debate about tactics and ideology between those who wished to remain in the Labour Party and those who thought that the 1945 Labour government had so besmirched the ideal of socialism that the state had degenerated into an irredeemably ossified bureaucratic apparatus. There was also an ideological dispute about the status of Stalinist Russia between those, in what was to develop as the Socialist Labour League (SLL) and later the Workers Revolutionary Party (WRP), who saw it as a deformed workers' state and those – in what was to become the International Socialists (IS), later the Socialist Workers Party (SWP) – who interpreted it as a form of state capitalism. The Club, the Trotskyist successor to the RCP split, and the three major groupings which emerged from this and other factions, were divided over ideology and tactics. In general terms it can be said that the SLL caused the most headaches for the Labour Party in the 1950s and early 1960s, IS and the SWP from 1968 to about 1978, and from then to the present day the Militant Tendency.[10] The picture became more complicated in the later 1960s with the emergence of the 'new left', a loosely allied group of ex-communists, international Marxists, a Trotskyist faction and a workers' control group. Most of these were to go their separate ways into CND, the Labour Party or the political fringe. Perhaps the best known of the activists were the International Marxist Group.[11]

The common denominator of all these groups as far as the Labour Party was concerned was the appeal that revolutionary idealism made to alienated, disaffected youth. In 1936, 1940, 1955 and 1964 the Labour Party Young Socialists (LPYS) had been closed down after being taken over by Trotskyist elements. For much of the 1970s the LPYS was controlled by Militant Tendency, which through its influence on the Liverpool City Labour Party caucus between 1980 and 1986, also had significant leverage over the council which provoked a notorious confrontation with the Thatcher government and, more recently, the outbreak of disciplinary action and expulsions in the Labour Party. The continuing recurrence of the problem has led to continuing purges of Militant supporters in the later 1980s. Militant is still exerting influence in inner city areas in the nineties. The tactic of using immediate reformist demands, an impossibilist programme masking the revolutionary aims of the organization, as a propaganda weapon, have also been a factor in the case of so-called 'loony left' councils in their opposition to rate capping and the seemingly endless brake on local government expenditure initiated by Mrs Thatcher's administrations in the 1980s. As the Trotskyists have at most a few thousand dedicated adherents, the amount of trouble they have caused the Labour Party was out of all proportion to the numerical size of the various factions. At its peak in 1984 the most successful of these groups, Militant, only had just over 8,000 members, and its paper, *Militant,* sold 20,000.[12] As its ideological mentor, Ted Grant, was once described by an ex-collaborator as possessing the charisma of 'a gramophone record that got stuck forty years ago', the problems of the Labour Party in motivating reformist idealism become immediately apparent. The attractions of some Trotskyist sects, who spend as much energy in vituperative attacks on competing revolutionary groups as on denouncing the evils of capitalism or Stalinist communism, are sometimes difficult to understand.

Labour's opponents have been able to associate the party's image with what was seen as the disreputable activism of Militant by much popular opinion, despite the Labour Party's obvious hostility to Trotskyism, made absolutely clear even though the leadership moved to the left during the 1980s. Although there were other reasons, as I shall argue, why Labour failed to challenge Thatcherism effectively in the 1980s, deep-seated and unfounded propaganda smears about the unreliability of its organization and beliefs played their part.

What the role of the secret agencies of the state was in this development is still unclear. Whilst the official view – that the security service is neutral and operates to defend parliamentary democracy from its enemies – is true, the suspicion that historically the left has been subject to far more political surveillance than the right in British politics appears well founded. Although leakages from the post-1945 security services have produced a very one sided and somewhat unflattering view of the activities of MI5 and MI6, and the revelations of Peter Wright have highlighted some dubious areas, a few general points can be made from material now in the public domain.

Perhaps the most significant of these can be gleaned from reading in between the lines of *Spycatcher.* Whilst the seminal reorganization of MI5 took place in 1940, and there appear to have been refinements since to the structure then put in place, the division between counter espionage, aimed at Soviet threats, and the surveillance of British groups has become significant. Peter Wright has hinted that from the early 1970s his obsession with Soviet communism was not the only (or even the main) concern of MI5, given the emergence of new forms of extremism. Although Wright suggests that his activities involved work in Northern Ireland, and it appears that MI5 ousted MI6 from its role in Ulster, this remained basically the prerogative of Special Branch as well as the Royal Ulster Constabulary and the military until 1992. A concern about the development of international terrorism and possible links between British organizations, the Baader-Meinhoff group, the Red Brigades and radical Muslim fundamentalist sects, and other possible international paymasters like Libya or Iran, became at least as important as the red menace in the demonology of the security authorities from the 1970s. Native Trotskyist sects had fewer obvious international paymasters, although no doubt this was an area of some investigation by the authorities. Certainly Libya appears to have been significantly implicated in funding both Provisional IRA activities and international terrorism.

The other major area of concern for the authorities was the surveillance of what could be termed popular front activities and the extent to which these were controlled by foreign powers or extremist organizations. There is some anecdotal evidence to suggest that groups classified as extreme right, like the National Front and various mimetic Nazi organizations, have also been subject to surveillance. No doubt this is so, although whether there has been much need for MI5 to do more than invest in an annual subscription to the well informed independent left-wing anti-fascist magazine *Searchlight*, remains doubtful. Certainly this source has highlighted the international connections of the extreme right as well as help to organize a militant anti-racism campaign (which one suspects has occupied the attentions of the authorities rather more than the operations of racist organizations).

Whilst the secret state, despite Peter Wright and the Fluency Committee, showed a slowly diminishing obsession with the activities of communist subversion from the later 1960s, the activities of 'extremists' still worried the authorities with regard to criticism of the state. Whilst several examples could be given, the state's reaction to CND and the ANL will serve the purpose. These two cases show that if the level of analysis appears to have been more sophisticated than in the interwar period – for, as Peter Wright and other sources have informed us, MI5 acquired a research and analysis department in the 1970s – the same conspiracy mentality of the authorities still predominated in interpretations of these organizations, and the nature of the control of these groups.

The state is still highly suspicious of populist low politics, street corner oratory and mass demonstrations. The left, too, has developed its mirror image conspiracy of state manipulation and direction. Little has changed from the interwar period except the authorities' superior technology and more sophisticated methods of propaganda, organization and control, and expanded legal powers. This is certainly the case, although whether news manipulation by the authorities, and a generally hostile response by the media to the methods and techniques of low politics, outweighed the effects of investigative journalism and criticism of the authorities, the state and the police in newspapers and on television, is much more open to question. Whilst the judiciary have generally supported many of the new powers assumed by the state, the jury system has proved much more problematical for the authorities, as Clive Ponting's leakage of defence secrets in the aftermath of the Falklands War proved. Whilst the new Official Secrets Act of 1989 plugged the defence of public interest to disclose possible dubious behaviour, what a jury would make of any similar case is anybody's guess.

The attitude of the state to popular mass protest highlighted some of the problems faced by the secret state. It appeared that the main concern of the authorities with regard to such groups was the extent to which the ANL was controlled by the Trotskyist SWP, and CND by Soviet influence. Thus the secret state was more concerned with the agitational aspects of mass demonstrations complaining about overt racist behaviour and the horrors of nuclear war than they were about the substance of the issues being complained about. For the authorities, therefore, it was more important to maintain the legitimacy of state supervision, whether it be the activities of Special Patrol Groups in controlling demonstrations at Red Lion Square in 1974, when Kevin Gately was killed, and at Southall on 23 April 1979, when Blair Peach died allegedly after receiving a blow from a policeman, or in relation to the annual Aldermaston march of CND, most notably the 1,314 arrested in Trafalgar Square in 1961 and the 357 at the associated Holy Loch march at the same time.[13]

In these cases the public order aspects of the problem were of particular concern to the authorities. Although the Race Relations Acts have been used against the instigators of racist behaviour aimed at immigrant groups, it remains true that more arrests have been made against those who protest against racial violence than those who either foment it or who were directly responsible for it. Similarly, following inner city riots – from the Notting Hill and Nottingham disturbances in 1958 to the conflagrations in St Pauls, Bristol in 1980, and in Brixton, Toxteth and Moss Side in 1981 – more emphasis has been given to the criminal activities associated with the background to these events than to the social causes of the problem. Thus the police are now better equipped to deal with local disturbances, although little progress has been made in curing the causes of social alienation in ethnic communities.

Although the Scarman judicial enquiry into the Brixton riot in 1981 pointed out the necessity of addressing the community issues involved, improvements, if any, have been made at a snail's pace; the horrific murder of PC Blakelock at the Broadwater Farm Estate at Tottenham in 1987, when the authorities tried to restore order, illustrated the depth of the breakdown of trust between many inner city areas and the representatives of law and order.[14] The continuing controversy over the convictions in the case has done little to improve matters. Again there seem to be distinct parallels between official attitudes in the interwar period and today. Although the Race Relations legislation of 1965 and 1968, and various amendments since, together with the Public Order Act of 1986, which made it easier to prosecute for the offence of incitement to racial hatred, have given some belated protection to minorities as victims of racist abuse, the authorities find it as difficult today as in the 1930s to make the legislation work effectively. Ethnic communities, the victims of increasing racist abuse and outbreaks of violence, view cynically the inability of the police to protect the interests of minorities. This it should be stressed is due to the difficulties the authorities face in collecting evidence and proving allegations in such a difficult area, and in interpreting the law with regard to incitement, racial abuse and the retaliation against provoked insults. As in the 1930s, there does appear to be an unresolved difficulty between the wish of the authorities to crack down on the instigators of racial violence and the problems of police officers in collecting evidence to validate complaints. Police 'racism' is partially explained by this dilemma, although there is a worrying 300 per cent increase in complaints from members of ethnic minorities against officers in 1993. The political difficulties encountered by the authorities in this area are well illustrated by the debate in Cabinet over fascist activities and public order in 1962–3. Following the well publicized fracas between anti-racist protestors and the National Socialist Movement (NSM), the Cabinet discussed the issue of whether greater legal powers were needed by the police than those provided by the Public Meetings Act (1908) and the Public Order Act (1936). The matter was complicated by the appeals of the leaders of the NSM following legal proceedings. The court upheld the convictions in the case, even if sentence was reduced on some of the charges. The Cabinet considered the fascist provocation and anti-Semitic abuse involved an outrage, but declined to support a private member's bill making racial incitement a new offence or to increase penalties under the Public Order Act.

Several arguments were used to justify inactivity. Although there was much public disquiet over the activities of the NSM in 1962, the fact that it had only between 300 and 400 members, and that other radical right, racial populist or neo-fascist groups like Mosley's Union Movement (900 members) and John Bean's British Nationalist Party (300–400 members) made little impact, the case for stronger legal powers had not been proved, particularly as the convictions had been upheld. Specific legislation to protect individuals with regard to race or origin was denied on the grounds that it could be used to deny criticism of individuals on religious or political grounds, which would limit freedom of speech. Responsible members of the Jewish and coloured communities understood that greater resentment against protected minorities could result from such legislation. It might also create difficulty with regard to the expression of nationalist opinion on the Celtic fringe.

The government considered that whilst the provocation of the Jewish community was deplorable, the upholding of the conviction of the accused had shown that Sections 2 and 5 of the Public Order Act, banning paramilitary formations and making abusive words and behaviour an offence, were working satisfactorily. The Home Secretary, Henry Brooke, was prepared to consider the raising of sentences for these offences, but dropped the idea when government backbenchers signalled their objection with regard to a threat to freedom of speech. Such amendments to the law would also not strengthen the authorities against the much larger numbers of left-wing demonstrators who infringed Public Order legislation in direct response to real or alleged provocation. Such a barrage of objections led the Cabinet to adopt the traditional cautious approach to the minefield of Public Order legislation: only Ian Macleod was prepared to support the private member's bill against the arguments of the Home Secretary; he was concerned about the threat of anti-Semitism, even if communist opposition counted little, and Fenner Brockway's proposal to outlaw racial discrimination was 'political skywriting'.[15]

The difficulty of the authorities in this matter is that many of the inhabitants of localities, particularly inner city areas, which have either become or are perceived as being potential immigrant reception areas, feel threatened by the process. Competition for scarce jobs, housing and other social services, and a fear of 'cultural swamping', fanned by right-wing politicians including Mrs Thatcher, has led to ethnic tension.[16] Right-wing extremist groups like the National Front (NF) in the 1970s and the British National Party (BNP) in the 1990s have taken advantage of these problems. In political terms, the fact that Mrs Thatcher adopted a strong nationalist stance, as well as a highly restrictive and illiberal policy with regard to immigration, coupled with the fact that the 'Falklands factor' enabled her to adopt a credible Churchillian pose, meant that much of the potential support for the extreme right became dissipated from the outset. With strong government in control, wrapping oneself up in the Union Jack was not a very productive policy for the extreme right. Firm government prevented the emergence of political space within which an alternative low politics tradition could develop in the 1980s. Thus only when Mrs Thatcher fell from power could a credible political challenge from the extreme right emerge.

Moreover, the longstanding official and media disparagement of ethnocentric hostility within British political culture also accounted for the failure of anti-immigrant low politics during the Thatcher era. Britain, unlike much of the rest of Europe in the 1980s, did not experience the phenomenon of nearly ten per cent of its electorate supporting anti-immigrant or neo-fascist parties.[17] The failure of John Major to stamp his authority on the Conservative government, and the government's deep unpopularity, together with continuing divisions and a worry about the credibility of a Labour government (for reasons of both doctrine and electoral geography), have created the conditions for the possible revival of the extreme right. Its first local election victory since the 1970s, at Millwall in September 1993, is perhaps a symptom of this.

There was continuing suspicion of popular front type organizations like the ANL and CND by the authorities, which it was thought on no account should be given any official recognition whatsoever. This appears to have followed from the low politics of mass demonstrations and marches practised by both, and the belief that organizations allegedly controlled or influenced by 'extremists' should be given no credibility by the state. This was because the authorities concluded that the ANL had become a satellite organization of the SWP, and the security service was concerned about how CND could be manipulated in Soviet interests.

This suspicion extended so far that even liberal defenders of these organizations were put under surveillance as alleged subversives. The National Council for Civil Liberties (now called Liberty), for example, as in the 1930s, appears not to have improved its reputation in the eyes of the state. Following the revelations of Cathy Massiter, the European Court ruled there had been a breach of the European Human Rights Convention: Harriet Harman (now a Labour MP) and Patricia Hewitt (later a personal assistant to Labour leader Neil Kinnock) had been General Secretaries of the NCCL in the 1980s, and had been put under political surveillance by MI5. According to the Council of Europe this was a breach of their human rights; the Thatcher government argued this abuse was rectified with the introduction of the Security Service Bill of 1989 which put MI5 on to a statutory basis.

Whilst the manifest paranoia of elements within the state even today has led to continuing embarrassments for the government and the security authorities, there is also compensatory evidence which explains why political surveillance is still considered necessary. Perhaps the best recent example of this was the admission of two members of the Committee of 100, Michael Randle and Patrick Pottle, that they had been involved in aiding the escape from Wormwood Scrubs of George Blake, a fellow inmate, a Soviet spy and ex-MI6 employee, and helping him flee to Moscow. They objected to the 42-year prison sentence passed on him, which they considered to be excessive. Although they were later charged with helping Blake to escape, the jury accepted the explanation offered by the two men and acquitted them.

For the state authorities the case showed how idealists could be used by agents of a foreign power. The fact that so many convicted of political crimes, or that so many who had intelligence connections, had been allowed to congregate together in the same gaol, and that the confession was voluntary, highlighted the weaknesses of MI5. Political surveillance may be necessary, but by its very nature it is a very inexact science and produces more errors than unveilings of political or intelligence conspiracies. Possibly the continuing controversy over the abduction and death of the veteran antinuclear campaigner Hilda Murrell in 1984 is an example of this; the circumstances, despite official denials, bear comparison with subcontracted and deniable security operations which have run into difficulties in the the past.[18]

Similarly, the embarrassment of the resignation of the commission established by the NCCL during the miners' dispute, because they insisted on recognizing the civil rights of 'scab' miners who refused to strike, provided ammunition for justifying the state's hostility to that organization.[19]

b) 'The Enemy Within'

Activities of political 'extremists' have proved to be an irritant to the state since 1945, but the authorities have been more concerned about the threat posed by militant trade unionists to the structure of British government. Whilst much of the poor industrial relations record of a relatively strike prone British economy between 1945 and 1985 has rightly been blamed on economic disputes between management and workers over wages and conditions of employment, the actual or threatened miners' strikes of 1972, 1974 and 1984–5 had a more political dimension. The response to this was not to lead to a revival of the old communist menace, but it had more in common with the reactions of the state to the General Strike in 1926. The power of the authorities was pitted in a struggle against the economic power of the miners in a situation where the conditions of the battle had been rigged against the workers.

In short, conflict with the miners was the decisive confrontation in a war between state and trade union power whose outcome was to result in the collapse of the corporatist tradition in British society since 1945. Whilst the impact of Thatcherism will be assessed in the last section of this chapter, its role and influence cannot be understood except in relation to the decisive conflict of this social war, whose outcome was a landmark in the tragic decline of Britain's mining industry, and the devastation of so many of its communities.

The background to the industrial confrontation with the miners is seen with the changing nature of relative power between the state and trade unions since 1945. The Churchill coalition in 1940 saw the beginnings of a corporatist tradition: trade unions played an important role in stabilizing relationships between the state and civil society, and in ameliorating conflict.[20] This development was not always harmonious. Unofficial elements, from the 1940s to the 1980s, led working class resistance to greater state interference in the labour market, and to wage control. Industrial leadership, particularly in the Confederation of British Industry (CBI), remained steadfast over its demand for 'the right to manage'. The trade unions remained suspicious of Prices and Incomes policies, and whereas at times (such as the 1940s) they acquiesced tacitly in such arrangements, in the later 1960s, during the Heath administration from 1970 to 1974 and in the 'winter of discontent' in 1979, they opposed any accommodation with the state which restricted collective bargaining. This was the case irrespective of whether there was a Labour or Conservative administration in power.

Whereas both management and labour continued their traditional hostility to greater state involvement in collective bargaining, the triumph of corporatism during the era of Butskellism meant there was greater acceptance on both sides of industry of the idea that the framework of industrial relations should be regulated by the state. In an economic environment of full employment and the welfare state the repeal of the Trade Union Act of 1927 by the new Labour administration in 1945, and the development of mild inflationary pressures, led to the growth of the influence of the Trades Union Congress. This was recognized in the ill-fated National Plan of the 1964–6 Labour administration and the role of the National Economic Development Council in the 1970s.

If in general terms corporatism since the war was to see greater trade union power, higher living standards and better working conditions for British workers, for critics of the performance of the economy there was a considerable downside. Relative economic decline, lower productivity than our industrial rivals, slower rates of economic growth, poor rates of investment, balance of payments difficulties and the 'English disease' of restrictive practices in manufacturing industry threatened to turn Britain into an industrial museum of antiquated practices.[21] Attempts at modernizing the economy came up against a wall of vested interest and defensive action from trade unions fearful of losing economic power. The framework of the law and the decisions of the courts also tended to militate against change before 1979.

Whilst the era of Butskellism had seen an uneasy partnership between the state and the trade union movement, the authorities had managed frictional conflict in society through the greater managed coordination of elements of the secret state. As has already been shown, the Labour administration in 1945 reactivated the old Supply and Transport Organization and changed its name to the more innocuous Emergencies Committee in 1947. The Home Office Chief Constables Conference became the Association of Chief Police Officers in 1948, which fused the separate organizations of boroughs and county constabularies.[22] These changes were accelerated into providing greater central coordination to national disturbances following the industrial confrontations of the later 1960s and early 1970s. Similarly, both Labour and Conservative administrations, starting in the 1940s, used the military to aid the civil power in performing emergency work during strikes and ensuring the distribution of essential goods and services.[23]

During the Heath administration of the early 1970s this relatively corporatist consensus came under increasing strain. As has already been made clear, the relationship between state, industry and trade unions had always been an uneasy one, but between 1970 and 1974 it was in danger of breaking down completely. Of the twelve occasions between 1920 and 1982 when the Emergency Powers Act was invoked, five of them occurred between 1970 and 1974. The abrasive posture of the new administration towards the unions was spelt out immediately when the Emergency Powers Act was invoked to deal with a docks and an electricity workers' strike in 1970. It was, however, the confrontation between the miners and the Heath government in 1972 which redrew the familiar political landscape.

The background to the dispute has to be seen in terms of attempts to alter the balance of power in society. The Wilson administration lost the election in 1970 partly as a reaction to its failure to reform the trade unions who had successfully resisted attempts to curb their powers in 1969. The attempt by the Heath administration to introduce an Industrial Relations Act was like a red rag to a bull and soured the possibility of a harmonious relationship with the unions. This was made manifestly clear with the national miners' strike in January 1972, the first since 1926.

The confrontation with the miners followed an increasingly violent series of disputes in which militant pickets had intimidated or obstructed strike breaking 'scabs' in industrial conflicts. This had led to violent confrontations with the police, such as had ocurred at the Roberts-Arundel dispute at Stockport between 1966 and 1968. This picket line violence had been aided and abetted by the mass importation of so-called 'new left' activists, many associated with extremist groups who were not members of the trade union in dispute. The escalation in such tactics at the Saltley coke depot in Birmingham derived something from this development, although many of the 'flying pickets' were miners. It owed more to a ruthless strategy behind the confrontation,

18 A CND march through London, 1989. The march was timed to coincide with the anniversary of the founding of NATO

formulated by Arthur Scargill of the National Union of Mineworkers Barnsley area strike committee. Scargill, whose hero was A. J. Cook, the charismatic leader of the miners in 1926, fought the strike on the assumption that 'we were not playing cricket on the village green', and organized 15,000 massed secondary pickets to prevent 800 police from keeping the Saltley coke depot open.[24] Whilst the organization behind the dispute owed as much to a plan implemented by the NUM, under the leadership of Joe Gormley, which involved a ten weeks' overtime ban that ran down coal stocks, it was Scargill's militant tactics which led to the success of the strike after much of industry was reduced to a two-day week, and forced a pay offer which breached the incomes policy.[25]

The passing of the Industrial Relations Act in 1971, which challenged the closed shop and established the Industrial Relations Court, merely worsened a tense confrontation. In 1972 more days were lost in strikes than in any year since 1919, and steeply rising costs and the effects of quadrupling oil prices in 1973 exacerbated the situation. Although the rapid escalation of inflation owed most to the devaluation of the dollar in 1971 and the effects of the Arab–Israeli war of 1973, the Heath government's growth strategy and the so-called 'Barber boom', engineered by the Chancellor of the Exchequer, became the scapegoats for the Tory defeat. In the soul searching following the loss of power, the U-turn in 1972 signalling a return to a corporatist policy and a Prices and Incomes policy became the battleground which led to the decisive breakdown of political consensus.[26]

Mass picketing like that at Saltley developed in other disputes and led to the arrest of the 'Pentonville five' and a rash of sympathy dock strikes around the country. Eventually the dockers were released, although there was considerable violence at the Neap House dispute at Flixborough involving wharves that were not registered under the National Dock Labour Scheme.

The response of the state to this challenge to its authority consisted of the Heath government beefing up its planning with relation to emergencies. The Cabinet Office now took over responsibility for civil emergency planning from the

Home Office. A new, streamlined emergencies organization was created and called the Civil Contingencies Unit (CCU), sometimes referred to as 'Cuckoo', operating from a 'doomsday' operations Cabinet Office briefing room known as 'Cobra' which was able to communicate directly with regional officers and Chief Constables.[27] As a direct consequence of the Saltley débâcle, the National Reporting Centre was established in consultation with the Home Office to coordinate the response of local police forces in a national emergency.

Whilst the administrative framework to cope with national emergencies was revamped in 1972, a new crisis in the winter of 1973–4 led to the downfall of the Heath administration. The TUC objected to the implementation of 'stage three' of the government's Prices and Incomes policy, whilst the state was determined to resist inflationary wage claims. A work to rule by workers in the electricity supply industry, the cutback of production of oil supplies by OPEC following the Arab–Israeli war of 1973, and the declaration of a coal strike by the miners, led Edward Heath to declare a general election on the issue of who governs Britain. The inconclusive outcome to the February 1974 election led to a minority Labour administration. The miners were given a settlement which specifically exempted them from stage three, and a majority Labour administration was formed after a narrow Labour victory following a second election in October 1974.

A rather different confrontation with the Unions in Northern Ireland in May 1974 highlighted the political problems faced by the state with regard to direct action by militant workers. The fiercely loyal Orangemen of the Ulster Workers Council strangulated electricity supplies, breached the Sunningdale Agreement and forced the Power sharing executive to resign. Direct rule was imposed on Northern Ireland. The first attempt to limit the growing power of the trade unions had ended in failure.

The Wilson (1974–6) and Callaghan administrations (1976–9) tried to persuade Unions to moderate their demands through voluntary restraint, but when this proved insufficient to prevent inflationary pressures on the economy, and with the forced devaluation of 1976 in mind, the attempts to impose more statutory forms of restraint provoked immediate hostility from organized labour. The Labour governments invoked the amended version of the Emergency Powers Act (1964) and used troops in a strike breaking role against Glasgow dustmen (1975), and to drive the 'Green Goddesses' when the firemen came out between November 1976 and January 1978. On the latter occasion the troops were used illegally, as the authorities realized belatedly that under Queen's regulations they only had local powers to aid the civil power, whereas in the fire brigade dispute they had been used on a national scale. When this was pointed out by the radical journal *State Research*, the regulations were altered to justify even more creeping centralization of emergency powers.

The failure of Labour to curb picket line violence, as in the Grunwick dispute between 1976 and 1978, also alienated much public opinion. What was particularly interesting about this dispute was the growing public concern about alleged intimidatory tactics of strikers and mass pickets and the increasingly sympathetic response of much of the media to the frankly reactionary and hard line approach to strikers by strong voiced policemen like the Metropolitan Police Commissioner, Sir Robert Mark, and his successor Sir David McNee.[28] What led to the final collapse of the era of corporatism was the 'winter of discontent' in 1978–9, when a 5 per cent pay limit was attempted. Its failure was an important contributory factor to the defeat of the Labour government.

The second decisive change in the nature and structure of the British state during the twentieth century occurred in May 1979 with the election of Mrs Thatcher's first administration. Whilst this will be examined in greater detail in the next section, it was the willingness to adopt confrontational tactics with organized labour which enabled the 'Iron Lady' to introduce the 'Thatcher revolution'. The organisation of government was modernised to allow greater coordination and control of centralized administration during emergencies. This to a great extent had begun in the aftermath of the 1972 miners' strike, had been developed as a response to the Heath débâcle in 1974, and was approved by Mrs Thatcher once she had successfully ousted him as leader in 1975.

The Thatcher revolution in government was based on *ad hoc* committees of senior ministers and civil servants. Their prototypes were the groups which produced the Carrington and Ridley reports in opposition. The former came to the conclusion that there had been a fundamental shift in industrial power in favour of the unions, and that the best brains in Whitehall should be immediately asked to consider emergency planning procedures; also that attention should be given to publicity to ensure that the public would be fully primed about the government's case. The conclusions of the latter were leaked to the *Economist* in 1978. The central argument was that the government should carefully choose the best strategic moment to challenge the power of the unions to ensure a government victory.[29]

It was concluded that the most likely battleground between a new Conservative administration and the unions was in the coal industry. The government should prepare for such a confrontation by building up stocks of coal at power stations and at the pitheads; make contingency plans for the import of foreign coal during an emergency; encourage the employment of non-union lorry drivers; and build dual oil/coal fired power stations as quickly as possible. It must also be made more difficult for strikers to collect social security payments, and more contingency planning was necessary to ensure an adequate centrally coordinated mobile squad of riot police to deal with any eventuality. This was the blueprint for the Thatcher government's successful rolling back of union power.

Yet it would be an exaggeration to suggest that the Carrington and Ridley reports represented a preconceived conspiratorial agenda for union bashing, even if actual secret preparations in case of a confrontation bore some resemblance to these suggestions. Indeed, the first Thatcher administration of 1979–83 witnessed as many retreats from conflict with trade union power as direct challenges to undermining the authority of organized labour. In retrospect, Mrs Thatcher sometimes, in opposition to the majority in her own Cabinet, showed considerable political skill and tactical awareness in knowing when to retreat and compromise. Firm government rather than an ideological disregard of political reality became the hallmark of Mrs Thatcher's governments. Whilst Thatcherite strategy remained fairly constant, political tactics were more pragmatic, and sometimes involved taking two steps backwards in order to take one step forward.[30] This was not always the case – as the Howe budgets in the first administration, and the 'Community Charge' or Poll Tax, were to show before her fall.

With the benefit of hindsight in industrial policy, one can say that much of the legal framework reducing trade union powers, on which the government placed so much emphasis, even if they were reluctant to use the legislation or to encourage employers to do so, was put in place during the first administration, and before the decisive confrontation with the miners in 1984–5. The undermining of the authority of unions, the anti-inflation policy and the reduction of trade union influence to marginalized and infrequent National Economic Development Council meetings in the 1980s, was often subordinated to short-term constraints between 1979 and 1983.

In some ways Mrs Thatcher's use of kid gloves resembled the cautious approach of Stanley Baldwin before the General Strike, although the political rhetoric was far more aggressive. There was, however, a gradual trend towards a more confrontational pose perhaps best demonstrated by the increased legal restrictions placed on trade unions by the 1982 Employment Act. The replacement of the 'wet' Jim Prior by the 'dry' Norman Tebbit as Minister for Employment produced a more abrasive style, a reduction in legal immunities of unions in industrial disputes and the virtual outlawing of secondary picketing. This decisively shifted the delicate balance of industrial power away from the unions and towards management.

The similarity with the run-up to the General Strike was in the the policy of selective concessions to militant trade unions whilst preparing the machinery of state for a decisive confrontation. Thus several key committees and a beefed up national and regional administrative organization were established in secret. When confrontation developed, strategy was to be implemented by the Civil Contingencies Unit; this was a well oiled administrative machine using the most sophisticated communications and technological equipment under the direction of the Cabinet Office. Political control of state responses to emergencies was overseen by a secret committee called 'Misc 101' and chaired by the Prime Minister. In the miners' dispute in 1984–5 the illusion was created, in keeping with the anti-corporatist philosophy of the government, that the strike represented merely an industrial argument between management and labour. The official line was that the state had little role to play as an arbiter in the dispute. The only visible state involvement was in the astute public relations activities of the Energy Minister, Peter Walker (ironically, an unreconstructed 'wet'), who believed in corporatism, but who blamed the miners' strikes of 1972 and 1974 for the fall of Edward Heath. He acted as a coordinator between the political and administrative responses to the strike as well as being the government front man in the dispute.[31]

Mrs Thatcher's tactical caution and clever political management had been illustrated in her response to industrial unrest before the miners' strike. The anti-corporatist stance had been demonstrated in the state response to the steel strike in South Yorkshire between January and April 1980. Here the refusal to intervene by the state illustrated the benefits of supposed neutrality. The legal problems thrown up by the strike, most notably the Law Lords decision declaring secondary picketing at private sector steel works lawful, were addressed in the employment legislation of 1980 and 1982.

The problems of policing industrial disputes and of managing recalcitrant police authorities, who had more sympathy for the strikers than for management, was met by the reorganization of the Police Department of the Home Office, with greater national coordination and the response of specialist units, the PSU and SPG, specially trained in riot control and in containing industrial unrest. The Home Office, as it also did in the miners' strike, adopted a tough policy which forced local authorities to foot part of the bill for mutual aid, for importing police from other areas.[32] When the strike had been resolved on a fudged compromise, the government replaced Sir Charles Villiers as head of British

Steel by Ian Macgregor, who then introduced greater rationalization and job losses, in addition to those which had so embittered the dispute in the first instance. The appointment of Macgregor (who had a well deserved reputation for union busting in the USA) in 1984 as head of the Coal Board soured relations with the miners and increased the intransigence of the dispute.

A pragmatic response to industrial confrontation was adopted by Mrs Thatcher's first administration from the outset. When strikes threatened, a realistic appraisal was made as to whether strategic opposition or tactical retreat was the best response; when opposing industrial militancy became the preferred option, as in the steel strike in 1980 and the seamen's strike in 1981, management was encouraged to stand up to the unions, and indirect help was given through the forces of law and order, even though the government did not officially intervene. In other disputes discretion was judged the better part of valour and management was encouraged to settle quickly to avoid immediate conflict. Hence the decision in 1981 to avoid a confrontation with the miners over pit closures and to continue subsidizing coal, and the partial climbdown to avert water worker disputes in 1980 and 1981.[33]

It was, however, the eleven-month confrontation with the miners in 1984–5 which symbolised the loss of power of the union movement and that marked the real victory of the industrial policy of Thatcherism. The statistics of this bitter conflict make grim reading: 9,808 arrests were made in the course of the strike of which over half were charged with offences under the Public Order Act of 1936. There were 1.4 million officer days of mutual aid worked by police imported in from outside forces during the dispute; the cost of policing the strike was probably in the order of £225 million; 1,019 miners were dismissed for alleged or proven offences during the dispute, although 662 of these were reinstated by 1987.[34]

The longer-term consequences were no less worrying. Arthur Scargill's dire warnings about the future of the coal industry if market forces were allowed to determine the demand for coal were ridiculed as pessimistic propaganda in 1985. In fact Scargill underestimated the contraction of the industry. Within eight years British Coal was to close the majority of its mines; projections thereafter suggest that even an efficient privatized mining sector will have difficulty surviving after the first decade of the twenty-first century.

The miners' last stand was to represent the domestic triumph of Thatcherism and to illustrate the growing impotence of trade unions. The dispute proved that, unlike the 1970–4 period, no single union, even if it had the will like the miners, could effectively challenge the power of the state. The ghost of syndicalism was effectively laid to rest. The defeat of the miners resulted from several causes, including divisions within the miners' union itself, with the refusal of the National Executive to call a national ballot validating the strike. This led to the creation of the National Union of Democratic Mineworkers, the continuance of production in the Nottingham coal field, and the creation of bitter feuds between miners. Significant, too, were the inability of the TUC to provide more than lukewarm rhetorical support for the miners, the failure of the unions to give much practical assistance with sympathy action, and the Labour Party's criticism of the leadership of Arthur Scargill. Equally important was the failure of public opinion to back the cause of the miners. Whilst the disaster of the projection of the miners' case was partly due to an inept public relations exercise by the leadership of the union, and the inability of Arthur Scargill and others to develop beyond an outmoded cliché-ridden, class warfare rendition of a rhetorical style which struck few contemporary chords in the 1980s, it also owed much to media, as well as government hostility towards the miners' case.

The opposition to the strike in much of the national press was named by the left as a key factor in the defeat of the miners. It was true that many of the popular newspapers personalized the issues involved and made the figure of Arthur Scargill in particular a scapegoat for what was seen as a dispute the miners should not and could not win.[35] The demonization of the dispute, by the Murdoch press empire in particular, masked the fact that several newspapers at both the national and regional level, particularly the *Guardian*, gave remarkably objective accounts of the issues involved in the dispute. The NCCL and Policewatch also provided evidence which often conflicted with official versions of events, and it would be wrong to argue that the media only presented a slanted or censored version of the strike.

It would also be misleading, however, not to emphasize the manipulation by the state of events as they unfolded. Whilst it is false to argue that the government saw a national strike as inevitable, it was certainly not prepared, as it had been in 1981, to let the threat of such an eventuality force it to compromise or retreat. The strike was ostensibly about the issue of the closing of Cortonwood colliery in South Yorkshire. But this was only a symptom of the real issue, the retreat of the government from the *Plan for Coal* published in the aftermath of the Heath government's defeat at the hands of the miners between 1972 and 1974, which appeared to guarantee the future for the industry as the major source of Britain's energy needs. The recession of the early 1980s, the decline of industrial capacity, the threat of alternative power sources to domestic coal (notably natural gas and cheap coal imports), the need to protect the higher cost nuclear power industry, and the decline in the cost of oil since 1979, put pressure on the state to review its energy needs. The government decided, in tune with its free market policies, to end the privileged position of the protected coal industry; revenge for the defeat in 1972–4 was not a motive, but it was the state which chose the time and the place of the confrontation and ensured that its secret preparation for such an eventuality were far better planned than the fiascos of the 1970s.

The preparations included such practical issues as the stockpiling of coal at power stations to over a year's supply, the encouragement of the use of non-union labour in ports and road transport, the amendment of social security regulation to ensure that unions, rather than the state, were made more responsible for funding strike benefits, and the organization of regional administration to ensure that the strike did not seriously affect power, food supplies or communications. Behind the scenes the whole apparatus of the secret state was overhauled; although much of the detail still eludes us and has not been made public, it is now quite clear that though 'the government is not involved' it was the state, under close supervision of secret committees of Cabinet politicians and civil servants, which managed the official response to the strike, using the most sophisticated state of the art technology to coordinate local administration, the forces of law and order and the organization of supplies.

Two examples illustrate this point. It was the government who successfully persuaded employers not to use the new legislation to claim civil damages from the NUM, as the state did not wish to increase sympathy for the miners in the unions. Peter Walker after much argument finally persuaded Ian Macgregor to agree to a compromise with the supervisory union NACODS, to avoid the closure of the Nottinghamshire coalfield in October 1984.[36]

The Home Office, through its Police department and the Chief Constables Conference, organized a national framework for the policing of the strike in all but name, and never failed to back up or justify the police response to the pushing and shoving of the miners and their supporters. In particular, any attempt to control supplies of food and power, to intimidate 'scabs' or working miners, or to escalate the dispute through secondary picketing, was ruthlessly dealt with by the forces of law and order; good examples of this are provided by the protection given to the working miners in Nottinghamshire pit villages, and by the violence at Orgreave when the police stopped the miners' attempt at a strategic Saltley-type victory to close a coal depot.[37] Later court proceedings suggested the police were at least as responsible for the violence that transpired as the miners. Similarly, although there was some dispute about the funding of mutual aid from other authorities with Labour controlled police authorities, the state never failed to back the actions of Chief Constables in the conflict.

Although in retrospect the failure of the miners' strike appeared inevitable, the consequences were more complex. Mrs Thatcher gained little immediate political capital from the defeat of the miners. Although she triumphed in the 1987 election, poll findings suggest this was in spite of rather than because of the outcome of the miners' strike. It would be wrong also to see the quiescence of the trade unions since 1979 as due solely to the hostility of the government to organized labour. Whilst the Employment Acts of 1980, 1982 and 1986 have made it more difficult for unions to use the strike weapon or to apply mass picketing, the decrease in industrial confrontation has owed more to market forces, unemployment and changing public opinion.

Interestingly, soon after the end of the miners' strike the government pushed through a new Public Order Act in 1986. As in the 1936 bill, the legislation dealt with wider issues than those thrown up by the miners' strike, although no doubt it was influenced by that event and the inner city riots of the early 1980s. The act revised, codified and extended the common law offences of riot, unlawful assembly and affray; it widened the authorities' control on demonstrations and marches; the offence of incitement to racial hatred was broadened and additional powers to combat football hooliganism were introduced.

The authorities in 1986, as in 1936, despite bitter divisions in British society, and the deep alienation of the mining community, felt it only necessary to strengthen marginally the legal weapons at their disposal to maintain law and order. Despite muted objection criticizing the reduction of civil liberties, the act did not stop popular protest, although it aided the authorities in controlling the continuing hostility from the left to Mrs Thatcher's government, and after November 1990, John Major's administration. Perhaps the most notorious confrontation occurred at the 'Battle of Wapping' in 1987, when the authorities broke up the picketing of sacked employees of *The Times* after the transfer from Fleet Street.

Although the fall of Mrs Thatcher resulted from a high politics revolt of Conservative MPs, negative public opinion blaming the government for recession, high unemployment and the poll tax, was orchestrated by an effective low politics campaign involving mass demonstrations. This has to be seen as part of the immediate background to the dumping of the Iron Lady.

c) 'The Lady's not for turning'

The pronounced difference in style and approach of the Conservative administrations since 1979 necessitates a deeper consideration of the extent to which 'Thatcherism' represents a break in the way government is managed, and its influence on state and society in Britain. This is important because although much of the relevant documentation has not been released since 1945, the general argument of this book is for the most part a variation of 'the seamless web' interpretation. This tends to emphasize the areas of continuity in the state, whether the left or the right is in power – albeit with a gradual trend in the twentieth century for greater centralization of administration and control, despite the extension of democratic rights to practically all its citizens over the age of eighteen. This has reinforced the long-term trend of the creation of a conservative nation based on liberal principles.[38]

However, there have been three significant possible turning points in which the general political direction of government has significantly altered: the Lloyd George coalition between 1916 and 1922, the Labour governments of 1945–51 and Conservative administrations since 1979. In all three cases war provided the motor for change. The difficulties encountered by the state in the First World War led to the Lloyd George coalition, the Second World War created the social consensus behind the reforms of the third Labour government, and the victorious outcome of the Falklands War gave Mrs Thatcher the key to the door of 10 Downing Street for a second term with an increased majority which enabled her to impose a more radical direction on her administration's political programme. The Lloyd George coalition proved to be a turning point at which the wheels of change failed to turn, although it created a precedent for the more durable reforms set in motion by the Churchill coalition between 1940 and 1945. The consensus of Butskellism and the conviction politics of Mrs Thatcher represented more significant changes in direction.

The allegedly revolutionary agenda of Thatcherism has been emphasized both by friends and opponents of her governments. To Conservative propaganda since 1979 there appears to be little difference between the pale pinks of a centrist social democracy or liberalism, the democratic socialism of Labour, the marxist syndicalism of Arthur Scargill or of fringe groups, and Soviet communism. Mrs Thatcher and her friends advertise the road to Damascus conversion to 'true Conservatism' of Sir Keith Joseph in the latter days of the Heath administration in 1974, and the pioneering work of the Institute of Economic Affairs and the Centre for Policy Studies in propagating the values of the social market economy.

Whilst the originality of this development should not be exaggerated – as it bore a close similarity (apart from the Little Englandism and outspoken criticism of coloured Commonwealth immigrants) to Enoch Powell's earlier criticism of Butskellism and the policies of Edward Heath – it was to have a great significance. The ideology of Thatcherism became a British variant of the 'new right' which saw a synthesis of free market liberal economics with traditional Conservative social values. It represented in effect a synthesis of the 'new right' and 'libertarian right'. Thatcherism owed much to the Austrian school of supply-side thinkers, particularly Friedrich von Hayek, and the monetarist ideas of Milton Friedman. The key elements in its assault on welfarism, social democracy and Keynesian economic management were an emphasis on liberty of the individual, an attack on corporatism, a call for necessity of driving inflation out of the system, popular capitalism and the extension of share ownership, and advocacy of the need for markets rather than the state to allocate resources in the economy.

Whilst Mrs Thatcher and the Conservatives have been keen to emphasize the break with the past, so have her left-wing critics. The socialist journal *Marxism Today* published several articles from 'new left' authors, particularly influenced by Gramscian concepts, which have criticized the 'hegemonic project' of Thatcherism.[39] This unholy alliance of 'new left' and 'new right' has successfully raised the status of the Thatcher phenomenon to an 'ism', but there is a diametrically opposed interpretation of how this came about. For the libertarian right, the Conservative revolution was achieved by rolling back the boundaries of the state; for her Marxist critics, and the new right, the social market economy necessitated the creation of a strong state. There was an unresolved contradiction at the core of Thatcherism.

Perhaps the most influential challenge to these views has been expressed by Peter Riddell.[40] He has questioned the uniqueness of Thatcherism, has emphasized elements of continuity and pointed out that certain key ideas were not an intellectual monopoly of the new right. Thus monetarism came to the Treasury in 1976 during Denis Healey's tenure as Labour Chancellor. Similarly, the alleged Thatcherite agenda was slow to alter policy in key areas. Whilst privatization and the breakup of nationalized industries proceeded apace during the second and third terms, at no stage was there a reduction in real terms in public expenditure, despite incessant propaganda suggesting the contrary. There was, however, a transfer of wealth from local authorities and public corporations to the private sector and wealthy individuals. The recovery of the 1980s, which was proclaimed a result of squeezing inflation out of the system, to others was seen as a product of North Sea oil plugging a chronic balance of payments deficit which had led to stop–go cycles in the past, or a product of the failure to correct massive budget deficits in the United States.

Riddell has pointed out as well that Thatcherism as an ideology has only been a partial success in terms of converting the political culture to its values. Whilst it has made significant inroads into the working class vote, it still has to convert the more liberal middle classes. In spite of four successive Conservative victories since 1979, the vote for the Thatcher and Major administrations remained at just over 40 per cent. The negative message of Thatcherism – that socialism had failed both domestically and internationally – had more impact than its positive case. The leftward shift in the Labour Party in the 1980s, with Michael Foot and Neil Kinnock representing the 'soft left', was significantly rejected by many blue collar workers who voted Conservative. This process was aided by the split from Labour of the 'gang of four' in 1980, and the formation of the Social Democratic Party (SDP) with the Limehouse declaration in 1981.

19 The SAS storms the Iranian embassy in London during the embassy siege, 1980

The 'Thatcher revolution' was fuelled more by a bitterly divided opposition than by its own merits. The cause was not positive support for a radical Conservatism, even if with mass unemployment and the restructuring of the market that was the effect. Mrs Thatcher only became leader of the Conservative party in 1975 as a result of the obstinacy of Edward Heath, the temperamental unsuitability of Sir Keith Joseph, and the peculiarities of the leadership election – which had more similarities to a coup than the triumph of a new ideology. This process was aided by the quirks of electoral geography: Labour held its own in its industrial heartland and the Celtic fringe, but south and east of the Humber–Severn line the Alliance, or Liberals, became the main opposition to the government.

The policies associated with Thatcherism similarly have

been less than wholeheartedly endorsed. Privatization and 'popular capitalism' have been quite successful, but there is evidence that public opinion, although in favour of lower taxes, was resentful of cuts in services. Renewed recession in 1990, rising unemployment, the poll tax fiasco, and the resignations of Nigel Lawson and Sir Geoffrey Howe, led to the leadership challenge of Michael Heseltine and the resignation of Mrs Thatcher. Whilst she recovered from mid-term unpopularity in the two previous administrations, the fickleness of the electorate hardly amounted to a blanket endorsement of Thatcherism, in either its doctrinal or pragmatic mode. A more sceptical view of the Thatcher revolution, by David Marquand, challenged its alleged success and argued that her policies have neither halted the decline of Britain nor created a new political consensus. The deep unpopularity of the Thatcher medicine has only been made acceptable by a divided opposition who have attained a numerical majority of the votes in all elections since 1979, but who advocated a nostalgic vision of a return to a form of corporatism, with an increased role for the political centre.[41]

Since 1979 Conservative governments have adopted a strong stance to state security. In general there has been a reaffirmation of the cult of secrecy since 1979, with important exceptions. As the last two chapters have shown, Mrs Thatcher seemed to have inherited some of the more primeval responses to socialism generally associated with Unionist politicians and military and security chiefs of the post-First World War era. This was probably best exemplified by the GCHQ affair of 1984. The sudden decision to ban trade unions at Cheltenham was due to several influences: the work to rule and industrial disruption of 1981, the Geoffrey Prime arrest in 1983, and pressure from the Reagan administration, who saw trade unions and national security as even more incompatible than did Mrs Thatcher.

What was notable was the government's total refusal to compromise. The whole issue seemed to suggest that membership of a trade union jeopardized national security in the eyes of the government. Similarly, the exposure of the Zircon spy satellite was also seen as endangering the security of the realm and attempts were made to stop media investigations of the secret world.[42] Even the disaster of the Peter Wright affair, the hounding of a security hawk whose right-wing political views made Mrs Thatcher's appear anaemic by comparison, appeared not to deflect the security obsession. The new Official Secrets Act reinforced the national defences against leakages from the secret world.

Yet this was not the entire story. Whilst there is continuing caution about a more liberal release of state papers relating to policy decisions in the departments of state or of the more secret areas of the administration since the Second World War, or indeed about the introduction of a Freedom of Information Act, the balance sheet has not been entirely negative. The exposure of Sir Anthony Blunt in 1979 showed that Mrs Thatcher realized that there were higher principles than the need for secrecy on all occasions. Public pressure has also led to the early release of government papers by Mrs Thatcher's administration which have made this book possible: the Home Office files on British fascism, and on internment and the Channel Islands in the Second World War are examples. The 1993 White Paper following the Waldegrave initiative is to allow a much more liberal access to personal files and routine administrative material, although it has not relaxed the usual caveats about national security and the retention of sensitive material.

The Civil Service mandarin class has been to a certain extent neutralized through selective privatization, but also through the use of personal advisers in many departments of state, most particularly by the Prime Minister and by the Treasury – Sir Alan Walters and Sir Terence Burns being perhaps the most significant. Yet the administrative Civil Service has not declined in importance, and Mrs Thatcher came to appreciate its flexible approach to problems of state. Given her considerable powers of patronage and the longevity of her leadership, officials more amenable to the rationalisation and efficiency drive of Thatcherism have gradually replaced the leading mandarins of the Butskellite generation.

There was little evidence of the need for suspicion; the real administrative civil servants, although able to procrastinate, were also well versed in the need to conform to new political masters – indeed, career civil servants like Sir Robert Armstrong, the Cabinet Secretary and head of the Civil Service, Sir Bernard Ingham, her Press Secretary, and Sir Charles Powell, her foreign policy adviser, probably became better known than any previous civil servants because of their high profile in her administration.[43] In spite of the initial suspicion and hostility the Civil Service has adapted its role to become servants of the new regime, exactly as it did in 1945. This again was a symbiotic relationship, a necessary compromise between ideology and pragmatism.

Whilst fewer conclusions can be reached with regard to internal security because of the dearth of information, several points can be emphasized. Whilst public order and internal security have been given the highest priority, neither was immune from the Thatcherite drive for efficiency and rationality. Indeed, there is a similarity with the inter-war administrations, with greater commitments and fewer resources, at least in terms of humint operations, the employment of intelligence and security officers. The outward signs of this have been cutbacks in the armed forces. The various defence reviews since 1980 have cut resources at a faster rate than commitments; indeed, it appears that it was more by luck than judgement that sufficient capital ships were found to mount the Falklands armada in 1982. Whereas little is known about the real levels of financing received by the secret world under the Thatcher regime, it has been noted that both MI5 and MI6 are being moved to spacious new buildings and that GCHQ has not been starved of funds. It appears likely that humint expenditure has been reduced since the end of the Cold War.

The police in recent years have not been immune from reorganization. Whilst the Home Office has created more national coordination in police activities, particularly in the control of public order, the local responsibility in the shires and urban watch committees is still retained, even if their powers have been significantly reduced. Renewed criticism of many aspects of the administration of law and order has put renewed pressure on the authorities. The Sheehy report, despite the burying of its more radical proposals, was symptomatic of the desire to make the institutions of law and order more efficient and cost effective.

Thus, with relation to the state's management of political extremism, internal security and public order, as with many other aspects of the somewhat contradictory programme of Thatcherism, policy represents a pragmatic application of radicalism to traditional conservatism, which can often be rationalized in terms of historical administrative practice. But before a final conclusion can be ventured about the response of the British state to these matters in the twentieth century, the continuing 'troubles' in Northern Ireland since 1968 must be examined. Here a very different picture from the situation in the rest of the United Kingdom developed which led to new methods of political management of public order and social control.

9

THE ORANGE AND THE GREEN (1968–1993)

The exception to the general argument of this book – that the liberal traditions of the British state have successfully managed problems of political extremism, public order and internal security in the United Kingdom during the twentieth century – has been the inability to prevent intercommunity tensions, sectarian murders, terrorism and continuing violence in Northern Ireland since 1968. This failure has led to some highly illiberal features of government in the province: the ending of local self-government based in Stormont Castle, the termination of the jury system in criminal cases and the imposition of so-called Diplock courts, the internment without trial in 1971–2 of over 700, the use of uncorroborated evidence provided by 'supergrasses', and the permanent use of the military to aid the civil power since 1968.

This has entailed the permanent security presence of the British army, and intelligence operations of the secret state, to help maintain law and order. The legal basis for emergency legislation for the state in Northern Ireland, from its formation in 1922 until the introduction of Direct Rule in 1972, was provided by the Special Powers Act; this was the basis for the use of internment without trial in the early 1920s, from 1938 to 1945 and 1956 to 1961. Even more draconian infringements of civil rights were introduced under Direct Rule: the Emergency Provisions Act, first passed in 1973, and the Prevention of Terrorism Act of 1978, which applied throughout the United Kingdom, have been regularly renewed. The latter was made permanent in 1988.[1]

The firm response of the authorities, and of both Conservative and Labour administrations in London, has led to the adoption of policies and restrictions on civil liberties which would not be countenanced in the rest of the United Kingdom. This has led to the embarrassment of the British government at the bar of international public opinion: Amnesty International, the European Court and the United Nations have all denounced aspects of prison conditions, the alleged use of torture and the supposed 'shoot to kill' policy of the British army in various operations.

Whatever the merits of the catalogue of individual criticisms of British policy and administration in Northern Ireland since 1968, the historical and political background needs to be placed in a broad context. In chapter 3 I pointed out that the Irish dimension to British history was characterized by a long and bitter hostility which illustrated the intractability of the 'troubles'.[2] Lloyd George's 'solving' of the problem in 1921–2 was not accepted by those who refused to recognize the boundary with the six counties of Ulster, or who objected to the oath of allegiance to the British king. Whilst the latter ceased to be a problem after the creation of Eire, the Irish Free State, in 1937, the border question continued to frustrate the will of those who had never accepted the 1922 treaty.

For the purposes of this chapter several general points need to be stressed from the outset. The Ulster problem was a clash in Great Britain's back yard between the forces of liberalism and illiberal nationalism; between those who saw the will of the majority in a defined community as representing the wishes of the people, and those who argued that national identity was a higher principle than democratic rights.[3] Even then the issue was not clear-cut: if the wishes of the majority of those in Ireland, rather than the inhabitants of Ulster (and whether the province was defined in terms of the six counties with its Protestant majority, or the historic nine counties) represented the basis on which a solution was to be found, then very different 'democratic' answers to the Irish problem were possible. Certainly the complexities of the issue tested the political will of the British state to uphold the rule of law and maintain civil society. Whatever criticisms can be levelled at the British authorities, there was no diminution of the commitment to uphold the power of the state, to maintain the rule of law or to protect the whole community of Northern Ireland. The authorities proved once more not to be soft; the British state was forced to adopt illiberal measures to counteract the threat of a decline into anarchy.

In spite of the vast resources channeled into security, with the militarization of the police, the use of the British army to help maintain law and order, and the use of special forces including the SAS and a sophisticated intelligence apparatus, the authorities could only contain the threat posed by the guerrilla forces of the Provisional Irish Republican Army (PIRA) and the Irish National Liberation Army (INLA), and of sporadic sectarian terrorism initiated by the Protestant paramilitaries of the Ulster Volunteer Force (UVF) and the Ulster Freedom Fighters (UFF), with their links to the Ulster Defence Association (UDA).

It was not only internal security measures which were used to solve the problem. All British governments since 1968, from Harold Wilson to John Major, have used interventionist measures to stimulate economic recovery as far as conditions would permit; excepting Scotland, doctrinaire Thatcherism was not applied to the the Celtic fringe. As with Peter Walker's tenure at the Welsh Office, there have been direct attempts to stimulate revival, as well as provide compensation in Northern Ireland for the effects of terrorist outrage.[4]

It was not surprising that the British state would be unable to comprehend the fanaticism and single minded dedication of the PIRA. British administration, based as it was on the need for efficiency, fairness, democratic rights, compromise and the rule of law, failed to comprehend a nationalism, rooted in mystical and cultural traditions, which placed national sovereignty above the democratic will of the majority of Irish citizens, let alone those of the province of Ulster.[5] Perhaps more surprising was the failure of one of the best trained and equipped military and police security apparatuses in the world to overcome the irregular forces of the PIRA.[6] This was despite the conspicuous success of the British in defeating nationalist and communist guerrilla insurgencies in the retreat from Empire, such as in Kenya, Malaya and Cyprus during the 1950s.[7] The leading theorist of counter-insurgency, Sir Frank Kitson, himself served a term in Northern Ireland.[8]

The roots of the problem lay in the origins of the IRA: the belief that only military power could drive the British from Ireland, and that political solutions meant betrayal and the manipulation of Irish freedom for the benefit of British imperialism. Whilst the strategy of the PIRA evolved into seeing the necessity for a political dimension in the 1980s, the policy enunciated by Danny Morrison, of 'the armalite [a rifle] and the ballot box', still emphasized the role of a military solution. The earlier attempt by William Whitelaw, the Northern Ireland Secretary in Edward Heath's administration in 1972, to talk directly to the PIRA, after a ceasefire, foundered on the reefs of mutual incomprehension. The working class representatives of the PIRA distrusted the suave, sophisticated upper class politicians and mandarins on the other side of the negotiating table. The hedgehogs of the PIRA, who knew 'one big thing', were suspicious of the clever foxes of the British state. On their side, the establishment of the British state, the ultimate custodians of law and order, distrusted the PIRA negotiators, whom they basically regarded not as freedom fighters but common criminals. Mrs Thatcher's and John Major's administrations were to turn this perception into holy writ.

What also needs to be stressed is that whatever criticisms can be levelled at British rule, in the way a political democracy negates many of the civil rights of those citizens who resist the state itself and its laws, it has to be viewed in the context of parallel developments in Ireland, which with proportional representation could be seen as even more democratic than Great Britain. Since the granting of independence in 1922, the Irish government have shown a marked intolerance of IRA activity. A large minority of the political nation rejected the terms of the settlement, and the civil war that resulted between 1922 and 1924 led to escalating atrocities on both sides and permanently soured relations. The state shot political prisoners, including Erskine Childers, Rory O'Connor and Liam Mellowes, in retaliation for the murder of Michael Collins, other politicians and members of their families. Whilst Fianna Fáil came to represent the opponents of the original settlement coming to terms with political reality, the survival of the IRA was due to opponents of the settlement who never accepted the 'treason' of 1922, and who based their intransigence on the mystical allegiance to the supposed integrity of the 'second Dáil', which was given a timeless validity above constant shifts in public opinion or the wishes of political democracy.[9]

Indeed, Fianna Fáil were to prove as hostile to the IRA as other Irish governments. Even more than the United Kingdom, the Irish Free State was to deal ruthlessly with those who tried to use force to impose their will or undermine the political process. This included decidedly more unpleasant regimes of internment for IRA members in the Curragh during the Second World War and at other times of tension, than those operated by the British government. Between 1939 and 1945 400 IRA members were interned. The British government also used internment during the border campaign between 1956 and 1962, when 256 were detained without charge or trial.

The fact that both wings of the IRA have gone out of their way not to engage in hostilties against the Irish state since the 1930s reflects rather less on this decided animosity, or the wish to avoid fighting two enemies at once, but rather more on the tactical convenience of being able to use Eire as a kind of 'safe house', as a guerrilla base from which to plan operations against the British state, and by exploiting the legal loopholes which make it more difficult to extradite from Ireland to the United Kingdom those who can claim political motivation for crime. The constant hostility of the Irish government reinforced the limiting of the new campaign to Northern Ireland after political unrest broke out in Ulster in 1968, leading to a new campaign in 1970.[10]

The difference in security policy between Northern Ireland and the rest of the United Kingdom is also as noticeable today as it was earlier in the century. The tendency to shunt Irish matters into the sidings of British politics, until some particular outrage forces it back into the headlines, is as common now as it was in the Lloyd George era. There is also a grim determination that terrorist disruption should affect British politics as little as possible, despite several mainland campaigns in Britain, and aimed at British targets in Europe, including the murder of a government minister, Airey Neave, in the House of Commons car park in 1979, the murder of the Conservative MP and friend of Mrs Thatcher, Ian Gow in 1990, and attempts, which nearly succeeded, to kill Mrs Thatcher in Brighton in 1984 and to wipe out the British Cabinet in 1991. Various military targets have been attacked in West Germany, and the British Ambassador in the Netherlands was murdered in 1979. Lord Mountbatten, although assassinated in Ireland in 1979, was murdered because he was seen as a leading figure in the British establishment, with a relationship to the royal family. He died on the same day that another IRA bomb atrocity killed 18 at Warrenpoint.[11] The targeting of respected individuals, and the horrific consequences of premature explosions or mistaken calculations have led to civilian massacres, such as at Enniskillen war memorial on Remembrance Day 1987; in the Shankhill Road, Belfast, in October 1993; and the subsequent Protestant paramilitary sectarian reprisal at Greysteel, in County Londonderry. Not only does the evidence suggest that the initial premiss of the PIRA campaign – that the civilian population and the British authorities will wilt before the violence – is wrong, but 'own goals' reinforce both public opinion and the state in their steely determination to withstand the guerrilla warfare tactics. A Protestant Blitz mentality and resolution never to compromise, symbolized by the intransigent determination of the Reverend Ian Paisley and the Democratic Unionists, the emergence of the 'peace people' amongst those sickened by violence, and deep divisions within the Nationalist community, are some of the consequences of the tactics of PIRA.

Whatever the cost, the illusion of normality has to be maintained, particularly in Northern Ireland but also in the rest of the United Kingdom. Only if the government is seen to limit the rights of its citizens can the terrorist be thought to be winning. The aim is to deny the Provos publicity and to prevent them using propaganda to present their political case. The intention is to deny their civil liberties whilst maintaining British citizens' freedom of opinion within the law. Such seeming contradictions are difficult to justify before international opinion; the bizarre use of actors to read the lines of PIRA leaders' pronouncements in news broadcasts makes the attempt to silence the terrorists appear ridiculous. Yet any relaxation of such a policy whilst pleasing the Nationalist community and American opinion, would further alienate Unionist support.

a) Britain's Bosnia

The creation of Northern Ireland in 1920 marked the institutionalization of the Protestant ascendancy and led to a deep entrenchment of its power until 1968. It also led to the making of the British equivalent of the state of Bosnia-Hercegovina in ex-Yugoslavia. Whilst the main division between the communities in Northern Ireland is based on religion, the differences between Catholics and Protestants consist as much of separations of cultures and divergences of ethnic origins. The granting of what was in effect Home Rule to loyalist Ulster in 1921–2, whilst creating a form of independence within the Empire to the new Irish state, symbolized the British authorities' washing of their hands of the problem of Ireland. The basic point was that control of law and order in the province now became the responsibility of Stormont, not the British government. Whilst the reforms instituted by Sir John Anderson in Dublin Castle, following the Fisher commission in 1920, bequeathed a competent administrative apparatus in both Dublin and Belfast after partition, the political settlement in Ulster led to a permanent

Unionist government which was not slow to look after its own. The fact that the liberal British state tolerated within the United Kingdom government which actively discriminated against the large Catholic minority (representing more than one-third of its population), in terms of the political gerrymandering of its electoral constituencies, the blatant unfairness of the provision of housing and access to educational facilities, and the disproportionate skewing of the employment market in favour of the loyalist Protestant majority, created a festering resentment north and south of the border.[12]

This situation was compounded by the blatant injustices upheld by what can only be described as a partisan form of law enforcement, which reinforced the basic inequalities of the system. The creation of a Protestant-based armed Special Constabulary, the notorious B specials, meant that order was maintained by representatives of those who benefited most from an unjust system. It was therefore not surprising that Catholics complained that the Royal Ulster Constabulary, but particularly the B Specials, sided against them when intercommunity hostility degenerated into violence. Before 1968 the most notorious riots had occurred in 1932 and 1935, when so-called 'murder gangs' had been involved in alleged pogroms against the Catholic community. The outbreaks in the latter year led to 11 deaths and 574 injuries. The lack of an impartial police force to maintain law and order for the whole community resulted in the IRA becoming recognized in the Catholic community as providing a legitimate defence against Protestant rioters and against the failure of the authorities to impartially administer the law. In the eyes of some of the Catholic minority, the 'Orange State' blatantly abused its authority, and this was reinforced by the partiality of a police force who were seen as the upholder of Protestant power.[13]

One other important variable, other than religion, needs to be assessed as part of the background. The secret society tradition in Ulster had developed in a different direction from the rest of Ireland. Here Protestant ascendancy meant loyalty to the Union, rather than Irish independence, as the symbol of authority. The Orange order, named after William of Orange – whose troops had come to the aid of the Apprentice Boys and lifted the siege of Londonderry in 1689, and finally defeated the forces of the Catholic monarch James II in 1690 at the Battle of the Boyne – was an important behind-the-scenes anti-liberal influence in Unionist government. Its public persona was advertised to all during the 'marching season' in July and August, when Orange parades annually celebrated the triumph of good King Billy.

The IRA, in contrast, had been relatively weak in Northern Ireland until the rise of the PIRA after 1970. Historically its role in the slums of West Belfast and in Derry had been a defensive one, to protect Catholics against Protestant rioters. There had been 'border campaigns' against Ulster from Eire in 1939, and during 1956–62, but these had been more of a nuisance for the authorities than a serious threat. The 'Belfast Brigade' had always been relatively weak, and exhibited little in the way of initiative or independence until the 1970s.

What transformed the political situation in Northern Ireland was the sign of a split in the Unionist administration at Stormont in the later 1960s. The succession of the relatively liberal Terence O'Neill to the leadership of the Unionist party, replacing the conservative Lord Brookeborough, to become Prime Minister, and his meeting with the Irish leader, Sean Lemass in 1965, opened old wounds in the community. Protestant 'murder gangs' made an alleged reappearance in 1966 in Belfast. Young Catholics began to organize a radical democratic campaign to advertise their complaints about discrimination and injustice in Northern Ireland. The Campaign for Social Justice and the Northern Ireland Civil Rights Association (NICRA) developed out of this initiative, and began to demonstrate against perceived grievances.

This political activism led to a reaction amongst some equally annoyed Ulster Protestants. Those Loyalists who argued that any signs of a split within the majority population would be seized upon by their enemies as a sign of weakness, advocated that no concessions should be given to the Catholics. Only those who remained loyal to the state of Northern Ireland (in this version, Protestants by definition) should be allowed to receive the support of the government. This view was backed by many in the Protestant urban working class who felt threatened by catholic competition for employment and scarce resources. It also was tacitly agreed by many rural Protestants, sometimes evangelical supporters of the Reverend Ian Paisley's Free Presbyterian Church, who saw themselves as part of the Calvinist elect, and who wished to 'save' Northern Ireland from the Catholic contamination of the rule of bishops and the internationalist conspiracy centred on Rome; politically this meant no compromise and no contact with his alleged agents closer to home, the government of Eire. 'No Popery' became the convenient shorthand for no concessions to the Catholic community, and no truck with the conception of a united Ireland.

In political terms the fundamentalist old time religion espoused by Paisley and his allies represented the base of one of three major divisions within the Protestant community, although his Democratic Unionist Party was the only long-term survivor in competition with the Unionist Party. Both William Craig's Vanguard movement and Harry West's faction were reincorprated back into Official Unionism. The divisions between Unionists decisively weakened the Stormont government, an important factor in its loss of legitimacy in the eyes of the community and the British state.[14]

1968 was the time of student protest, of radical left demonstrations and riots throughout the Western world; the eddy of such turmoil was felt late in the year in the Britain and in Northern Ireland. It developed from the confrontation of radical Catholics and militant Protestants, in a political environment where the Stormont government, supporting liberal Unionism, was advocating peaceful change. In this it was encouraged by Harold Wilson's Labour government in London. The conflict between radical Catholics and militant Protestants, and the inability of the authorities to contain violence, led to a succession of Enquiries which emphasized the need for continuing reform, enhanced security and a reestablished rule of law.[15]

The failure of the authorities to ban a Protestant march

20 Extra troops are put on the streets of Belfast in a bid to combat tit-for-tat sectarian killings, 1991

in Armagh in November 1968, and the serious rioting in Derry in 1969, led to the use of the military to aid the civil power, initially to protect the Catholic community. This was the beginning of the end for both Stormont and liberal Unionism. O'Neill resigned in 1969, and his successor, James Chichester Clarke, in April 1971.

The perception of the function of the British army changed markedly as a result of the events of 'Bloody Sunday' in January 1972, when 13 civil rights demonstrators were shot dead by members of the Parachute Regiment in Londonderry. From that time on the British army was seen in its traditional role as the upholder of the Protestant ascendancy by many in the Catholic community. The British army is still providing essential help to the civil authorities in Northern Ireland. What needs to be stressed is that the IRA played little initial role in the disturbances which led to the collapse of the government at Stormont.

The pronounced position of the IRA in Protestant and Unionist demonology as a threat to the stability of Northern Ireland bore little relation to the facts until the 1970s. Historically the IRA was a small problem in the province. The beginning of the 'troubles' arose from the essentially peaceful protests organized by NICRA and others, with their nationalist, middle class, moral force reform leaders like John Hume and Bernadette Devlin. Whilst socialists and other radicals represented important elements in the NICRA coalition, the IRA (although involved) was a minor force. Indeed, the lack of visibility of the IRA during the early period of the troubles lent some plausibility to the joke that IRA stood for 'I Ran Away'.

The events of 1968 exposed the inconsistencies and divisions within an IRA organization which had always been an unstable alliance between romantic nationalism and revolutionary socialism. Unfortunately, in the Irish context the two ingredients were often basic contradictions: Marxist-Leninism failed to coexist with conservative Catholic nationalist elements. The later 1960s were the heyday of the idea of proletarian internationalism; this intellectual fashion made a distinct mark on the IRA leadership in Dublin. Under the leadership of Cathal Goulding and Ray Johnston, the IRA developed the idea that the ultimate aim of the organization was to work for a socialist revolution in Ireland which united the Protestant and Catholic working class against the bourgeois state, both north and south of the border. In the context of Ulster this was a hopelessly utopian enterprise, as it defied the political law of gravity of the province; bitterly opposed protestant and catholic working class organizations had few traits in common, and most notable of these was their social and political conservatism.

The lack of impact of the IRA before 1971 led to increased criticism inside the organization, especially from survivors of the border campaign of 1956–62 and those who believed in the use of physical force rather than dabbling in politics. This included the unrealistic political dreams of the leadership. After an acrimonious dispute there followed a murderous split in the organization in 1970, leading to a division between the 'Official' and 'Provisional' IRA. The former remained true to its new internationalist ideology, and after a period declared a cessation of hostilities with the authorities in 1972; the latter are still involved in their undeclared war with the British state.[16]

Whilst the PIRA have undergone political development since 1970, it has been their commitment to the traditional military conception of the IRA which has shaped their approach to the conflict with the British state. The demise of NICRA in the early 1970s has made nationalist politics a competition between the reformist Social Democratic Labour Party (SDLP), under John Hume, and Sinn Fein, with its traditional close political links with the IRA. Whilst successive Northern Ireland Secretaries, after the imposition of Direct Rule, have managed to supervise a string of ultimately fruitless political initiatives in Northern Ireland – between the SDLP, the Unionist groups and the middle ground of the Alliance party – nobody has established a forum where the Unionists have been prepared to talk to the IRA or Sinn Fein.

Thus the problem in Northern Ireland has been to find a political solution to the troubles given the entrenched position of both communities, and the British government's reluctance to be seen as negotiating with rebels, or compromising with terrorism. Political initiatives have been forthcoming, both directly and indirectly, but the encouragement of dialogue has always failed to break down the mutually incompatible conditions for agreement even about talks, such has been the animosity and suspicion in both Catholic and Protestant communities. This has meant that attempted military and security solutions to the troubles have been the main feature of recent Ulster history, with terrorist atrocities being met with a clampdown on the civil liberties of those accused of being involved in extremist military activities. In short, violence has led to counter-violence, and a spiralling of paramilitary atrocities has led to terrorism and alleged disregard for the rules of combat by the forces of law and order.

The statistics of this vicious circle makes for grim reading. Between 1969 and 1988 there were over 30,000 shooting incidents, 8,000 explosions, 6,000 malicious fires, and 12,000 armed robberies in Ulster. Since 1969 over 2,500 have been killed and 26,000 injured as a result of the troubles. The peak was in 1972 in the aftermath of internment, when 467 were killed, comprising 146 members of the security forces, 75 paramilitaries and 246 civilians. In the less murderous 1980s the death toll still averaged 76 per year. This included an average of 15 RUC officers, 9 from the Ulster Defence Regiment (UDR), 8 from the British Army, 10 paramilitaries and 34 civilians. Of this grim total Protestant paramilitaries are thought to have been responsible for one-third of the deaths, with a higher percentage in the early 1970s and in 1992–3, when it rose to over half.[17]

What these statistics signify is that the majority Protestant community has lost 50 per cent more, as a proportion, than did the USA population during the Vietnam war, and that if the 1980s statistics are any guide, one in twenty RUC officers will be shot by the IRA. It is hardly surprising that this level of guerrilla warfare has been met with intransigence by most Protestants, and that the hardline position of both the Ulster Unionists and Ian Paisley's DUP, of no concessions to violence and no talks with the IRA (what might be called Orangeism writ large), represented the basic view of practically the entire majority community. The failure of the British security policy led to the reemergence of a new underground hardline leadership of Protestant paramilitaries in the UDA and UFF, which retaliated directly against the Catholic community with sectarian murder campaigns as revenge for PIRA atrocities, or bombing campaigns directed at military or paramilitary targets which killed innocent civilians.

Since the reemergence of the IRA, with the campaign of the Provisionals since 1971, the Catholic community has been divided in the support it provides for Sinn Fein. Whilst support for republicanism and nationalism remains strong, both amongst those who loathe violence and those who see it as a tactical necessity, the majority support is for the political campaigning of the SDLP and its policy of peaceful political reforms in the province. The tentative attempts to further a political solution to the Ulster problem in 1993, with talks between the SDLP and Sinn Fein (the Hume–

Adams initiative), was an attempt to bypass stalled inter-community talks brokered by the British government. These collapsed as a result of Unionist suspicions of the role of the Irish government, a bone of contention in any solution to the Ulster problem. The attempt by both Dublin and London to include the other constitutional parties in discussions following the Hume–Adams talks is made more difficult by such entrenched positions.

Hostility to any British constitutional agreement with Eire, no matter how vague, has ended the traditional alliance between Ulster Unionism and the British Conservative Party. Any Anglo-Irish declarations – like the Anglo-Irish summit in 1981, the Hillsborough Agreement in 1985 (which established the Council of Ireland) and the Downing Street Declaration in 1993 – have been boycotted on principle by the Unionists. This has been the case despite great care taken over the language used to ensure the maximum area of agreement, and the search for a form of words which will not alienate Protestant or Catholic, Nationalist or Unionist. Local attempts, such as the Round Table conferences in 1991, to find areas of agreement have foundered at the talks stage, with little in the way of an agreed agenda.[18] Such have been the difficulties in trying to resolve the issue.

There would be progress if the Protestant community would agree, in return for a ceasefire, to an indirect role in the solution being given to the Provisionals. This seems unlikely at present, as deep intercommunity wounds have not healed, and mutual suspicions and recriminations between the Orange and the Green are still the underlying realities of Ulster politics. Initial reactions suggest that Protestant opinions may be less united in condemnation at such developments than is traditionally the case, although the murder campaign of outlawed extremist groups in 1993 suggests that little has changed around the basic faultlines of Ulster politics. The rhetoric of the Major government, which expressed horror at continued terrorist outrage in Northern Ireland in 1993, and used the coded message that there would be no compromise with political violence, whilst meanwhile the general suspicion remained that there were already informal contacts with the PIRA, suggested a new initiative in the Lloyd George tradition, of trying to build new bridges over a wide and deep chasm. Such behaviour is regarded as duplicity in Unionist circles; however, it is difficult to see how the level of violence can be abated except by the use of unorthodox methods, given the fact that security solutions have never worked in the Irish context. The insistence that there has to be a permanent end to violence before a political solution can be found also comes up against traditional objections: it has never worked before, and is seen purely as a political tactic to divide the PIRA. Meanwhile, guerrilla warfare continues.

b) Irish Terrorism and the British State

The strategy of the British state in defeating, or at least containing violence in, Northern Ireland involved both a political and a military dimension. The deteriorating security situation in 1969 necessitated the calling in of the military to aid the civil power, in an attempt to end sectarian violence and confrontation between the Protestant and Catholic communities. The failure to prevent this led to the reemergence of the IRA, and the rise of a young northern leadership, which effectively transformed its nature and prompted a PIRA split, a new and highly effective guerrilla force. This occurred despite the highly sophisticated technology of, and rigorous intelligence and security operations organized by, the authorities, which at best only contained the level of violence.

The political response included an unsuccessful attempt by the Northern Ireland Secretary, William Whitelaw, to negotiate with the PIRA leadership in 1972; and the failure of various initiatives involving round table conferences between the main political parties pursuing a peaceful solution from the 1970s through to 1991. This included most notably the collapse of the power sharing executive in 1974 after the general strike had forced an end to the experiment. The attempt to involve the Irish government in the process, with the Sunningdale Agreement in 1973, the Anglo-Irish Summit in 1981 and the Hillsborough Agreement in

1985, was the main reason for the failure to find a political solution. The influence of Democratic Unionism was to a certain extent diminished with the failure to repeat the success of the 1974 strike in 1977. The most important point was the refusal of the politicians, after the failure of Whitelaw's initiative, to sit down with those at war with the British state: this led inevitably to political stalemate, and a failure to end the conflict between the authorities and the perpetrators of violence.[19]

The inability to find a political solution meant the undeclared war had to be fought with military and security measures. Whilst the authorities have, not surprisingly, been less than forthcoming about the nature of the activities of the secret state in Ulster, enough has percolated through the security clampdown to suggest several areas of controversy and concern. There appear also to be distinct continuities with several earlier conclusions about the historical record in such areas. Thus, for example, although steps have now apparently been taken to make intelligence collection more coordinated, and to ensure adequate dissemination of intelligence amongst those with a need to know, frictional rivalries between different agencies have hindered operations. Many of the same criticisms have been levelled against the modern secret state in Ulster as were levelled at Sir Basil Thomson with regard to political surveillance in Ireland during the First World War.

The operators in the field in Northern Ireland have included MI5, MI6, Special Branch, Military Intelligence (14 Intelligence Company) and the Royal Ulster Constabulary. There has also been the shadowy role of the SAS units serving in Northern Ireland. There certainly was tension between MI5 and MI6, which was resolved by the former taking over the main responsibility for counter-intelligence to avoid unnecessary duplication. Sir Maurice Oldfield was removed from his post as security coordinator in Northern Ireland after less than a year in 1980, although personal reasons were involved in this decision. There were also jurisdictional problems with Special Branch, and rivalries between the military and the police.

To a certain degree this dilemma was tackled in 1976 with

the establishment of the doctrine of Police Primacy, but the continuing duplication of intelligence failed to cure the problem. The secrecy with which security policies have been operated within Northern Ireland has often created difficulties over the cooperation of competing agencies. The 'need to know' principle has also meant that security operations have not always been adequately monitored, and government has sometimes been in the dark about such matters. This has led to several *causes célèbres* during the period of the troubles.[20]

In spite of the massive security operation the results of political intelligence have been mixed. The activities of those at the sharp end of secret state activities in Northern Ireland have evoked vigorous public controversy both in the media and in the House of Commons. There are, however, several factors which need to be assessed before the main areas of public concern can be analysed. The main problem is that for reasons of national security, and with the danger of compromising current operations, it is often very difficult for the authorities to comment on matters of alleged wrongdoing by the military, the police, or the security and intelligence services operating in Northern Ireland. Very often the political authorities are quite legitimately, on the 'need to know' principle, not informed about current operations. When such activities turn sour the media may pick up hints of alleged wrongdoing.

Often this relates to instinctive reaction of men protecting their own security, who play safe rather than risk putting themselves into danger, by applying Queen's regulations to the letter. In theory the actions of the military and the police are judged as no different from those of the general public under the common law, and the doctrine of the use of minimum force to maintain the public peace is followed at all times. In practice the problems posed by guerrilla warfare have meant that there has been a certain bending of the literal meaning of regulations, which has been recognized by the legal system. The important *McElhone* judgement in the House of Lords in 1975 effectively allowed people to be shot on sight, so long as the soldier afterwards could plausibly argue that the target was a terrorist, and that by following Queen's Regulations his own life may have been put in danger.

The controversy over 'shoot to kill' also needs to be seen in terms of the undeclared war waged by the PIRA and their use of guerrilla tactics to murder and maim the security forces, both British soldiers and Ulster (Protestant) policemen. The fact that the security forces have arrested more alleged PIRA and INLA terrorists than Protestant paramilitaries, who have often deliberately engaged in purely sectarian murders, is a propaganda point made by Sinn Fein, which hints at alleged close ties between the security forces and the Protestant militias.

It also remains true that the function of the security forces is to maintain law and order, and uphold the peace under very difficult circumstances, and that much of their work has been designed to protect civil society from the effects of terrorist outrage. Mistakes have been made: 'Bloody Sunday' in January 1972 being perhaps the most costly in terms of permanently alienating many in the Catholic community, and acting as a recruiting sergeant for the PIRA; but the security forces have maintained the rule of law in conditions which at times approach those of an undeclared civil war.

It is quite clear, then, that British policy in Northern Ireland is predicated on the assumption that a political solution of the Ulster problem acceptable to both the Protestant and Catholic communities, and which is supported by a majority of the population, must be the basis of an eventual settlement. This would include a role (perhaps leading to eventual unification) for the Irish government. Hence the significance of the Anglo-Irish conference, where British and Irish ministers have met periodically to discuss political and security issues with relation to Ulster since 1985. Until those conditions are in place there can be no question of compromise, or accommodation, with those who seek a solution through force, and the necessary security measures have been implemented to defeat terrorist outrage. This policy is a matter of principle and will be followed no matter what the cost, in financial or human terms. Such commitment will of necessity mean adopting illiberal policies; force must be met with force, so the law can be upheld. Ways must be found of squaring the circle; if the lion cannot lie down with the lamb, a form of words must be found so that Protestants can compromise with Catholics, and the men of force and violence can be defeated or agree to negotiate a solution with the political parties, a suitable period of time after a ceasefire. This is the logic behind the Downing Street Declaration of 1993.

There are perhaps four areas in particular where the activities of the secret state in Ulster can be partially examined, as a result of public discussion of controversial policies. These are: security and the 'shoot to kill' controversy; intelligence and the employment of 'supergrasses'; the use of Diplock courts and emergency powers; and the treatment of political prisoners, internees and terrorists.

The 'shoot to kill' controversy reached particular prominence following the sacking of Manchester's Assistant Chief Constable, John Stalker, from an enquiry in 1986 into three separate incidents in Ulster in 1982–3, when the security forces killed unarmed civilians.[21] Other unrelated episodes have also fuelled this controversy over the years, particularly the shooting of three suspected IRA members in Gibraltar in 1988, although these were the most notorious cases. Such criticism has involved accusations against special forces in Ulster, the SAS and 14 Intelligence Company. Whilst the latter cases are less satisfactory because the accusations are impossible to substantiate, the 'shoot to kill' controversy involves accusations that the security forces are out of control, and that it is impossible to adequately monitor their behaviour because of the institutional cover-up, the lack of parliamentary scrutiny of security policy, and the official rationalization of alleged misdeeds. In essence this debate has revolved round arguments that the death of innocent or unarmed civilians is unfortunate, but that such mistakes are a regrettable but understandable consequence of the rules of war, and of soldiers ensuring their own protection in a dangerous situation. Sinn Fein have not been slow to make the propaganda point that alleged cavalier disregard for civilian life could be compared to the reprisal activities of the Black and Tans after the First World War.

Indeed, the Stalker enquiry related to three cases which

occurred in Armagh following the deaths of three RUC officers, blown up by an IRA bomb in the same county in October 1982. In three separate incidents in the following months, unarmed civilians were shot without having offered any form of provocation. Three were members of the PIRA, two of INLA and the last, perhaps a case of mistaken identity, was a youth with no connection to any Republican organization.[22]

The Stalker enquiry was set up as a result of discrepancies in the evidence, and after the Diplock courts had exonerated the officers involved and found them not guilty of murder. The particular point at issue was the extent to which Special Branch had failed to cooperate with the authorities, had coached witnesses and tried to cover up the evidence. The RUC had been vigorously defended by their Chief Constable, Sir John Hermon, who wished to bolster the morale of the force. John Stalker was appointed to head an enquiry into the allegations in May 1984, and diligently investigated the case until he was replaced in 1986. In essence the liberal policeman, John Stalker, failed to develop a satisfactory relationship with Hermon, who felt that the energetically pursued enquiry was undermining the integrity of the RUC.

The problem was compounded by the battle of wills that developed between the Stalker enquiry, the RUC and MI5 over alleged tapes which may have recorded the shooting of the three PIRA men in a hayshed near Lurgan. These had apparently been installed by MI5 but had failed to work when explosives had been removed and were used in a terrorist campaign against RUC officers. Stalker concluded that Special Branch had become too powerful within the RUC, was organizing a cover-up of the shootings and was obstructing his enquiry. Stalker was removed from the investigation as a result of his social connections with Kevin Taylor, a Manchester businessman who had alleged associations with a group of criminals in Manchester. When Taylor was later charged with an offence, he was found not guilty.

Stalker was replaced by Colin Sampson, the Chief Constable for West Yorkshire. He concluded that officers had conspired to cover up what had occurred in the three incidents but that no action would be taken for reasons of national security. Sir John Hermon claimed in his 1988 annual report that no evidence had been found to substantiate the 'shoot to kill' allegations. Stalker argued that what he discovered was that no announcement of such a policy was stuck up on a noticeboard, but that the officers involved had a clear impression that that was what was expected of them.

A similar controversy arose over the shooting of three unarmed Irish citizens in Gibraltar in 1988. Here members of the Special Forces testified behind curtained screens that they had shot the three suspects rather than arrest them because they felt their movements when challenged could have been interpreted as potentially putting some of the soldiers in danger of retaliatory fire. A conflict of evidence with witnesses resulted, which, despite attempts by the authorities to question the reliability and veracity of those who challenged the official account, still left important questions unanswered.

Similarly, there has been a conflict of evidence with regard to problems of connections between the security forces and Protestant paramilitaries. Two ex-members of Military Intelligence in Northern Ireland, Fred Holroyd and Colin Wallace, have gone public with their accounts of alleged dubious behaviour on the part of the authorities.[23] Other ex-intelligence officers have challenged their main accusations, and the authorities have argued that both had grudges against the Army, one needing psychiatric treatment, the other losing a civil service job in Lisburn and later serving a prison sentence for killing a Sussex antiques dealer, a crime he had always denied. A later tribunal found that Wallace had been unfairly dismissed and recommended compensation. Wallace also claimed that 'black propaganda' had been used to smear Harold Wilson.

The Holroyd accusations included specific accusations against Captain Robert Nairac of 14 Intelligence Company, who was captured and killed by the IRA in May 1977. According to Holroyd, who was in the Special Military Intelligence Unit, Nairac showed him photographs of the corpse of John Francis Green, with fresh blood on the ground.

Green was a prominent Republican who was killed in January 1975. Holroyd claims that he may also have been involved in the Miami showband killings in the same year, as one of the weapons used appears to have been the same in both cases. He alleged that the army and Special Branch worked closely with loyalist terrorists. All these claims have been vigorously denied by the authorities, who posthumously awarded Nairac the George Cross for his bravery. Colin Wallace's claims that most of the 35 Catholics murdered by sectarian Protestant terror groups, were acting as agents for the security services, and using weapons supplied by them, have also been flatly denied by both the authorities and the soldiers involved.[24]

Such accusations have proved problematical for the authorities because use has been made of information which military intelligence has undoubtedly discovered from Protestant paramilitary sources. Whilst republican organizations have long since pointed to alleged connections between clandestine loyalist organizations and the security forces, the issue was raised above the level of propaganda by the trial of Brian Nelson in 1992. He had been the Chief Intelligence Officer of the UDA, whilst at the same time acting as a double agent for British Military Intelligence between 1983 and 1985, and for a period after 1987. He allegedly played an intricate double game, telling the authorities about the activities of the UDA and linked terrorist groups, whilst at the same time reputably feeding the paramilitaries details of intelligence files about the IRA.[25]

As a result of Nelson's activities the authorities claimed they were able to foil many planned murders by Protestant terror groups, including that of the Sinn Fein president, Gerry Adams. But it was alleged that Nelson did not inform the authorities of all the information at his disposal, and it was for this that he was given a long prison sentence. Whatever the truth of this claim the case highlighted a tactic, which the MI5 had used against fascist groups in the inter-war period: the infiltration of agents into the intelligence structure of extremist groups under political surveillance. The case also embarrassed the security authorities, as Nelson was imprisoned for his part in aiding terrorist activity.

There is an interesting point of comparison with interwar political surveillance of perceived extremist groups.

Whereas the PIRA was the ultimate enemy to whom no quarter is given, and is viewed in a similar way as the CPGB was, the attitude towards the Protestant paramilitaries was more ambivalent. Whilst official military and police leadership viewed sectarian murder with horror, the security forces came dangerously close to complicity in the Brian Nelson case: this was comparable to the use made of the intelligence departments of the British Fascists and the British Union of Fascists in the interwar period. Arresting Nelson proved to be counter-productive. The authorities lost a major source close to the centre of Protestant extremist operations as well as accelerated the emergence of a more violent young leadership amongst the loyalist community who remain scornful of both the trustworthiness of the security forces and their ability to prosecute a successful war against the PIRA.

The somewhat dubious activities of elements associated with British intelligence in Ireland had earlier been exposed in the case of the Littlejohn brothers. It was alleged that MI6 had encouraged them to rob banks in the Republic of Ireland. This was vehemently denied when the Irish authorities found their fingerprints after a raid in 1972. Whatever the validity of this denial, the case of the British authorities was not helped by the fact that the extradition proceedings were held in camera for reasons of national security. Similarly, the arrest in 1973 of John Wyman, who was believed to have been an MI6 officer, for receiving information from an officer of the Gardai Special Branch, also played a part in the decision to scale down MI6 operations against the IRA in Britain, and the ultimate decision to make MI5 rather than MI6 responsible for British civilian security operations in Northern Ireland.[26]

That is not to say that there were no security successes for British intelligence. Although the authorities have not been able to stop the supply of weapons or sources of finance for IRA terrorist campaigns, the interception of several cargoes of sophisticated armaments destined for Ireland from Libyan and American origins provided evidence of considerable

21 Soldiers on patrol in Belfast, 1991

assistance from both radical Arab and traditional Irish-American sources. Thus in 1983 five tons of arms from Libya on board the freighter *Claudia* were seized at Antwerp. This included seven RPG-7 rocket launchers and 36 rockets. Armalites, machine guns and ammunition were seized by Irish naval vessels from the *Valhalla* following a tipoff from British intelligence in 1984.[27] The PIRA has also benefited from the proceeds of bank robberies in both Eire and the United States, allegedly including much of the proceeds of one of the largest heists in history, in Rochester, New York, in 1993.

The counter-intelligence tactic which worried the Irish terrorist organizations most however was the use of so-called 'supergrasses'. This tactic involved the British authorities providing protection, new identities and a fresh start for members of illegal organizations who provided testimony in open court against others allegedly involved in terrorist crime. Christopher Black, a PIRA member, was the first to testify under such an arrangement in 1981, and 35 of the 38 defendants were convicted as a result of his testimony. During 1981 and 1982 more than 200 people were arrested on the evidence of supergrasses, and the PIRA organization in Derry was decimated as a result of supergrass testimony. Those convicted included members of the PIRA, INLA and 70 members of the various Protestant terrorist organizations who were found guilty of serious crimes.

The credibility of the uncorroborated testimony of terrorists quickly began to unravel, however, and many of the convictions were overturned on appeal. Of the 120 people convicted on the evidence of the ten main supergrasses, 67 were subsequently released on appeal and the authorities abandoned the use of the system. Whilst British security thought much of the evidence given was genuine, the fact that it originated in such unreliable sources and was uncorroborated meant it obviously fell short of the usual standard of British justice.[28]

The use of 'turned' supergrasses highlighted the abnormal nature of law and order in Ulster. It was necessary because of the success of the PIRA in repeating the achievement of Michael Collins during and after the First World War with regard to effective counter-intelligence measures against political surveillance. The move from a brigade to a cell structure of organization, and the operation of a need to know principle, so that few IRA secrets would be compromised by individual arrests, was a tactic which the British security forces found difficult to counter.

The introduction of emergency powers, the imposition of Direct Rule and the ending of the jury system in courts in order to prevent intimidation, meant Northern Ireland became an exceptional case whose civil turmoil contrasted with the relative peace of the rest of the United Kingdom.

Diplock courts had no place in the legal tradition of the common law. Although the authorities had taken exceptional measures, the steady trickle of violence in Ulster, sometimes erupting into a more tragic dimension after particularly severe outrage, failed to heal the deep divisions in Northern Ireland. Indeed, the current situation is as gloomy as ever. The sickening increase in Protestant paramilitary sectarian murders is a sympton of extremist response to the belief that despite its illiberalism British security policy in Northern Ireland has failed.

The attempt to use a double barrelled policy involving harsh security measures in tandem with political initiatives led to a failure to reassure either the Protestant or Catholic communities in Northern Ireland, to close the rift between the two, or instil much confidence that any British government could repeat Lloyd George's fudge, let alone build bridges to heal the deep wounds in Ulster society. Whereas the British troops had been welcomed in 1969, the twin disasters of internment and Bloody Sunday provided a propaganda gift for the PIRA. Liberal and international opinion became progressively alienated from the harsh security measures of the authorities, no matter how necessary they were to restore law and order. The PIRA, in particular, was not slow to reactivate traditional forms of revolt against prison conditions, demand political prisoner status, and engage in hunger strikes, as well as pioneer new forms of indiscipline, like the dirty protest in the Maze. These were effective propaganda weapons which discredited the British government in the eyes of international opinion.[29]

The introduction of internment in August 1971 was the mistake from which British policy in Ulster never recovered: 342 men were detained initially, of whom only 2 were protestants. Altogether by the end of 1971 700 were held without charge or trial. The counter-productiveness of the policy was evident from the outset. Before August there had been 30 deaths as a result of terrorism; another 143 died before the end of the year. Internment appeared to have strengthened the allegiance of internees to the PIRA and acted as a spur to educational indoctrination of internees, a kind of crash university course.

The effective ending of internment in 1972 was

accompanied by the suspension of Stormont, the imposition of Direct Rule from Westminster, and the introduction of Diplock Courts.[30] In recognition of the unusual situation and the draconian suspension of the operation of the common law, paramilitary prisoners both loyalist and republican were given 'special category status', in effect they were recognized as political prisoners. This meant they were kept in separate prisons from those who had committed 'normal' crimes, and were allowed not to wear prison uniform. Indeed, they were permitted to control their own discipline, and all orders from the authorities were communicated via the paramilitaries' commanding officers in the 'H' blocks of the Maze prison.

The oscillation or U-turn in the Heath administration's policy with regard to Northern Ireland mirrored that of the change in industrial policy in 1972. Whilst the Wilson and Callaghan Labour governments of 1974–9 exhibited a hardening of attitude towards the political violence in Ulster, with the return to a criminalization policy after March 1976, Mrs Thatcher regarded the Heath government's 'soft' Ulster policy as a prime example of wetness in action. According to such an analysis, more concern was given to the perpetrators than the victims of political crimes, and this view led to a relative consensus on the political management of terrorist violence in Northern Ireland. The main difference was that the Labour Party envisioned a long-term goal of a united Ireland to be obtained by political consent, whereas the Conservatives emphasized more their traditional concerns about the democratic wishes of the majority in Ulster. Both, however, were united in their insistence that there could be no compromise with terrorist violence.

If the British state saw the need for continuing the military presence, then both Labour and Conservative administrations recognized the need for the 'Ulsterization' of security measures, to relieve both the stresses on the British army and the loss of local control on the government of Northern Ireland. Locally recruited forces, based on the expansion of the RUC, and the newly created Ulster Defence Regiment (UDR), were seen as the answer. The UDR had been created in 1970 to replace the notorious B Specials.

The relative political consensus within the British state

across party lines did not affect the administrative experiments on how to handle 'political prisoners'. The developments in the 1970s and 1980s mirrored previous debates over the acknowledgement of the issue, both with relation to the IRA between 1916 and 1923, suffragettes between 1905 and 1914, and British fascist internees in the Second World War. Whereas the authorities had traditionally opposed the granting of political status, the necessity to appease militant, respectable middle and upper class suffragettes, the fear of the propaganda effects of IRA martyrdom, and the insistence that fascist internees should receive more privileges and not be regarded as criminals, were all relevant precedents which affected British attitudes to political crimes in Northern Ireland.

The new criminalization policy after 1976 was opposed from the outset by the PIRA paramilitaries. For several years republican prisoners wore blankets rather than submit to accept prison uniforms. They also adopted a 'dirty protest', fouling their cells and refusing to cooperate with the authorities. When a new Conservative government under Mrs Thatcher showed no sign of a less firm attitude, the prisoners upped the stakes and several went on hunger strike in the autumn of 1979. Although a negotiated settlement which fudged the uniform issue appeared to be on offer over Christmas, the failure of the apparent concessions to materialize created renewed intransigence on the part of the prisoners. Under the leadership of Bobby Sands, ten republican prisoners died after a renewed hunger strike.[31]

Whilst the British government stood firm and failed to compromise with the hunger strikers, the PIRA effectively won the propaganda war. The election of Bobby Sands to the Westminster parliament for Fermanagh and South Tyrone, and of two other members of Sinn Fein to the Dáil Eireann, including a hunger striker, provided much international publicity for the PIRA. This resulted in a fundamental reappraisal of PIRA tactics which led to the abandonment of traditional IRA abstentionism in politics. Henceforth the policy of 'the armalite and the ballot box' was to give a much greater profile to the role of Sinn Fein, whose function now was to attempt to provide a bridge to the political arena for the men of violence. The authorities responded with great suspicion to this development, seeing Sinn Fein as a wolf in sheep's clothing which tries to negotiate a political solution using the blackmail of continued force and violence of the PIRA, whose tactics they understand and do not disown.

Although Mrs Thatcher had stood firm, the prison authorities in practice allowed the paramilitaries to reassert their own discipline and control over much of prison conditions during the later 1980s. This trend continued despite outbreaks of violence against prison warders and the murder of several officers, although a form of uneasy truce has distinguished relations for the most part. Both Mrs Thatcher and John Major have taken steps to mute the propaganda of Sinn Fein. British ears are not allowed to hear the Irish brogue of Gerry Adams or Martin McGuinness, although actors can read their lines. Gerry Adams was banned from entry into England in 1993. The British government has censored the views of a significant section of Ulster republican politics; this is not so much a reflection of a change in the traditional state views on allowing extremist political elements to put forward their political programme, but a criticism of their failure to renounce the use of violence by the PIRA.

c) The Mainland Campaign

Since the murder of Sir Henry Wilson in 1923, the IRA has exported its struggle with the British government to mainland Britain. This has included a shortlived campaign in 1939 which led to the deaths of innocent civilians, and the hanging of an IRA man. Similarly, the border campaign in 1956–62 had included a United Kingdom dimension with raids on public school and military armouries, leading to the imprisonment of Sean Macstiofain and Cathal Goulding. The renewal of hostilities in 1970, however, was punctuated by the activities of the PIRA active service units in the United Kingdom, with campaigns including the bombing of civilian and military targets, the murder of Airey Neave, Ian Gow, and Ross McWhirter amongst others, and attempts to target main institutions for maximal disruption and destruction in British society.

Whilst other sources of terrorist outrage have emerged for short periods, it is the persistence and recurrence of PIRA activity which have chiefly been responsible for the reorganization of Britain's security defences on the mainland, most notably the Prevention of Terrorism Act and the formation of the Anti-Terrorist Squad (SO13) under George Churchill Coleman and David Tucker. Outrages in 1974, with 21 deaths and 162 injured, as the result of the bomb explosions at two Birmingham pubs, and 7 more deaths from similar atrocities in Guildford and Woolwich in the same year, were the harbingers of several more mainland campaigns.[32] The PIRA argued that if guerrilla warfare failed to bring about the withdrawal of British troops from Northern Ireland, then the terrorist campaign must be spread to the rest of the United Kingdom to persuade public opinion that the defence of Ulster was not worth the cost of the spread of the troubles to England. The immutable belief that political outrage and terror produced meek compliance to the wishes of the perpetrators was to prove as much wishful thinking on the mainland as in Protestant Ulster. Horror, a stiff upper lip and the Blitz mentality punctuated the general response of the usual bored indifference of public perception to the troubles and traumas of Ulster.

The statistics of the PIRA campaign in England in the 1980s and early 1990s suggested a no-win situation for either side. There have been 20 mainland atrocities, accounting for 35 deaths, 544 injuries and £1.5 billion worth of damage.[33] The worst carnage was experienced at the Royal Marines School of Music at Deal, Kent, in 1989, with 11 fatalities, and at Harrods at Christmas 1983 with 6 deaths and 91 injured. The bomb which just missed Mrs Thatcher at Brighton in 1984 killed 5 and injured 30. Bombs in 1992 and 1993 caused hundreds of millions of pounds of damage and 4 deaths at the Baltic Exchange and at Bishopsgate in the City of London. With all this mayhem only three terrorists have been convicted. What successes there have been seem to have arisen as much from luck as good intelligence, such as the Balcombe Street siege in 1975.

Indeed, the problem of security against terrorist outrage has produced little in the way of results, or of preventing further violence. Whilst several PIRA cells have been broken up, the increasingly sophisticated security apparatus have been unsuccessful in putting an end to the menace. The failure of Special Branch, traditionally in charge of dealing with Irish terrorism, and of the specially created Anti-Terrorist Branch (SO13), led in 1992 to MI5 being given the leading role in combatting Irish terrorism. This appears to have changed little, apart from the moving around of the deckchairs on the Titanic. In the time honoured tradition of British government, a review of security had decided that there was too much overlapping of intelligence function and that there should be a streamlining of the system to make it more efficient.

Whilst Special Branch objected to this change, the Association of Chief Police Officers also contributed to several botched operations, such as Octavian in 1989. The problem of a lack of a coordinated national police force, institutional jealousies and operational difficulties has led to a far less successful counter-intelligence operation against the PIRA than most Continental police forces conduct against their home grown terrorist organizations (such as the Baader-Meinhof gang in West Germany, the Red Brigades in Italy, Action Directe in France, ETA in Spain and CCC in Belgium). Critics of British counter-intelligence, such as James Adams, argue fairly convincingly that much of the blame for this should be attributed to the failure of British security to coordinate adequately the response of overlapping agencies to the activities of terrorists.[34] The authorities were often hamstrung by the necessity of having to work within the law.

The problem was that since the days of Michael Collins' counter-intelligence operations between 1918 and 1922, the British security authorities have generally found it difficult to infiltrate the IRA or to operate an effective political surveillance.[35] This was particularly the case after the PIRA moved, after internment, from a brigade to a cell unit of organization, and the use of terror, of the murder of those suspected of informing to the authorities.

The PIRA and INLA have kept well away from known IRA sympathizers in Great Britain. The illegal Protestant terror organizations, of which the authorities have more knowledge, do not operate on the mainland, as they desire to remain part of the United Kingdom and do not wish to alienate British public opinion. As a result, most concern on the mainland is expressed about the activities of the PIRA, even though more deaths in the last two years have been caused by Protestant paramilitaries operating in Ulster. In Northern Ireland the authorities claim to know who the men of violence are on both sides but are hindered by their inability to provide the evidence which would satisfy even a Diplock court. The need to protect the source of information has prevented the authorities from acting against the men of terror, or so it is claimed. This is seen as an argument to justify the reintroduction of internment.

Long experience has taught the British authorities to be wary of such a ruthless move. Ever since the Boer War, incarcerating security risks without charge or trial has rebounded against the authorities and has provided more difficulties than it has solved. Only in the case of the fascists in the Second World War was there little objection to such a move by liberal public opinion. This caution is reinforced by the memory of the disaster of locking up the IRA in 1971–2. On the mainland it is quite clear that the authorities have little knowledge of the whereabouts of the perpetrators of violence, and the main successes have resulted from chance discoveries of arms dumps and bomb factories.

What has also hampered the police in trying to control the PIRA has been public unease about methods employed by the authorities to convict alleged perpetrators of atrocities. The eventual release in 1989 and 1990 of the so-called Guildford four, the Birmingham six and the Maguire seven after their convictions had been declared unsafe, highlighted the dilemma for the authorities. The calling into question of forensic evidence, the scientific doubts about alleged confessions, and the methods used to extort confessions cast doubts on the integrity of police methods and the standards of British justice.[36]

Whilst the eventual quashing of the cases against the accused, after 15 or 16 years in jail, came as little surprise to anybody, given the evidence had been discredited for some considerable time, the prosecution of the police officers involved has not helped to clear the matter up. The acquittal of all those concerned raised serious questions about police methods and British justice. Those accused of the dreadful crimes were innocent; but there was nothing wrong with the way in which the authorities gained false confessions.

The episode has severely damaged the reputation of the British police. This appears to have resulted from a combination of placing too much reliance on now discredited forensic evidence, and using this supposedly scientific proof as the necessary justification for applying dubious interrogation techniques to produce confessions. It was the intense pressure for the police to obtain convictions in these cases which led to questionable interrogation techniques being employed. This together with the misleading forensic evidence led the jury to convict. A combination of these factors has produced other notorious miscarriages of justice in criminal cases, such as that of Stephan Kisko, which has severely embarrassed the police and undermined their reputation as the upholders of justice as well as law and order.

The inability of the authorities to contain terrorism successfully, despite the massive resources that have been employed to neutralize it, increased the pressure for a more centralized if not authoritarian management of a national police force. There were also demands for unitary control and direction of political surveillance, and the collection and analysis of intelligence. Whilst the requirement of efficiency and better utilization of resources has led to demands such as that proposed by the Sheehy report (turning the operation of the police into a normal business), the failure of high cost technology to improve the rate of success against terrorist outrage has raised embarrassing questions. This has also threatened civil liberties and made the Home Office cautious in speeding up the process of greater centralization, despite pressures from the authorities and Mrs Thatcher between 1979 and 1990.

Although it is quite clear that the forces of law and order and the secret state will not be subject to radical restructuring, piecemeal tinkering will no doubt continue to be the response to the failure of the authorities to defeat the PIRA either in Ulster or on the mainland. Whilst it is quite clear that local sensibilities, traditionally the reason for the patchwork quilt development of the management of law and order in Britain, are a declining factor, and that adequate political accountability is as far away as ever, the Major administration is at least more sensible and less secretive about these matters than the governments dominated by his predecessor.

The problem of Northern Ireland has proved the most intractable of all the difficulties facing the security authorities in the twentieth century. It has become the First World War of the secret state, with entrenched attitudes on both sides, and whilst initiatives on how to break the stalemate have shown imagination and perseverance, the response to such activity has been predictable in its negativity. The need for a political solution will not compromise with the use of force to resolve the conflict; the constitutional parties will not sit down with the men of violence; Unionists will not discuss any solution which compromises the position of Northern Ireland within the United Kingdom, nor allow a role for the Irish government; the PIRA will not contemplate laying down its arms until British troops are out of Northern Ireland. In fact, both sides appear to be adopting the strategy which won Ronald Reagan and George Bush the Cold War: implacable opposition to the 'evil empire' and building up arsenals of weapons to break the will of the enemy, or make it too expensive in human or financial terms for the other side to compete. Lloyd George managed to fudge the issue and provided a solution of sorts, but this can be said to have led to intermittent outbreaks of violence which degenerated into a prolonged outbreak of guerrilla warfare since 1970. There is little sign of a new 'Welsh Wizard' on the horizon, despite new initiatives set in train by the Major administration in an attempt to widen the scope of discussions within the nationalist community, and draw in participants from the Protestant political parties. Countering Irish terrorism now accounts for half of the work of MI5.

CONCLUSION

In some ways this has been a frustrating book to write. Whatever its defects, the author can legitimately use as a partial excuse the cult of secrecy which has hindered a more rapid release of state papers. Whilst the attitude of the present government, and the White Paper announcing the Waldegrave initiative is to be welcomed, as is the current expansion of storage facilities at the PRO at Kew, even such positive steps stop short of the public right to access to information, personal files and state papers which has been provided under the Freedom of Information Act in the United States since 1975.

Whilst this comparison can be overstated, as legislation on confidentiality and national security in the USA parallels that in Great Britain, it nevertheless remains true that Americans can see a greater range of material, including FBI files, than in this country. Ironically, they can also consult more secret material on the British state and political extremism, public order and internal security than can citizens of the United Kingdom, as a result of a secret intelligence treaty of 1917. This led to an exchange of material, including MI5 and Special Branch reports on communism and fascism in Britain amongst other subjects, which is to be found in the London embassy files at the National Archives in Washington. Since John Costello pointed this out, the authorities have clamped down on unofficial disclosures and memoirs of the secret world and, following the Official Secrets Act of 1989, has made it next to impossible to leak unauthorized information, no matter what the source or antiquity. The virtual collapse of self-regulation through the D-Notice committee has made publication in this area more problematic.

Having made the ritual complaint about often unnecessary secrecy in the declassification of material, I need to stress that for those willing and able to mine the treasure trove of state papers there is a considerable body of material which throws light on the subject matter of this book. In one sense the censorship of material is an advantage to the historian: the authorities have made the historian's task more manageable by only allowing access to a representative sample of the documentation kept under lock and key. By choosing the material which historians can consult the state has provided clues about the nature of the secret state. It must be realized, however, that to a certain degree the state has released more on relatively uncontroversial or less important areas like the BUF, than on others which were of greater state concern, such as papers pertaining to the CPGB or the IRA. It nevertheless remains true that much of relevance has been declassified. Much can be learned, for example, from the state surveillance of British fascism, which is also applicable to more delicate areas. Private papers also can help us fill in some of the gaps.

It is entirely right that there should be a thorough declassification procedure even on historical material with regard to the IRA, as this remains an ongoing problem for the authorities. Perhaps there is a strengthening argument for the more rapid release of material on the CPGB, given the collapse of that organization in 1991. There are imminent plans, according to *The Times*, for the release of up to 200 more files on the BUF, and for the indexing of up to a further 500,000, although what that implies for access is not clear.[1] The Cabinet Office, too, is diligently reviewing much of its more secret material up to 1950.

With relation to the Second World War there have been recent releases of Joint Intelligence Committee minutes and papers for the 1939–41 period. The rest of the Second World War material will be released in January 1994, and the review has been extended to the early Cold War. Some of the surviving SOE papers have also been declassified, and there is a continuing assessment of the Security Executive and its associated committees during the Second World War. In this sense the Home and Cabinet Offices are following in the footsteps of the Foreign Office, which has had a more liberal attitude towards the declassification of files, particularly in the General Correspondence (FO 371). The official histories of various aspects of intelligence and security during the Second World War have also appeared at regular intervals, including the volume relating to the subject matter of this book.

Whilst many areas show improvement in terms of material available, the continuing black hole is the unavailability of the papers of the most secret agencies of state, most notably those of Special Branch, MI5 and MI6. Whilst the authorities are now more rational about the existence and the objectives of these organizations, there is little likelihood of even material of historical interest only being made available for consultation. In short, the nature of the evidence at best is patchy, but improving in many areas. There is need for greater pressure on the authorities to review and declassify material which has little more than historical interest. To that extent it should be possible to release more files than are currently available in all areas up to at least the end of the Second World War. The work of the Institute of Contemporary British History and of the Study Group on Intelligence, both of which request reviews of classified material, is a useful *ad hoc* initiative in which consumer demand generates more releases of important material.

Several points can be made about files that are declassified. Where there is an issue of confidentiality, misleading information or unsubstantiated and unprovable rumour about individuals, then the liberal application of the blue pencil is called for, rather than the failure of the document to appear at all. As in many areas of the state, the greatest limitation on the declassification of material is not the lack of will but the lack of resources to assess the files. There is also the need to double-check that state security and the principle of confidentiality are not being impeded; and to that extent, as well as protecting their own depository, MI5 are probably responsible for the slow process of the review of files in several departments. Certainly compared with the United States the British process of declassification is slow, and is an area where greater efficiency is called for, a concern which is supposedly at the heart of modern Conservatism and the 'Thatcher revolution'. A final suggestion would be to speed up the process whereby more series are brought into the orbit of the 30-year rule: the important HO 144 series respecting demonstrations and disturbances would benefit historians more if its 75- to 100-year closure period were reduced to 30 years, rather than relying on special exceptional reviews like those on British fascism and the Channel Islands, which led to early declassification.

If there is still a continuing need for some material to be made available, this does not mean that conclusions are more difficult to sustain. The evidence assessed in this book suggests paradoxically that there is both a continuity of response by the British state to political extremism, public order and internal security during the twentieth century, and unresolved tensions between the different levels of the state on how best to manage these phenomena. Whilst only tentative conclusions can be drawn for the period after 1950, because of the dearth of relevant state papers, there is an underlying conflict between administrative practice and the work of the security agencies. It nevertheless remains true that despite the application of modern technology, greater rationalization and efficiency, and a trend towards centralization of resources in the Thatcher era, the tension within the state between the often contradictory pull of the liberal traditions of political and administrative practice, have met with resistance from the erratic and often haphazard growth of the security agencies of the state.

Indeed, the greatest difficulty has been to define the nature of the state, and its attitude towards the subject matter of this book. The problem has partly been secrecy, but also the authorities' conflicting attitudes about the concept of public order.

In general it may be argued that Victorian liberalism, with its suspicion of 'Continental practices' and neglect of security concerns, has led to a slowly diminishing residue of governmental distaste for the need for secret political policemen during the twentieth century. In this sense the atmosphere of John le Carré's spy novels, where the seedy secret world of Smiley's people is kept at arms length from the work of government by the administrative intermediary from Whitehall, is instructive. Not only does such an arrangement remove responsibility for dubious activities from politicians in the fictional world, but it also enables them to pretend that they are not aware of what is allegedly going on, that if it is illegal it will be dealt with, for such behaviour is not the British way.

This establishment distaste for secret plans and dirty tricks has been forced to compromise with the real world during the twentieth century. The knowledge that others were not playing by the rules of the game, and were doing their best to undermine the nation, and the suspicion that that they were aided and abetted by rogue elements within British society, which led to the perceived need to extend the secret areas of the state into the more morally dubious areas of intelligence and security.

This development in mainland Britain arose from the practical need to defend society from terrorism, originally from the Fenians in the 1880s; its twentieth-century growth owed most to the need to organize and plan many aspects of society as a byproduct of the British state's response to the First and Second World Wars. In that sense 'war socialism' necessitated state initiatives not only to plan the use of manpower and the output of munitions, but to discover intelligence which would aid in the battle with the enemy, and provide counter-intelligence measures which would prevent the enemy discovering British secrets or sabotaging the war effort. The initiatives included managing industrial unrest and pacifist sentiment in an attempt to stop them damaging the war effort, presenting such activity as unpatriotic. It also meant that perceived necessary limitations on civil liberties were justified usually with reference to alleged, and mainly imaginary, connections with the enemy. War ensured that 'the worst case scenario' became the justification for ensuring that internal security was accorded the highest possible priority, and that the secret agencies of the state usurped the working of the common law, as emergency powers became the basis for the regulation of public order.

Whilst it needs to be stressed that wartime infringements of civil liberties proved to be temporary, and an understandable reaction, the insidious growth of the security dimension of the secret state arose from the perceived continuation of threats to the maintenance of order, and of alleged conspiracies instigated by foreign powers against the United Kingdom during the peace. Of particular significance here was the conspiracy hatched by the Comintern and their Soviet masters in Moscow, a threat which was to dominate the secret state from 1917 until 1990. Such was the concern about potential problems instigated by this source that it was felt necessary to put on to the statute book in 1920 provision for the state to adopt wartime emergency powers during periods of political crisis.

Thus the security aspects of the secret state in Britain owed much to suspected external enemies, most notably Germany (spy scare in Edwardian England, 'hidden hand' in the First World War, Nazism in the 1930s and 1940s) and the Soviet Union, with the Red Menace orchestrated from Moscow. These were sometimes combined as part of the management team behind home grown political violence and terrorism such as the IRA.

Ireland provided the conflict which led to the breakdown of Victorian complacency about the extension of the secret state into that of the management of public order. In the twentieth century old concerns about trying to keep Irish problems over the water became harder to substantiate. It remained true, however, that Whitehall attempted to keep the Irish troubles at arm's length, both by giving responsibility for security to Stormont, with the creation of Northern Ireland in 1922, and the establishment of the Northern Ireland Office following the implementation of Direct Rule in 1972. Whilst the British state has been forced reluctantly to concede that events in Ireland do have significance for security and public order in Britain, it would be wrong to jump from this conclusion to the argument of Tony Benn's that the operation of the secret state in Northern Ireland is a stalking horse, an experimental laboratory for the implementation of technologically sophisticated surveillance techniques, which will soon be used against political non-conformists in the rest of the United Kingdom. The need in 1993 to be Janus-faced, to face both directions at the same time, denouncing IRA terrorism whilst placating Unionist objections to contact with the men of violence, shows that basic realities have not altered significantly since the days of Lloyd George. The attempt to send an arms shipment to Protestant paramilitaries in 1993 in Larne also has distinct echoes of 1914 about it. The suspicion remains that despite the many millions of pounds poured down the political and security drain of Northern Ireland, it is still the Orange and the Green which call the shots.

In historical terms, however, it does remain true that the Ulster question did play a significant part in the extension of the security role of the secret state. Many of those involved with the expansion of political surveillance to include radicals, socialists and trade unionists in the rest of the United Kingdom during and after the First World War were intransigent Unionists who themselves had first-hand experience of defying the authority of the British government. Whilst security conscious policemen may hanker for greater powers to curtail the threat posed by civil disobedience, the mandarins of the Home Office and Whitehall's political and administrative supervision ensure that the hallowed tradition of negative liberalism, of freedom of opinion and expression within the law, although frayed a little at the edges, is still sacrosanct.

Thus the general argument presented by this book is that although there have been changes in the management of political extremism, internal security and public order in the twentieth century, and the state has equipped itself with more powers to deal adequately with civil disruption, the quest for greater efficiency has not impaired civil liberties, except where minority power threatens to disrupt the entire community. To this end the administrative practice put in place by Sir John Anderson in the 1920s, utilizing the arguments of negative freedom enunciated by John Stuart Mill, and the tradition of the common law followed by Anderson's predecessors in the Home Office, has allowed those seen as political extremists to spout hot air to true believers whilst denying them recognition and publicity. The fact that so many of Anderson's acolytes rose to become top civil servants in the Home and Cabinet Offices during the succeeding half century made his influence on the administration of civil liberties and public order, as in other areas of government, a seminal one.

Whilst there has been a decline in the role of the military to aid the civil power except as a force of last resort, and as a means by which essential supplies can be kept flowing, the militarization of the administration of the forces of law and order, following closely the advice of General Macready before the Desborough Committee in 1919, has been consistently developed during the twentieth century – although, of course, our policemen and secret policemen do not usually carry firearms. Again Macready's disciples were to ensure his influence on the sharp end of the maintenance of public order long after his retirement.

Although it would be an exaggeration to say that policy enunciated in government represents the synthesis or compromise of liberal politicians and conservative policemen, working within the framework of law and precedent adjudicated by Whitehall administrators, it nevertheless remains true that the authorities are reluctant either to alter the law or to increase the powers of the police except where absolutely necessary. There have been right-wing law and order Home Secretaries, including Sir William Joynson Hicks in the 1920s and the present incumbent, Michael Howard, but the general pattern has been a significant degree of political consensus throughout the twentienth century with regard to state policy on political extremism, public order and internal security.

The major unanswered question is who surveills the surveillers? Whilst the ripping yarn memoirs of Peter Wright and disclosures from other disgruntled security officers have raised disturbing thoughts on this, it nevertheless remains true that there is no adequate accountability for secret policemen. Although the material in the public domain is probably misleading in a number of respects, and the Major government appears to have come to the same conclusion as its predecessors, that for reasons of national security it is best to let sleeping dogs lie, it assumes that the management and control of secret and security organizations is best dealt with internally, although there are plans in the pipeline for partial parliamentary oversight. Whilst the reorganizations instituted under Sir Dick White and others have made for more efficient management, the whole thrust of Thatcherite reforms and the style of John Major's administration has been to make institutions more accountable to government and consumers: except intelligence and security organizations. Secrecy is nearer to godliness in this one special instance it seems, although it will be interesting to see whether John Major's plan for limited parliamentary oversight is anything more than window dressing.

The insidious growth of the secret state throughout the twentieth century has represented more a technological than a manpower revolution. Indeed there are grounds for thinking that until at least the 1970s political distaste for the secret world led to starvation of resources, at least as far as humint investment was concerned. In the interwar period the police, despite increasing responsibility for the maintenance of public order, were not immune to considerable cutbacks in expenditure. Since the Second World War, although police pay has been protected for the most part, and the information revolution has made sigint even more important and expensive, managerial efficiency has been used to minimize unit costs. Certainly the less than generous attempts to make local authorities foot some of the bill for policing the miners' strike in 1984–5 must be seen as part of this process, as well as a political weapon aimed at Labour authorities who were too sympathetic to the needs of the strikers.

Whatever our final judgement is on the role of secrecy within government, it needs to be stressed that (comparatively) Britain has avoided the worst excesses of administrative government, and illegal activities as a routine measure by unaccountable secret policemen. Whilst not as open as the United States of America or Germany, the United Kingdom has avoided the horrors of the Soviet Union or Sadaam Hussein's Iraq. Secrecy in Great Britain is a nuisance to the historian and a continuing source of worry for those who believe in the maximization of civil liberties; but the state, whilst increasing its sphere of activity, has not significantly undermined the basis of a free society.

Finally, an instructive analogy to the subject of this book has been provided by Rosamund Thomas in her discussion of the differences between the British and American systems of public administration between 1900 and 1930.[2] She argues that the basic difference between the two systems is that British practice is characterized by synthesis between ethical idealism and scientific principle, as compared to the role of scientific management in American administration. The argument of this book has been that although there is no distinct ideology behind British administrative practice, the mixture of ethical idealism and scientific principle holds good in the principle of the common law, but there have been two significant turning points: the 1945–51 Labour government, where ethical concerns became more pronounced, and the advent of Thatcherism, where American scientific management techniques were applied across a broad section of policy.

NOTES

Introduction

1 K. Robertson, *Public Secrets* (London, 1982).
2 F. H. Hinsley and C. A. G. Simkins, *British Intelligence in the Second World War,* vol. 4, *Security and Counter-Intelligence* (London, 1990); C. Andrew, *Secret Service* (London, 1985); B. Porter, *The Origins of the Vigilant State* (London, 1987); B. Porter, *Plots and Paranoia* (London, 1989); N. Hiley, 'The Failure of British Counter-Espionage against Germany, 1907–1914', *Historical Journal* 28 (1985), pp. 835–62; N. Hiley, 'Counter-Espionage and Security in Great Britain During the First World War', *English Historical Review* 101 (1986), pp. 100–26.
3 J. Pellew, *The Home Office 1848–1914* (London, 1982), pp. 33–92; Sir E. Troup, *The Home Office* (London, 1925).
4 Porter, *The Origins of the Vigilant State,* p. 4.
5 F. C. Mather, *Public Order in the Age of the Chartists* (Manchester, 1959), pp. 171–80; D. Thompson, *The Chartists* (London, 1984), pp. 83–4.
6 S. Palmer, *Police and Protest in England and Ireland 1780–1850* (Cambridge, 1988), p. 517; P. Thurmond Smith, *Policing in Victorian London* (Westport, 1985), pp. 202–6.
7 B. Porter, *The Refugee Question in Mid-Victorian Politics* (Cambridge, 1979), p. 47.
8 B. Porter, *Plots and Paranoia,* p. 31.
9 K. Morgan, 'High and Low Politics of Labour: Keir Hardie to Michael Foot', in M. Bentley and J. Stevenson, eds, *High and Low Politics in Modern Britain* (Oxford, 1983), pp. 285–312.
10 Andrew, *Secret Service,* pp. 108–14, 247, 306–7.
11 Hinsley and Simkins, *British Intelligence,* pp. 3–27.
12 A. Thorpe, ed., *The Failure of Political Extremism in Inter-War*

Britain (Exeter, 1989), p. 1; C. Townshend, *Making the Peace* (Oxford, 1993), p. 23.

13 E. P. Thompson, *The Making of the English Working Class* (London, 1965), pp. 77–101.

14 D. S. Lewis, *Illusions of Grandeur* (Manchester, 1987).

15 A. Palmer, 'The History of the D-Notice Committee', in C. Andrew and D. Dilks, eds, *The Missing Dimension: Governments and Intelligence Communities in the Twentieth Century* (London, 1984), pp. 227–49.

16 C. Holmes, 'Internment, Fascism and the Public Records', *Bulletin of the Society for the Study of Labour History* 52, no. 1 (1987), pp. 17–22.

17 C. Holmes, 'Government Files and Privileged Access', *Social History* 6 (1981), pp. 335–50.

18 Holmes, 'Internment, Fascism and the Public Records', p. 17.

19 Hinsley and Simkins, *British Intelligence.*

20 J. Costello, *Mask of Treachery* (London, 1989).

1 The Strange Death of Liberal England (1900–1914)

1 G. Dangerfield, *The Strange Death of Liberal England* (London, 1970); A. O'Day, ed., *Conflict and Stability* (London, 1979); D. Reed, ed., *The Edwardian Age: Conflict and Stability* (London, 1982).

2 J. R. Hay, *The Origins of the Liberal Welfare Reforms, 1906–14* (London, 1975).

3 J. D. Fair, *British Interparty Conferences 1867–1921* (Oxford, 1980), pp. 77–102.

4 R. A. Rempel, *Unionists Divided* (Newton Abbott, 1972); K. O. Morgan, *The Age of Lloyd George* (London, 1971), pp. 17–37; K. W. Aikin, *The Last Years of Liberal England 1900–14* (London, 1972), pp. 9–31.

5 M. Bentley and J. Stevenson, eds, *High and Low Politics in Modern Britain* (Oxford, 1983).

6 G. Stedman Jones, *Outcast London* (London, 1976).

7 R. Kamm, 'The Home Office, Public Order and Civil Liberties, 1880–1914' (University of Oxford D.Phil. thesis, 1987), pp. 90–2.

8 J. Morgan, *Conflict and Order* (Oxford, 1987), p. 31; L. Lustgarten, *The Governance of the Police* (London, 1986).

9 PRO MEPO 2/248; MEPO 2/250; Kamm, The Home Office, Public Order and Civil Liberties, 1880–1914', pp. 3–4.

10 Ibid., pp. 80, 105–7.
11 V. Bailey, 'Salvation Army riots, the "Skeleton Army" and Legal Authority in a Provincial Town', in A. P. Donajgrodzki, ed., *Social Control in Nineteenth Century Britain* (London, 1977), pp. 231–53; PRO MEPO 2/168; PRO HO 45/9629/A22415.
12 PRO HO 144/204/A47976/8.
13 PRO MEPO 2/248; MEPO 2/250.
14 PRO HO 144/704/107039; HO 144/659/V36777; D. M. MacRaild, 'The Irish in North Lancashire and West Cumberland *c.*1850–1906: Aspects of the Social History of Barrow in Furness, Cleator Moor and Their Hinterlands' (University of Sheffield Ph.D. thesis, 1993,) pp. 260–383.
15 G. Phillips, *The Diehards* (London, 1979); G. Phillips, 'The Diehards and the Myth of the Backwoodsmen', *Journal of British Studies* 16 (Spring 1977), pp. 105–20.
16 R. Rempel, *Unionists Divided*; A. Sykes, *Tariff Reform in British Politics* (Oxford, 1979).
17 B. Harrison, 'The Act of Militancy: Violence and the Suffragettes, 1904–14', in B. Harrison, ed., *Peaceable Kingdom* (Oxford, 1982), pp. 26–81.
18 PRO HO 144/1257/235545/12, HO 144/1204/221826/5, HO 144/1196/220301/6.
19 PRO HO 144/1038/180965/3.
20 PRO MEPO 2/1438.
21 B. Porter, *The Origins of the Vigilant State* (London, 1987), p. 165; PRO HO 144/1043/183461/1; PRO MEPO 2/1297.
22 PRO HO 144/1033/175878/70.
23 PRO HO 144/1042/183256/2a.
24 PRO HO 144/1042/183256/3.
25 PRO HO 144/1042/183256/17.
26 PRO HO 144/1042/183256/21, 30a.
27 PRO HO 144/1107/200655/6.
28 PRO HO 144/1195/220196/658.
29 PRO HO 144/1041/182749/9.
30 PRO HO 144/1052/187234/20.
31 PRO HO 144/1052/187234/40.
32 PRO HO 144/1042/183256/18.
33 PRO HO 144/1038/180965/3.
34 PRO HO 144/1042/183256/20.
35 PRO HO 144/1205/221862/22.
36 PRO HO 144/1457/314179/3.
37 See R. Thurlow, *Fascism in Britain* (Oxford, 1987).
38 B. Harrison, 'Women's Suffrage at Westminster, 1866–1928',

in M. Bentley and J. Stevenson, eds, *High and Low Politics in Modern Britain*, pp. 80–122; A. Wiltsher, *Most Dangerous Women* (London, 1985), p. 2.

39 T. Kennedy, *The Hound of Conscience* (Fayetteville, 1981), p. 65.

40 J. Pellew, *The Home Office 1848–1914* (London, 1982), pp. 198–9.

41 PRO CAB 37/118/14.

42 R. Geary, *Policing Industrial Disputes 1893–1985* (Cambridge, 1985), pp. 6–24.

43 PRO MEPO 3/200, Blue Book on Strike Disturbances.

44 PRO HO 144/1022/163219/6.

45 PRO HO 144/1551/199768/55.

46 PRO CAB 37/107/70, CAB 37/110/62.

47 R. Church, 'Edwardian Labour Unrest and Coalfield Militancy 1890–1914', *The Historical Journal* 30, no. 4 (1987), pp. 841–57.

48 PRO HO 144/1160/212987/13.

49 H. Pelling, *A Short History of the Labour Party*, 8th edn (London, 1986), p. 13.

50 PRO MEPO 3/206; PRO HO 144/1211/223877.

51 Porter, *The Origins of the Vigilant State*, p. 169; PRO MEPO 3/206.

52 PRO HO 45/10608/192905/50; B. Weinberger, *Keeping the Peace?* (Oxford, 1991), pp. 20–36.

53 R. Church et al., *The History of the British Coal Industry*, vol. 3, 1830–1917 (Oxford, 1986), pp. 742–3; Weinberger, *Keeping the Peace?*, pp. 37–68; G. Brown, *Sabotage* (Nottingham, 1977), pp. 23–40.

54 PRO HO 144/1551/199768 to HO 144/1554/199768.

55 J. Morgan, *Conflict and Order*, pp. 154–64.

56 B. Weinberger, 'Police Perceptions of Labour In the Inter-war Period: The Case of the Unemployed and Miners on Strike', in F. Snyder and D. Hay, eds, *Labour, Law and Crime* (London, 1987), p. 164.

57 Sir N. Macready, *Annals of an Active Life* (London, 1924), pp. 136–57.

58 PRO HO 144/1553/199768/300.

59 J. Blake, 'Civil Disorder in Britain 1910–39: The Roles of Civil Government and Military Authority' (University of Sussex D.Phil. thesis, 1979), p. 136.

60 PRO HO 144/1551/199768/41a.

61 PRO HO 144/1551/199768/55.

62 C. Andrew, *Secret Service* (London, 1985), p. 284.
63 PRO MEPO 3/200, Blue Book on Strike Disturbances.
64 Weinberger, 'Police Perceptions', p. 164.
65 PRO HO 144/1553/199768/251, 294.
66 B. Holton, *British Syndicalism* (London, 1976), pp. 40–4.
67 J. Morgan, *Conflict and Order*, pp. 164–87; PRO HO 45/10648/210615/6, 10, 26, 26a, 43a; HO 45/10649/210615/66, 67.
68 PRO HO 45/10655/212470/206.
69 F. C. Mather, *Public Order in the Age of the Chartists* (Manchester, 1959), pp. 171–80; D. Thompson, *The Chartists* (London, 1984), pp. 83–4.
70 PRO HO 45/10648/210615/10, 26; HO 45/10649/210615/67.
71 PRO HO 45/10649/210615/65, 82; MEPO 3/219; HO 144/1157/212342/116.
72 PRO HO 45/10654/212470/103.
73 PRO HO 144/1163/213549/2.
74 PRO HO 144/1192/220104/5.
75 PRO HO 144/1157/212342/53.
76 Morgan, *Conflict and Order*, p. 40; PRO HO 144/1022/163219/8; PRO MEPO 2/360.
77 PRO HO 45/10654/212470/100.
78 PRO MEPO 3/217, 'Disturbances at Rotherhithe'.
79 Ibid.
80 Holton, *British Syndicalism*, p. 135.
81 PRO CO 904/158/3.
82 Morgan, *Conflict and Order*, p. 276; Weinberger, *Keeping the Peace?*, pp. 112–13.
83 R. Davidson, *Whitehall and the Labour Problem in Late Victorian and Edwardian Britain* (London, 1985), pp. 3–33.
84 F. H. Hinsley and C. G. Simkins, *British Intelligence in the Second World War*, vol. 4, *Security and Counter-Intelligence* (London, 1990), p. 4; N. Hiley, 'The Failure of British Counter-espionage against Germany, 1907–1914', *Historical Journal* 28, no. 4 (1985), pp. 835–62.
85 P. Kennedy, *The Rise of the Anglo-German Naval Antagonism* (London, 1980), pp. 441–63.
86 A. Palmer, 'The History of the D-Notice Committee', in C. Andrew and D. Dilks, eds, *The Missing Dimension* (London, 1984), p. 228.
87 PRO MEPO 2/1297; Porter, *The Origins of the Vigilant State*, p. 164.

88 Ibid., p. 166.
89 D. French, 'Spy Fever in Britain 1900–1915', *Historical Journal* 21, no. 2 (1978), pp. 355–70; C. Andrew, *Secret Service*, pp. 34–85; A. J. A. Morris, *The Scaremongers* (London, 1984); I. F. Clarke, 'The Battle of Dorking 1871–1914', *Victorian Studies* 8 (1965), pp. 309–27.
90 B. Porter, *Plots and Paranoia* (London, 1989), p. 126.
91 PRO CAB 16/8; Hinsley and Simkins, *British Intelligence in the Second World War*, p. 30
92 Ibid., p. 4.
93 Porter, *Plots and Paranoia*, p. 127; Lady Kell, 'Secret Well Kept', SVK 1, Imperial War Museum, pp. 122 and 124.
94 PRO HO 45/10254/X36450/77; Kamm, 'The Home Office, Public Order and Civil Liberties 1880–1914', p. 251.
95 Porter, *The Origins of the Vigilant State*, pp. 73–4.
96 Porter, *Plots and Paranoia*, p. 120.
97 Palmer, 'The History of the D-Notice Committee', pp. 227–49.
98 D. Hooper, *Official Secrets* (London, 1987), p. 29.
99 C. Townshend, *Britain's Civil Wars* (London, 1986), p. 52; B. Ash, *The Lost Dictator* (London, 1968), pp. 118–33.
100 C. Townshend, *Making the Peace* (Oxford, 1993), p. 36.

2 The First World War (1914–1918)

1 B. Porter, *The Refugee Question in Mid Victorian Politics* (Cambridge, 1979); B. Porter, *The Origins of the Vigilant State* (London, 1987).
2 C. Andrew, *Secret Service* (London, 1985), pp. 174–202; B. Porter, *Plots and Paranoia* (London, 1989), pp. 120–50; N. Hiley, 'Counter-Espionage and Security in Great Britain During the First World War', *English Historical Review*, 101, no. 3 (July 1986), pp. 635–70.
3 D. Englander, 'Military Intelligence and the Defence of the Realm: The Surveillance of Soldiers and Civilians in Britain During the First World War', *Bulletin of the Society for the Study of Labour History* 52, no. 1 (1987), pp. 24–32; A. W. Brian Simpson, *In the Highest Degree Odious* (Oxford, 1992), pp. 5–7.
4 R. J. Q. Adams, *Arms and the Wizard* (London, 1978), pp. 71–89; R. J. Q. Adams and P. Poirier, *The Conscription Controversy in Great Britain 1900–18* (London, 1987), pp. 160–76; A. Marwick, *The Deluge* (London, 1976); Simpson, *In the Highest Degree Odious*, pp. 15–33.

5 Sir A. Dixon, 'The Emergency Work of the Police Forces in the Second World War' (Home Office, 1963), pp. 5–6; Sir A. Dixon, 'The Home Office and the Police Between the World Wars' (Home Office, 1966). Both these documents are kept at the Bramshill Police College Library, Hampshire.
6 PRO AIR 1/550/16/15/27; AIR 1/551/16/15/29; AIR 1/558/16/15/55, 56, 57.
7 PRO INF 4/9; PRO WO 32/10776; N. Hiley, 'Internal Security in Wartime: The Rise and Fall of PMS 2, 1915–17', *Intelligence and National Security* 1, no. 3 (1986), p. 395.
8 PRO CAB 23/4 W.C.274 (17); M. Swartz, *The Union of Democratic Control in British Politics During the First World War* (Oxford, 1971), p. 190.
9 PRO CAB 24/13 GT 733; C. Nottingham, 'The State and Revolution in Britain, 1916–26' (University of Sheffield Ph.D. thesis, 1985), p. 38.
10 PRO HO 45/22901/446727/1, 2.
11 F. H. Hinsley and C. A. G. Simkins, *British Intelligence in the Second World War*, vol. 4, *Security and Counter-Intelligence* (London, 1990), p. 5.
12 Ibid., p. 6; Andrew, *Secret Service*, pp. 282–3; E. O'Halpin, 'Sir Warren Fisher and the Coalition 1919–1922', *The Historical Journal* 24, no. 4 (1981), pp. 922–4; B. Porter, *Plots and Paranoia*, pp. 55–155.
13 Englander, 'Military Intelligence', p. 24; B. Weinberger, *Keeping the Peace?* (Oxford, 1991), p. 128.
14 PRO AIR 1/550/16/15/27; AIR 1/551/16/15/28; AIR 1/551/16/15/29; AIR 1/558/16/15/55; AIR 1/558/16/15/56; AIR 1/558/16/15/57.
15 PRO HO 144/1484/63.
16 PRO HO 144/1650/15.
17 PRO HO 144/22936/1C.
18 Lord Ironside, *Archangel 1918–1919* (London, 1953), p. 188.
19 PRO WO 32/5553/1a.
20 PRO WO 32/5467.
21 IWM 73/1/4. May 11 1919, April 4 1921, Field Marshal Sir Henry Wilson Diaries.
22 Andrew, *Secret Service*, pp. 174–7.
23 CAB 17/90; J. C. Bird, 'Control of Enemy Alien Civilians in Great Britain 1914–1918' (University of London D.Phil. thesis, 1981), p. 22.
24 Sir A. Dixon, 'The Emergency Work of the Police Forces', pp. 35–8; P. Panayi, *The Enemy in Our Midst* (Oxford, 1991), p. 97.

25 PRO AIR 1/550/16/15/27.
26 PRO AIR 1/551/16/15/29.
27 PRO AIR 1/551/16/15/28.
28 PRO HO 45/10727/74.
29 PRO HO 45/10727/66.
30 Andrew, *Secret Service*; pp. 179–202; N. Hiley, 'Counter-Espionage', pp. 635–70.
31 J. C. Bird, 'Control of Enemy Alien Civilians', pp. 15–17; Panayi, *Enemy in Our Midst*, p. 97.
32 PRO HO 45/10729/45.
33 Ibid., PRO HO 45/10760/47; Panayi, *Enemy in Our Midst*, pp. 223–58; P. Panayi, 'Anti-German Riots in Britain During the First World War', in Panayi, ed., *Racial Violence in Britain* (Leicester, 1993), pp. 65–91.
34 PRO HO 45/10729/45; Simpson, *In the Highest Degree Odious*, pp. 24–5.
35 PRO AIR 1/550/16/15/27.
36 Bird, 'Control of Enemy Alien Civilians', p. 96.
37 Ibid., p. 116; Simpson, *In the Highest Degree Odious*, pp. 15–16, 20–1.
38 PRO HO 45/10729/153.
39 PRO HO 45/10760/192.
40 PRO MEPO 2/1633.
41 Bird, 'Control of Enemy Alien Civilians', p. 147; PRO HO 45/10946/35.
42 C. Holmes, *John Bull's Island* (London, 1989), p. 64.
43 P. Panayi, 'The Hidden Hand: British Myths about German Control of Britain During the First World War', *Immigrants and Minorities* 7 (1988).
44 M. Ceadel, *Pacifism in Great Britain 1914–45* (Oxford, 1980), pp. 1–8; A. J. P. Taylor, *The Trouble Makers* (London, 1957), p. 51n.
45 Swartz, *The Union of Democratic Control*, pp. 118–19; PRO HO 45/10741/88.
46 PRO FO 395/140/25424/168072.
47 PRO HO 45/10834.
48 H. Weinroth, 'Norman Angell and *The Great Illusion*: An Episode in pre-1914 Pacifism', *Historical Journal* 27, no. 3 (1974), pp. 551–74; J. Hinton, *Protests and Visions* (London, 1989), pp. 27–32.
49 PRO HO 45/10834/2.
50 Ibid.
51 PRO HO 45/10834/3.

52 PRO HO 144/1459/1.
53 PRO HO 45/10814/10.
54 PRO HO 45/10741/2.
55 PRO AIR 1/560/16/15/60.
56 PRO HO 45/10741/75; A. Wiltsher, *Most Dangerous Women* (London, 1985), p. 66.
57 PRO HO 45/10801/74.
58 PRO HO 45/10744/367, 378.
59 PRO HO 45/10743/274, 295.
60 PRO HO 45/10742/219.
61 T. Kennedy, *The Hound of Conscience* (Fayetteville, 1981).
62 PRO CAB 23/10 WC 553 WM 1, 3 April 1919.
63 R. J. Q. Adams and P. P. Poirier, *The Conscription Controversy in Great Britain* (London, 1987), pp. 118–241.
64 J. Rae, *Conscience and Politics* (London, 1970), p. 134.
65 Kennedy, *The Hound of Conscience*, pp. 134–61.
66 PRO WO 32/2051–5.
67 Kennedy, *The Hound of Conscience*, pp. 178–96; Rae, *Conscience and Politics*, pp. 201–33; D. Boulton, *Objection Overruled* (London, 1967), pp. 242–66.
68 Rae, *Conscience and Politics*, pp. 162–90.
69 PRO CAB 24/12/677.
70 Rae, *Conscience and Politics*, pp. 207–15; PRO CAB 23/4/257(3).
71 R. Barker, *Conscience, Government and War: Conscientious Objection in Great Britain 1939–1945* (London, 1982), pp. 16–82.
72 K. Jeffery and P. Hennessy, *States of Emergency* (London, 1983), p. 2.
73 G. Askwith, *Industrial Problems and Disputes* (New York, 1974), pp. 414–16.
74 Swartz, *The Union of Democratic Control*, p. 199.
75 C. J. Wrigley, *David Lloyd George and the British Labour Movement* (Hassocks, 1976), p. 165; G. Brown, *Sabotage* (Nottingham, 1977), pp. 165–94.
76 R. J. Q. Adams, *Arms and the Wizard* (London, 1978), pp. 82–9.
77 Adams and Poirier, *The Conscription Controversy*, pp. 136–245.
78 Wrigley, *David Lloyd George*, pp. 122–8.
79 R. K. Middlemas, *The Clydesiders* (London, 1965), pp. 64–5; J. Hinton, *The First Shop-Stewards Movement* (London, 1973); J. Hinton, 'The Clyde Workers Committee and the Dilution Struggle', in A. Briggs and J. Saville, eds, *Essays in Labour History 1886–1923* (London, 1971), pp. 152–85.
80 PRO MUN 5/56/300/108; CAB 24/24 GT 1822.

81 PRO CAB 24/24 GT 1849.
82 PRO CAB 24/26 GT 2073; J. Turner, *British Politics and the Great War* (London, 1992), pp. 227–52, 334–89.
83 PRO MUN 5/56/300/108.

3 John Bull's Other Island (1910–1923)

1 C. Townshend, *Britain's Civil Wars* (London, 1986), pp. 57–61.
2 J. Lee, *Ireland 1912–1985* (Cambridge, 1989), pp. 1–2.
3 G. Dangerfield, *The Damnable Question* (London, 1977), p. 111; A. Jackson, *The Ulster Party* (Oxford, 1989), pp. 322–6.
4 C. Townshend, *Political Violence in Ireland* (Oxford, 1983), p. 335.
5 Dangerfield, *The Damnable Question*, pp. 76–82.
6 A. T. Q. Stewart, *The Ulster Crisis* (London, 1969).
7 Lee, *Ireland 1912–1985*, p. 6.
8 A. T. Q. Stewart, *Sir Edward Carson* (Dublin, 1981), p. 79.
9 PRO CO 904/29/2.
10 Ibid.
11 Dangerfield, *The Damnable Question*, p. 111; PRO CO 904/29/1.
12 PRO CO 904/27. *Belfast Newsletter* 22 September 1913.
13 PRO CO 904/28/2.
14 Ibid.
15 PRO CO 906/18/2.
16 PRO CO 904/27.
17 Ibid.
18 Ibid.
19 PRO CO 904/28/1.
20 PRO CO 904/29/2.
21 General Sir N. Macready, *Annals of an Active Life*, vol. 1 (London, 1924), p. 198.
22 J. D. Fair, *British Interparty Conferences 1867–1921* (Oxford, 1980), pp. 103–19.
23 PRO CO 904/29/2.
24 PRO CO 904/28/2.
25 Add 62461 Viscount Cave Papers.
26 Add 62463 Viscount Cave Papers.
27 E. O'Halpin, 'British Intelligence in Ireland, 1914–21', in C. Andrew and D. Dilks, eds, *The Missing Dimension* (London, 1984), p. 55.
28 Ibid., p. 70.

29 75146/12. Field Marshal Sir John French Papers.
30 PRO CO 904/23/3.
31 O'Halpin, 'British Intelligence in Ireland', p. 59.
32 C. Andrew, *Secret Service* (London, 1985), p. 247; Admiral Sir W. James, *The Eyes of the Navy* (London, 1955), pp. 110–15.
33 PRO CO 904/28/2.
34 O'Halpin, 'British Intelligence in Ireland', pp. 67–9.
35 PRO CO 904/23/2.
36 Townshend, *Britain's Civil Wars*, p. 54.
37 PRO CO 903/19/2.
38 PRO HO 144/1455/313106/1 and 661.
39 PRO HO 144/1455/313106/2.
40 PRO HO 144/1455/313106/1.
41 PRO CO 903/19/2.
42 PRO HO 144/1455/313106/57a.
43 PRO CAB 24/16 GT 1027; CAB 23/3 WC 163/19.
44 PRO HO 144/1496/362269/1.
45 PRO HO 144/1459/316398/2.
46 PRO CO 904/157/1.
47 PRO HO 144/1453/311980/31.
48 PRO HO 144/1453/311980/112.
49 PRO HO 144/1458/316093/5.
50 PRO HO 144/1457/314179/3, 5.
51 PRO HO 144/1454/312169/1a.
52 PRO HO 144/1457/321387/41.
53 PRO HO 144/1458/315300/5.
54 PRO HO 144/1458/315663/30; S. Lawlor, *Britain and Ireland 1914–23* (Dublin, 1983), pp. 11–12.
55 PRO HO 144/1465/321387/1.
56 PRO HO 144/1465/321387/6.
57 PRO HO 144/1465/321387/14.
58 PRO HO 144/1465/321387/41.
59 PRO HO 144/1463/319502/3.
60 E. O'Halpin, *The Decline of the Union* (Dublin, 1987), pp. 157–79.
61 Townshend, *Political Violence in Ireland*, p. 289; C. Townshend, 'Policing Insurgency in Ireland, 1914–1923', in D. M. Anderson and D. Killingray, *Policing and Decolonisation* (Manchester, 1992), p. 30.
62 T. P. Coogan, *The IRA* (London, 1987), pp. 40–3.
63 Ibid., p. 44.
64 PRO CO 904/121.
65 PRO CO 904/150.

66 C. Townshend, *The British Campaign in Ireland, 1919–21* (Oxford, 1975), pp. 129–31; T. P. Coogan, *Michael Collins* (London, 1988), pp. 121–56.
67 Andrew, *Secret Service*, p. 254.
68 J. McColgan, *British Policy and the Irish Administration 1920–22* (London, 1983), p. 132.
69 PRO CO 904/188/2.
70 Townshend, *The British Campaign in Ireland*, p. 75.
71 PRO CO 904/188/22.
72 PRO CO 904/150. C. Townshend, 'One Man You Can Hang If Necessary: The Discreet Charm of Nevil Macready', in J. B. Hattendorf and M. H. Murfett, eds, *The Limitations of Military Power* (London, 1990), pp. 141–59.
73 Townshend, *The British Campaign in Ireland*, p. 141.
74 K. Middlemas, ed., *Thomas Jones: A Whitehall Diary*, vol. 3 (Oxford, 1971), p. xix.
75 Ibid., p. 49.
76 Ibid., p. 77.
77 Ibid., pp. 180–1.
78 P. Canning, *British Policy Towards Ireland 1921–1941* (Oxford, 1985), pp. 50–85.

4 Reds in the Bed (1917–1939)

1 N. Hiley, 'British Internal Security in Wartime: The Rise and Fall of PMS2, 1915–17', *Intelligence and National Security* 1, no. 3 (September 1986), p. 402.
2 Ibid., pp. 395–415.
3 PRO AIR 1/560/16/15/59.
4 PRO CAB 24/16 GT 1049; S. White, 'Soviets in Britain: The Leeds Convention of 1917', *International Review of Social History* 19, no. 3 (1974).
5 PRO AIR 1/560/16/15/59.
6 PRO CAB 24/4 GT 1849.
7 PRO CAB 24/16 GT 1049.
8 K. Morgan, *Consensus and Disunity* (Oxford, 1979).
9 K. Middlemas and T. Jones, eds, *Whitehall Diary*, vol. 1 (London, 1969), p. 99.
10 B. Ash, *The Lost Dictator* (London, 1968).
11 Middlemas and Jones, *Whitehall Diary*, p. 103.
12 B. Porter, *Plots and Paranoia* (London, 1989), pp. 151–74; C. Andrew, *Secret Service* (London, 1985), pp. 224–45.
13 C. Wrigley, *Lloyd George and the Challenge of Labour* (London, 1990), p. 24.

14 Porter, *Plots and Paranoia*; Andrew, *Secret Service.*
15 Sir B. Thomson, *Queer People* (London, 1922), p. 292.
16 L. J. Macfarlane, *The British Communist Party* (London, 1966), p. 302.
17 H. Pelling, *The British Communist Party* (London, 1975), p. 104.
18 J. Morgan, *Conflict and Order* (Oxford, 1987), p. 122.
19 F. H. Hinsley and C. A. G. Simkins, *British Intelligence in the Second World War*, vol. 4, *Security and Counter-Intelligence* (London, 1990), p. 9.
20 PRO T 160/6139/053; E. O'Halpin, 'Financing British Intelligence: The Evidence up to 1945', in K. G. Robertson, ed., *British and American Approaches to Intelligence* (London, 1989), pp. 187–217.
21 K. Jeffery, 'The British Army and Internal Security, 1919–39', *The Historical Journal* 24, no. 2 (1981), pp. 377–97.
22 J. Hope, 'Fascism, the Security Service and the Curious Careers of Maxwell Knight and James McGuirk Hughes', *Lobster* 22, pp. 1–5; J. Hope, 'British Fascism and the State, 1917–27: A Re-examination of the Documentary Evidence', *Labour History Review* 57, no. 3 (1992), p. 74; J. Hope, 'Fascism and the State in Britain: The Case of the British Fascists 1923–31', *Australian Journal of Politics and History* 39, no. 3 (1993), pp. 367–80; J. Hope, 'Surveillance or Collusion? Maxwell Knight, MI5 and the British Fascisti', *Intelligence and National Security* 9, no. 4 (October 1994).
23 PRO HO 144/13864/517164/97.
24 Thomson, *Queer People*, pp. 279–302; Sir W. Childs, *Episodes and Reflections* (London, 1930), pp. 209–25.
25 Andrew, *Secret Service*, pp. 259–97; C. Andrew, 'Codebreakers and Foreign Offices: The French, British and American Experience', in C. Andrew and D. Dilks, eds, *The Missing Dimension: Government and Intelligence Communities in the Twentieth Century* (London, 1984), pp. 42–8.
26 K. Morgan, *Against Fascism and War* (Manchester, 1989), p. 8; K. Morgan, *Harry Pollitt* (Manchester, 1993); N. Fishman, 'The British Communist Party and the Trade Unions 1933–1945: The Dilemmas of Revolutionary Pragmatism' (University of London Ph.D. thesis, 1991).
27 PRO AIR 1/556/16/15/49.
28 PRO AIR 1/554/16/15/44.
29 PRO AIR 1/560/16/15/59.
30 PRO CAB 24/74 GT 6713.

31 PRO CAB 24/79 GT 7218.
32 PRO AIR 1/554/16/15/43; S. R. Ward, 'Intelligence Surveillance of British Ex-servicemen, 1918–20', *The Historical Journal* 16, no. 1 (1973), pp. 179–88; D. Englander and J. Osborne, 'Jack, Tommy and Henry Dubb: The Armed Services and the Working Class in Britain, 1917–21' *The Historical Journal* 21, no. 3 (1978), pp. 593–621.
33 PRO AIR 1/553/16/15/41.
34 PRO CAB 24/96 CP 462.
35 C. Nottingham, 'The State and Revolution in Britain (1916–26)' (University of Sheffield Ph.D. thesis, 1985), pp. 139–69.
36 G. D. Anderson, *Fascists, Communists and the National Government* (London, 1983), pp. 15–27.
37 Morgan, *Conflict and Order*, pp. 98–9.
38 A. Rothstein, *The Soldiers Strike of 1919* (London, 1980), pp. 37–83; C. Wrigley, *Lloyd George and the Challenge of Labour* (London, 1990), pp. 24–52.
39 Morgan, *Conflict and Order*, p. 85.
40 PRO CAB 23/10 WC 577 WM1; CAB 23/11 WC591 WM1; CAB 24/80 GT7329; Sir A. Dixon, 'The Home Office and the Police Between the Two World Wars', (Home Office, 1966), pp. 5–20; Morgan, *Conflict and Order*, p. 83; Wrigley, *Lloyd George and the Challenge of Labour*, pp. 53–79.
41 Reynolds and Judge.
42 B. Weinberger, *Keeping the Peace?* (Oxford, 1991), pp. 163–9.
43 T. A. Critchley, *A History of the Police in England and Wales* (London, 1978), pp. 197–8.
44 PRO HO 144/22556/534204/5.
45 PRO HO 144/22936/257009/9.
46 PRO HO 45/17913/400508.
47 PRO WO 32/5611; Jeffery, 'The British Army and Internal Security', pp. 377–80.
48 PRO WO 32/5467; CAB 23/12 WC 627, WM1; Wrigley, *Lloyd George and the Challenge of Labour*, pp. 217–25.
49 PRO HO 144/1603/390739/5.
50 PRO HO 144/1603/390739/18.
51 W. C. May, *Recollections and Reflections of a Country Policeman* (Ilfracombe, 1979), pp. 69–78.
52 Morgan, *Conflict and Order*, pp. 191–2.
53 PRO HO 144/1747/417250/178.
54 PRO CAB 23/9 WC523 WM1.
55 K. Jeffery and P. Hennessy, *States of Emergency* (London, 1983),

pp. 10–39; PRO CAB 27/82 Appendix; CAB 23/18 Appendix; CAB 27/74 TC 29.

56 R. Desmarais, 'Lloyd George and the Development of the British Government's Strikebreaking Organization', *International Review of Social History* 20 (1975), pp. 1–15.

57 R. Desmarais, 'The Supply and Transport Committee 1919–26' (University of Wisconsin Ph.D. thesis, 1970), pp. 86–107.

58 Jeffery and Hennessy, *States of Emergency*, pp. 6–7.

59 A. Marwick, *The Deluge* (London, 1975); Morgan, *Consensus and Disunity*, p. 56.

60 J. Turner, 'British Politics and the Great War', in J. Turner, ed., *Britain and the First World War* (London, 1988), p. 133.

61 M. Cowling, *The Impact of Labour, 1920–24* (Cambridge, 1971), p. 1.

62 N. Whiteside, 'The British Population at War', in J. Turner, ed., *Britain and the First World War*, pp. 85–98; N. Whiteside, 'Industrial Welfare and Labour Regulation in Britain at the Time of the First World War', *International Review of Social History* 25, no. 3 (1980), pp. 307–31; J. M. Winter, *The Great War and the British People* (London, 1985), pp. 108–15; D. Englander, *Landlord and Tenant* (Oxford, 1983), pp. 205–31.

63 C. Wrigley, *Lloyd George and the Challenge of Labour*, pp. 96–109.

64 Whiteside,'The British Population at War', pp. 92–3.

65 Ibid., p. 91.

66 Morgan, *Consensus and Disunity*, p. 72; Jeffery and Hennessy, *States of Emergency*, pp. 62–3; J. Jenkinson, 'The 1919 Riots', in P. Panayi, ed., *Racial Violence in Britain 1840–1940* (Leicester, 1993), pp. 92–111; J. Jenkinson, 'The Glasgow Race Disturbances of 1919', *Immigrants and Minorities* 4 (1985), pp. 43–67.

67 J. Mahon, *Harry Pollitt* (London, 1976), pp. 79–83.

68 R. Challinor, *The Origins of British Bolshevism* (London, 1977).

69 W. Kendall, *The Revolutionary Movement in Britain* (London, 1969), pp. 244–5.

70 Wrigley, *Lloyd George and the Challenge of Labour*, p. 294.

71 Ibid., p. 82.

72 Andrew, *Secret Service*, pp. 265–70; C. Andrew, 'The British Secret Service and Anglo-Soviet Relations in the 1920s, Part 1', *The Historical Journal* 20, no. 3 (1977), pp. 673–706; Jeffery, 'British Military Intelligence following World War One', in K. Robertson, *British and American Approaches*, pp. 59–63.

73 73/1/4 Diary of Sir Henry Wilson, 18 February, 18 and 24 August 1920. IWM.
74 F/203/1/4 Lloyd George MSS, HLRO; Andrew, *Secret Service*, pp. 267–8; A. J. Williams, *Trading with the Bolsheviks* (Manchester, 1992), pp. 55–95.
75 Andrew, *Secret Service*, pp. 298–308.
76 A. Thorpe, 'Labour and the Frustration of the Extreme Left', in A. Thorpe, ed., *The Failure of Political Extremism in Inter-War Britain* (Exeter, 1988), pp. 11–28.
77 J. Jupp, *The Radical Left in Britain, 1931–41* (London, 1982); K. Morgan, *Against Fascism and War*, pp. 254–76; B. Pimlott, *Labour and the Left in the 1930s* (Cambridge, 1977), pp. 155–61.
78 N. Branson, *History of the Communist Party of Great Britain 1927–41* (London, 1985), pp. 110–29; Morgan, *Against Fascism and War*, p. 19; N. Fishman, 'The British Communist Party and the Trade Unions', pp. 1–208.
79 M. Beloff, 'The Whitehall Factor: The Role of the Higher Civil Service 1919–39', in G. Peele and C. Cook, eds, *The Politics of Reappraisal 1918–39* (London, 1975), pp. 209–31.
80 J. Wheeler Bennett, *Sir John Anderson* (London, 1959).
81 PRO HO 144/20159/102–3.
82 R. Thurlow, *Fascism in Britain* (Oxford, 1987), p. 113.
83 PRO CAB 24/118 CP 2455.
84 E. O'Halpin, 'Sir Warren Fisher and the Coalition 1919–22', *The Historical Journal* 24, no. 4 (1981), p. 924.
85 PRO CAB 24/160 CP 297.
86 Sir W. Childs, *Episodes and Reflections*, p. 223.
87 PRO 30/69/220. Report on Revolutionary Movements No. 253.
88 PRO T 164/78/22.
89 PRO HO 144/20159/107.
90 PRO CAB 23/90B.
91 PRO WO 32/3948/110/Gen/4771; CAB 24/175 CP420; Anderson, *Fascists, Communists and the National Government*, pp. 63–90; Andrew, *Secret Service*, p. 366.
92 SVK 12. Lecture notes on Socialism. Major-General Sir Vernon Kell papers. Imperial War Museum.
93 PRO HO 45/24871/5, 29.
94 PRO HO 45/24871/97; M. Heinemann, 'The People's Front and the Intellectuals', in J. Fryth, ed., *Britain, Fascism and the Popular Front* (London, 1986), p. 171.
95 Hinsley and Simkins, *British Intelligence*, pp. 7–8.
96 Andrew, *Secret Service*, pp. 278–9.

97 C. Andrew and O. Gordievsky, *The KGB* (London, 1990), pp. 79–185.
98 PRO FO 371/11O28/N3625; R. Martin, *Communism and British Trade Unions* (Oxford, 1969).
99 PRO FO 371/8170/N9113.
100 PRO FO 371/9366/N4499.
101 PRO CAB 24/180 CP236 (26).
102 PRO CAB 24/180 CP244 (26).
103 J. Valtin, *Out of the Night* (New York, 1941), p. 326.
104 S. White, *Britain and the Bolshevik Revolution 1920–1924* (London, 1979), p. ix.
105 PRO FO 371/10478/N7838; FO 371/12602/N2289.
106 PRO HO 45/25521; FO 371/16336/N1370; J. Costello and O. Tsarev, *Deadly Illusions* (London, 1993), p. 143.
107 B. Weinberger, ed., 'Communism and the General Strike', *Bulletin of the Society for the Study of Labour History* 48 (Spring 1984), p. 32.
108 K. Middlemas and T. Jones, eds, *Whitehall Diary*, vol. 2 (London, 1969), pp. 48–53.
109 Mahon, *Harry Pollitt*, pp. 116–17.
110 PRO HO 144/13864/31, 39, 138, 156.
111 PRO HO 144/13864/152.
112 PRO HO 144/13864/195.
113 PRO HO 144/13864/90.
114 J. Degras, *Documents of the Third International* (London, 1963); A. Ullman, *Anglo-Soviet Relations* (London, 1974).
115 PRO CAB 24/118 CP 2452.
116 PRO HO 45/24871/57; J. Costello, *Mask of Treachery* (London, 1989).
117 PRO HO 45/14449/7.
118 PRO HO 45/24861.
119 PRO HO 45/24834/18.
120 PRO CAB 24/161 CP 314 (23).
121 PRO CAB 27/205 Minutes of STC 17 July 1923.
122 Jeffery and Hennessy, *States of Emergency*, pp. 76–87.
123 PRO CAB 23/50 42 (25).
124 PRO CAB 27/260 ST (24) 7; CAB 27/261 ST (24) 14; HO 45/12336/11.
125 PRO CAB 24/175 CP 420 (25); CAB 23/50 45 (25) Min 6.
126 W. Hannington, *Unemployed Struggles* (London, 1973), p. 137.
127 PRO HO 45/12431/18.
128 A. Mason, *The General Strike in the North East* (Hull, 1969), pp. 70–1.
129 PRO HO 144/12051/1a.

130 A. McIntyre, *Little Moscows* (London, 1983).
131 B. Weinberger, 'Police Perceptions of Labour in the Inter-war Period: The Case of the Unemployed and the Miners on Strike', in F. Snyder and D. Hay, eds, *Labour, Law and Crime* (London, 1987), pp. 163–75.
132 PRO HO 144/6902/17.
133 PRO WO 32/3455.
134 Morgan, *Conflict and Order*, p. 115; S. Peak, *Troops in Strikes* (London, 1987); A. Babington, *Military Intervention in Britain* (London, 1991), pp. 133–52.
135 Sir A. Dixon, 'The Home Office and the Police', p. 248.
136 Morgan, *Conflict and Order*, p. 123.
137 Ibid., p. 125.
138 PRO HO 144/22556/5; B. Weinberger, *Keeping the Peace?*, p. 167; C. Nottingham, 'Recasting Bourgeois Britain', *International Review of Social History* 31, no. 3 (1986), pp. 31–6.
139 R. Croucher, *We Refuse to Starve in Silence* (London, 1987); P. Kingsford, *The Hunger Marches in Britain* (London, 1982).
140 Weinberger, 'Police perceptions of Labour', p. 151.
141 J. Stevenson, 'The Politics of Violence' in Peele and Cook, eds, *The Politics of Reappraisal*, pp. 147–8; A. J. P. Taylor, *English History, 1914–1945* (Oxford, 1965), p. 149.
142 PRO CAB 24/139 CP 4207.
143 PRO CAB 24/128 Report 125 Revolutionary Organisations in the United Kingdom, 15 September 1921.
144 PRO CAB 24/159 CP 194; R. Flanagan, *Parish Fed Bastards* (London, 1991), pp. 167–78.
145 PRO HO 45/17928; Weinberger, 'Police Perceptions of Labour', p. 156.
146 H. J. Harmer, 'The National Unemployed Workers Movement in Britain: Failure and Success' (London School of Economics Ph.D. thesis, 1987), p. 257; PRO MEPO 2/3064, meeting of the London District Council NUWM, 24 October 1932.
147 R. Hayburn, 'The Police and the Hunger Marchers', *International Review of Social History* 17 (1972).
148 Hannington, *Unemployed Struggles*, p. 141.
149 Mahon, *Harry Pollitt*, pp. 122–3.
150 PRO HO 144/20149/19.
151 PRO HO 144/20149/105–7.
152 PRO HO 144/20149/68–9.
153 Stevenson, 'The Politics of Violence', p. 149; PRO MEPO 3/548.
154 PRO MEPO 2/3071. Minute of National Hunger March to London, October and December 1934.

155 PRO MEPO 2/3064. Précis of further information *re* Hunger Marches.
156 Stevenson, 'The Politics of Violence', p. 160; PRO MEPO 3/546.
157 Morgan, *Conflict and Order*, p. 160.
158 Stevenson, 'The Politics of Violence', p. 162.
159 PRO MEPO 2/3064. Ministry of Health. Memorandum to General Inspectors, Unemployed March 1932.
160 PRO MEPO 2/5507. Cinematograph Pictures of the Unemployed Marches 1936; MEPO 2/3069. Taking of Pictures by Film Companies, 1934.
161 PRO MEPO 2/3097. Jarrow March. Letter to the Chief Constable, Hendon.
162 Harmer, 'The NUWM in Britain', p. 349.
163 Croucher, *We Refuse to Starve*, pp. 141–4.
164 Morgan, *Conflict and Order*, p. 264.
165 Kingsford, *The Hunger Marches*, pp. 192–3.
166 H. Harmer, 'The Failure of the Communists, The NUWM 1921–1939: A Disappointing Success', in A Thorpe, ed., *The Failure of Political Extremism in Inter-War Britain* (Exeter, 1989), pp. 21–37.
167 J. Halstead, R. Harrison and J. Stevenson, 'The Reminiscences of Sid Elias', *Bulletin of the Society for the Study of Labour History* 38 (Spring 1979), p. 41.
168 Harmer, 'The NUWM in Britain', pp. 156–89.
169 PRO HO 45/25519 Home Office Minute 25–1–38.
170 Croucher, *We Refuse to Starve*, pp. 202–10.
171 J. Fyrth, *The Signal was Spain* (London, 1986), pp. 19–42.
172 PRO HO 45/25463/36–53.
173 R. Kidd, *British Liberty in Danger* (London, 1940), pp. 141–7.
174 PRO HO 45/25462/7–8.
175 PRO HO 45/25462/28.
176 PRO HO 45/25463/283.

5 The March of the Blackshirts (1923–1939)

1 R. Thurlow, 'The Mosley Papers and the Secret History of British Fascism, 1939–40', in K. Lunn and A. Kushner, eds, *Traditions of Intolerance* (Manchester, 1989), pp. 173–95.
2 PRO HO 144/20141/294–322; HO 144/20142/108–22, 215–35; HO 144/20144/123–32, 262–70; HO 144/21060/53–6; HO 144/21062/44–7; HO 45/25385/38–49.
3 A. Cave Brown, *The Secret Servant* (London, 1988), pp. 678–83.

4 R. Thurlow, *Fascism in Britain: A History 1918–85* (Oxford, 1987), pp. 46–61; K. Lunn, 'The Ideology and Impact of the British Fascists in the 1920s', in Lunn and Kushner, *Traditions of Intolerance*, pp. 140–54.
5 PRO FO 371/11384/C9108. I would like to thank John Hope for this reference and for giving me a copy of A981/1 from Australian archives.
6 PRO HO 144/19069/21–3.
7 PRO 30/69/221; C. Nottingham, 'The State and Revolution in Britain, 1906–26' (University of Sheffield Ph.D. thesis, 1985), pp. 317–18.
8 G. Webber, *The Ideology of the British Right* (London, 1987).
9 B. Farr, 'The Development and Impact of Right Wing Politics in Great Britain, 1903–32' (University of Illinois Ph.D. thesis, 1976), pp. 53–108; Webber, *Ideology of the British Right.*
10 PRO HO 144/19069/85; HO 45/25386/37–40.
11 PRO FO 371/11384/C9880.
12 A. Masters, *The Man who was M* (Oxford, 1984), pp. 55–75.
13 W. J. West, *Truth Betrayed* (London, 1987), pp. 216–17; PRO 283/43/33; J. Hope, 'Fascism, the Security Service and the Curious Careers of Maxwell Knight and James McGuirk Hughes', *Lobster* 22 (1991), pp. 1–5; J. Hope, 'British Fascism and the State 1917–27: A Re-examination of the Documentary Evidence', *Labour History Review* 57, no. 3 (1992), pp. 72–83.
14 PRO HO 144/22454/51–2.
15 PRO HO 144/22454/52.
16 PRO HO 45/24967/105.
17 PRO HO 283/28/11.
18 PRO HO 283/45/62–3.
19 PRO HO 283/45/37–8.
20 PRO HO 144/21062/408–10.
21 PRO HO 45/25385/17–20.
22 N. Mosley, *Rules of the Game* (London, 1982); N. Mosley, *Beyond the Pale* (London, 1983).
23 R. Skidelsky, *Oswald Mosley* (London, 1975), pp. 93–298.
24 B. Coleman, 'The Conservative Party and the Frustration of the Extreme Right', in A. Thorpe, ed., *The Failure of Political Extremism in Inter-War Britain* (Exeter, 1989), pp. 49–66.
25 G. Webber, 'The British Isles', in D. Muhlberger, ed., *The Social Basis of European Fascist Movements* (London, 1987), p. 144.
26 R. Thurlow, 'The Failure of British Fascism, 1932–40', in Thorpe, ed., *The Failure of Political Extremism*, pp. 67–84.

27 T. Jones, *Whitehall Diary*, ed. K. Middlemas (London, 1969) vol. 2, p. 195.
28 290 HC Debs 5s, 11 June 1934, 1935–7, 1952–3.
29 317 HC Debs 5s, 5 November 1936, 294–7.
30 309 HC Debs 5s, 27 February 1936, 1932.
31 PRO HO 144/21062/10–45.
32 PRO HO 144/20140/7–8.
33 PRO HO 144/20141/51.
34 PRO HO 144/20710/3; MEPO 2/5507; West, *Truth Betrayed*, p. 91.
35 G. Anderson, *Fascists, Communists and the National Government* (Columbia, 1983); D. S. Lewis, *Illusions of Grandeur* (Manchester, 1987), pp. 145–80; J. Morgan, *Conflict and Order* (Oxford, 1987), pp. 229–75.
36 Lewis, *Illusions of Grandeur*, pp. 149, 159; R. Kidd, *British Liberties in Danger* (London, 1940), p. 258.
37 PRO HO 45/24996/13.
38 E. O'Halpin, 'Financing British Intelligence: The Evidence up to 1945', in K. G. Robertson, ed., *British and American Approaches to Intelligence* (London, 1987), pp. 187–217.
39 PRO HO 144/20158/304–9.
40 PRO HO 144/21086/17.
41 P. Cohen, 'The Police, the Home Office and Surveillance of the British Union of Fascists', *Intelligence and National Security* 1, no. 3 (September 1986), pp. 416–39; R. Thurlow, 'British Fascism and State Surveillance, 1934–45' *Intelligence and National Security* 3, no. 1 (January 1988), pp. 77–99; PRO HO 45/25462/131–2.
42 A. Boyle, *Trenchard* (London, 1962), pp. 665–8; Sir A. Dixon, 'The Home Office and the Police Between the Two World Wars' (Home Office, 1966), pp. 206–7; Morgan, *Conflict and Order*, p. 276.
43 Boyle, *Trenchard*, pp. 665–8.
44 PRO HO 144/20158/272; HO 144/20143/107.
45 MFC 76/1/314/25, Trenchard Papers, Trenchard to Gilmour, 28.9.34.; PRO HO 144/20158/186–7, 350–7.
46 PRO HO 144/20158/162–3.
47 PRO HO 144/20158/186–7.
48 PRO HO 144/20159/155–62.
49 B. Foott, *Dismissal of a Premier: The Philip Game Papers* (Sydney, 1968); A. Moore, 'Sir Philip Game's Other Life: The Making of the 1936 Public Order Act in Britain', *Australian Journal of Politics and History* 36, no. 1 (1990), pp. 62–72.

50 PRO HO 144/21087/367–70.
51 PRO HO 144/21087/208–10, 215–19, 225–31.
52 PRO MEPO 2/3109; MEPO 2/3127. BUF meetings of A. R. Thomson and Mick Clarke, Victoria Park, Bethnal Green, 1937; S. M. Cullen, 'Political Violence: The Case of the British Union of Fascists', *Journal of Contemporary History* 28, no. 2 (April 1993), pp. 245–67.
53 PRO MEPO 2/3127. Memo Superintendents' Conference 1.8.39.
54 PRO HO 144/21381/186.
55 PRO MEPO 2/3043. *Aide-mémoire* on Jew baiting 22 July, 1936 and Commissioner's Memorandum 29.6.37.
56 PRO MEPO 2/3043. Special Branch Report, December 1938.
57 PRO HO 144/20141/306; HO 144/20142/114–15, 216.
58 PRO HO 144/20142/211–12.
59 G. Webber, 'Patterns of Membership and Support for the British Union of Fascists', *Journal of Contemporary History* 19 (1984), pp. 575–606; S. Cullen, 'The British Union of Fascists, 1932–40: Ideology, Membership, Meetings' (University of Oxford M.Litt. thesis, 1987), pp. 43–62.
60 PRO HO 144/20142/225.
61 PRO HO 144/20142/222.
62 PRO HO 144/20162/404.
63 PRO HO 144/20710/38–42.
64 B. Porter, *The Refugee Question in Mid-Victorian Politics* (Cambridge, 1979), pp. 175–219; C. Holmes, *Anti-Semitism and British Society, 1876–1939* (London, 1979), pp. 175–219; C. Holmes, *John Bull's Island* (London, 1988).
65 PRO HO 144/21381/186; J. A. Cross, *Sir Samuel Hoare* (London, 1977), pp. 284–5.
66 PR0 HO 45/24967/52.
67 PRO HO 45/24967/62.
68 PRO HO 144/21381/188–9.
69 PRO HO 45/25398/278–9.
70 Thurlow, 'British Fascism', p. 83; PRO HO 144/21379/36–7.
71 PRO MEPO 2/3112, Home Office Minute, 25 June 1937; HO 45/25462.
72 PRO HO 144/20147/314–17; HO 45/25463/7–46.
73 PRO HO 144/21061/93; R. Kidd, *British Liberty in Danger* (London, 1940), pp. 69–70.
74 PRO HO 144/21061/193.
75 Morgan, *Conflict and Order*, pp. 265–6; Lewis, *Illusions of*

Grandeur, pp. 163–5; W. C. May, *Recollections and Reflections of a County Policeman* (Ilfracombe, 1979), pp. 163–74; PRO MEPO 3/549.

76 PRO HO 144/20140/58.
77 PRO HO 144/20158/350.
78 PRO MEPO 2/3043 and 2/3127; Kidd, *British Liberty in Danger*, pp. 24–9.
79 PRO HO 144/20159/171–8.
80 PRO HO 144/21060/231–7.
81 Ibid.
82 Anderson, *Fascists, Communists and the National Government*, p. 186; Kidd, *British Liberty in Danger*, p. 141.
83 PRO HO 144/21086/10.
84 PRO HO 144/21086/16.
85 Anderson, *Fascists, Communists and the National Government*, p. 177; Lewis, *Illusions of Grandeur*, pp. 145–80.
86 Lewis, *Illusions of Grandeur*, p. 160; Kidd, *British Liberty in Danger*, p. 75; PRO HO 144/20729/8, 10.
87 Morgan, *Conflict and Order*, pp. 229–75; R. Croucher, *We Refuse to Starve in Silence* (London, 1987).
88 Thurlow, *Fascism in Britain*, p. 115; C. Cook and J. Stevenson, *The Slump* (London, 1979).
89 PRO HO 144/21086/245.
90 PRO HO 144/21087/201.
91 PRO HO 144/21087/268, 350.
92 PRO HO 45/25386/54–9.
93 J. D. Blake, 'Civil Disorder in Britain, 1910–39: The Roles of Civil Government and Military Authority' (University of Sussex Ph.D. thesis, 1978), p. 228.
94 PRO HO 144/20140/112; HO 144/20145/222–5.
95 PRO HO 144/21377/306.
96 PRO HO 45/25385/48; HO 144/20140/251–2.
97 PRO HO 144/20144/137.
98 PRO HO 283/45, Aubrey Lees to Norman Birkett, 26 August 1940.
99 Hope, 'Fascism, the Security Service and the Curious Cases of Maxwell Knight and James McGuirk Hughes', p. 4.; PRO HO 283/54/23–4, 31; HO 45/25463/290; T. Bunyan, *The Political Police in Britain* (London, 1976), pp. 18–20.
100 West, *Truth Betrayed*, pp. 216–17; PRO HO 283/40/22.
101 PRO HO 144/20144/135–9, 155–61.
102 N. Mosley, *Beyond the Pale*, pp. 174–5.
103 J. Christian, ed., *Mosley's Blackshirts* (London, 1986), p. 38.

104 Thurlow, *Fascism in Britain,* p. 149; PRO HO 283/13/107–10.
105 J. Drennan, *BUF, Mosley and British Fascism* (London, 1934).
106 PRO HO 144/21381; HO 144/22454. C6/10/29, C6/9/2/1, Board of Deputies of British Jews; Thurlow, *Fascism in Britain,* pp. 78–84; R. Pilkington,'Captain A. H. M. Ramsay: Patriot or Traitor?' (Polytechnic of Central London MA thesis, with distinction, 1988).
107 PRO HO 144/21381/236–7.
108 PRO HO 144/21379/237; HO 144/22454/136.
109 C6/10/29. Letter N. Laski to Inspector Keeble, BDBJ.
110 PRO HO 144/22454/51.
111 PRO HO 144/21381/279.
112 PRO HO 144/20141/305.
113 PRO HO 144/20144/126.
114 P. G. Taylor to R. Saunders, 11 May 1939, Saunders Papers, University of Sheffield.
115 PRO HO 144/20141/300–6.
116 J. Parker, *King of Fools* (London, 1988).
117 PRO HO 144/20144/127; Cohen, 'The Police, the Home Office and Surveillance of the British Union of Fascists', p. 430.
118 PRO HO 144/20160/53.
119 O. Mosley, *My Answer* (London, 1946), p. 4; N. Mosley, *Beyond the Pale,* pp. 30–4; D. Irving, *Focal Point* (30 October 1981); Thurlow, *Fascism in Britain,* pp. 136–9.
120 PRO HO 283/10/9.
121 PRO HO 144/20141/14–18.
122 PRO HO 144/20142/221.
123 PRO HO 144/21060/55.
124 J. and P. Barnes, 'Oswald Mosley as Entrepreneur', *History Today* 40, no. 3 (March 1990), pp. 11–16.
125 Thurlow, 'The Mosley Papers', in Lunn and Kushner, eds, *Traditions of Intolerance,* pp. 173–95.

6 The Second World War (1939–1945)

1 F. Hinsley and C. Simkins, *British Intelligence in the Second World War,* vol. 4, *Security and Counter-Intelligence* (London, 1990).
2 J. Miller, *One Girl's War* (Dublin, 1987); C. Ponting, *Secrecy in Britain* (Oxford, 1990), pp. 58–9.

3 *Intelligence Digest* 242 (January 1959).
4 Ibid. 270 (May 1961).
5 Ibid. 271 (June 1961).
6 D. Reynolds, 'Churchill and the British "Decision" to Fight On in 1940: Right Policy, Wrong Reasons', in R. Langhome, ed., *Diplomacy and Intelligence During the Second World War: Essays in Honour of F. H. Hinsley* (Cambridge, 1985), pp. 147–66; J. Costello, *Ten Days that Saved the West* (London, 1991), pp. 308–13; J. Charmley, *Churchill: The End of Glory* (London, 1993), pp. 371–500.
7 H. M. Hyde, *George Blake Superspy* (London, 1967), p. 60.
8 W. R. Rock, *British Appeasement in the 1930s* (London, 1977), pp. 41–53; Royal Institution of International Affairs, *Political and Strategic Interests of the United Kingdom* (London, 1939), pp. 3–99; M. Cowling, *The Impact of Hitler* (Cambridge, 1975), pp. 97–208; W. Mommsen and L. Kettenecker, eds, *The Fascist Challenge and the Policy of Appeasement* (London, 1983), pp. 79–206.
9 Cowling, *Impact of Hitler*, p. 368.
10 G. Roberts, *The Unholy Alliance* (London, 1989), pp. 5–6, 267–8.
11 Sir A. Dixon, 'The Emergency Work of the Police Forces in the Second World War' (Home Office, 1963), p. 33.
12 PRO CAB 52/1; PRO 52/3, Wel 99, Annex 1–3; N. Stammers, *Civil Liberties in Britain During the Second World War* (London, 1983), pp. 1–8.
13 PRO CAB 52/3, Wel 99, p. 3.
14 Stammers, *Civil Liberties in Britain*, pp. 18–19.
15 R. Kidd, *British Liberty in Danger* (London, 1940), p. 43.
16 Sir John Wheeler Bennett, *John Anderson, Viscount Waverley* (London, 1959).
17 PRO CAB 75/3 Memo WL (39) 27; CAB 75/3 HPC (39) 17th meeting; Stammers, *Civil Liberties in Britain*, pp. 19–21; Dixon, 'The Emergency Work of the Police Forces', pp. 76–7.
18 R. Thurlow, *Fascism in Britain: A History 1918–85* (Oxford, 1987), pp. 163–87.
19 N. Mosley, *Beyond the Pale* (London, 1983), pp. 159–60.
20 K. Morgan, *Against Fascism and War* (Manchester, 1989).
21 Hinsley and Simkins, *British Intelligence*, pp. 29–32; L. Sponza, 'The anti-Italian Riots, June 1940', in P. Panayi, ed., *Racial Violence in Britain 1840–1940* (Leicester, 1993), pp. 130–48.
22 Ibid., p. 39.

23 PRO CAB 67/6 WP (40) 131, 17 May 1940; CAB 81/97 JIC (40) 95, 1 June 1940.
24 F. W. Winterbotham, *The Nazi Connection* (London, 1978), p. 5.; Charmley, *Churchill.*
25 A. Cave Brown, *The Secret Servant* (London, 1988), pp. 208–23.
26 R. McCleod and D. Kelly, eds, *The Ironside Diaries 1937–40* (London, 1962), p. 93.
27 Fuller Diaries, 27 September 1939, Liddell Hart Centre for Military Archives, Kings College, London.
28 J. Parker, *King of Fools* (London, 1988), p. 180; C. Higham, *Wallis* (London, 1988), pp. 239–40; M. Gilbert, *Winston S. Churchill,* vol. 6 (London, 1983), pp. 698–709; *Documents on German Foreign Policy 1918–45,* series D, vol. 8, p. 785; P. Ziegler, *King Edward VIII* (London, 1990), pp. 435–6; Cave Brown, *The Secret Servant,* pp. 177–80.
29 PRO HO 144/20141/305.
30 File 39, 59 and 154, *Mass Observation File Reports 1940*; I. McClaine, *Ministry of Morale* (London, 1979), pp. 34–61.
31 PRO HO 283/45/83; HO 45/25728.
32 PRO HO 45/25724.
33 A. Masters, *The Man who was M* (Oxford, 1984), pp. 33–4.
34 PRO CAB 66/35 WP (43) 109, 13 March 1943; J. Hinton, ed., 'Killing the People's Convention', *Bulletin of the Society for the Study of Labour History* 39 (Autumn 1979), p. 27 n. 3.
35 PRO CAB 66/7 WP (40) 153, 10 May 1940. Appendix to Annexe 2.
36 PRO HO 45/25549/5.
37 PRO HO 45/24895/3–4, 27, 35; HO 45/25754 Home Office minute September 1939.
38 PRO HO 144/22454/86–9, Domvile Diary 56, 19 September, 18 October, 12 November 1939. Thurlow, *Fascism in Britain,* pp. 178–87; R. Thurlow, 'The Mosley Papers and the Secret History of British Fascism 1939–40', in A. Kushner and K. Lunn, eds, *Traditions of Intolerance* (Manchester, 1989), pp. 173–95.
39 PRO HO 45/25728 Special Branch Report 8 June 1940; PRO HO 144/21993/330; A. W. Brian Simpson, *In the Highest Degree Odious* (Oxford, 1992), pp. 146–71.
40 PRO 283/28/82.
41 PRO CAB 98/18 Committee on Communist Activity, first meeting 20 January 1941.
42 Costello, *Ten Days,* pp. 105–63; R. Thurlow, 'British Fascism

and State Surveillance 1934–45', *Intelligence and National Security* 3, no. 1 (January 1988), p. 90.

43 PRO HO 45/25521.

44 PRO CAB 66/35 WP (43) 109; J. Haslam, 'The British Communist Party, the Comintern, and the Outbreak of War, 1939: "A Nasty Taste in the Mouth" ', *Diplomacy and Statecraft* 3, no. 1 (1992), pp. 147–54; F. King and G. Matthews, eds, *About Turn: The Communist Party and the Outbreak of the Second World War* (London, 1990); K. Mcdermott, 'Rethinking the Comintern: Soviet Historiography, 1987–1991', *Labour History Review* 57, no. 3 (1992), pp. 46–8; K. Morgan, *Harry Pollitt* (Manchester, 1993), pp. 89–118.

45 PRO HO 45/25549/9; K. Morgan, *Against Fascism and War*, pp. 134–45.

46 Morgan, *Against Fascism*; J. Attfield and S. Williams, eds, *1939, The Communist Party and the War* (London, 1984).

47 PRO HO 45/25549/44–52; CAB 66/40 WP (43) 359.

48 PRO INF 1/910 Roger Hollis to MOI 25 October 1940.

49 PRO INF 1/913 Morton to Churchill, 14 November 1941; PREM 4/64/5 Morton to Churchill, 27 April 1942.

50 CAB 66/19 WP (41) 229.

51 PRO HO 45/25549/58–113; D. Childs, 'The Communist Party and the War 1939–41: Old Slogans Revived', *Journal of Contemporary History* 12, no. 2 (April 1977), pp. 237–54.

52 PRO INF 1/265 'The Anti-Lie Bureau'.

53 W. J. West, *Truth Betrayed* (London, 1987), p. 201.

54 PRO HO 45/25792 John Lingshaw to Special Branch 16 June 1945.

55 PRO HO 45/25628 Intelligence Unit Print out of NBBS broadcast, 4 September 1940; West, *Truth Betrayed*, p. 205.

56 PRO INF 1/910; HO 144/21540/126; Hinsley and Simkins, *British Intelligence*, p. 47.

57 PRO HO 144/21540/180–2.

58 PRO INF 1/849 and INF 1/910. Minutes of the Committee on Communist Activities, 1 October 1940 and 5 February 1941.

59 PRO INF 1/849 Lord Swinton to MOI 3 September 1940.

60 K. Jefferies, *The Churchill Coalition and Wartime Politics 1940–45* (Manchester, 1991), pp. 9–34

61 J. Christian, ed., *Mosley's Blackshirts* (London, 1984), p. 66.

62 PRO CAB 66/7 WP (40) 153, 10 May 1940; CAB 81/87 JIC (40) 43 26th meeting, 1 May 1940.

63 Hinsley and Simkins, *British Intelligence*, p. 48.

64 PRO CAB 67/6 WP (40) 131, 17 May 1940; FO 371/25189 W 7984G
65 Thurlow, 'British Fascism', p. 90.
66 Thurlow, 'British Fascism', pp. 194–5; Miller, *One Girl's War*, pp. 21–37; Costello, *Ten Days*, pp. 100–63; Brian Simpson, *In the Highest Degree Odious*, pp. 146–54, 431–3; R. Bearse and A. Reed, *Conspirator: The Untold Story of Churchill, Roosevelt and Tyler Kent, Spy* (London, 1991).
67 Masters, *The Man Who Was M*, pp. 88–9; Bearse and Reed, *Conspirator*, p. 147.
68 PRO HO 45/25748, Minute on Maule Ramsay.
69 Higham, *Wallis*, p. 239.
70 PRO HO 144/22454/116–17a.
71 McCleod and Kelly, *The Ironside Diaries*, p. 221; W. Schellenberg, *Memoirs* (London, 1956), p. 118.
72 *Documents on German Foreign Policy*, series D, vol. 8, p. 785.
73 PRO CAB 65/13 WM 133 (40) 22 May 1940.
74 PRO CAB 65/7 WM 133 (40).
75 R. Croucher, *Engineers at War* (London, 1983), pp. 87–8.
76 PRO HO 45/24891/49.
77 N. Longmate, *If Britain had Fallen* (London, 1975), p. 116.
78 Hinsley and Simkins, *British Intelligence*, pp. 65–78; PRO FO 371/32583/W14560; FO 371/29523/N5572.
79 A. Boyle, *Trenchard* (London, 1962), pp. 717–19.
80 McCleod and Kelly, *The Ironside Diaries*, p. 384.
81 C. Andrew, *The Secret Service* (London, 1985).
82 PRO HO 45/25758 Major-General Liardet to Chief Constable of Kent 2 June 1940.
83 Hinsley and Simkins, *British Intelligence*, p. 55.
84 *Comrade* 1 March 1986.
85 PRO HO 144/21540/180–2
86 PRO HO 45/25123; HO 45/25475/116; Croucher, *Engineers at War*, pp. 40–1.
87 PRO HO 144/21540/206; HO 199/419; HO 199/437; N. Bowes, 'The People's Convention', (University of Warwick M.A. thesis, 1976), pp. 67–8.
88 PRO CAB 65/8 WM (40) 193–4, 4 July 1940; CAB 67/7 WP (40) 171, 3 July 1940.
89 Hinsley and Simkins, *British Intelligence*, pp. 56–8; PRO HO 45/25552/172.
90 S. R. Broomfield, 'South Wales During the Second World War: The Coal Industry and its Community' (University of Wales (Swansea) Ph.D. thesis, 1979). Hinsley and Simkins, *British Intelligence*, p. 320.

91 PRO HO 144/21540/2–9.
92 PRO HO 144/21540/212–20.
93 PRO HO 144/21540/210–11.
94 PRO HO 144/21540/199–202.
95 PRO HO 144/21540/231–3.
96 PRO CAB 98/18. First meeting on Communist activities, 28 January 1941; J. Hinton, ed., 'Killing the People's Convention', *Bulletin of the Society for the Study of Labour History* 39 (Autumn 1979), pp. 27–32; D. Hyde, *I Believed* (London, 1950), pp. 90–113.
97 PRO HO 144/21540/266.
98 *Times Law Report*, 14 November 1941, *Liversidge* v. *Anderson*, *Greene* v. *Secretary of State*; C. K. Allen, 'Regulation 18b and Reasonable Cause', *Law Quarterly Review* 58 (1942), pp. 232–42; Brian Simpson, *In the Highest Degree Odious*, pp. 333–80.
99 Thurlow, *Fascism in Britain*, pp. 188–232; Bellamy, 'We Marched with Mosley', pp. 932–1052.
100 PRO HO 45/25768 Review of orders made before the revision of DR 18b.
101 PRO HO 45/24895/9–12; HO 45/25115/1–3.
102 Hinsley and Simkins, *British Intelligence*, pp. 319–20.
103 Trevelyan Scholarship Project, 'The British Union of Fascists in Yorkshire', (1960), p. 19.
104 J. Charnley, *Blackshirts and Roses* (London, 1990).
105 PRO CAB 66/20 WP (41) 279.
106 PRO CAB 65/40 WM (43) 156 minute 4.
107 PRO HO 45/25729; HO 45/25700 note by W. H. Lines of meeting with Ramsay, Domvile et al., 4 November 1942; HO 45/25753 note on forced feeding of H. U. Bowman.
108 West, *Truth Betrayed*, p. 175.
109 PRO HO 283/6/7.
110 PRO HO 45/24891/253; F. Hinsley and Simkins, *British Intelligence*, pp. 341–2; Brian Simpson, *In the Highest Degree Odious*, pp. 239–44.
111 A. Raven Thomson, 'Ham Common', *Union* (19 June 1948); J. L. Battersby, *The Bishop Said Amen* (Poynton, 1947), p. 29; Bellamy, 'We marched with Mosley', pp. 932–1052.
112 Charlie Watts, 'It has happened here', *Comrade* 2 (June 1986), p. 45.
113 PRO HO 45/24967/105.
114 PRO HO 45/25754 Minutes of the Home Defence (Security) Executive October 15 and 31, and 6 November 1940.
115 PRO HO 45/25754 Minute from A. S. Hutchinson Home Office n.d.

116 PRO HO 283/22 Memorandum by Norman Birkett, 5 March 1941; CAB 65/10 WM (40) 283, 21 November 1940; Stammers, *Civil Liberties,* p. 65.
117 Masters, *The Man Who Was M,* pp. 135–67.
118 PRO HO 45/25698 Minute from Herbert Morrison, 6 January 1942.
119 PRO HO 283/28/5 Intelligence Officer, Peveril Camp to Home Office, 20 January 1943.
120 PRO 283/16/28.
121 Brian Simpson, *In the Highest Degree Odious,* pp. 200–29.
122 P. M. H. Bell, *John Bull and the Bear* (London, 1990), pp. 25–105; PRO FO 371/24856/N6005.
123 Hinsley and Simkins, *British Intelligence,* pp. 82–3, 283; Morgan, *Against Fascism,* p. 317; J. Hinton, 'Coventry Communism: A Study of Factory Politics in the Second World War', *History Workshop* 10 (Autumn 1980), pp. 90–118.
124 PRO FO 371/29523/N5832. Minutes HD(S)E 49 meeting 1 October 1941; P. Shipley, *Hostile Action* (London, 1989), pp. 91–4, 178–88; N. Fishman, 'The British Communist Party and the Trade Unions 1933–45: The Dilemmas of Revolutionary Pragmatism' (Birkbeck College, University of London Ph.D. thesis, 1991), pp. 209–45.
125 PRO CAB 66/35 WP (43) 109, 13 March; 148, 14 April 1943; CAB 65/34 WM (43) 60, 28 April 1943; Hinsley and Simkins, *British Intelligence,* p. 284.
126 Croucher, *Engineers at War,* pp. 363–85; G. Brown, *Sabotage* (Nottingham, 1976), pp. 271–93; PRO FO 371/29523/N5832, N7216, SE minutes 50th (1 Oct 1941) and 55th (16 December 1941) meetings; M. Upham, 'The History of British Trotskyism to 1949' (University of Hull Ph.D. thesis, 1980), pp. 527–33; PRO CAB 66/49 WP (44) 202.
127 Hinton, 'Coventry Communism', pp. 90–118.
128 McClaine, *Ministry of Morale,* pp. 186–216; PRO INF 1/676 Bragg to Parker 10 October 1941; Croucher, *Engineers at War,* pp. 308–11.
129 PRO INF 1/292 MOI Home Office Intelligence Report 48, 27 August to 3 September 1941.
130 PRO INF 1/292 MOI Home Office Intelligence Report 56, 20–7 October 1941; 77, March 1942; Morgan, *Harry Pollitt,* p. 131.
131 Box 41/4 Harold Nicolson to NCCL, 23 December 1943, National Council of Civil Liberties archive, University of Hull.
132 PRO HO 45/24892/252, 257.

133 PRO HO 45/24893/11.
134 PRO INF 1/292 MOI Home Office Intelligence report 165, 2 December 1943.
135 PRO INF 1/292 MOI Home Office Intelligence report 166, 9 December 1943.
136 R. Cecil, 'The Cambridge Comintern', in C. Andrew and D. Dilks, eds, *The Missing Dimension* (London, 1984), p. 197.
137 J. C. Masterman, *The Double Cross System* (London, 1973); Hinsley and Simkins, *British Intelligence*, p. 138; Andrew, *Security Service*, p. 382.
138 B. Penrose and S. Freeman, *Conspiracy of Silence* (London, 1987), pp. 293–308.
139 P. Knightley, *Philby* (London, 1988); R. Cecil, *A Divided Life* (London, 1988); P. Knightley, *The Second Oldest Profession* (London, 1986), pp. 271–96; PRO FO 371/29523/N5832.
140 A. Glees, *The Secrets of the Service* (London, 1987); A. Glees, *Exile Politics During the Second World War* (London, 1983).
141 Hyde, *George Blake Superspy*, pp. 146–8.
142 Hinsley and Simkins, *British Intelligence*, p. 286; Knightley, *The Second Oldest Profession*, pp. 179–80, 206–7; D. C. Watt, 'Francis Herbert King: A Soviet Source in the Foreign Office', *Intelligence and National Security* 3, no. 4 (October 1988), pp. 62–83.
143 A. Sinclair, *The Red and the Blue* (London, 1986), pp. 90–1.

7 The Cold War (1946–1989)

1 C. Cruickshank, *The German Occupation of the Channel Islands* (London, 1975).
2 R. Thurlow, 'The State and the Radical Right in Italy, France and Britain – A Historical Perspective', Conference on the Radical Right in Western Europe, University of Minnesota (November 1991), p. 35.
3 PRO HO 144/23276/2; HO 45/25792.
4 PRO HO 144/22237/I. W. 701655/37. R. P. S. 2510 Appendix B.
5 PRO HO 144/22829/19.
6 PRO HO 144/22835/587.
7 PRO HO 45/22399/6.
8 PRO HO 45/22399/22.
9 PRO HO 45/22424/3.
10 PRO HO 45/22399/22.

11 PRO HO 45/22399/5.
12 PRO HO 144/22237/I. W. 701655/37. R. P. S. 2510 Appendix A; HO 144/22834/426.
13 PRO HO 144/22834/543.
14 *Daily Express*, 6 January 1993.
15 PRO HO 144/22833/281.
16 PRO HO 144/22237/I. W. 701655/37 R. P. S. 2508.
17 PRO HO 144/22176/122.
18 PRO HO 144/22829/13.
19 PRO HO 144/22237/I. W. 701655/37 R. P. S. 2122, 2141.
20 J. A. Cole, *Lord Haw-Haw* (London, 1964), pp. 257–304; J. W. Hall, ed., *The Trial of William Joyce* (London, 1946).
21 R. Thurlow, *Fascism in Britain 1918–87* (Oxford, 1987), p. 199; PRO HO 45/25834–6, 25817–20.
22 D. Sassoon, 'The Rise and Fall of West European Communism, 1939–48', *Contemporary European History* 1, no. 2 (1992), pp. 139–69.
23 S. Brooke, *Labour's War* (Oxford, 1992), pp. 1–11.
24 PRO HO 45/25399/83.
25 PRO HO 45/25399/93–5.
26 PRO HO 45/24968/116; MEPO 3/546; M. Beckman, *The 43 Group* (London, 1993).
27 A. Glees, 'War Crimes: The Security and Intelligence Dimension', *Intelligence and National Security* 7, no. 3 (July 1992), pp. 242–67; T. Bower, *Blind Eye to Murder* (London, 1981); D. Cesarani, *Justice Delayed* (London, 1992); B. Heuser, 'Covert Action within British and American Concepts of Containment', in R. Aldrich, ed., *British Intelligence, Strategy and the Cold War 1945–51* (London, 1992), pp. 65–84.
28 J. Loftus, *The Belarus Secret* (New York, 1982), pp. 8–57.
29 PRO FO 371/86906/ NS 2195/4; FO 371/86905/NS 2195/3.
30 *ABN Correspondence* 6, nos 5–6 (May–June 1955).
31 Loftus, *Belarus Secret*; T. Bower, *The Red Web* (London, 1989).
32 PRO FO 371/86715/NS1016/3, 8; FO 371/86905/NS2194/3.
33 S. Ambrose, *The Rise to Globalism* (Harmondsworth, 1988), pp. 54–180; L. Halle, *The Cold War as History* (New York, 1991); N. Lowles, 'Cold War Warriors, The OUN-Bandera 1939–53' (University of Sheffield B A dissertation, 1993).
34 K. Morgan, *Labour in Power 1945–51* (Oxford, 1984), p. 41; R. Eatwell, *The 1945–51 Labour Government* (London, 1979), pp. 32–44.
35 Sassoon, 'The Rise and Fall', pp. 139, 157–8.

36 Morgan, *Labour in Power*, p. 295.
37 F. Claudin, *The Communist Movement from Comintern to Cominform* (London, 1975), pp. 455–79; K. Morgan, *Harry Pollitt* (Manchester, 1993), pp. 155–84.
38 Hall, ed., *The Trial of William Joyce.*
39 P. Addison, *The Road to 1945* (London, 1975); A. Calder, *The People's War: Britain 1939–45* (London, 1969).
40 PRO FO 371/56763/N4065; A. Deighton, *The Impossible Peace: Britain, the Division of Germany, and the Origins of the Cold War* (Oxford, 1993), pp. 223–35; R. Merrick, 'The Russia Committee of the British Foreign Office and the Cold War, 1946–47', *Journal of Contemporary History* 20, no. 3 (1985); J. Zametica, 'Three Letters to Bevin: Frank Roberts at the Moscow Embassy 1945–46', and V. Rothwell, 'Robin Hankey', in J. Zametica, ed., *British Officials and Foreign Policy 1945–1950* (Leicester, 1990), pp. 39–97 and 156–88. I would like to thank Pauline Elkes for discussing these matters with me.
41 PRO FO 371/56763/N4156; R. Aldrich and M. Coleman, 'The Cold War, the JIC and British Signals Intelligence, 1948', *Intelligence and National Security* 4, no. 3 (July 1989), pp. 535–49; A. Gorst, 'Military Planning for Post-War Defence 1943–45', in A. Deighton, ed., *Britain and the First Cold War* (Basingstoke, 1990), pp. 91–107.
42 B. Jones, *The Russia Complex* (Manchester, 1977), pp. 147–73; J. Saville, 'Ernest Bevin and the Cold War 1945–50', *Socialist Register* (1981), pp. 147–73; P. Weiler, *Ernest Bevin* (Manchester, 1993), pp. 144–87, P. Hennessy, *Never Again* (London, 1993), pp. 245–72.
43 Loftus, *Belarus Secret.*
44 PRO CAB 129/25 CP (48) 72; P. Weiler, *British Labour and the Cold War* (Stanford, 1988), pp. 189–229; J. Bloch and P. Fitzgerald, *British Intelligence and Covert Action* (London, 1983), pp. 90–1; W. Scott Lucas and C. J. Morris, 'A Very British Crusade: The Information Research Department and the Beginning of the Cold War', in Aldrich, ed., *British Intelligence*, pp. 85–110.
45 PRO PREM 8/1081; R. Aldrich, 'Secret Intelligence for a Post-War World: Reshaping the British Intelligence Community, 1944–51', in Aldrich, ed., *British Intelligence*, pp. 30–5.
46 PRO CAB 130/46 GEN 291/4.
47 PRO PREM 8/1289.
48 PRO PREM 8/1290.
49 PRO PREM 8/673; K. Jeffery and P. Hennessy, *States of Emergency* (London, 1983), pp. 143–80.

50 Jeffery and Hennessy, *States of Emergency*, p. 218; J. T. Richelson and D. Ball, *The Ties that Bind* (Hemel Hempstead, 1985), p. 87.
51 S. Peak, *Troops in Strikes* (London, 1984); G. Ellen, 'Labour and Strike Breaking 1945–1951', *International Socialism* no. 24 (1984), p. 45.
52 Weiler, *British Labour*, pp. 230–69; P. Weiler, 'British Labour and the Cold War', in J. Cronin and J. Schneer eds, *Social Conflict and Political Order in Modern Britain* (London, 1982), pp. 146–78; Jeffery and Hennessy, *States of Emergency*, pp. 181–221.
53 Weiler, *British Labour*, p. 266; H. Wilson, *The Labour Government 1964–70: A Personal Record* (London, 1974), pp. 295–314; E. P. Thompson, *Writing by Candlelight* (London, 1980), pp. 159–60.
54 Jeffery and Hennessy, *States of Emergency*, p. 222; J. Callaghan, *British Trotskyism* (Oxford, 1984).
55 CAB 130/65 Gen 341/1 World Peace Congress; P. Wright with P. Greengrass, *Spycatcher* (New York, 1987), pp. 368–72.
56 D. Leigh, *The Wilson Plot* (London, 1989); PRO CAB 21/2554/14/31/172; P. Ziegler, *Harold Wilson* (London, 1993), pp. 475–6; B. Pimlott, *Harold Wilson* (London, 1993).
57 R. Rovere, *Senator Joe McCarthy* (London, 1969); D. Caute, *The Great Fear* (London, 1978).
58 Weiler, *British Labour*, p. 228; R. Whitaker, 'Fighting the Cold War on the Home Front', *Socialist Register* (1984), pp. 3–43.
59 P. Hennessy and G. Brownfeld, 'Britain's Cold War Security Purge: The Origins of Positive Vetting', *Historical Journal* 25, no. 4 (1982).
60 PRO CAB 128/19 CM (51) 42 (3).
61 Cmd 9577, 'Report Concerning the Disappearance of Two Foreign Office Officials', 23 September 1955; V. Newton, *The Cambridge Spies* (Lanham, 1991), p. 338; N. West, *Molehunt* (London, 1987), pp. 250–63; P. Hennessy and K. Townsend, 'The Documentary Spoor of Burgess and Maclean', *Intelligence and National Security* 2, no. 2, pp. 291–301; S. Kerr, 'The Secret Hotline to Moscow: Donald Maclean and the Berlin Crisis of 1948', in Deighton, ed., *Britain and the First Cold War*, pp. 71–87.
62 PRO CAB 128/29 CM (55) 36 (6).
63 PRO CAB 128/29 CM (55) 39 (1).
64 PRO CAB 129/78 CP (55) 161; A. Horne, *Macmillan 1894–1956* (London, 1988), pp. 365–6.
65 Wright with Greengrass, *Spycatcher*, pp. 226–8.

66 Ibid., pp. 188–9, 278–86.
67 J. Rusbridger, *The Intelligence Game* (London, 1989).
68 West, *Molehunt*, pp. 234–41.
69 J. Costello, *Mask of Treachery* (London, 1989), pp. 570–80.
70 A. Summers and S. Dorrill, *Honeytrap* (London, 1987), pp. 72–91; PRO CAB 129/113 C (63) 99, 100.
71 PRO CAB 128/37 CC (63) 40, 262.
72 PRO CAB 129/109 C (62) 51.
73 A. Boyle, *The Climate of Treason* (London, 1979).
74 Costello, *Mask of Treachery*, pp. 557–8; B. Penrose and S. Freeman, *Conspiracy of Silence* (London, 1986), pp. 433–59.
75 Wright with Greengrass, *Spycatcher*.
76 C. Pincher, *The Spycatcher Affair* (London, 1987), p. 44.
77 N. West, *MI5 1945–72: A Matter of Trust* (London, 1982); C. Pincher, *Their Trade is Treachery* (London, 1981).
78 Pincher, *The Spycatcher Affair*.
79 M. Turnbull, *The Spycatcher Trial* (London, 1988), pp. 59–168.
80 Rusbridger, *The Intelligence Game*, pp. 85–104; C. Andrew and O. Gordievsky, *KGB: The Inside Story of its Foreign Operations from Lenin to Gorbachev* (London, 1990), pp. 437–8, 441–2, 501, 506.
81 W. J. West, *The Truth about Roger Hollis* (London, 1988); Pincher, *Their Trade is Treachery*.
82 A. Glees, *The Secrets of the Service: British Intelligence and Communist Subversion 1939–1951* (London, 1987), pp. 318–99; S. Kerr, 'Roger Hollis and the Dangers of the Anglo-Soviet Treaty of 1942', *Intelligence and National Security* 5, no. 3 (July 1990), pp. 148–58.
83 Andrew and Gordievsky, *KGB*, pp. 571–2.
84 A. Cavendish, *Inside Intelligence* (London, 1990).
85 Wright with Greengrass, *Spycatcher*, pp. 55–8.
86 M. Thatcher, *The Downing Street Years 1979–1990* (London, 1993).
87 C. Pincher, *Too Secret Too Long* (London, 1984).
88 Rusbridger, *The Intelligence Game* pp. 207–17; R. Thomas, *Espionage and Secrecy* (London, 1991), pp. 207–19.
89 L. P. Weinberg, *After Mussolini* (Washington, 1979).
90 D. Bell, ed., *The Radical Right* (New York, 1964); Rovere, *Senator Joe McCarthy*.
91 Newton, *The Cambridge Spies*, p. xiii.

8 Pushing and Shoving (1958–1994)

1 A. M. Scott and I. Macleay, *Britain's Secret War* (Edinburgh, 1990), p. 202.

2 R. Sked and C. Cook, *Post War Britain* (London, 1987).
3 V. Bogdanor and R. Skidelsky, eds, *The Age of Affluence 1951–1964* (London, 1970); P. Hennessy, *Never Again* (London, 1993), pp. 379–80.
4 S. Hall, 'The Great Moving Right Show', in S. Hall and M. Jacques, eds, *The Politics of Thatcherism* (London, 1983), p. 23.
5 R. Skidelsky, ed., *Thatcherism* (Oxford, 1989); K. Minogue and M. Biddiss, eds, *Thatcherism, Personality and Politics* (London, 1987).
6 C. Andrew and O. Gordievsky, *KGB* (London, 1990), pp. 302–543.
7 K. Jeffery and P. Hennessy, *States of Emergency* (London, 1983), p. 222–69; T. Bunyan, *The Political Police in Britain* (London, 1976), pp. 58–101; J. T. Richelson and D. Ball, *The Ties that Bind* (Hemel Hempstead, 1985), pp. 17–22, 283–300.
8 S. McCabe et al., *The Police, Public Order and Civil Liberties* (London, 1988), p. 41.
9 M. Kettle, 'The National Reporting Centre and the 1984 Miners Strike', in B. Fine and R. Millar, eds, *Policing the Miners Strike* (London, 1985), pp. 23–33.
10 J. Callaghan, *British Trotskyism* (Oxford, 1985), pp. 27–197.
11 P. Shipley, *Revolutionaries in Modern Britain* (London, 1976), pp. 105–29.
12 M. Crick, *The March of Militant* (London, 1986), p. 173.
13 National Council for Civil Liberties, *Southall, 23 April 1979* (London, 1979); R. Taylor and C. Pritchard, *The Protest Makers* (Oxford, 1980), p. 11.
14 M. Barker, *The New Racism* (London, 1981).
15 PRO CAB 128/37 CC (63) 28 Min 3; CC (63) 34.5; CAB 129/111 C (62) 156; CAB 129/113 C (63) 70, 71.
16 C. Husbands, *Racial Exclusionism and the City* (London, 1983), pp. 140–1.
17 L. Cheles, R. Ferguson and M. Vaughan, eds, *Neo-fascism in Europe* (London, 1991).
18 M. Randle and P. Pottle, *The Blake Escape* (London, 1989), pp. 225–44; G. Murray, *Enemies of the State* (London, 1993), pp. 143–208.
19 McCabe et al., *The Police, Public Order and Civil Liberties*, pp. 1–8.
20 P. Weiler, *Ernest Bevin* (Manchester, 1993).
21 A. Gamble, *Britain in Decline*, 3rd edn (Basingstoke, 1990); S. Pollard, *The Wasting of the British Economy* (London, 1982); C. Barnett, *The Audit of War* (London, 1986).

22 M. Kettle, 'The National Reporting Centre', in Fine and Millar, *Policing the Miners Strike*, p. 23.
23 S. Peak, *Troops in Strikes* (London, 1984), pp. 83–164.
24 Jeffery and Hennessy, *States of Emergency*, p. 233.
25 R. Geary, *Policing Industrial Disputes* (London, 1986), pp. 67–78; T. Bunyan, 'From Saltley to Orgreave via Brixton', *Journal of Law and Society* 12, no. 3 (Winter 1985), pp. 293–303.
26 J. Campbell, *Edward Heath* (London, 1993), pp. 289–622.
27 Jeffery and Hennessy, *States of Emergency*, p. 237.
28 Geary, *Policing Industrial Disputes*, pp. 83–91.
29 M. Marshall, 'The Last Battle: Contingency Planning during the 1984–5 Miners Strike' (University of Sheffield BA dissertation, 1991), pp. 5–7.
30 M. Adeney and J. Lloyd, *The Miners Strike 1984–1985* (London, 1986), pp. 202–17.
31 Ibid., pp. 207–12.
32 S. Spencer, *Police Authorities During the Miners Strike* (London, 1985), p. 27; J. Coulter, S. Miller and M. Walker, *State of Siege* (London, 1984), p. 19.
33 H. Young, *One of Us* (London, 1989), pp. 135–246.
34 McCabe et al., *The Police, Public Order and Civil Liberties*, pp. 161–9.
35 J. and R. Winterton, *Coal, Crisis and Conflict* (Manchester, 1989), pp. 167–71.
36 Geary, *Policing Industrial Disputes*, pp. 136–42.
37 R. Samuel, B. Bloomfield and C. Boanas, eds, *The Enemy Within: Pit Villages and the Miners Strike 1984–1985* (London, 1986), pp. 118–19; B. Jackson and T. Wardle, *The Battle for Orgreave* (Brighton, 1986).
38 A. Gamble, *The Conservative Nation* (London, 1974).
39 A. Gamble, *The Free Economy and the Strong State* (Basingstoke, 1988), p. 26.
40 P. Riddell, *The Thatcher Era and its Legacy* (Oxford, 1991), pp. 204–18.
41 D. Marquand, *The Unprincipled Society* (London, 1988).
42 C. Ponting, *Secrecy in Britain* (Oxford, 1990), pp. 58, 78.
43 P. Hennessy, *Whitehall* (London, 1989).

9 The Orange and the Green (1968–1993)

1 M. J. Cunningham, *British Government Policy in Northern Ireland 1969–1989* (Manchester, 1991), pp. 40–74, 90–122.
2 See pp. 74–106 above.

3 R. Griffin, 'Nationalism', in R. Eatwill, ed., *Contemporary Political Ideologies* (London, 1973), pp. 147–68.
4 F. Gaffikin and M. Morrissey, *Northern Ireland: The Thatcher Years* (London, 1990), pp. 7–39.
5 T. P. Coogan, *The IRA* (London, 1988), pp. 15–58.
6 M. Urban, *Big Boys' Rules* (London, 1993); J. Adams, *The New Spies* (London, 1994).
7 C. Townshend, *Making the Peace* (Oxford, 1993).
8 F. Kitson, *Low Intensity Operations* (London, 1974); D. Hamill, *Pig in the Middle* (London, 1984), pp. 41–4.
9 P. Bishop and E. Mallie, *The Provisional IRA* (London, 1992), pp. 16–46.
10 Ibid., pp. 119–38.
11 J. J. Lee, *Ireland 1912–1985* (Cambridge, 1985), pp. 455, 495.
12 R. Rose, *Northern Ireland: A Time of Choice* (London, 1976), pp. 33–70.
13 M. Farrell, *Northern Ireland: The Orange State* (London, 1976); L. de Paor, *Divided Ulster* (London, 1970), pp. 103–73.
14 S. Bruce, *God Save Ulster* (Oxford, 1986), pp. 93–120.
15 A. Babington, *Military Intervention in Britain* (London, 1990), pp. 153–75; 'Disturbances in Northern Ireland. Report of the Commission appointed by the Governor of Northern Ireland, September 1969', Cmd 532 (1969); 'Violence and Civil Disturbances in Northern Ireland in 1969. Report of the Tribunal of Enquiry under Mr Justice Scarman', Cmd 566 (1972).
16 Bishop and Mallie, *The Provisional IRA*, pp. 275–86.
17 B. Rowthorn and N. Wayne, *Northern Ireland: The Political Economy of Conflict* (Oxford, 1988), pp. 176–83.
18 Rose, *Northern Ireland*, pp. 139–66.
19 Lee, *Ireland*, pp. 411–57.
20 Urban, *Big Boys' Rules*, pp. 238–47.
21 J. Stalker, *Stalker* (London, 1988).
22 Urban, *Big Boys' Rules*, p. 152.
23 P. Foot, *Who Framed Colin Wallace?* (London, 1990).
24 Urban, *Big Boy's Rules*, p. 77.
25 *Sunday Times*, 26 January 1992.
26 Urban, *Big Boys' Rules*, pp. 21–2.
27 Ibid., p. 34.
28 Cunningham, *British Government Policy*, pp. 156–7.
29 Bishop and Mallie, *The Provisional IRA*, pp. 338–76.
30 Cunningham, *British Government Policy*, pp. 141–58.
31 Coogan, *The IRA*, pp. 623–31.
32 *Sunday Times*, 23 May 1993.

33 R. Adams, 'Bungled', *Sunday Times,* 7 November 1993.
34 Adams, 'Bungled'.
35 T. P. Coogan, *Michael Collins* (London, 1988), pp. 121–56.
36 *Sunday Times,* 25 February 1990.

Conclusion

1 *The Times,* 28 September 1993.
2 R. Thomas, *The British Philosophy of Administration* (London, 1978).

SELECT BIBLIOGRAPHY

The purpose of this bibliography is to draw to the reader's attention the main primary and secondary sources used in the compilation of this work. The aim is to highlight the main classes of documents consulted in the Public Record Office, other private collections and several interesting unpublished theses, as well as an ever lengthening list of books and articles on aspects of the main themes. The latter list is selected for its relevance for this book, and not necessarily on academic merit. As such, this bibliography contains elements of the sublime and the ridiculous; but what even those of more dubious merit lack in accuracy they often make up for in readability or more oblique significance.

Primary Sources

The main classes consulted at the PRO at Kew included the HO 45, 144 and 283 series; CAB 23, 24, 66, 67, 128 and 129 series; FO 371; CO 204; INF 1; and AIR 1.

Other primary sources consulted included the Sir Henry Wilson and Sir John French Papers at the Imperial War Museum, the Lord Trenchard Papers at the RAF Museum Colindale, the Lloyd George Papers at the House of Lords Record Office, the Sir Henry Cave Papers at the British Library, the Ramsay MacDonald and Sir John Anderson collections at the Public Record Office, and the National Council for Civil Liberties Archive at the University of Hull. Also consulted were Mass Observation File Reports.

Theses, Dissertations

The following theses were also invaluable with regard to both references and ideas which stimulated the production of this book:

Bird, J. C., 'Control of Enemy Alien Civilians in Great Britain 1914–1918' (University of London, Ph.D., 1981).
Blake, J., 'Civil Disorder in Britain 1910–1939: The Roles of Civil Government and Military Authority' (University of Sussex, D.Phil., 1979).
Bowes, N., 'The People's Convention' (University of Warwick, MA, 1976).
Broomfield, S. R., 'South Wales During the Second World War: The Coal Industry and its Community' (University of Wales (Swansea), Ph.D., 1979).
Cullen, S., 'The British Union of Fascists 1932–1940: Ideology, Membership, Meetings' (University of Oxford, M. Litt., 1987).
Desmerais, R., 'The Supply and Transport Committee 1919–1926' (University of Wisconsin, Ph.D., 1970).
Farr, B., 'The Development and Impact of Right Wing Politics in Great Britain 1903–1932' (University of Illinois, Ph.D., 1976).
Fishman, N., 'The British Communist Party and the Trade Unions 1933–45: The Dilemmas of Revolutionary Pragmatism' (Birkbeck College, the University of London, Ph.D., 1991).
Harmer, H. J., 'The National Unemployed Worker Movement in Britain, Failure and Success' (London School of Economics, Ph.D., 1987).
Kamm, R., 'The Home Office, Public Order and Civil Liberties 1880–1914' (University of Oxford, D.Phil., 1987).
Macraild, D. M., 'The Irish in North Lancashire and West Cumberland *c.*1850–1906: Aspects of the Social History of Barrow in Furness, Cleator Moor and Their Hinterlands' (University of Sheffield, Ph.D., 1993).
Marshall, M., 'The Last Battle: Contingency Planning During the 1984–1985 Miners Strike' (University of Sheffield, BA dissertation, 1991).
Nottingham, C., 'The State and Revolution in Britain 1916–1926' (University of Sheffield, Ph.D., 1985).
Upham, M., 'The History of British Trotskyism to 1949' (University of Hull, Ph.D., 1980).

Secondary Sources

Adams, J., *The New Spies* (London, 1994).

Aldrich, R., *British Intelligence, Strategy and the Cold War 1945–51* (London, 1992).

Aldrich, R., 'Secret Intelligence for a Postwar World: Reshaping the British Intelligence Community, 1944–1951', in Aldrich (1992).

Aldrich, R. and Coleman, M., 'The Cold War, the JIC and British Signals Intelligence 1948', *Intelligence and National Security* 4, no. 3 (1989), pp. 535–49.

Anderson, G. D., *Fascists, Communists and the National Government* (Columbia, 1983).

Andrew, C., *Secret Service* (London, 1985).

Andrew, C. and Gordievsky, O., *KGB: The Inside Story of its Foreign Relations from Lenin to Gorbachev* (London, 1992).

Andrew, C. and Dilks, D., eds, *The Missing Dimension: Government and Intelligence Communities During the Twentieth Century* (London, 1984).

Attfield, J. and Williams, S., eds, *1939: The Communist Party and the War* (London, 1984).

Babington, A., *Military Intervention in Britain* (London, 1991).

Bearse, R. and Reed, A., *Conspirator: The Untold Story of Churchill, Roosevelt and Tyler Kent, Spy* (London 1991).

Bennett, J. W., *Sir John Anderson* (London, 1959).

Bentley, M. and Stevenson, J., eds, *High and Low Politics in Modern Britain* (Oxford, 1983).

Bishop, P. and Mallie, E., *The Provisional IRA* (London, 1992).

Boyle, A., *Trenchard* (London, 1962).

Boyle, A., *The Climate of Treason* (London, 1979).

Brown, A. C., *The Secret Servant* (London, 1988).

Bruce, S., *The Red Hand: Protestant Paramilitaries in Northern Ireland* (Oxford, 1992).

Bunyan, T., *The Political Police in Britain* (London, 1976).

Callaghan, J., *British Trotskyism* (Oxford, 1985).

Ceadel, M., *Pacifism in Great Britain 1914–45* (Oxford, 1980).

Cecil, R., *A Divided Life* (London, 1988).

Cecil, R., 'The Cambridge Comintern', in Andrew and Dilks, eds.

Cesarani, D. and Kushner, A., eds, *The Internment of Aliens in Twentieth-Century Britain* (London, 1993).

Childs, W., *Episodes and Reflections* (London, 1930).

Cohen, P., 'The Police, the Home Office and Surveillance of the British Union of Fascists', *Intelligence and National Security* 1, no. 3 (September 1986), pp. 416–39.

Coogan, T. P., *The IRA* (London, 1988).
Coogan, T. P., *Michael Collins* (London, 1988).
Costello, J., *Mask of Treachery* (London, 1989).
Costello, J., *Ten Days that Saved the West* (London, 1991).
Costello, J. and Tsarev, O., *Deadly Illusions* (London, 1993).
Cox, B., *Civil Liberties in Britain* (Harmondsworth, 1975).
Crick, M., *The March of Militant* (London, 1986).
Croucher, R., *Engineers at War* (London, 1983).
Croucher, R., *We Refuse to Starve in Silence* (London, 1987).
Cullen, S., 'Political Violence: The Case of the British Union of Fascists', *Journal of Contemporary History* 28, no. 2 (April 1993), pp. 245–67.
Cunningham, M. J., *British Government Policy in Northern Ireland 1969–1989* (Manchester, 1991).
Deighton, A., ed., *Britain and the First Cold War* (Basingstoke, 1990).
Deighton, A., *The Impossible Peace: Britain, the Division of Germany, and the Origins of the Cold War* (Oxford, 1993).
Dixon, Sir A., 'The Emergency Work of the Police Force in the Second World War' (Home Office, 1963).
Dixon, Sir A., 'The Home Office and the Police Between the World Wars' (Home Office, 1966).
Englander, D., 'Military Intelligence and the Defence of the Realm: The Surveillance of Soldiers and Civilians during the First World War', *Bulletin of the Society for the Study of Labour History* 52, no. 1 (1987), pp. 24–32.
Fine, B. and Millar, R., eds, *Policing the Miners Strike* (London, 1985).
Foot, P., *Who Framed Colin Wallace?* (London, 1990).
Gamble, A., *The Conservative Nation* (London, 1974).
Gamble, A., *The Free Economy and the Strong State* (Basingstoke, 1988).
Geary, R., *Policing Industrial Disputes 1893–1903* (Cambridge, 1985).
Glees, A., *Exile Politics during the Second World War* (London, 1983).
Glees, A., *The Secrets of the Service: British Intelligence and Soviet Subversion 1939–51* (London, 1987).
Glees, A., 'War Crimes: The Security and Intelligence Dimension', *Intelligence and Security* 7, no. 3 (July 1992), pp. 242–67.
Gorst, A., 'Military Planning for Post-War Defence 1943–45', in Deighton, ed.
Hamill, D., *Pig in the Middle* (London, 1985).
Hannington, W., *Unemployed Struggles* (London, 1973).
Haslam, J., 'The British Communist Party, the Comintern and the Outbreak of War 1939: "A Nasty Taste in the Mouth"', *Diplomacy and Statecraft* 3, no. 1 (1992), pp. 147–54.

Hennessy, P. and Brownfeld, G., 'Britain's Cold War Security Purge: The Origins of Positive Vetting', *Historical Journal* 25, no. 4 (1982).

Hennessy, P. and Townsend, K., 'The Documentary Spoor of Burgess and MacClean', *Intelligence and National Security*, 2, no. 2 (1987), pp. 291–301.

Hennessy, P., *Whitehall* (London, 1989).

Hennessy, P., *Never Again* (London, 1993).

Higham, C., *Wallis* (London, 1988).

Hiley, N., 'The Failure of British Counter-Intelligence against Germany 1907–1914', *Historical Journal* 28, no. 4 (1985), pp. 835–62.

Hiley, N., 'Internal Security in Wartime: The Rise and Fall of PMS 2, 1915–1917', *Intelligence and National Security* 1, no. 3 (1986), pp. 395–415.

Hiley, N., 'Counter Espionage and Security in Great Britain During the First World War', *English Historical Review* 101 (1986), pp. 100–26.

Hiley, N., 'Sir Hedley le Bas and the Origins of Domestic Propaganda in Britain, 1914–1917', *Journal of Advertising History* 10, no. 2 (1987), pp. 30–46.

Hinsley, F. H. and Simkins, C. A. G., *British Intelligence in the Second World War*, vol. 4, *Security and Counter-Intelligence* (London, 1990).

Hinton, J., *Protests and Visions* (London, 1989).

Holmes, C., 'Government Files and Privileged Access', *Social History* 6 (1981), pp. 335–50.

Holmes, C., 'Internment, Fascism and the Public Records', *Bulletin of the Society for the Study of Labour History* 52, no. 1 (1987), pp. 17–22.

Hooper, D., *Official Secrets* (London, 1987).

Hope, J., 'Fascism, the Security Service and the Curious Careers of Maxwell Knight and James Mcguirk Hughes', *Lobster* 22.

Hope, J., 'British Fascism and the State 1917–27: A Reexamination of the Evidence', *Labour History Review* 57, no. 3 (1992).

Hope, J., 'Fascism and the State in Britain: The Case of the British Fascisti 1923–31', *Australian Journal of Politics and History* 39, no. 3 (1993), pp. 367–80.

Hope, J., 'Surveillance or Collusion? Maxwell Knight, MI5 and the British Fascisti', *Intelligence and National Security* 9, no. 4 (October 1994).

Hyde, H. M., *George Blake, Superspy* (London, 1967).

James, Sir W., *The Eyes of the Navy* (London, 1955).

Jeffery, K., 'The British Army and Internal Security 1919–39', *The Historical Journal* 24, no. 2 (1981), pp. 377–97.

Jeffery, K. and Hennessy, P., *States of Emergency* (London, 1983).
Kerr, S., 'The Secret Hotline to Moscow: Donald Maclean and the Berlin Crisis of 1948', in Deighton, ed., pp. 71–87.
Kerr, S., 'Roger Hollis and the Dangers of the Anglo-Soviet Treaty of 1942', *Intelligence and National Security* 5, no. 3 (July 1990), pp. 148–58.
Kerr, S., 'Familiar Fiction not the Untold Story', *Intelligence and National Security* 9, no. 1 (January 1994), pp. 128–75.
Kidd, R., *British Liberty in Danger* (London, 1940).
King, F. and Matthews, G., eds, *About Turn: The Communist Party and the Outbreak of the Second World War* (London, 1990).
Kitson, F., *Low Intensity Operations* (London, 1974).
Knightley, P., *The Second Oldest Profession* (London, 1986).
Lee, J. J., *Ireland 1912–1985* (Cambridge, 1985).
Leigh, D., *The Wilson Plot* (London, 1989).
Lewis, D. S., *Illusions of Grandeur* (Manchester, 1987).
Lucas, W. Scott and Morris, C. J., 'A Very British Crusade: The Information Research Department and the Beginning of the Cold War', in Aldrich, ed.
Lustgarten, L., *The Governance of the Police* (London, 1986).
Macready, Sir N., *Annals of an Active Life*, 2 vols (London, 1924).
Masters, A., *The Man who was M* (Oxford, 1984).
McCabe S., et al., *The Police, Public Order and Civil Liberties* (London, 1988).
McLaine, I., *Ministry of Morale* (London, 1979).
Mcdermott, K., 'Rethinking the Comintern: Soviet Historiography 1987–1991', *Labour History Review* 57, no. 3 (1992).
Merrick, R., 'The Russia Committee of the British Foreign Office and the Cold War 1946–1947', *Journal of Contemporary History* 20, no. 3 (1985).
Messinger, G. S., *British Propaganda and the State in the First World War, 1914–1918* (London, 1992).
Middlemas, K., *Thomas Jones: A Whitehall Diary* (Oxford, 1971).
Moore, A., 'Sir Philip Game's Other Life: The Making of the 1936 Public Order Act in Britain', *Australian Journal of Politics and History* 36, no. 1 (1990), pp. 62–72.
Morgan, J., *Conflict and Order* (London, 1987).
Morgan, K., *Against Fascism and War* (Manchester, 1989).
Morgan, K., *Harry Pollitt* (Manchester, 1993).
Murray, G., *Enemies of the State* (London, 1993).
Newton, V., *The Cambridge Spies* (Lanham, 1991).
O'Halpin, E., 'Sir Warren Fisher and the Coalition 1919–22', *The Historical Journal* 24, no. 4 (1981).
Panayi, P., *The Enemy in our Midst* (Oxford, 1991).

Panayi, P., ed., *Racial Violence in Britain 1840–1940* (Leicester, 1993).
Parker, J., *King of Fools* (London, 1988).
Peak, S., *Troops in Strikes* (London, 1987).
Peele, G. and Cook, C., eds, *The Politics of Reappraisal* (London, 1975).
Pellew, J., *The Home Office 1848–1914* (London, 1982).
Penrose, B. and Freeman, S., *Conspiracy of Silence* (London, 1987).
Pincher, C., *Their Trade is Treachery* (London, 1981).
Pincher, C., *The Spycatcher Affair* (London, 1987).
Ponting, C., *Secrecy in Britain* (Oxford, 1990).
Porter, B., *The Origins of the Vigilant State* (London, 1987).
Porter, B., *Plots and Paranoia* (London, 1989).
Randle, M. and Pottle, P. *The Blake Escape* (London, 1989).
Riddell, P., *The Thatcher Era and its Legacy* (Oxford, 1991).
Robertson, K. G., *Public Secrets* (London, 1982).
Robertson, K. G., ed., *British and American Approaches to Intelligence* (London, 1989).
Roskill, S., *Hankey, Man of Secrets*, vols 1 and 2 (London, 1970).
Rothwell, V., *Britain and the Cold War* (London, 1988).
Rothwell, V., 'Robin Hankey' in Zametica, ed., pp. 156–88.
Rusbridger, J., *The Intelligence Game* (London, 1989).
Sanders, M. L. and Taylor, P. M., *British Progaganda during the First World War, 1914–1918* (London, 1982).
Saville, J., 'Ernest Bevin and the Cold War 1945–50', *Socialist Register* (1981), pp. 147–73.
Scott, A. M. and Macleay, I., *Britain's Secret War* (Edinburgh, 1990).
Shipley, P., *Revolutionaries in Modern Britain* (London, 1976).
Shipley, P., *Hostile Action* (London, 1989).
Simpson, A. W. B., *In the Highest Degree Odious* (Oxford, 1992).
Sinclair, A., *The Red and the Blue* (London, 1986).
Stammers, N., *Civil Liberties in Britain During the Second World War* (London, 1983).
Stevenson, J., 'The Politics of Violence', in G. Peele and C. Cook, eds, *The Politics of Reappraisal* (London, 1975), pp. 146–65.
Stevenson, J., 'The BUF, the Metropolitan Police and Public Order', in K. Lunn and R. Thurlow, eds, *British Fascism* (London, 1980), pp. 135–49.
Thomas, R., *The British Philosophy of Administration* (London, 1978).
Thomas, R., *Espionage and Secrecy* (London, 1991).
Thomson, Sir B., *Queer People* (London, 1923).
Thorpe, A., ed., *The Failure of Political Extremism in Interwar Britain* (Exeter, 1989).
Thurlow, R., *Fascism in Britain 1918–85* (Oxford, 1987).

Thurlow, R., 'British Fascism and State Surveillance 1934–45', *Intelligence and State Security* 3, no. 1 (January 1988), pp. 77–99.
Thurlow, R., 'The Mosley Papers and the Secret History of British Fascism 1939–40', in K. Lunn and A. Kushner, eds, *Traditions of Intolerance* (Manchester, 1989), pp. 173–95.
Thurlow, R., 'Blaming the Blackshirts: The Authorities and the Anti-Jewish Disturbances in the 1930s', in Panayi, ed., pp. 112–29.
Thurlow, R., 'Internment in the Second World War', *Intelligence and National Security* 9, no. 1 (January 1994), pp. 123–7.
Tomlinson, J., *Left, Right: The March of Political Extremism in Britain* (London, 1981).
Townshend, C., *The British Campaign in Ireland 1919–21* (Oxford, 1975).
Townshend, C., *Political Violence in Ireland* (Oxford, 1983).
Townshend, C., *Britain's Civil Wars* (London, 1986).
Townshend, C., 'One Man You Can Hang If Necessary', in J. B. Hattendorf and M. H. Murfett, *The Limitations of Military Power* (London, 1990), pp. 141–59.
Townshend, C., *Making the Peace* (Oxford, 1993).
Troup, Sir E., *The Home Office* (London, 1925).
Turnbull, M., *The Spycatcher Trial* (London, 1988).
Urban, M., *Big Boys' Rules* (London, 1993).
Valtin, J., *Out of the Night* (New York, 1941).
Weiler, P., 'British Labour and the Cold War', in J. Cronin and J. Schneer, eds, *Social Conflict and Political Order in Modern Britain* (London 1982), pp. 146–78.
Weiler, P., *British Labour and the Cold War* (Stanford, 1988).
Weiler, P., *Ernest Bevin* (Manchester, 1993).
Weinberger, B., 'Police Perceptions of Labour in the Inter-War Period: The Case of the Unemployed and Miners On Strike', in F. Snyder and D. Hey, eds, *Labour, Law and Crime* (London, 1987).
Weinberger, B., *Keeping the Peace?* (Oxford, 1991).
Weinberger, B., ed., 'Communism and the General Strike', *Bulletin of the Society for the Study of Labour History* 48 (Spring 1984).
West, N., *MI5 1945–72: A Matter of Trust* (London, 1982).
West, N., *Molehunt* (London, 1987).
West, W. J., *Truth Betrayed* (London, 1987).
West, W. J., *The Truth about Roger Hollis* (London, 1988).
Wilkinson, P., *Terrorism and the Liberal State* (Basingstoke, 1986).
Wright, P., with P. Greengrass, *Spycatcher* (New York, 1987).
Wrigley, C., *Lloyd George and the Challenge of Labour* (London, 1990).

Zametica, J., 'Three Letters to Bevin: Frank Roberts at the Moscow Embassy 1945–46', in Zametica, ed., pp. 39–97.

Zametica, J., ed., *British Officials and Foreign Policy 1945–1950* (Leicester, 1990).

INDEX